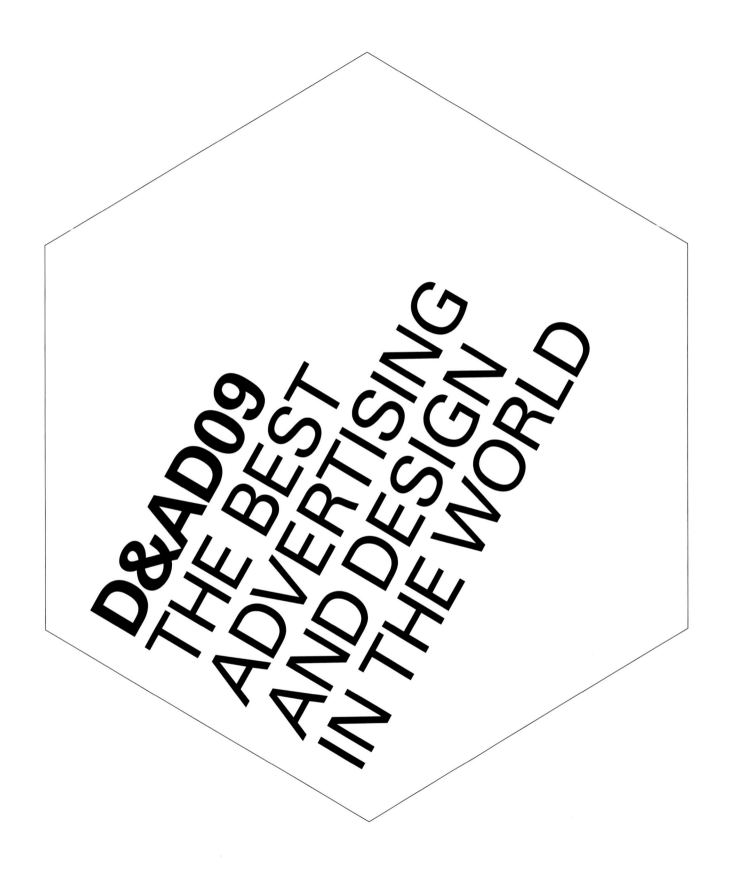

TASCHEN

HONG KONG KÖLN LONDON LOS ANGELES MADRID PARIS TOKYO

Contents / Inhalt / Sommaire

7   Introduction
8   Einleitung
9   Introduction

10   Some words from the judges
12   Einige Zitate der Juroren
14   Quelques mots des membres du jury

17   D&AD Black Pencil Winners

23   Poster Advertising
75   Press Advertising
95   Direct
125   Ambient
137   Integrated
147   TV & Cinema Advertising
171   TV & Cinema Communications
179   Broadcast Innovations
187   Music Videos
201   Radio
211   Graphic Design
287   Magazine & Newspaper Design
303   Book Design
323   Branding
341   Environmental Design
359   Packaging Design
379   Product Design
387   Art Direction
407   Illustration
431   Photography
443   Typography
449   Writing for Design
459   Writing for Advertising
473   TV & Cinema Crafts
501   Websites
523   Online Advertising
539   Mobile Marketing
551   Viral
563   Digital Installations

569   Index
574   Acknowledgements / Danksagungen / Remerciements

D&AD is a not-for-profit organisation that represents the international design, advertising and creative communities. More than any other organisation, D&AD sets industry standards, educates and inspires the next generation and promotes the importance of creativity, innovation and ideas within the business community. For more information, please visit dandad.org

Tim O'Kennedy's career began at Saatchi & Saatchi London in the early 1980s, following which he was hired by Jay Chiat as 'one of the first Account Planners in the US advertising industry'. Following two years at Wieden + Kennedy Portland steering the original 'Just Do It' campaign, he became International Marketing Director at Nike. O'Kennedy returned to Europe with Nike in 1994 and later joined The Lowe Group Europe as Chief Operating Officer. He was a founding partner of marketing agency Circus in 1998 and subsequently became Managing Director at Wieden + Kennedy Amsterdam, where he remained until the end of 2007. O'Kennedy joined D&AD in 2009 and he currently serves as a non-executive director of digital creative agency Perfect Fools in Stockholm and of communications agency Indie in Amsterdam. He also serves as an advisor to DIESEL Industries in Molvena.

Introduction

Standards matter.

In all walks of life, we make progress by understanding what excellence in any given field looks like, and then striving to beat that standard. Simple to say, but very much more difficult to achieve, and nowhere more so than in the field of commercial creativity, where originality, conceptual bravery and craftsmanship are all held in tension with a practical imperative: the need for the work in question to perform a clear function. It could be to help make a product more attractive or easy to use, create an affinity with a brand, or make it easier to navigate one's way through a crowded airport – but in every case (and in contrast with the art one finds in galleries), the starting point is always functional and usually commercial.

And that's what makes the best examples of work in this field so exciting and so uplifting: the often breathtaking ingenuity involved in marrying function with pure creative expression. Commercial creativity – at its best – confirms that even mundane tasks can be accomplished with flair and imagination, and enrich us all for having done so.

For forty-seven years now, D&AD has nurtured and celebrated excellence in this field: principally design and advertising, but increasingly in interactive communications. D&AD awards are, in the eyes of the creative community, the absolute reference for creative excellence worldwide.

And 2009 was no exception: over 270 experienced and highly-lauded judges met at London's Olympia in April, and sat on 29 specialist juries ranging from Music Videos to Graphic Design, TV Advertising, Illustration and Websites. From over 20,000 entries, submitted from 64 countries, 747 pieces of work were selected to be included in the D&AD annual – an achievement in itself.

Of these, 174 were nominated for further recognition.

A scant 54 received a Yellow Pencil, and just four went on to win a Black Pencil: representing just 0.02% of the work entered, this is a rarefied standard indeed, and without question the most coveted in the industry.

The contents of the book you now hold were, until this year, available only to D&AD members. It contains, simply, the best advertising and design work produced anywhere in the world during 2008. It is inspiring, uplifting, and confirms that even in the most challenging of economic circumstances, the best remedy is still a sharp pencil, imaginatively wielded.

We hope you enjoy it.

Tim O'Kennedy
CEO

D&AD ist eine nicht kommerzielle Organisation, die internationale Arbeitsgemeinschaften aus den Bereichen Design, Werbung und Kreativität repräsentiert. Mehr als irgendeine andere Organisation setzt D&AD Standards für die Branche, bildet die nächste Generation aus, inspiriert sie und engagiert sich für die Bedeutung von Kreativität, Innovation und Ideen innerhalb der Business-Community. Weitere Informationen finden Sie unter dandad.org

Die Karriere von Tim O'Kennedy begann in den frühen 80er-Jahren bei Saatchi & Saatchi in London. Anschließend wurde er von Jay Chiat als einer „der ersten Account Planner in der amerikanischen Werbebranche" eingestellt. Nachdem er zwei Jahre lang bei Wieden + Kennedy Portland die ursprüngliche „Just Do It"-Kampagne von Nike betreut hatte, wurde er bei Nike International Marketing Director. O'Kennedy kehrte mit Nike 1994 nach Europa zurück und ging später als Chief Operating Officer zur Lowe Group Europe. 1998 war er Gründungspartner der Marketingagentur Circus und wurde anschließend Managing Director bei Wieden + Kennedy in Amsterdam. Dort blieb er bis Ende 2007. O'Kennedy trat 2007 dem D&AD bei und ist momentan als nicht am Management beteiligter Director der digitalen Kreativagentur Perfect Fools in Stockholm sowie für die Kommunikationsagentur Indie aus Amsterdam tätig. Außerdem berät er die DIESEL Industries in Molvena.

Einleitung

Standards sind wichtig

In jeglichem Bereich erzielen wir erst Fortschritte, wenn wir verstehen, was als exzellent betrachtet wird. Dann müssen wir danach streben, diesen Maßstab zu überbieten. Das ist einfach gesagt, aber um so vieles schwerer zu erreichen. Und nirgendwo sonst gilt das so wie im Bereich der kommerziellen Kreativität, wo Originalität, Mut in der Konzeption und gutes handwerkliches Können durch einen ganz praktischen Imperativ in Schach gehalten werden: die Pflicht, dass die fragliche Arbeit eine klare Funktion zu erfüllen hat. Dabei kann es darum gehen, ein Produkt attraktiver oder unkomplizierter in der Handhabung zu machen, dafür Sorge zu tragen, dass eine bestimmte Marke bevorzugt wird, oder es schlicht einfacher zu gestalten, den Weg durch einen überfüllten Flughafen zu finden. Aber in jedem Fall (und das ist der Kontrast zu jener Kunst, die man in Galerien findet) ist der Ausgangspunkt immer funktional und normalerweise auch kommerziell.

Genau das macht die besten Beispiele der Arbeiten aus diesem Bereich so spannend und so erhebend: die oft atemberaubende Genialität, die erforderlich ist, um Funktion mit reinem kreativem Ausdruck zu verschmelzen. Die kommerzielle Kreativität bestätigt im besten Fall, dass sogar banale Aufgaben mit Fingerspitzengefühl und Ideenreichtum umgesetzt werden können, und am Ende alle mit dem erzielten Ergebnis zufrieden sind.

Seit mittlerweile 47 Jahren fördert und feiert D&AD in diesem Bereich Spitzenleistungen: vornehmlich bei Design und Werbung, aber in steigendem Maße auch bei der interaktiven Kommunikation. Die Auszeichnungen des D&AD sind in den Augen der Kreativen die absolute Referenz für weltweite kreative Top-Performances. Und 2009 war hier keine Ausnahme: Über 270 erfahrene und hochgelobte Juroren trafen sich im April im Londoner Hotel Olympia. Sie bildeten 29 Spezialjurys, die sich mit Themen von Musikvideos und Grafikdesign über Fernsehwerbung bis hin zu Illustrationen und Websites beschäftigten. Aus mehr als 20.000 Arbeiten aus 64 Ländern wurden 747 ausgewählt, die in das D&AD-Jahrbuch aufgenommen werden sollten – allein das ist schon eine Errungenschaft. Davon erhielten 174 Arbeiten eine weitere Nominierung.

Gerade einmal 54 der eingesandten Beiträge bekamen einen Yellow Pencil. Lediglich vier wurden dann mit einem Black Pencil bedacht, was nur 0,02 Prozent aller eingereichten Arbeiten entspricht: Das ist wirklich eine äußerst exklusive und zweifelsohne die begehrteste Auszeichnung der ganzen Branche.

Die Inhalte dieses Buches, das Sie in Händen halten, standen bis zu diesem Jahr nur Mitgliedern des D&AD zur Verfügung. Es enthält schlicht und einfach die besten Arbeiten aus Werbung und Design, die im Laufe des Jahres 2008 irgendwo auf der Welt geschaffen wurden. Diese Arbeiten sind inspirierend und erbaulich und bestätigen, dass auch unter größten ökonomischen Belastungen das beste Gegenmittel immer noch ein spitzer Bleistift ist, der erfindungsreich eingesetzt wird.

Wir hoffen, dass Ihnen dieses Buch Freude macht.

Tim O'Kennedy, CEO

Introduction

De l'importance des critères

Dans tous les domaines de la vie, on progresse en étudiant les critères de l'excellence, puis en cherchant à les dépasser. Facile à dire, mais beaucoup plus difficile à faire, surtout dans le domaine de la créativité commerciale, où l'originalité, l'audace conceptuelle et le savoir-faire sont sous-tendus par un impératif pratique : le travail produit doit remplir une fonction clairement définie. Il peut s'agir de rendre un produit plus séduisant ou plus facile à utiliser, de créer une affinité avec une marque, ou d'aider les gens à trouver leur chemin dans un aéroport bondé. Mais dans tous les cas (et contrairement à l'art que l'on trouve dans les galeries), le point de départ est toujours fonctionnel et généralement commercial.

Et c'est pour cela que les meilleurs exemples de projets dans ce domaine sont si passionnants et réjouissants : l'ingéniosité déployée pour allier la fonction à l'expression purement créative est souvent époustouflante. La crème de la créativité commerciale montre que même le travail le plus terre-à-terre peut être accompli avec style et imagination, et nous enrichir.

Cela fait maintenant quarante-sept ans que D&AD nourrit et rend hommage à l'excellence dans ce domaine : principalement pour le design et la publicité, mais aussi et de plus en plus pour la communication interactive. Dans la communauté des métiers de la créativité, les D&AD Awards sont la référence absolue de l'excellence mondiale.

Et l'année 2009 ne fait pas exception à la règle : plus de 270 juges expérimentés et très cotés se sont rencontrés au centre des expositions Olympia à Londres, au sein de 29 jurys spécialisés dans les clips musicaux, le graphisme, la publicité télévisée, l'illustration ou encore les sites web. Parmi les 20 000 projets participants, issus de 64 pays, 747 ont été sélectionnés pour « l'Annual » de D&AD, ce qui en soi est déjà un exploit.

Parmi ceux-là, 174 sont passés à la phase suivante.

Seulement 54 ont reçu un Yellow Pencil, et quatre d'entre eux ont gagné un Black Pencil, ce qui représente 0,02 % des projets en compétition : un critère d'excellence réellement draconien, sans aucun doute le plus convoité du métier.

Le livre que vous tenez entre vos mains contient des informations qui étaient jusqu'à présent réservées aux membres de D&AD. Il présente tout simplement les meilleurs projets de publicité et de design créés n'importe où dans le monde en 2008. Il vous inspirera et vous encouragera, et il confirme que même dans la situation économique la plus problématique, le meilleur remède est un crayon bien taillé, manié avec imagination.

Bonne lecture.

Tim O'Kennedy
Directeur général

Some words from the judges

UK Coinage Reverse Designs
Matt Dent
Page 20

"Matt's designs are likely to remain in production until the Queen is succeeded. It's nice to know that something as good as this will be around for a few years. I wish I'd designed them."
– Ben Terrett

Whopper Sacrifice
Crispin Porter + Bogusky
Page 525

"'Whopper Sacrifice' brought out the cliché in all the judges: it was the one piece of work they wish they'd done themselves when they heard about it."
– Dave Bedwood, Lean Mean Fighting Machine

Woman Whisperer
Clemenger BBDO Melbourne
Page 156

"With those three words, 'The Woman Whisperer', you've got a joke that every bloke in every pub will laugh at and repeat."
– Dave Trott, CST

Rabbit
Goodby Silverstein and Partners
Pages 150, 461, 498

"When you take great visuals and add great words, then you've really got something. 'Rabbit' does this brilliantly. Just when you think they can't ramp it up any higher, it carries on. Superb."
– Simon Veksner, BBH London

Oasis 'Dig Out Your Soul' –
in the Streets
BBH New York
Pages 126, 127, 143

"The concept of seeding the new Oasis album through buskers performing tracks was mind-blowing. Totally different, brave, and big. A sure-fire D&AD Nomination."
– Mike O'Sullivan, Saatchi & Saatchi New Zealand

Million
Droga 5
Page 22

"By first identifying the problem then bringing together the New York School system, Verizon and Samsung, Droga5 have created a genuinely useful programme wrapped up in a powerful creative message that can really make a difference."
– Mark Cridge, glue London

It's Mine
Wieden + Kennedy Los Angeles
Pages 149, 474

"'It's Mine' is the kind of ad you can watch again and again. The epic, filmic scale feels just right, the music is spot on, and the direction stunning – it just all comes together so effortlessly. A genuinely uplifting moment from an iconic brand."
– Mark Waites, Mother

Yoda Melvin / Statistic Spencer /
Ego Ed
Saatchi & Saatchi New York
Page 204

"Beautifully observed characters, witty dialogue and hilarious performances. These radio ads will be a favourite among listeners and marketers alike."
– Ralph van Dijk, Eardrum

Crime
Murray & Sorrell FUEL
Page 305

"There was an obvious attention to detail in the design of the book, and the intelligent way it had been produced. A reminder that a large print budget alone is not enough."
– Jamie Keenan, Keenan Design

Trouble Maker Condoms
HanTang Communications Group
Page 361

"The idea behind the 'Trouble Maker' condoms makes the most impact on the packaging itself. It really takes advantage of that personal connection that great packaging design can have with consumers."
– Bruce Duckworth, Turner Duckworth

MacBook Air
Apple Industrial Design Team
Page 380

"The design development of the MacBook Air is focused strongly on the future user experience. The bold deletion of extraneous conventional features makes it lightweight and portable. It's a great leap forward in laptop design."
– Sebastian Conran, Conran & Partners

Davidson / Gill / Ledwidge / Silburn
Dye Holloway Murray
Pages 390, 391

"This campaign was chosen because it worked in the way great pieces of art direction should work. Fresh and free-spirited, the art direction sprang from the page."
– Brian Connolly, Spark London

WERK No.16: Joe Magee Special
Joe Magee
Pages 214, 408

"Beautifully printed, considered and with a rawness to it, this publication really is quite special."
– Marion Deuchars, M Deuchars

Faces of Evil
Das Comitee
Page 432

"An extraordinary (if slightly crazy) concept, supported by exhaustive research and executed impeccably."
– Tony Chambers, Wallpaper*

Christopher Doyle Identity Guidelines
Christopher Doyle
Pages 232, 337, 451

"Chris Doyle's personal identity guidelines harmonise words and visuals beautifully (and hilariously), with an obvious love for the craft of language."
– Mike Reed, Reed Words

Hotel 626
Goodby Silverstein and Partners
Pages 502, 528

"A unanimous choice, one of the most amazing sites of the year. The concept pushes interactive branded content to the limit, creating an incredible and terrifying experience."
– Mauricio Mazzariol, Wieden + Kennedy Portland

Kei-tai Traveler K-TRA
Dentsu Tokyo
Page 541

"This campaign was genius. I wish that we'd thought of it – and that's what D&AD is all about."
– Dan Rosen, AKQA

The Great Schlep
Droga 5
Pages 18, 19, 139

"This was the year that US politics entered the digital world. The Great Schlep was hysterical, timely and brought about change."
– Michael Lebowitz, Big Spaceship

Kinetic Sculpture for the BMW Museum
ART+COM
Pages 21, 564

"Although 'Kinetic Sculpture' is technically very impressive, narrative is at the heart of this work, informing and fascinating simultaneously."
– Matt Clark, United Visual Artists

Einige Zitate der Juroren

UK Coinage Reverse Designs
Matt Dent
Seite 20

„Matts Designs werden wahrscheinlich so lange produziert, bis die Queen abgedankt hat. Es ist schön zu wissen, dass es etwas so Gutes wie das hier noch ein paar Jahre geben wird. Ich wünschte, seine Designs wären von mir."
– Ben Terrett

Whopper Sacrifice
Crispin Porter + Bogusky
Seite 525

„Der ‚Whopper Sacrifice' löste bei allen Jurymitgliedern die gleiche Reaktion aus: In dem Moment, in dem sie davon hörten, wünschten sich alle, es wäre ihre Idee gewesen."
– Dave Bedwood, Lean Mean Fighting Machine

Woman Whisperer
Clemenger BBDO Melbourne
Seite 156

„Mit den beiden Worten ‚Der Frauenflüsterer' hast du einen Gag, den jeder Kerl in jeder Kneipe zum Totlachen findet und weitererzählt."
– Dave Trott, CST

Rabbit
Goodby Silverstein and Partners
Seiten 150, 461, 498

„Wenn man tolle Bilder verwendet und sie mit einem Supertext unterlegt, entsteht etwas Großartiges. ‚Rabbit' macht das auf brillante Weise: erstaunliche Bildfolgen (dank ein paar technologischer Tricks) und ein hypnotisches Voice-over. Immer, wenn man glaubt, dass das nicht noch weiter beschleunigt werden kann, legt das Video noch 'nen Zahn zu. Hervorragend."
– Simon Veksner, BBH London

Oasis „Dig Out Your Soul" –
in the Streets
BBH New York
Seiten 126, 127, 143

„Das Konzept, das neue Oasis-Album dadurch bekannt zu machen, dass Straßenmusiker die Stücke der neuen CD spielen, ist absolut genial. Total anders, supermutig und riesig. Eine todsichere D&AD-Nominierung."
– Mike O'Sullivan, Saatchi & Saatchi Neuseeland

Million
Droga 5
Seite 22

„Indem sie zuerst das Problem identifizierte und dann das New Yorker Schulsystem mit Verizon und Samsung zusammenbrachte, schuf Droga5 ein äußerst nützliches Programm, verpackt in eine schlagkräftige, kreative Botschaft, die wirklich etwas bewegen kann."
– Mark Cridge, glue London

It's Mine
Wieden + Kennedy Los Angeles
Seiten 149, 474

„‚It's Mine' ist die Art von Werbung, die man sich immer wieder anschauen kann. Die epische Filmlänge fühlt sich genau richtig an, die Musik trifft auf den Punkt genau, und die Regieleistung ist überwältigend – alles fließt völlig mühelos zusammen. Ein echt erhebender Moment dieser Kultmarke."
– Mark Waites, Mother

Yoda Melvin / Statistic Spencer /
Ego Ed
Saatchi & Saatchi New York
Seite 204

„Wunderbar beobachtete Charaktere, geistreiche Dialoge und urkomische Auftritte. Diese Radiospots werden bei Hörern und Marketingleuten gleichermaßen abräumen."
– Ralph van Dijk, Eardrum

Crime
Murray & Sorrell FUEL
Seite 305

„Man hat dem Design des Buches wirklich angesehen, wie sehr auf die Details geachtet und mit welchem Anspruch es produziert wurde. Wieder mal ein Hinweis darauf, dass ein großes Budget für Print allein nicht ausreicht."
– Jamie Keenan, Keenan Design

Trouble Maker Condoms
HanTang Communications Group
Seite 361

„Die Idee hinter den ‚Trouble Maker'-Kondomen wäre auch für eine Plakatkampagne geeignet. Aber auf der Packung selbst hat sie den größten Effekt. Denn sie nutzt geschickt die persönliche Verbindung aus, die ein großartiges Verpackungsdesign zu seinen Verbrauchern aufbauen kann."
– Bruce Duckworth, Turner Duckworth

MacBook Air
Apple Industrial Design Team
Seite 380

„Die Designentwicklung des MacBook Air war stark darauf konzentriert, zukünftigen Usern ein neuartiges Erlebnis zu bieten. Durch das mutige Weglassen irrelevanter, herkömmlicher Features wird das MacBook Air leicht und gut tragbar. Ein Riesenschritt in Richtung Zukunft im Bereich Laptopdesign, das die konventionelle Konstruktion auf den Kopf stellt und perfekt durchdachte Produkte abliefert."
– Sebastian Conran, Conran & Partners

Davidson / Gill / Ledwidge / Silburn
Dye Holloway Murray
Seiten 390, 391

„Diese Kampagne wurde ausgewählt, weil sie genauso funktionierte, wie man es von ausgezeichneten Beispielen aus dem Bereich Artdirection erwartet. Unverbraucht und unkonventionell fällt die künstlerische Arbeit völlig aus dem Rahmen und bringt einen dazu, sich mit der Idee zu beschäftigen und sie zu absorbieren."
– Brian Connolly, Spark London

WERK No.16: Joe Magee Special
Joe Magee
Seiten 214, 408

„Bildschön gedruckt, durchdacht und mit einer gewissen Ungeschliffenheit ist diese Publikation wirklich etwas ganz Besonderes."
– Marion Deuchars, M Deuchars

Faces of Evil
Das Comitee
Seite 432

„Ein außergewöhnliches (wenn auch leicht verrücktes) Konzept, unterstützt durch umfassende Recherchen und makellos ausgeführt."
– Tony Chambers, Wallpaper*

Christopher Doyle Identity Guidelines
Christopher Doyle
Seiten 232, 337, 451

„Chris Doyles Leitfaden für die Personal Identity vereint Worte und Bilder auf eine wunderschöne (und urkomische) Art und Weise und zeigt deutlich seine offensichtliche Liebe für das Handwerk der Sprache."
– Mike Reed, Reed Words

Hotel 626
Goodby Silverstein and Partners
Seiten 502, 528

„Eine einhellige Entscheidung: ‚Hotel 626' ist eine der erstaunlichsten Internetseiten des Jahres. Das Konzept treibt den interaktiven markenbezogenen Inhalt auf die Spitze und schafft mithilfe der Website, auf die man nur nachts zugreifen darf, eine unglaubliche und zugleich verstörende Erfahrung. Ein detailgenaues und nahezu unfassbares Spiel."
– Mauricio Mazzariol, Wieden + Kennedy Portland

Kei-tai Traveler K-TRA
Dentsu Tokyo
Seite 541

„Diese Kampagne war genial. Ich wünschte, sie wäre uns eingefallen – und genau darum geht es doch bei D&AD."
– Dan Rosen, AKQA

The Great Schlep
Droga 5
Seiten 18, 19, 139

„Es war das Jahr, als die US-Politik in die digitale Welt eintrat. ‚The Great Schlep' war völlig abgedreht, zeitgemäß und konnte tatsächlich etwas verändern."
– Michael Lebowitz, Big Spaceship

Kinetic Sculpture
for the BMW Museum
ART+COM
Seiten 21, 564

„Obwohl ‚Kinetic Sculpture' technisch sehr beeindruckend ist, steckt im Kern dieser Arbeit eine Geschichte, die gleichermaßen informativ wie faszinierend ist."
– Matt Clark, UnitedVisualArtists

Quelques mots des membres du jury

UK Coinage Reverse Designs
Matt Dent
Page 20

« Les pièces portant les revers dessinés par Matt resteront sans doute en circulation jusqu'à la fin du règne de la Reine. C'est agréable de savoir qu'un projet aussi réussi restera disponible pendant quelques années. J'aurais aimé en être l'auteur. »
– Ben Terrett

Whopper Sacrifice
Crispin Porter + Bogusky
Page 525

« ‹ Whopper Sacrifice › a fait ressortir le vieux cliché chez tous les juges : c'était LE projet dont ils auraient tous voulu être l'auteur dès qu'ils en ont entendu parler. »
– Dave Bedwood, Lean Mean Fighting Machine

Woman Whisperer
Clemenger BBDO Melbourne
Page 156

« Avec ces trois mots : ‹ The Woman Whisperer › (‹ l'homme qui murmurait à l'oreille des femmes ›), vous obtenez une blague que tous les hommes dans tous les bars trouveront drôle et auront envie de répéter. »
– Dave Trott, CST

Rabbit
Goodby Silverstein and Partners
Pages 150, 461, 498

« Lorsque vous prenez des images brillantes, et que vous leur ajoutez des mots brillants, vous obtenez vraiment quelque chose de bien. ‹ Rabbit › fait cela avec maestria : des images inouïes (grâce à la magie de la technologie) et une voix off envoûtante. Quand on croit qu'ils ont atteint l'accélération maximale, ça va encore plus loin. Superbe. »
– Simon Veksner, BBH London

Oasis « Dig Out Your Soul » –
in the Streets
BBH New York
Pages 126, 127, 143

« Lorsque l'un des frères Gallagher présente votre idée, c'est plutôt un bon début, pour n'importe quel projet. Le concept consistant à lancer le nouvel album d'Oasis en demandant à des musiciens de rue d'en reprendre les morceaux, c'est sidérant. Totalement différent, courageux, et grand. Une nomination D&AD assurée. »
– Mike O'Sullivan, Saatchi & Saatchi New Zealand

Million
Droga 5
Page 22

« En commençant par identifier le problème, puis en faisant collaborer le système new-yorkais de l'éducation, Verizon et Samsung, Droga5 a créé un programme vraiment utile emballé dans un message créatif puissant qui peut vraiment faire changer les choses. »
– Mark Cridge, glue London

It's Mine
Wieden + Kennedy Los Angeles
Pages 149, 474

« ‹ It's Mine › est le genre de spot de publicité que l'on peut regarder 1000 fois. L'échelle cinématographique et épique est parfaite, la musique met dans le mille, et la réalisation est superbe. Tout se met en place naturellement. C'est un moment vraiment réjouissant offert par une marque emblématique. »
– Mark Waites, Mother

Yoda Melvin / Statistic Spencer /
Ego Ed
Saatchi & Saatchi New York
Page 204

« Des personnages magnifiquement observés, des dialogues pleins d'esprit et un jeu d'acteur hilarant. Ces publicités pour la radio vont faire un malheur chez les auditeurs et chez les annonceurs. »
– Ralph van Dijk, Eardrum

Crime
Murray & Sorrell FUEL
Page 305

« L'attention apportée aux détails était évidente dans la conception du livre, et dans l'intelligence de la façon dont il a été produit. Le résultat montre bien qu'un gros budget d'impression ne suffit pas. »
– Jamie Keenan, Keenan Design

14

Trouble Maker Condoms
HanTang Communications Group
Page 361

« L'idée des préservatifs ‹ Trouble Maker › est suffisamment forte pour faire une campagne d'affichage, mais son impact le plus important est sur l'emballage lui-même. Elle exploite vraiment la connexion personnelle qu'un emballage bien conçu peut établir avec les consommateurs. »
– Bruce Duckworth, Turner Duckworth

MacBook Air
Apple Industrial Design Team
Page 380

« Le design du MacBook Air est très orienté vers l'expérience des futurs utilisateurs. La suppression audacieuse des fonctions extérieures habituelles le rend léger et portable. C'est un grand bond en avant dans la conception des ordinateurs portables. »
– Sebastian Conran, Conran & Partners

Davidson / Gill / Ledwidge / Silburn
Dye Holloway Murray
Pages 390, 391

« Cette campagne a été choisie parce qu'elle fonctionne comme les grandes œuvres de direction artistique devraient fonctionner. Originale et non conformiste, la direction artistique crève la page. »
– Brian Connolly, Spark London

WERK No.16: Joe Magee Special
Joe Magee
Pages 214, 408

« Magnifiquement imprimée et pensée, avec un certain caractère brut, cette publication est vraiment très spéciale. »
– Marion Deuchars, M Deuchars

Faces of Evil
Das Comitee
Page 432

« Un concept extraordinaire (et quand même un peu fou), soutenu par des recherches exhaustives et une exécution impeccable. »
– Tony Chambers, Wallpaper *

Christopher Doyle Identity Guidelines
Christopher Doyle
Pages 232, 337, 451

« Le guide de l'identité personnelle de Chris Doyle harmonise à merveille (et avec beaucoup d'humour) les mots et les images, et démontre un amour évident de l'art du langage. »
– Mike Reed, Reed Words

Hotel 626
Goodby Silverstein and Partners
Pages 502, 528

« ‹ Hotel 626 › est l'un des sites les plus brillants de l'année, il a fait l'unanimité. Le concept explore les limites des contenus de marque interactifs, et crée une expérience incroyable et terrifiante sur le site, que l'on ne peut visiter que de nuit. »
– Mauricio Mazzariol, Wieden + Kennedy Portland

Kei-tai Traveler K-TRA
Dentsu Tokyo
Page 541

« Cette campagne est géniale. J'aurais aimé y avoir pensé. Et c'est bien de ça qu'il s'agit chez D&AD. »
– Dan Rosen, AKQA

The Great Schlep
Droga 5
Pages 18, 19, 139

« C'est l'année où la politique américaine est entrée dans le monde numérique. Le ‹ Great Schlep › était hilarant, est arrivé au bon moment, et a vraiment fait changer les choses. »
– Michael Lebowitz, Big Spaceship

Kinetic Sculpture for the BMW Museum
ART+COM
Pages 21, 564

« La ‹ Kinetic Sculpture › est très impressionnante du point de vue technique, mais au cœur de ce projet il y a une histoire qui nous est contée, qui nous informe et nous fascine simultanément. »
– Matt Clark, United Visual Artists

The D&AD Black Pencil

The Black Pencil is the rarest of prizes. Awarded to only the most ground-breaking work of the year, just 104 have been awarded in D&AD's 47 year history. Some years no Black Pencils are awarded, most recently in 2003.

Past winners include Apple for the iMac in 1999; *The Times Newspapers* won in 1969; and the UK's Channel 4 has won Black Pencils twice for its corporate identity – in 1983 and 2005. New York agency Droga5 set a new standard in 2009, being the first advertising agency to win two Black Pencils for different pieces of work.

The Black Pencil Jury is split into 3 groups; Advertising, Design and Digital. The groups look at the nominations from their respective disciplines and each jury representative has the opportunity to champion work they think has redefined the boundaries of creative communication. It's a long day filled with debate – of the healthy and the heated variety. Eventually each jury member casts a final, anonymous vote. The results are announced at the Awards Ceremony soon after.

Der Black Pencil des D&AD

Der Black Pencil ist die seltenste aller Auszeichnungen und wird nur an die herausragendste und bahnbrechendste Arbeit eines Jahres verliehen. Deswegen ist der Black Pencil in der 47-jährigen Geschichte des D&AD bisher nur 104 Mal vergeben worden. In manchen Jahren gibt es gar keinen Preisträger – so zum Beispiel im Jahr 2003.

Zu den früheren Preisträgern gehörten 1969 die Zeitung *The Times*, die Firma Apple mit dem iMac im Jahre 1999 und der britische Channel 4. Er bekam sogar zwei Black Pencils für seine Corporate Identity – 1983 und 2005. Die New Yorker Agentur Droga5 setzte 2009 schließlich neue Maßstäbe: Als erste Werbeagentur gewann sie gleich zwei Black Pencils für verschiedene Arbeiten.

Die Jury für den Black Pencil teilt sich in drei Gruppen: Advertising, Design und Digital. Die Mitglieder der einzelnen Gruppen betrachten die Nominierungen aus Sicht ihrer jeweiligen Disziplin. Danach bekommt jeder Juryrepräsentant die Möglichkeit, sich für die Arbeit einzusetzen, von der er denkt, dass damit die Grenzen der kreativen Kommunikation neu definiert werden. Es folgt ein langer Tag voller hitziger Debatten, an dessen Anschluss jedes Jurymitglied anonym endgültig seine Stimme abgibt. Die Ergebnisse werden kurz darauf in der Preisverleihung verkündet.

Le Black Pencil de D&AD

Le Black Pencil est la plus rare de toutes les récompenses. Elle n'est accordée qu'aux projets les plus révolutionnaires de l'année, et seulement 104 ont été remises au cours des 47 années d'existence de D&AD. Certaines années, aucun Black Pencil n'est décerné, par exemple en 2003.

Parmi ses lauréats, on trouve notamment Apple pour l'iMac en 1999, *The Times Newspapers* en 1969, et la chaîne de télévision anglaise Channel 4, qui a gagné deux Black Pencils pour son identité d'entreprise, en 1983 et en 2005. L'agence new-yorkaise Droga5 a battu un nouveau record en 2009, car c'est la première agence de publicité à remporter deux Black Pencils pour des projets différents.

Le jury du Black Pencil est divisé en trois groupes : publicité, design et numérique. Les groupes se penchent sur les nominations du point de vue de leurs disciplines respectives, et chaque représentant du jury peut défendre le projet qui selon lui a repoussé les limites de la communication créative. C'est une longue journée remplie de débats intenses et passionnants, au terme de laquelle chaque juré émet un vote définitif et anonyme. Les résultats sont annoncés peu après, lors de la cérémonie de remise des prix.

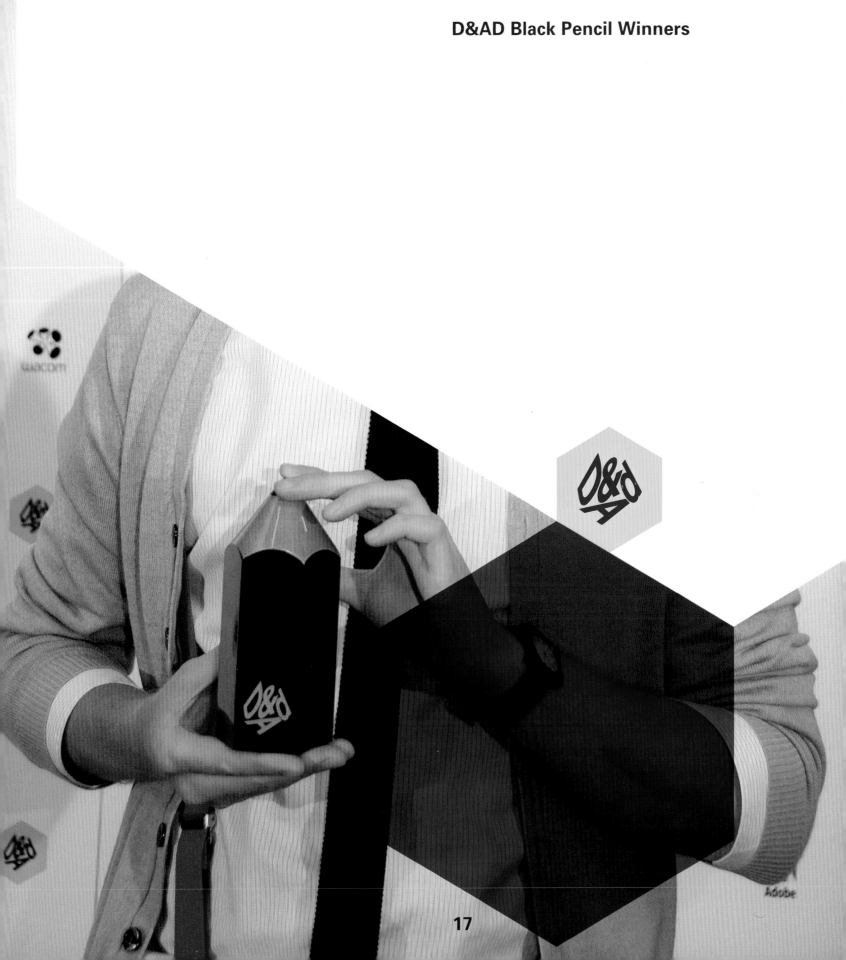

Copywriter	**Digital Creative**	**Advertising Agency**	**Head of Integrated**
Isaac Silverglate	**Director**	Droga5	**Production**
Writers	Scott Witt	**Digital Agency**	Sally-Ann Dale
Sarah Silverman	**Executive Creative**	Liberty Concepts	**Client**
Dan Sterling	**Director**	**Agency Producer**	Jewish Council of
Director	Ted Royer	Craig Batzofin	Education
Wayne McClammy	**Creative Chairman**	**Editor**	& Research
Art Director	David Droga	Josh Reynolds	**Brand**
Jeff Anderson	**Executive Producer**	**Director of**	The Great Schlep
Interactive Designer	Heidi Herzon	**Photography**	
Kenny Kim	**Production**	Rhet Bear	
	Company	**Music Composer**	
	Black Gold Films	Adam Berry	

Writing

Droga5
for Jewish Council of Education & Research

The Great Schlep
In Florida, elderly Jewish voters are a crucial voting block. In 2008, they were beginning to lean towards John McCain. To target them in a way they couldn't refuse, we encouraged their pro-Obama grandchildren to talk to them about Obama. We spread the word with a viral video featuring comedienne Sarah Silverman and a website that united and inspired a younger generation. Millions viewed the video and thousands of media outlets covered the campaign. For the first time in 12 years a Democratic nominee won Florida. Also selected in Viral Films.

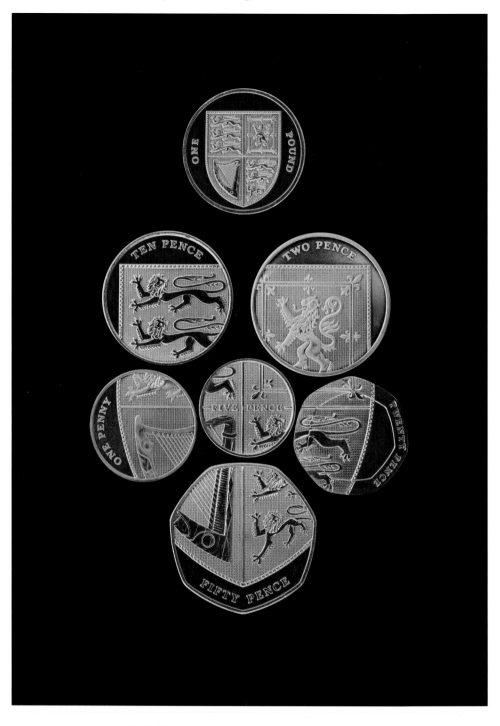

Designer
Matt Dent

Sculptor
John Bergdhal

Production
The Royal Mint

Client
The Royal Mint

Applied Print Graphics

Matt Dent
for The Royal Mint

UK Coinage Reverse Designs
A public competition was launched by The Royal Mint in August 2005, to find new reverse designs for UK circulating coins from the penny to the fifty pence, replacing the current set which has been in circulation for almost 40 years. My approach to the challenge was to use a single image, the shield of the Royal Coat of Arms, spread over the six coins, inviting people to assemble the design for themselves – an unprecedented approach to coinage. The coins illustrate how the separate elements of the shield come together and how different countries make up the UK. The pound coin was later introduced to act as the solution to the puzzle: the jigsaw box's lid.

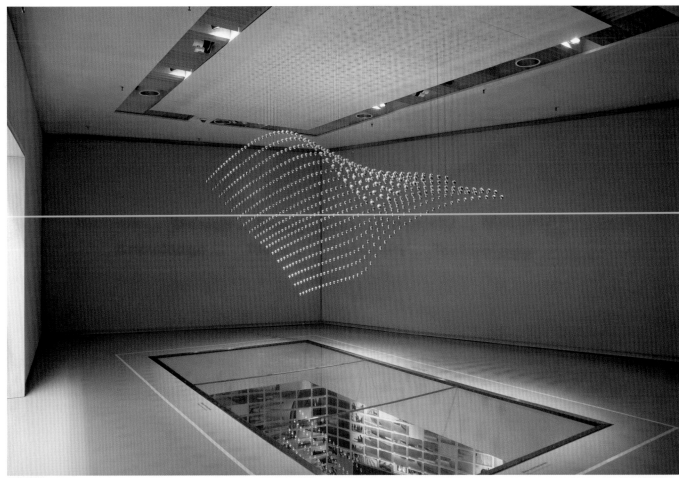

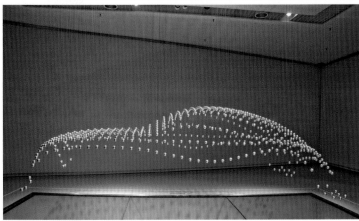

Designer	Art Directors	Design Group	Client
Susanne Traeger	Patrick Kochlik	ART+COM	BMW Group
Technical Designers	Petra Trefzger	**Museum Director**	**Brand**
Simon Schießl	**Creative Director**	Dr Ralf Rodepeter	BMW
David Siegel	Joachim Sauter		

Installations

ART+COM
for BMW Group

Kinetic Sculpture for the BMW Museum
The Kinetic Sculpture is a metaphorical translation of the process of form-finding in design. Covering an area of six square metres, it comprises 714 metal spheres, hanging from thin steel wires attached to individually controlled stepper motors to animate a seven-minute long mechatronic narrative. Moving chaotically at first, the sculpture evolves through several competing forms and eventually resolves into a final shape whose profile hints at one of many well known, historic and current, BMW automobiles. Shortly after the opening of the BMW Museum, the Kinetic Sculpture became the most watched video worldwide in the automotive category on YouTube for a week.

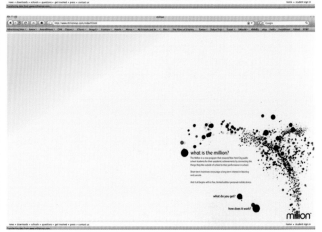

Art Directors
Cam Blackley
Matty Burton
Ben Nott
Copywriters
Cam Blackley
Matty Burton
Ben Nott
Designer
David Park

Executive Creative Director
Duncan Marshall
Digital Creative Director
Scott Witt
Creative Chairman
David Droga

Advertising Agency
Droga5
Agency Producers
Craig Batzofin
Thomas Beug
Head of Integrated Production
Sally-Ann Dale
Digital Agency
POKE New York

Account Handler
Julia Alba
Client
New York City
Department
of Education
Brand
Million

Integrated

Droga5
for NYC Department of Education

Million
We were asked to rebrand scholastic achievement for New York City's public school students by re-enforcing the connection between academic performance and success. Launched in 2008, the Million is already in the hands of more than 3,000 NYC public school students. Within two weeks of the launch, teachers, principals and administrators recognised marked improvements in students' attendance, behaviour, homework completion and grades. As the Million continues its New York City rollout, school districts around the world have already expressed interest in piloting the Million programme, giving it the potential to become the largest global communications network. And it all started with a free, fully-functional mobile device.

The jury:
Tay Guan Hin, JWT Singapore (Jury Foreman)
Damien Bellon, Mother
Jonathan Burley, Leo Burnett London
Damon Collins, RKCR/Y&R
Andy DiLallo, Leo Burnett Sydney
David Hobbs, Miles Calcraft Briginshaw Duffy
Christian Mommertz, Ogilvy & Mather Frankfurt
Alan Moseley, Hurrell Moseley Dawson & Grimmer
Johnny Tan, BBH China

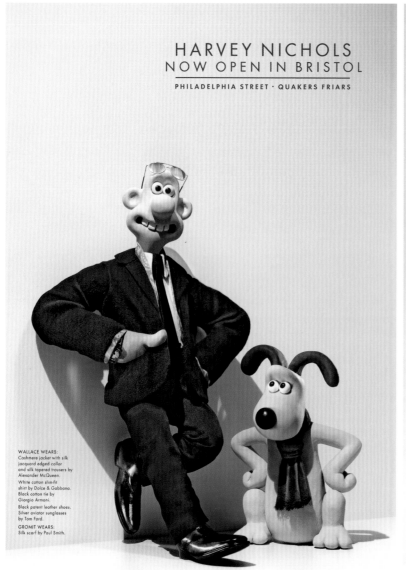

HARVEY NICHOLS
NOW OPEN IN BRISTOL
PHILADELPHIA STREET · QUAKERS FRIARS

WALLACE WEARS:
Prince of Wales
check three piece
wool suit
by Paul Smith.

GROMIT WEARS:
Purple stripe silk
scarf by Duchamp.
Ray-Ban Wayfarers.

Art Director
Grant Parker
Copywriter
Grant Parker
Photographer
Giles Revell
Typographer
Pete Mould
Creative Director
Jeremy Craigen

Retouchers
Greg Champman
Steve Sanderson
Andy Walsh
Advertising Agency
DDB London
Planner
Georgina Murray-Burton

Production Company
Aardman Animations
Model Making
Aardman Animations
Animator
Loyd Price
Art Buyer
Sarah Thomson
Project Manager
Caroline Tripp

Account Handlers
Philip Heimann
Briony Small
Marketing Manager
Shona Campbell
Marketing Officer
Mimi Morrish
Marketing Director
Julia Bowe
Client
Harvey Nichols

Poster Advertising Campaigns

DDB London
for Harvey Nichols

Wallace in Alexander McQueen & Gromit in Paul Smith / Lady Tottington in Alexander McQueen / Wallace in Paul Smith & Gromit in Duchamp
The campaign for the opening of the new Harvey Nichols Bristol store featured Wallace, Gromit and Lady Tottington.

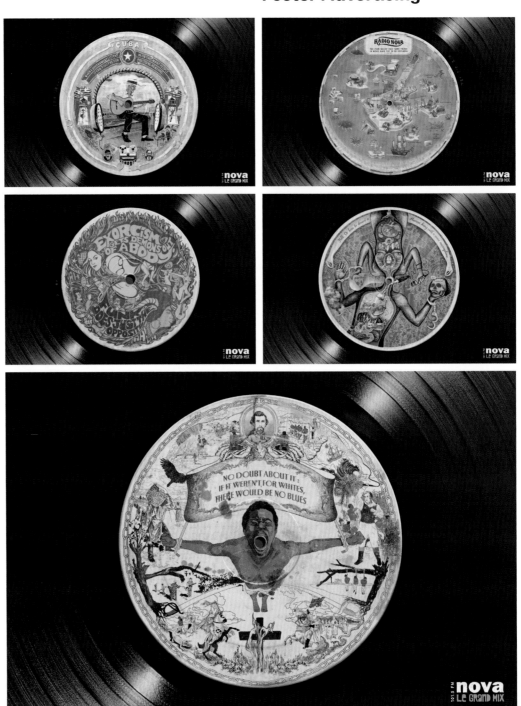

Art Director
Jessica Gerard-Huet
Copywriter
Jean-Francois
Bouchet
Photographer
Roger Turqueti
Creative Direction
Les Six

Illustrators
Jean-Francois
Bouchet
Jessica Gerard-Huet
Richard Mongenet
Jean Spezial
François Valla
Illustration
Am I Collective
Production Plein Soleil

Retoucher
Grazielle @ Asile
Advertising Agency
Young & Rubicam
France
Account Handlers
Geraldine Hincelin
Claire Nicaise-
Schindler

Brand Managers
Bruno Delport
Marc H'limi
Eric Karnbauer
Client
Nova Radio
Brand
Le Grand Mix

Poster Advertising Campaigns

Young & Rubicam France
for Nova Radio

Cuba / Electro / Funk / Folk / Blues / Jazz / Rap / Ska / James Brown / India
Nova is not your usual radio station. No one plays as many different styles of music as it does. The station started in 1981, and helped rap, world music and electro emerge in France. It is truly different. Very open. However, Nova had not run any ad campaigns for ten years. Fortunately, it liked ours because it was not trying to sell anything. It was not about the station itself, but about music. And (pleasant surprise!) Nova even asked for more ads, in order to make the campaign as 'musically wide' as possible, and to express its identity, well summed up by 'Le Grand Mix'.

27

Art Director	Typographer	Advertising Agency	Brand Manager
Nick Allsop	Chris Chapman	BBH London	Michael Joubert
Copywriter	**Creative Directors**	**Planner**	**Client**
Simon Veksner	Alex Grieve	Patricia McDonald	Levi Strauss EMEA
Photographer	John Hegarty	**Account Handlers**	**Brand**
Joseph Rodriguez	Adrian Rossi	Mel Exon	Levi Strauss
		Paisley Wright	

Roadside Posters

BBH London
for Levi Strauss EMEA

Cheerleaders / Audience / Cops

The brief from the client was to move away from product focused communications and to inject some attitude and desirability back into the brand. Each execution is shot from the first person point-of-view of a Levi's-wearing hero, capturing the reaction this person provokes in people who rigidly uphold convention and abhor difference. Unsurprisingly, they regard our heroes with disdain, suspicion and antipathy. So much the better. These are not people whose approval we want; they're the opposite of the Levi's wearer, the epitome of conformity.

29

Jeep

Jeep

Art Directors
Eric Hor
Willeon Leong
Gary Lim
MUN
Copywriters
Kevin Le
Ronald Ng

Creative Directors
MUN
Ronald Ng
Designers
Willeon Leong
Gary Lim
MUN
Illustrators
Willeon Leong
Gary Lim

Advertising Agency
BBDO/Proximity
Malaysia
Print Producer
Dickson Teh
Account Handlers
Tieh Pui Yen
Dong Hyun Yoo

Brand Manager
Sally Hong
Client
Chrysler Korea
Brand
Jeep

Point of Sale Posters
BBDO/Proximity Malaysia
for Chrysler Korea

Husky & Camel / Bushman & Eskimo / Mountain Goat & Crocodile
To promote Jeep's superior all-terrain capability, we overlapped two images of objects that are polar opposites to form the outline of the car, creating the impression that Jeep can go anywhere. As for applying a clean design style to the concept, well, we hope that it will make Jeep stand out from all the advertising in the car galaxy.

31

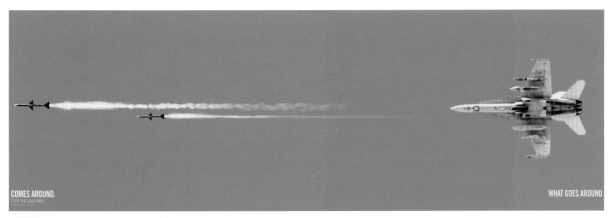

Art Directors
Frank Anselmo
Alfred S Park
Jeseok Yi

Copywriters
Francisco Hui
William Tran
Creative Director
Alfred S Park

Executive Creative Director
Richard Wilde
Advertising Agency
Big Ant International

Client
Global Coalition for Peace
Brand
Peace Campaign

Poster Advertising Campaigns

Big Ant International
for Global Coalition for Peace

What Goes Around Comes Around – Gun / Tank / Jet / Grenade
The Global Coalition for Peace wanted a campaign to reassert the importance of an immediate withdrawal from Iraq, while also building awareness of the organisation. We came up with a simple and elegant outdoor campaign that focused on the spiralling cycle of war; that what goes around, comes around. most likely to be motivated into direct action, either through volunteering or making donations. Support was overwhelming during the time that these pieces ran, with a significant increase in donations of both time and money.

Art Directors
Chris Fong
Nicky Sun
Cherry Yiu
Copywriters
Terry Tsang
Wong Wai
Photographer
U Hei Shing

Creative Directors
Chris Fong
Nick Lim
Terry Tsang
Spencer Wong
Designers
Chris Fong
Nicky Sun
Cherry Yiu

Advertising Agency
McCann
Worldgroup Hong
Kong
Account Handlers
Calton Chu
Yen Lee
Penelope Yau

Brand Managers
Mandy Liu
Jacqueline Tse
Marketing Manager
Amy Wu
Client
Nike Hong Kong

Poster Advertising Campaigns

McCann Worldgroup Hong Kong
for Nike Hong Kong

Paper Battlefield Campaign
Competing in and being a part of the most prestigious and competitive Nike League is the dream of every aspiring young basketballer. It is also an opportunity for the teens to show off their skills. So we took the spirit of competition and literally translated it into posters. Images of the top ten players with their individual skill were used as printing templates. The players were invited to our silkscreen workshop to print their image on top of each other. They handmade 350 posters. The posters became the battlefield; the random cross-printing, the battles. More importantly, the process conveyed our message.

Art Director
Attila Kiraly
Copywriters
Björn Persson
Mikael Ström

Creative Director
Björn Ståhl
Advertising Agency
Ogilvy Stockholm

Account Handler
Kristiina Mullersdorf
Brand Manager
Bonian
Golmohammadi

Marketing Manager
Maria Andersson
Client
United Nations
Sweden

Poster Advertising Campaigns

Ogilvy Stockholm
for United Nations Sweden

True Evidence of War
Our assignment was to make people aware of the terrible civilian suffering in Georgia after the war, and raise donations for the refugees. We went to Georgia and collected personal belongings abandoned in the rubble. These items, accompanied by their stories, were placed into billboards, demonstrating that the war may have ended but the suffering had only just begun.

Art Director
Rob Messeter
Copywriter
Mike Crowe
Photographers
Drew Leavy
Rob Messeter
Wayne Parker
Typographer
Pete Mould

Creative Directors
Emer Stamp
Ben Tollet
Retoucher
Steve Sanderson
Advertising Agency
DDB London
Project Manager
Lexie Linnert

Account Manager
Matt Bundy
Account Director
Paul Billingsley
Business Director
Anna Hopwood
**Global Strategy
Director**
Lucy Jameson

**Global Marketing
Director**
Frances Brindle
**Head of Global
Brand**
Caroline Halliwell
Client
Financial Times

Poster Advertising Campaigns

DDB London
for Financial Times

Global Downturn
This campaign for the Financial Times features billboards that have been stripped almost bare. The objective is to question the slashing of advertising budgets by businesses as a result of the economic downturn.

Art Director
Kerstin Eberbach
Copywriter
Lars Huvart
Photographer
Jo Bacherl

Creative Directors
Thomas Hofbeck
Lars Huvart
Designer
Kerstin Eberbach
Producer
Fabian Schrader

Advertising Agency
Ogilvy Frankfurt
Art Buyers
Martina Diederichs
Caroline Walczok
Account Handlers
Marco Bisello
Sascha Riedel

Marketing Manager
Jens Helfrich
Client
IKEA Germany
Brand
IKEA

Enhanced, Interactive & Digital Posters

Ogilvy Frankfurt
for IKEA Germany

Bigger Storage Ideas
German flats and apartments are full of messy corners. That's why IKEA produces practical boxes and drawers in all shapes and sizes for all storage needs. Frankfurt IKEA asked us to promote their storage solutions, targeted particularly at people living in smaller apartments, with a big outdoor idea. We played with the widely recognisable shapes and designs of the IKEA storage range and put them into a new and surprising context. By redesigning the front of an apartment building in a busy Frankfurt street with giant mock-ups of IKEA drawers and cardboard boxes, we generated the highest level of attention, and literally linked the product to where it belongs: in small flats and apartments.

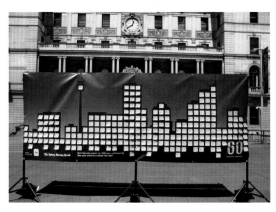

Art Directors
Mela Advincula
Dave Ladd
Copywriters
Cey Enriquez
Raoul Panes
Rupert Taylor
Alvin Tecson

Creative Director
Mark Collis
Designer
Dave Ladd
Retoucher
Dave Ladd
**Advertising
Agencies**
Leo Burnett Manila
Leo Burnett Sydney

Production Manager
Mark Dillon
Planner
Rupert Taylor
Account Handler
Sam McGown
Brand Manager
Liz Potter

Marketing Manager
Andy Ridley
Client
WWF
Brand
Earth Hour

Enhanced, Interactive & Digital Posters

Leo Burnett Manila & Leo Burnett Sydney
for WWF

Lights Off
As a reminder to join in Earth Hour 2008, we set up mobile billboards in city centres around Australia. The billboards featured a city skyline at night; post-it-note stickers represented the lights in the windows of the buildings. When people took one, they turned off a light on the billboard, and were reminded to turn theirs off for Earth Hour.

Art Directors	Creative Director	Producers	Advertising Agency
Yang Yong Liang	Yang Yeo	Yuncheng An	JWT Shanghai
Lillie Zhong	**Designer**	Xue Wu	**Agency Producer**
Copywriters	Sean Tang	**Editors**	Jane Zhang
Rafael Freire	**Illustrator**	Chun Huang	**Account Handler**
Jacqueline Ye	Yang Yong Liang	Jing Li	Betty Tsai
Photographer	**Director**	**Music Composer**	**Client**
Yang Yong Liang	Hailong Li	Jiangzhou Feng	CEPF

Enhanced, Interactive & Digital Posters

JWT Shanghai
for CEPF

Shan Shui
This campaign is the result of a collaboration with famous Shanghai artist Yang Yong Liang.
It looks like a beautiful landscape painting, but when zoomed in, it's neither mountain nor
stream, but factory buildings and cars. The China Environment Protection Fund wanted to warn
people with these striking images that if we don't take any more action to reduce pollution of
the environment, there will come a day when all the beautiful landscapes will have disappeared.

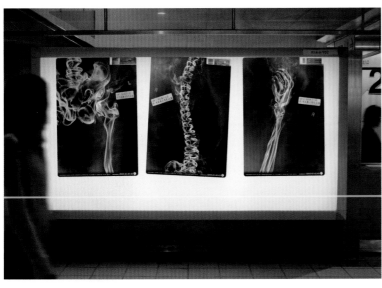
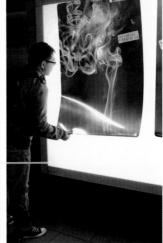

Art Directors
Ronny Hsu
Nelson Liu
Richard Yu

Copywriters
Renee Chen
Lion Tsai
Creative Directors
Ronny Hsu
Lion Tsai
Richard Yu

Illustrator
Nelson Liu
Advertising Agency
Bates Taiwan

Brand Manager
Lyiy Wu
Client
Taiwan Smokers'
Helpline

Enhanced, Interactive & Digital Posters

Bates Taiwan
for Taiwan Smokers' Helpline

X-Ray Photo Light Box
The aim of this campaign was to show that when smokers need a cigarette to relax, not only is smoking unlikely to help, but it also causes osteoporosis. We used smoke to compose loose bones to look like X-ray of the spine, carpal bones, and pelvis. These visuals were projected through the outdoor light boxes in an exact imitation of X-ray photo examiners in hospitals. When smokers saw the ads, it was like they were looking at their own X-ray, and they understood how harmful smoking is to their health.

Art Directors
Al Brown
Algy Sharman
Copywriters
Al Brown
Algy Sharman
Photographer
Rick Guest

Typographer
Rich Kennedy
Creative Directors
Nick Allsop
Simon Veksner
Designer
Rich Kennedy

Retouchers
Gary Meade
Joseph O'Dwyer
Advertising Agency
BBH London
Planner
Rob Ward
Account Handlers
Nick Phelps
Nick Stringer

Brand Manager
Paul Ridsdale
Marketing Manager
Anna Bateson
Client
ITV

Roadside Posters

BBH London
for ITV

Milkman
This advert was devised to promote coverage of the FA Cup on ITV. The FA Cup is unique because non-league teams – whose players have ordinary day jobs like postmen or milkmen – can get to play against the biggest teams in the country. Their lives may be very different, but out on the pitch they suddenly become just eleven men against eleven, and for 90 minutes only, all men are equal.

Roadside Posters

Draftfcb Johannesburg
for Drive Alive

Roadblock
South Africa has one of the worst drink driving problems in the world. Most people consider it acceptable to drive drunk, just as long as they don't get caught. Our mobile billboards were deployed at busy intersections on Friday and Saturday nights. From a distance, they appeared to be police roadblocks, and being unable to turn around and escape, drivers were forced to come face to face with our message: 'If you got nervous, you shouldn't be driving'.

Art Director	**Creative Directors**	**Advertising Agency**	**Marketing Manager**
Gerhard Myburgh	Brent Liebenberg	Draftfcb	Moira Winslow
Copywriter	Rob McLennan	Johannesburg	**Client**
Brent Liebenberg	Gerhard Myburgh	**Account Handler**	Drive Alive
		Gerhard Myburgh	

Transport Posters

Publicis London
for British Army

Victoria Cross
To counter the perception that black soldiers in the British Army are singled out because of their race, we used history to show how they have been singled out for their actions with the Victoria Cross, the highest military award for valour.

Art Director	**Executive Creative**	**Advertising Agency**	**Regional Marketing**
Robert Amstell	**Directors**	Publicis London	**Coordinator**
Copywriter	Tom Ewart	**Planner**	Katie Dulake
Matthew Lancod	Adam Kean	Mike Wade	**Clients**
Photographer	**Designers**	**Account Handler**	British Army
Derek Hiller	Bob Hanson	Guy Norwell	COI
	Simon Tomlin		

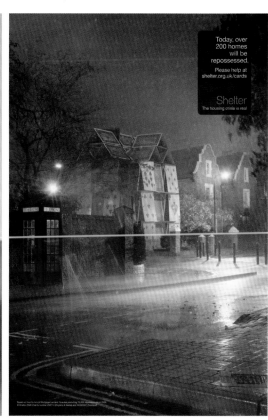

Art Directors	Typographer	Image Manipulation	Account Handler
Richard Brim	Lance Crozier	Saddington Baynes	Gary Simmons
Jay Hunt	**Executive Creative**	**Advertising Agency**	**Acting Head of**
Copywriters	**Director**	Leo Burnett London	**Brand & Marketing**
Daniel Fisher	Jonathan Burley	**Print Producer**	Rachel Murphy
Peter Gosselin	**Retouching**	Simon Keyworth	**Client**
Photography	Saddington Baynes	**Planner**	Shelter
Blinkk		Gary Simmons	

Transport Posters

Leo Burnett London
for Shelter

Morning / Daytime / Evening

These executions were developed to raise awareness of the housing crisis currently gripping the UK, and explain Shelter's unique positioning as a support to the many thousands of households affected. The fragility of a house of cards is used in this work to explain the complexity of different housing issues. Such are the UK's housing problems that this creative idea can be used to explain the truth about repossessions or temporary and social housing, as well as Shelter's call for the basic human right to have a place to call home.

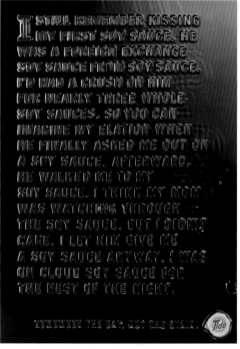

Transport Posters

Saatchi & Saatchi New York
for Procter & Gamble

Forget the Cheese Sauce / Forget the Ketchup / Forget the Soy Sauce
Stains ruin lives. Well, not really. But they can ruin the moment, leaving the memory of it tarnished forever. Tide challenged Saatchi & Saatchi New York to create a campaign that could shine a spotlight on that truth. We went with long copy because, why not? And we stained it, not only figuratively, but also literally, to drive home the ketchup. I mean point.

Art Director	**Creative Directors**	**Designer**	**Planner**
Alan Vladusic	Icaro Doria	Aaron Padin	Wanda Pogue
Copywriter	Audrey Huffenreuter	**Advertising Agency**	**Client**
Ashley Davis-Marshall	**Chief Creative Officer**	Saatchi & Saatchi New York	Procter & Gamble
Photographer	Tony Granger	**Art Buyer**	**Brand**
Dimitri Daniloff		Alli Taylor	Tide

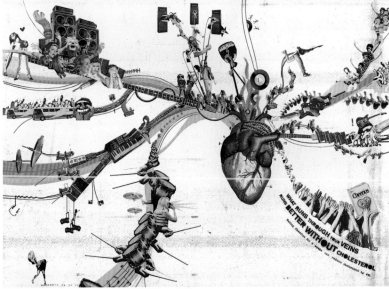

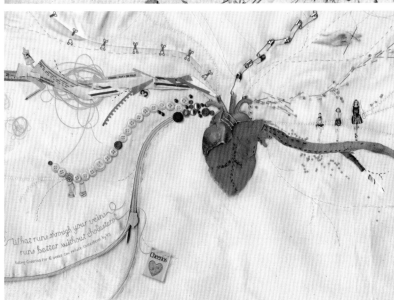

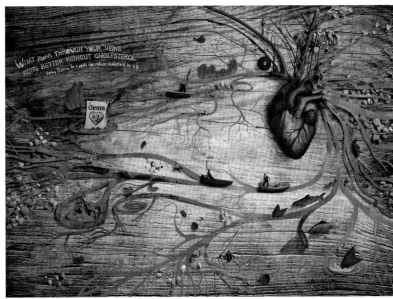

Art Director
Jaclyn Rink
Copywriter
Icaro Doria
Typographers
Hamish McArthur
Jaclyn Rink
Creative Directors
Icaro Doria
Ann Hayden

Chief Creative Officer
Tony Granger
Designers
Yan Apostolides
Aaron Padin
Illustrator
Dave Wheeler

Advertising Agency
Saatchi & Saatchi
New York
Art Buyer
Maggie Sumner
Account Handlers
Stephanie Lederman
Will Platt-Higgins

Client
General Mills
Brand
Cheerios

Transport Posters

Saatchi & Saatchi New York
for General Mills

Gardening / Rock 'n' Roll / Fashion / Fishing
Cheerios is the most popular brand of cereals in the US. In recent years, it has strived to make the claim 'Eating Cheerios for six weeks can reduce cholesterol by four per cent' a household fact. However this claim lacks the warmth that most Americans have grown to love about the brand. As the pursuit of a healthier life should not be cold and scientific, we came up with a campaign that showed what runs through people's veins, as a reference to their passions in life. 'Gardening', 'Rock 'n' Roll', 'Fashion' and 'Fishing' all show in a very visual way that health claims don't need to be boring.

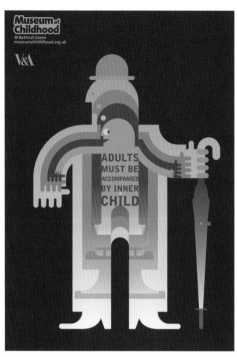

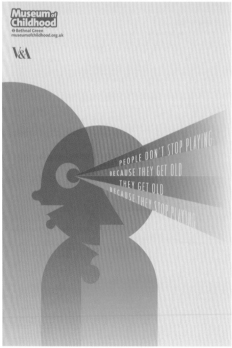

Art Director
Paul Pateman
Copywriter
Mike Nicholson
Creative Director
Paul Brazier

Creative Group
Heads
Mike Nicholson
Paul Pateman
Designer
Paul Pateman

Advertising Agency
Abbott Mead Vickers
BBDO
Print Producer
Linda Carlos

Account Handler
James Drummond
Client
Museum of
Childhood

Pavement Posters
Abbott Mead Vickers BBDO
for Museum of Childhood

Memory Back Guarantee / Playing / Inner Child
The objective was to encourage the public to visit The Museum of Childhood. The museum really takes you back to your youth. To dramatise this, we devised a campaign that literally encouraged you to relive your childhood.

46

Art Director
Cedric Auzannet
Copywriters
Lessly Chmil
Mathieu Grichois

Photography
Corbis
Creative Director
Andrea Stillacci
Illustration
David Martin &
Benoît Monceau

Advertising Agency
Callegari Berville Grey
Planner
Anouk Benlolo
Account Handler
Jessica Not

Marketing Manager
Frederic Guffroy
Client
123fleurs.com

Point of Sale Posters

Callegari Berville Grey
for 123fleurs.com

Airplanes
Don't try too hard. When you love someone, flowers are the best gift you can give.
And the safest...

Art Directors
Pebble Goh
Eric Hor
MUN
Copywriter
Joanne Chow

Creative Directors
MUN
Ronald Ng
Designers
Pebble Goh
Eric Hor
MUN

Advertising Agency
BBDO/Proximity
Malaysia
Print Producer
Dickson Teh

Brand Manager
Pierre Dievart
Client
Century Fiesta
Costume Shop

Point of Sale Posters

BBDO/Proximity Malaysia
for Century Fiesta Costume Shop

Name Cards
This poster doubles up as business cards for Pierre Dievart, owner of Century Fiesta Costume
Shop. Each card shows Pierre donning a different hat – coinciding with a fancy costume that's
available at the shop. All in all, it was a poster that had sixty logos, which is every client's dream
come true.

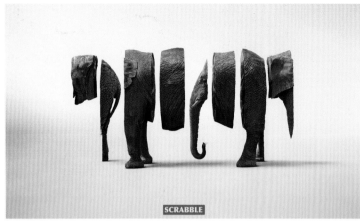

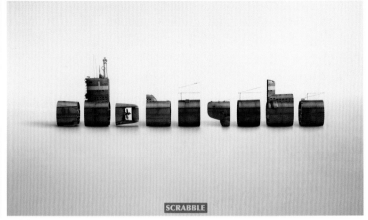

Art Director	**Creative Directors**	**Retoucher**	**Brand Manager**
Matias Lecaros	Leo Farfan	Cristian Gastelo	Pablo Espinosa
Copywriters	Matias Lecaros	**Advertising Agency**	**Marketing Manager**
Matias Lecaros	Sergio Rosati	JWT Chile	Phillip Norton
Tomas Vidal	**Designers**	**Planner**	**Client**
Photographer	Tomas Neely	Sara Munizaga	Mattel Chile
Cristian Gastelo	Israel Urrutia	**Account Handler**	**Brand**
Typographer	**Illustrator**	Cecilia Galaz	SCRABBLE
Boris Berstel	Boris Berstel		

Point of Sale Posters

JWT Chile
for Mattel Chile

EEEANFTL / NAOIMSBRU / RUTAAGRI
The objects are cut into the same number of pieces as there are letters in the word.

Art Director	**Illustrator**	**Agency Producers**	**Account Handlers**
Eirma Webster	Tye Sok Kuan	Ken Lee	Frances Great
Copywriter	**Artworkers**	D'Or Tey	Lesley-Anne Johns
Angie Featherstone	Ken Lee	Asmanic Yang	**Client**
Creative Directors	Loh Heng Loong	**Print Production**	Levi's Strauss Asia
Steve Elrick	**Advertising Agency**	**Managers**	Pacific
Todd Waldron	BBH Asia Pacific	D'Or Tey	**Brand**
		Asmanic Yang	Levi's

Point of Sale Posters

BBH Asia Pacific
for Levi's Strauss Asia Pacific

Levi's Kids – Humpty / Pigs / Jack
The brief was to promote Levi's new season of kids clothing. The objective was to communicate the superiority of the products as long-lasting, hardy clothes for children. As kids love pretending to be heroes when they play, we used familiar imagery from childhood tales and rhymes to engage parents by taking a cheeky poke at play behaviour commonly seen in children. The campaign also engaged children with a twist on stories they identify with. The point of sale medium, such as placement of posters in fitting rooms and shopping areas, was chosen based on the insight that mothers often shop with children in tow, and the posters would allow for interaction between mother and child.

Point of Sale Posters

David&Goliath
for Universal Studios Hollywood

Green Lisa
To launch the new Simpsons ride at Universal Studios Theme Park, we created this poster of Lisa Simpson, everyone's favourite yellow-skinned know-it-all, looking uncharacteristically green. The posters were placed around the park, to pique interest and drive foot traffic to the exciting new attraction.

Art Directors	**Copywriter**	**Creative Directors**	**Advertising Agency**
Federico Callegari	David Povill	David Angelo	David&Goliath
Adam Nelson		Colin Jeffery	**Client**
		Ben Purcell	Universal Studios
			Hollywood

Point of Sale Posters

Ogilvy Singapore
for GSK Singapore

Menstrual
Menstrual cramps can be a real pain, and not just for women. In fact, one would best stay at a safe distance from the potentially explosive situation. Better send in a bomb-disposal robot with a pack of Panadol Menstrual.

Art Director	**Photographer**	**Illustrator**	**Client**
Ashidiq Ghazali	Xuan	Dave	GSK Singapore
Copywriter	**Group Executive**	**Advertising Agency**	**Brand**
Troy Lim	**Creative Director**	Ogilvy Singapore	Panadol
	Todd McCracken		

Art Directors
Aaron Phua
Elisa Tan
Copywriter
Ed Cheong

Creative Directors
Tay Guan Hin
Ali Shabaz
Illustrator
Joseph Griffith

Advertising Agency
JWT Singapore
Account Handler
Chin Chew
Creative Services Director
Mercy Wong

Brand Manager
Pang
Client
Canelé Chocolate Pâtisserie
Brand
Canelé

Point of Sale Posters

JWT Singapore
for Canelé Chocolate Pâtisserie

Ouija / Voodoo
Beyond their eye-catching Victorian boutiques and artful creations, little is known about
Canelé's impressive range of dark chocolate specialties. Inspired by the artistry of Mark Ryden,
nothing says 'equally sweet equally dark' quite like these adorable kids with a subtle dark streak.

Art Director
Tim Holmes
Copywriter
Brendon Guthrie
Photography
Attic Fire Photography

Creative Director
Ant Shannon
Retouching
Electric Art
Advertising Agency
Grey Melbourne

Account Handler
Jane Callister
Brand Manager
Lisa Rizzardo
Marketing Manager
Tara Lordsmith

Client
Simplot Australia
Brand
John West

Indoor Posters

Grey Melbourne
for Simplot Australia

Peli-can
From bears to sharks, John West advertising has always had strong links to the natural world. In this poster, we chose yet another of nature's experts on high quality seafood, to prove that the fish in a John West can really is the best.

Art Directors
Ariyawat Juntaratip
Suthisak
Sucharittanonta
Supparat Thepparat

Copywriters
Subun Khow
Kongpope
Siriwattanagarn
Chanatthapol Tiensri

Photographers
Ekapon Hiranphart
Anuchai
Secharunputong
Creative Directors
Subun Khow
Suthisak
Sucharittanonta

Advertising Agency
BBDO Bangkok
Client
Ekchai Distribution
Systems
Brand
Tesco Lotus

Indoor Posters

BBDO Bangkok
for Ekchai Distribution Systems

Crab in the Pack / Prawn in the Pack / Squid in the Pack
We believe that simple ideas can create stunning visuals. In this poster campaign we used a visual with a twist: a hand grabbing our product from the pack to demonstrate how fresh it is.

BBH London
for Barnardo's

Shouting
Because of the tough experiences they have been through, some of the children Barnardo's helps can come across as hostile and difficult. Their sometimes less-than-perfect behaviour is often in reality a cry for help. The fact that 'shouting' can refer to either 'shouting abuse' or 'shouting for help' unlocked the concept. During the shoot, which was taken in a rough part of East London, a nearby pile of boxes started to move; a tramp had been sleeping underneath. The model, swearing at the photographer at the top of his voice, had woken him up.

Art Director
Nick Allsop
Copywriter
Simon Veksner
Photographer
Zed Nelson

Typographer
Chris Chapman
Creative Director
Nick Gill
Advertising Agency
BBH London
Planner
John Harrison

Account Handlers
Helen James
Lucy Kennedy
**Head of Brand &
New Media**
Collette Collins

**Director of
Communications**
Diana Tickell
Client
Barnardo's

Saatchi & Saatchi Malaysia
for Guinness Anchor Berhad

Stop
We wanted to demonstrate the fact that the brain processes information at a much slower rate when intoxicated. The objective of this advert is to make party-goers think twice before driving home after a night of drinking.

Art Director
Ong Kien Hoe
Copywriter
Christie Herman
Photographer
Alex Tow

Creative Directors
Edmund Choe
Adrian Miller
Retoucher
Choyue Chen

Advertising Agency
Saatchi & Saatchi
Malaysia
Account Handler
Aaron Taylor

Client
Guinness Anchor
Berhad
Brand
Guinness

Art Director
Gumpon
Laksanajinda
Copywriters
Kulvadee Doksroy
Khanitta Wichit-
sakonkit

Photographer
Anuchai Secha-
runputong
Creative Directors
Wisit Lumsiric-
haroenchoke
Nopadol Srikiea-
tikajohn

Advertising Agency
Ogilvy & Mather
Thailand
Account Handler
Phannika Vongsayan
Marketing Manager
William Schaedla

Client
WWF Thailand
Brand
WWF

Indoor Posters
Ogilvy & Mather Thailand
for WWF Thailand

Tree
The objective of this advert was to make the problem of deforestation a human one, something we can all understand and relate to. As WWF Thailand had a limited media budget, the piece had to work hard to carry momentum and grow awareness of WWF. The advert was launched in selected magazines and distributed as posters for WWF Forests for Life nationwide road show. The magazines and road show were targeted at young adult Thais.

Art Director
Benjamin Marchal
Copywriter
Olivier Lefebvre

Photographer
David Stewart
Creative Director
Alexandre Hervé

Advertising Agency
DDB Paris
Art Buyer
Sophie Mégrous
Account Manager
Thomas Granger

Brand Manager
Georges Djen
Client
Live Poker

Indoor Posters
DDB Paris
for Live Poker

Black Guy
Whaaaaooooouuuuuh!

Indoor Posters

BJL Manchester
for Eurocamp

Great Dane
People don't think they can take their dogs on holiday, so they put them into kennels. Dogs are welcome at Eurocamp, so they too can return home with tan marks.

Art Director
Adrian Dews
Copywriter
Richard Hague

Photographer
Euan Myles
Creative Directors
Pete Bastiman
Billy Mawhinney
Tom Richards

Retoucher
Rob Wilford
Advertising Agency
BJL Manchester
Account Handler
Becky Richards

Brand Manager
Chris Hilton
Client
Eurocamp

Indoor Posters

RKCR/Y&R
for British Library

Fist
The British Library needed a launch campaign for 'Taking Liberties', their exhibition about the historic struggle for our rights and freedoms. We decided to use the visual language of the protest poster, and a provocative headline which would make us think about whether we were now taking our rights for granted.

Art Director
Steve Williams
Copywriter
Adrian Lim
Typographer
Anthony Burrill

Creative Director
Damon Collins
Advertising Agency
RKCR/Y&R
Planner
Lori Meakin

Account Handler
Priya Patel
Brand Manager
Jane Richardson

Marketing Manager
Heather Norman-Soderlind
Client
British Library

Art Director	**Creative Directors**	**Advertising Agency**	**Account Handler**
Jolyon Finch	Damon Collins	RKCR/Y&R	Kate Uniowski
Copywriter	Mark Roalfe	**Planner**	**Brand Manager**
Steve Moss	**Illustrator**	Jo Bamford	Nick Futcher
Photographer	James Taylor	**Art Buyer**	**Client**
David Lidbetter	**Retoucher**	Hettie Rifkin	Oxfam
Typographer	Stuart Frost		
Jolyon Finch			

Indoor Posters

RKCR/Y&R
for Oxfam

Pen / Heart / Grenade
The brief was to motivate a younger audience to get involved with Oxfam's campaign against the global arms trade. The stencil device was used to give the brand a sense of dynamism and political activism.

Art Directors
Edmund Choe
Ong Kien Hoe
Lydia Lim
Copywriters
Andy Greenaway
Ong Kien Hoe
Lydia Lim
Adrian Miller

Photographers
Fulvio Bonavia
Allen Dang
Typographer
Lydia Lim
Creative Directors
Edmund Choe
Adrian Miller

3D Artist
Wayne Ho
Retouchers
James Teoh
Karen Yap

Marketing Manager
Raman Krishnan
Client
Silverfish Books
Brand
Penguin Books

Saatchi & Saatchi Malaysia
for Silverfish Books

Affair / Liberty / Psycho / Candlestick
The campaign is aimed at encouraging the movie-going, internet-surfing generation to get interested in books, by demonstrating how nothing gives you the complete story quite like a book. Each execution features a Penguin classic. The sequence of page numbers in the visuals refer to the sequence of events in a scene as it unfolds.

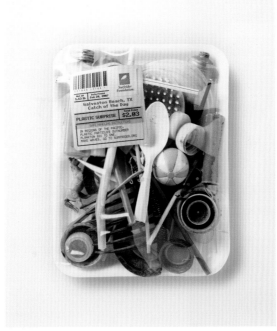

Art Director
Juan Cruz Bobillo
Copywriter
Raymond Hwang
Photographer
Matt Cobliegh

Creative Director
Felipe Bascope
Executive Creative Director
Harvey Marco

Associate Copy Director
Raymond Hwang
Retouching
Rocket
Advertising Agency
Saatchi & Saatchi
Los Angeles

Marketing Manager
Matt McClain
Client
Surfrider Foundation

Poster Advertising Campaigns

Saatchi & Saatchi Los Angeles
for Surfrider Foundation

Butts n' Bits / Condom Strips / Plastic Surprises / Styrofoam Bites
Actual beach garbage was packaged to look like seafood and displayed at local farmers' markets. The goods were also shot as print and posters.

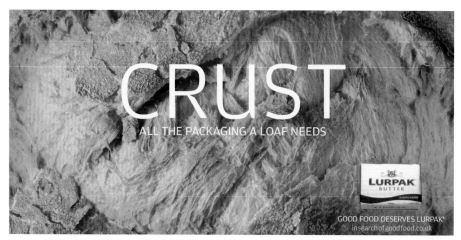

Art Directors	Copywriters	Photographers	Advertising Agency
Sophie Bodoh	Sophie Bodoh	Colin Campbell	Wieden + Kennedy
Matt Joiner	Matt Joiner	David Sykes	London
Ian Perkins	Ian Perkins	**Creative Directors**	**Account Handler**
Matt Powell-Perry	Matt Powell-Perry	Matt Gooden	Emma Wiseman
		Ben Walker	**Client**
		Designer	Lurpak
		Karen Jane	

Poster Advertising Campaigns

Wieden + Kennedy London
for Lurpak

Crust / Ping / Fear Not
Lurpak is the UK's favourite butter brand. It's a lactic butter, a firm favourite among chefs, and has a premium status and definite sense of authority when it comes to things in the kitchen.
We needed to demonstrate Lurpak's passion and belief in good, simple, quality food.
We continued to position Lurpak as the champion of good food by contributing to the noise around food, and asserting Lurpak's opinion on ingredients and cooking.

60

Art Director
Matias Lafalla
Copywriter
Mariana Peluffo
Creative Directors
Mariela Simirgiotis
Mercedes Tiagonce

Retoucher
Pablo Romanos
Advertising Agency
Del Campo Nazca
Saatchi & Saatchi

Account Handler
Paula Gambardella
Brand Manager
Emilio Laugier
Marketing Manager
Laura Salles

Client
Zoo de Buenos Aires
Brand
Guided Visits

Poster Advertising Campaigns
Del Campo Nazca Saatchi & Saatchi
for Zoo de Buenos Aires

Bird / Chameleon / Frog / Insect
The focus of the idea is to make the benefit of taking a guided visit evident to the consumer: that they will discover things about animals that are not obvious at first sight. The concept of using animal mimicry responds to the client's historical mandatory request: animals always have to be the main characters in zoo ads.

Art Directors
Brigid Alkema
Mark Harricks
Paul Nagy
Paul Young
Copywriters
Brigid Alkema
Mark Harricks
Paul Nagy
Paul Young

Photographer
Mat Blamires
Typographer
Geoff Francis
Creative Director
Mark Harricks
Deputy Creative Director
Paul Nagy

Executive Creative Director
Philip Andrew
Advertising Agency
Clemenger BBDO
Production Manager
Scott McMillan

Account Executive
Sean Keaney
Client
New Zealand
Transport Agency

Poster Advertising Campaigns
Clemenger BBDO
for New Zealand Transport Agency

Bridge / Creek / Tree
We created a print campaign showing the aftermath of three horrific fatal fatigue crashes. In each execution everything was true to how a crash scene would look; the only difference was, we replaced the smashed cars with smashed beds.

Art Director	Creative Directors	Advertising Agency	Client
Ian Lee	Edmund Choe	Saatchi & Saatchi	Procter & Gamble
Copywriter	Adrian Miller	Malaysia	Malaysia
James Yap	**Designer**	**Account Handlers**	**Brand**
Photographers	Xuxulyn	Diana Boo	Safeguard
Jesse Choo	**Retoucher**	Tina Tong	Antibacterial Soap
Edmund Leong	James Teoh		

Poster Advertising Campaigns

Saatchi & Saatchi Malaysia
for Procter & Gamble Malaysia

Alley / Toilet / Park
The aim was to enlighten the general public on the importance of personal hygiene, as the transmission of germs from object to person is shockingly easy.

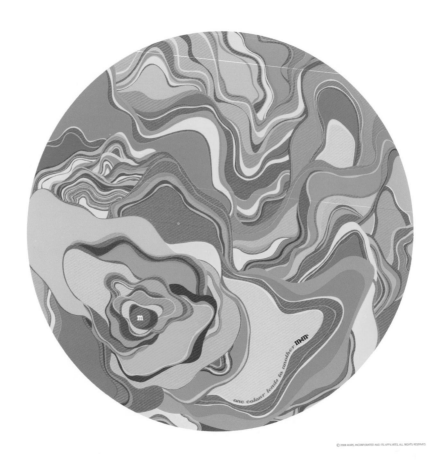

Art Director
KC Chung
Designer
KC Chung
Copywriter
Eddie Azadi

Creative Director
Graham Kelly
Advertising Agency
TBWA\Tequila
Singapore

Print Producer
Sam Tan
Account Handler
Eunice Tan
Marketing Manager
Sibylle Geisert

Client
Mars
Brand
M&M's

Poster Advertising Campaigns

TBWA\Tequila Singapore
for Mars

Wow / Yummy / Mmmm

Can the point-of-sale be a point of interesting discussion? M&M's certainly hoped so. As a chocolate candy synonymous with colour, its appeal had started to fade among young adults who felt they had outgrown the brand. Staying true to its playful and colourful nature, a change was made without changing what the brand stood for. Using an M&M at the heart of every design, evocative eye candy was created to arouse interest. What seemed like elaborate modern art actually conveyed two simple messages about M&M's: it's astoundingly colourful and it's addictively delicious.

64

Art Director
Richard Brim
Copywriter
Daniel Fisher
Photographer
Paul Belford

Executive Creative Director
Jonathan Burley
Designer
Paul Belford
Retouchers
Paul Belford
Tony Parsons

Advertising Agency
Leo Burnett London
Planner
Nick Docherty
Account Handler
Nick Morrell
Brand Manager
Nicola Edwards

Marketing Manager
Fiona Seymour
Client
UK Government, Department for Transport
Brand
Think!

Poster Advertising Campaigns

Leo Burnett London
for UK Government, Department for Transport

Career / Christmas / Relationship / Summer
This campaign was devised to encourage our young men to resist the temptation of that extra pint before getting behind the wheel. We wanted to make them realise the catastrophic effects a drink driving conviction can have on different aspects of life. Each execution features a photo of a typical treasured moment being ruined by a spilt drink: a wrecked graduation photo signifies a ruined career, a wedding photo is spoilt to suggest a damaged relationship and seasonal executions have been created with summer holiday and Christmas photographs.

65

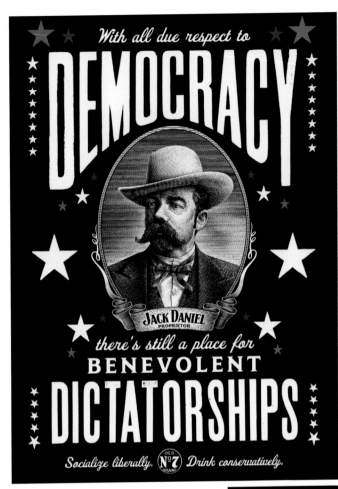

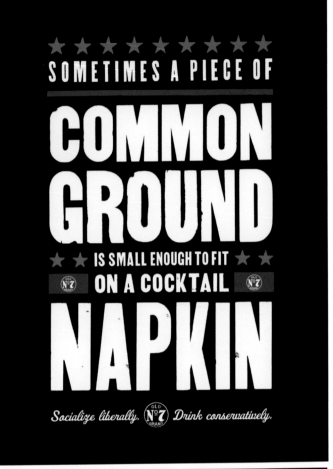

Art Director
Tim Mahoney
Copywriters
Lawson Clarke
Craig Johnson
Gregg Nelson

Creative Directors
Wade Devers
Pete Favat
Wade Paschall
Art Producer
Jessica Hunter

Letterpress
Yee Haw Industries
Advertising Agency
Arnold
Production Managers
Wendy Donnelly
Jim Spadafora

Planner
Dan Sarmiento
Account Handler
Paul Nelson
Brand Manager
Rachel Zigman
Client
Jack Daniel's

Poster Advertising Campaigns

Arnold
for Jack Daniel's

Benevolent Dictatorships / Common Ground / Champagne / Jack Supports all Parties / The Other Kind of Socialist
During the most spectacular election in US history, Jack Daniel's decided to weigh in on the one issue we had any right to weigh in on: whiskey. Combining Jack Daniel's iconography and classic 50s and 60s American political design, we created a series of authentic letterpress campaign posters. We covered the cities hosting the Republican and Democratic national conventions with posters and wild postings. Because if there's one thing that people need during the political process, it's a drink.

66

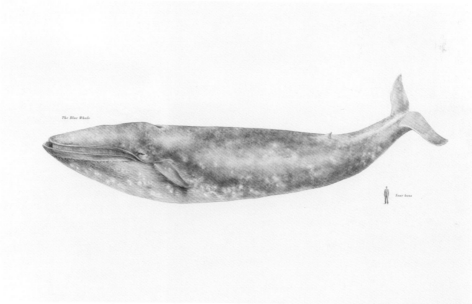

Art Director
Michael Lees-Rolfe
Copywriter
Kelly Putter

Creative Director
Christopher Gotz
Illustrator
Karen Cronje

Advertising Agency
Ogilvy Cape Town
Art Buyer
Merle Bennett
Account Handler
Greg Tebbutt

Client
Volkswagen South
Africa
Brand
Touareg

Poster Advertising Campaigns

Ogilvy Cape Town
for Volkswagen South Africa

Perspectives – Angel Falls / Redwood / Blue Whale
We encouraged people to get some perspective in their lives by considering what was really important. This was done by contrasting the grandeur and scale of the natural world with the mundane aspects of urban life.

Art Directors
Chris Moreira
Mark Schoeller
Copywriters
Chris Moreira
Mark Schoeller

Photographer
Dean Zillwood
Creative Directors
Jay Benjamin
Andy Dilallo

Retoucher
Lee Turner
Advertising Agency
JWT Sydney
Account Handler
Peter Bosilkovski

Client
Olympus
Brand
Ultra Zoom SP-570

Poster Advertising Campaigns

JWT Sydney
for Olympus

Elastic Campaign
This campaign is a simple visual demonstration of the powerful zoom capabilities of the Olympus Ultra Zoom SP-570 digital camera.

Art Directors
Anthony
Chelvanathan
Paul Giannetta
Copywriters
Sean Barlow
Steve Persico

Creative Directors
Sean Barlow
Israel Diaz
Paul Giannetta
Judy John

Advertising Agency
Leo Burnett Toronto
Account Handlers
David Buckspan
Natasha Dagenais

Client
James Ready Beer
Brand
James Ready

Poster Advertising Campaigns

Leo Burnett Toronto
for James Ready Beer

The Share our Billboard Campaign
For the last few years, James Ready, a discount beer brand, has engaged their loyal drinkers in its cause: 'Help us keep this beer a buck'. This year, to keep the cost of billboards down, James Ready asked drinkers to share their billboard space. Over 100 different billboards were selected from participants who became celebrities in their local communities.

Art Director	Typographer	Executive Creative	Advertising Agency
Suzana Haddad	José Roberto	**Director**	AlmapBBDO
Copywriter	Bezerra	Marcello Serpa	**Marketing Manager**
Renan Tommaso	**Creative Directors**	**Illustrator**	Joana Fernandes
Photography	Dulcídio Caldeira	Kako	**Client**
Corbis	Luiz Sanches	**Illustration**	Cia. das Letras
Photographer		6B Studio	**Brand**
Hugo Treu		Corbis	Cia. de Bolso

Poster Advertising Campaigns

AlmapBBDO
for Cia. das Letras

Che Guevara / Kafka / Roman Empire
The objective was to spread the word about the Company of Pocket, the pocket versions of publications from Companhia das Letras. Items small enough to be kept in a pocket were inserted in these scenes, to create the impression that the action was taking place inside a pocket.

Art Directors
Marcus Kawamura
Ary Nogueira
Copywriter
Eduardo Andrietta
Photographers
Mario Daloia
Hugo Treu
Typographer
José Roberto Bezerra

Creative Directors
Dulcídio Caldeira
Luiz Sanches
Executive Creative Director
Marcello Serpa
Illustrators
Daniel Battaini
Hugo Cafasso
José Cortizo Junior
Ellyson Lifante

Advertising Agency
AlmapBBDO
Media Planners
Laerte Mendonça
Zuleide Rampazzo
Cássio Soares
Account Supervisors
Filipe Bartholomeu
Fernão Cosi
Camila Figueiredo

Marketing Managers
Ricardo Alouche
Ana Maria Oliveira
Client
Volkswagen Trucks

Poster Advertising Campaigns

AlmapBBDO
for Volkswagen Trucks

Volkswagen Customised Trucks – Beer Box / Egg Box / Milk Box / Fruit Box
The aim of this campaign is to remind the audience that Volkswagen trucks are 'the only ones in Brazil tailored for your business'. Throughout the campaign, the main element is packaging designed to look like Volkswagen trucks. Wooden boxes contain large amounts of produce and have paintings on the side; they are transformed into trucks designed specifically to transport delicate products, such as milk, drinks or eggs.

It's your turn.
Visit wwf.sg

It's your turn.
Visit wwf.sg

It's your turn.
Visit wwf.sg

Art Director
Christiano Choo
Copywriter
Pradeep D'Souza

Creative Directors
Tay Guan Hin
Ali Shabaz
Advertising Agency
JWT Singapore
Account Handler
Peter Cheung

Creative Services Director
Mercy Wong
Brand Manager
Amy Ho

Managing Director
Amy Ho
Client
WWF

Poster Advertising Campaigns

JWT Singapore
for WWF

Earth / Shark / Tree
In the fight to save the environment, even a small decision can make a big difference. To get this message across, we used a popular game to remind us that it's all about making the right choice.

Art Director
Luke Duggan
Copywriter
Paul Bootlis

Creative Director
Rob Martin Murphy
Head of Art
Paul Fenton

Retouching
Electric Art
Advertising Agency
The Furnace

Client
Skins™

Poster Advertising Campaigns

The Furnace
for Skins™

Skins Uneven Playing Fields – Football / Rugby / Tennis
The objective was to create a new brand campaign for Skins™, highlighting the physical benefits of wearing the product. We used the concept that when you're playing sport, wearing Skins™ tips the balance of power in your favour. Our target market was any athlete who has the desire to be better than he or she currently is.

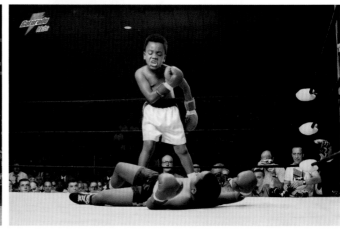

Art Director	Typographer	Advertising Agency	Account Supervisors
Renato Fernandez	José Roberto	AlmapBBDO	André Furlanetto
Copywriter	Bezerra	**Planners**	Ricardo Taunay
Gustavo Sarkis	**Creative Directors**	Fernanda Barone	**Marketing Manager**
Photographer	Dulcídio Caldeira	Valter Bombonato	João Paulo Lucena
Fernando Nalon	Luiz Sanches	Cintia Gonçalves	**Client**
Photography	**Executive Creative**	**Media Planners**	Pepsi
Conteúdo Expresso	**Director**	Gisele Carnielli	**Brand**
Getty Images	Marcello Serpa	Flávio de Pauw	Gatorade Kids
LatinStock		Maira Toledo	

Poster Advertising Campaigns

AlmapBBDO
for Pepsi

Soccer / Basketball / Boxer
Gatorade Kids is a campaign where we've re-shot some classic photos in the world of sport, replacing the sacred athletes with children. This shows how a child's dream of becoming a great champion can one day become a reality.

The jury:

Rosie Arnold, BBH London (Jury Foreman)
Dylan de Backer, DDB Amsterdam
Danny Higgins, Saatchi & Saatchi Dubai
Troy Lim, Ogilvy & Mather Singapore
Adrian Miller, Saatchi & Saatchi Malaysia
Guy Moore, Leo Burnett London
Ed Morris, Freelance
George Prest, Delaney Lund Knox Warren
Russell Ramsey, JWT London

HARVEY NICHOLS
NOW OPEN IN BRISTOL

PHILADELPHIA STREET · QUAKERS FRIARS

WALLACE WEARS:
Prince of Wales
check three piece
wool suit
by Paul Smith.

GROMIT WEARS:
Purple stripe silk
scarf by Duchamp.
Ray-Ban Wayfarers.

Art Director	**Retouchers**	**Animator**	**Marketing Manager**
Grant Parker	Greg Chapman	Loyd Price	Shona Campbell
Photographer	Steve Sanderson	**Project Manager**	**Marketing Officer**
Giles Revell	Andy Walsh	Caroline Tripp	Mimi Morrish
Typographer	**Planner**	**Account Handlers**	**Marketing Director**
Pete Mould	Georgina Murray-	Philip Heimann	Julia Bowe
Creative Director	Burton	Briony Small	**Client**
Jeremy Craigen	**Production Company**	**Art Buyer**	Harvey Nichols
Advertising Agency	Aardman Animations	Sarah Thomson	
DDB London			

Newspaper Press Advertising Colour

DDB London
for Harvey Nichols

Wallace in Alexander McQueen & Gromit in Paul Smith / Lady Tottington in Alexander McQueen / Wallace in Paul Smith & Gromit in Duchamp
The campaign for the opening of the new Harvey Nichols Bristol store featured Wallace, Gromit and Lady Tottington.

Art Director
Paul Kreitmann
Copywriter
Alexis Benoit
Creative Directors
Gilles Fichteberg
Jean-François
Sacco

Illustrator
Paul Kreitmann
Advertising Agency
CLM BBDO Paris
Art Buyer
Sylvie Etchémaïté

Account Handlers
Séverine Autret
Claire Roy-Thermes
Marketing Manager
Clotilde Masson

Client
Bayer
Brand
Alka-Seltzer

Newspaper Press Advertising Colour

CLM BBDO Paris
for Bayer

Bear / Mafia / Magician / Paparazzi / Prison
The campaign features characters that swallow awkward objects to get out of embarrassing situations. With this twist on the classic stomach ache, the Alka-Seltzer brand stands out in a sector that can often be a little conventional. The campaign offers a way to 'dissolve' your psychological as well as physical (digestive) problems.

Art Directors
Graeme Hall
Noah Regan
Copywriters
Graeme Hall
Noah Regan
Photographer
Jonathan de Villiers
Typographer
Pete Mould

Creative Director
Jeremy Craigen
Advertising Agency
DDB London
Planner
Georgina Murray-
Burton
Project Manager
Caroline Tripp

Account Handlers
Philip Heimann
Briony Small
Art Buyer
Sarah Thomson
Marketing Manager
Fran Page
Marketing Director
Julia Bowe

**Advertising &
Promotions
Manager**
Shona Campbell
Client
Harvey Nichols

Magazine Press Advertising Colour
DDB London
for Harvey Nichols

Bathroom / Fountain / Cafe

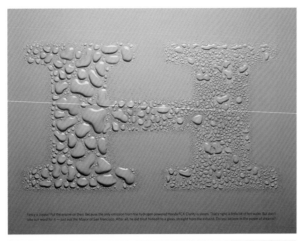

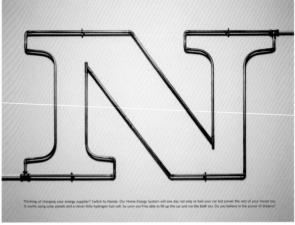

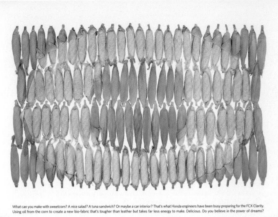

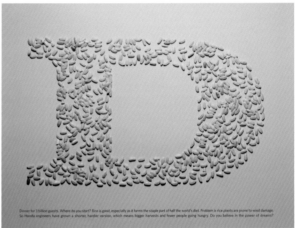

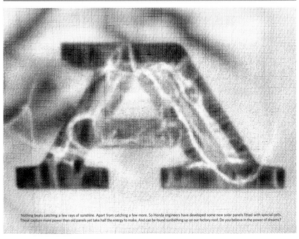

Art Directors
Guy Featherstone
Chris Groom
Copywriter
Stuart Harkness
Photographer
Guido Mocafico

Typographer
Guy Featherstone
Creative Directors
Tony Davidson
Kim Papworth
Model Maker
Gaël Langevin

Retouchers
Danny Holden
Dan Richardson
Advertising Agency
Wieden + Kennedy
London
Project Manager
Mark D'Abreo

Account Handlers
Ryan Fisher
Jonathan Tapper
Client
Honda
Brand
Honda Environment

Magazine Press Advertising Colour

Wieden + Kennedy London
for Honda

H / O / N / D / A
Honda wanted to showcase some of the things it has done to try to reduce its impact on the environment. We ran a campaign that used the letters of the car manufacturer to represent the technologies and initiatives that Honda has invested in. Honda also sponsored a series of environment supplements in the 'Daily Telegraph' where this work ran.

Art Director	Typographer	Advertising Agency	Brand Manager
Nick Allsop	Chris Chapman	BBH London	Michael Joubert
Copywriter	**Creative Directors**	**Planner**	**Client**
Simon Veksner	Alex Grieve	Patricia McDonald	Levi Strauss EMEA
Photographer	John Hegarty	**Account Handlers**	**Brand**
Joseph Rodriguez	Adrian Rossi	Mel Exon	Levi Strauss
		Paisley Wright	

Magazine Press Advertising Colour

BBH London
for Levi Strauss EMEA

Levi Strauss
The brief from the client was to move away from product focused communications and to inject some attitude and desirability back into the brand. The execution is shot from the first person point-of-view of a Levi's-wearing hero, capturing the reaction this person provokes in cheerleaderpeople who rigidly uphold convention and abhor difference. Unsurprisingly, they regard our heroes with disdain, suspicion and antipathy. So much the better. These are not people whose approval we want; they are the opposite of the Levi's wearer, the epitome of conformity.

Art Directors
Graeme Hall
Noah Regan
Copywriters
Graeme Hall
Noah Regan
Photographer
Andy Grimshaw
Typographer
Pete Mould

Creative Director
Jeremy Craigen
Illustrator
Al Murphy
Retoucher
Andy Walsh
Advertising Agency
DDB London

Account Handlers
Simon Alexander
George Roberts
Art Buyer
Sarah Thomson
Project Manager
Kirstie Petrie
Business Director
Jon Busk

Marketing Manager
Noam Buchalter
Marketing Executive
David Titman
Client
Unilever
Brand
Marmite Snacks

Magazine Press Advertising Colour

DDB London
for Unilever

GuzzlePuke / DropCatch / BogMouth / TrashCupboard / YukYum
To launch Marmite's new range of snacks, we created these press ads that not only show the products in their full glory, but also show people either loving or hating them, depending on which way up you hold the page.

Magazine Press Advertising Colour

JWT New York
for Kimberly-Clark

Boss Baby
Don't irritate your new boss.

Art Director
Tony Rizzuto
Copywriter
Cynthia Wills
Photographer
Tony D'Orio
Creative Directors
Richie Glickman
Roald van Wyk

Executive Creative Director
Walt Connelly
Chief Creative Officers
Harvey Marco
Ty Montague
Retouching
S05
Advertising Agency
JWT New York

Print Producer
Lauren Eberhardt
Project Manager
Lani de Rose
Account Director
Amy Frisch
Account Manager
Stephanie Reedy

Art Buyer
Dorreen Huff
Client
Kimberly-Clark
Brand
Huggies Gentle Care
Sensitve Wipes

Magazine Press Advertising Colour

TBWA\ESPAÑA
for SONY Computer Entertainment

Handcuffed
A man is arrested in the street by two policemen. To stop him from getting away, they detain him at a streetlamp. But instead of using handcuffs, they use a PlayStation Portable. It's more effective.

Art Director
Bernardo Hernández
Copywriter
Vicente Rodríguez
Photographer
Txema Yeste
Creative Directors
Bernardo Hernández
Vicente Rodríguez

Executive Creative Directors
Guillermo Ginés
Juan Sánchez
Advertising Agency
TBWA\ESPAÑA
Planner
Jesús Fuertes

Account Handler
Inés Díaz-Casariego
Brand Managers
Jorge Huguet
Cristina Infante
Marketing Manager
Javier Martínez-Avial

Client
SONY Computer Entertainment
Brand
PSP

Art Directors
Edmund Choe
Ong Kien Hoe
Lydia Lim
Copywriters
Andy Greenaway
Ong Kien Hoe
Lydia Lim
Adrian Miller

Photographers
Fulvio Bonavia
Allen Dang
Typographer
Lydia Lim
Creative Directors
Edmund Choe
Adrian Miller

3D Artist
Wayne Ho
Retouchers
James Teoh
Karen Yap
Advertising Agency
Saatchi & Saatchi
Malaysia

Marketing Manager
Raman Krishnan
Client
Silverfish Books
Brand
Penguin Books

Magazine Press Advertising Colour

Saatchi & Saatchi Malaysia
for Silverfish Books

Affair / Liberty / Psycho / Candlestick
This campaign is aimed at encouraging the movie-going, internet-surfing generation to get interested in books, by demonstrating how nothing gives you the complete story quite like a book. Each execution features a Penguin classic. The sequence of page numbers in the visuals refer to the sequence of events in a scene as it unfolds.

Magazine Press Advertising Colour

TBWA\Tequila Singapore
for Photolibrary

Emergency
Here's the thing with image banks: they all tend to share the same images. So while others are inclined to promote content to the advertising trade, Photolibrary aims to promote creativity. So, with a mountain load of images to play with, a new take on a simple demonstration became an easy sell to Photolibrary.

Art Director	**Photography**	**Retoucher**	**Account Handler**
KC Chung	Photolibrary	Jane Lai	Jun Shea
Copywriter	**Creative Director**	**Advertising Agency**	**Marketing Manager**
Eddie Azadi	Graham Kelly	TBWA\Tequila	Matthew Howden
		Singapore	**Client**
			Photolibrary

Magazine Press Advertising Colour

Leo Burnett Toronto
for Diageo

Keep Walking
How do we get more attention for Johnnie Walker in a magazine dedicated to the business man of the year, in a way that stays true to the brand? Break tradition: instead of just creating a congratulatory Johnnie Walker ad on page 24, let's get on the cover where most of the attention is focused. Let's prove just how progressive the brand is by placing the Johnnie Walker striding man 'breaking through' the actual bar code. The goal was to communicate that Johnnie Walker, like the person who has been named Business Man of the Year, is successful because he has overcome the obstacles he has encountered.

Art Director	**Creative Directors**	**Advertising Agency**	**Client**
Mike Lo Nam	Israel Diaz	Leo Burnett Toronto	Diageo
Copywriter	Judy John		**Brand**
Appanna Chetranda	Marcus Sagar		Johnnie Walker

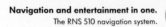

Art Directors
Kristoffer Heilemann
Gabriel Mattar
Copywriters
Ludwig Berndl
Philip Bolland
Ricardo Wolff

Photographer
Sven Schrader
Executive Creative Directors
Bert Peulecke
Stefan Schulte

Advertising Agency
DDB Berlin
Brand Manager
Hartmut Seeger
Marketing Manager
Jochen Sengpiehl

Client
Volkswagen
Brand
RNS 510 Navigation
System

Magazine Press Advertising Colour

DDB Berlin
for Volkswagen

Travolta / Freddie / Michael
The RNS 510 Navigation System from Volkswagen is more than a GPS, as it allows drivers to enjoy their favourite films and music. We demonstrated this in a simple yet effective way.

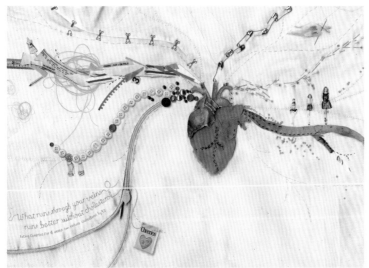

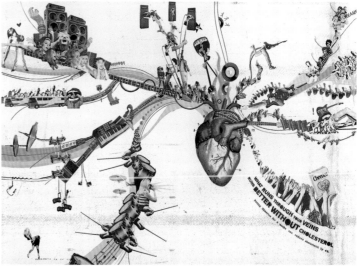

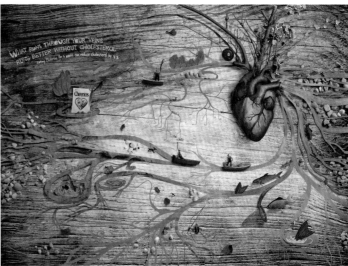

Art Director	**Creative Directors**	**Illustrator**	**Art Buyer**
Jaclyn Rink	Icaro Doria	Dave Wheeler	Maggie Sumner
Copywriter	Ann Hayden	**Advertising Agency**	**Client**
Icaro Doria	**Chief Creative**	Saatchi & Saatchi	General Mills
Typographers	**Officer**	New York	**Brand**
Hamish McArthur	Tony Granger	**Account Handlers**	Cheerios
Jaclyn Rink	**Designers**	Stephanie Lederman	
	Yan Apostolides	Will Platt-Higgins	
	Aaron Padin		

Magazine Press Advertising Colour

Saatchi & Saatchi New York
for General Mills

Fashion / Rock 'n' Roll / Gardening / Fishing
Cheerios is the most popular brand of cereals in the US. In recent years, it has strived to make the claim 'Eating Cheerios for six weeks can reduce cholesterol by four per cent' a household fact. However this claim lacks the warmth that most Americans have grown to love about the brand. As the pursuit of a healthier life should not be cold and scientific, we came up with a campaign that showed what runs through people's veins, as a reference to their passions in life. 'Gardening', 'Rock 'n' Roll', 'Fashion' and 'Fishing' all show in a very visual way that health claims don't need to be boring.

Art Directors	Copywriters	Creative Directors	Art Buyer
Nicolas Chauvin	Dimitri Guerassimov	Anne de Maupeou	Jean-Eric Leconiac
Romin Favre	Eric Jannon	Frederic Temin	**Client**
	Photographer	**Advertising Agency**	DIESEL
	Laurie Bartley	Marcel Paris	

Magazine Press Advertising Colour

Marcel Paris
for DIESEL

Baby / Blind / Lipstick / Prayer / Stitches
We didn't waste our time writing something so don't waste yours reading this. Live fast.

Art Directors
Marcus Kawamura
Ary Nogueira
Copywriter
Eduardo Andrietta
Photographers
Mario Daloia
Hugo Treu
Typographer
José Roberto
Bezerra

Creative Directors
Dulcídio Caldeira
Luiz Sanches
Executive Creative Director
Marcello Serpa
Illustrators
Daniel Battaini
Hugo Cafasso
José Cortizo Junior
Ellyson Lifante

Advertising Agency
AlmapBBDO
Account Supervisors
Filipe Bartholomeu
Fernão Cosi
Camila Figueiredo
Media Planners
Laerte Mendonça
Zuleide Rampazzo
Cássio Soares

Marketing Managers
Ricardo Alouche
Ricardo Barion
Ana Maria Oliveira
Client
Volkswagen Trucks

Magazine Press Advertising Colour

AlmapBBDO
for Volkswagen Trucks

Volkswagen Customised Trucks – Beer Box / Egg Box / Milk Box
The aim of this campaign is to remind the audience that Volkswagen trucks are 'the only ones in Brazil tailored for your business'. Throughout the campaign, the main element is packaging designed to look like Volkswagen trucks. Wooden boxes contain large amounts of produce and have paintings on the side; they are transformed into trucks designed specifically to transport delicate products, such as milk, drinks or eggs.

Art Directors	Copywriters	Illustration	Advertising Agency
Adrian Chan	Troy Lim	Magic Cube	Ogilvy Singapore
Ashidiq Ghazali	Serene Loong	**Group Executive**	**Client**
Andrew Goh	**Photographers**	**Creative Director**	FHM Singapore
Eric Yeo	Jeff Chen	Todd McCracken	**Brand**
	Jimmy Fok		FHM

Magazine Press Advertising Colour

Ogilvy Singapore
for FHM Singapore

Paintings / Graphic Novel

Before FHM, boys used to ogle at women in biology references, 'National Geographic' and other seemingly unsexy tomes. With this in mind, we created a campaign that featured such genres of books but cut away everything that men wouldn't be interested in – leaving only the bits with scantily clad women.

Newspaper Press Advertising Colour

BBDO/Proximity Malaysia
for Chrysler Korea

Bushman & Eskimo / Husky & Camel / Mountain Goat & Crocodile
To promote Jeep's superior all-terrain capability, we overlapped two images of objects that are polar opposites to form the outline of the car, creating the impression that Jeep can go anywhere. As for applying a clean design style to the concept, well, we hope that it will make Jeep stand out from all the advertising in the car galaxy.

Art Directors	**Creative Directors**	**Advertising Agency**	**Brand Manager**
Eric Hor	MUN	BBDO/Proximity	Sally Hong
Willeon Leong	Ronald Ng	Malaysia	**Client**
Gary Lim	**Designers**	**Print Producer**	Chrysler Korea
MUN	Willeon Leong	Dickson Teh	**Brand**
Copywriters	Gary Lim	**Account Handlers**	Jeep
Kevin Le	MUN	Tieh Pui Yen	
Ronald Ng	**Illustrators**	Dong Hyun Yoo	
	Willeon Leong		
	Gary Lim		

Newspaper Press Advertising Colour

JWT London
for Crimestoppers

Knife
Knife crime has reached epidemic numbers in the UK. Last year, police recorded more than 20,000 offences in England. For the campaign, we created the illusion that every reader of the daily newspaper City AM was carrying a knife. In order to position the knife exactly where readers hold the newspaper, we got City AM to change the layout of their back page by moving the paper's master-head to the side for the first time.

Art Directors	**Photography**	**Executive Creative**	**Account Handler**
Ronnie Vlcek	Getty Images	**Director**	Paul Kirkley
Bruno Xavier	**Designers**	Russell Ramsey	**Head of**
Copywriters	Ronnie Vlcek	**Advertising Agency**	**Communications**
Ronnie Vlcek	Bruno Xavier	JWT London	Hannah Daws
Bruno Xavier	**Creative Director**		**Client**
	Jason Berry		Crimestoppers

Newspaper Press Advertising Colour

RKCR/Y&R
for Land Rover

Cow
We wanted to inject a bit of fun into the usually dry commercial vehicles category. The unrivalled capability of a Land Rover means the driver can get more enjoyment out of his working day. So we came up with the 'Makes work play' line. To dramatise this thought and bring it to life, we used photographic 'tilt and shift' lenses to make the working vehicles, animals and people look like toys.

Art Director	**Photographer**	**Advertising Agency**	**National Advertising**
Jerry Hollens	Nadav Kander	RKCR/Y&R	**Manager**
Copywriter	**Typographer**	**Planner**	Les Knight
Mike Boles	Lee Aldridge	Angie Ma	**Client**
	Creative Directors	**Account Handler**	Land Rover
	Damon Collins	Lucy Harries	**Brand**
	Mark Roalfe		Defender

The jury:

Ian Haworth, WWAV Rapp Collins (Jury Foreman)
Mark Buckingham, Publicis Dialog
Emma de la Fosse, OgilvyOne Worldwide London
Duncan Gray, Proximity London
Justine Lee, TBWA\Tequila Singapore
Gavin McLeod, M&C Saatchi/Mark
Mike Musachio, Fathom Communications
Martin Riesenfelder, Wunderman Frankfurt
Glynn Venter, Draftfcb Cape Town

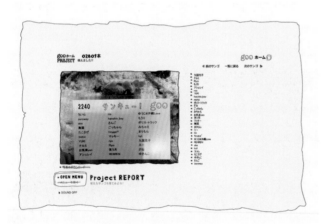

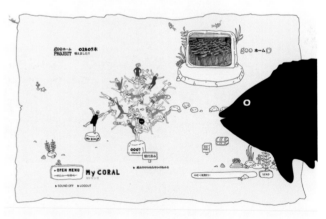

Art Directors
Jeong-Ho Im
Takumi Oguri
Director
Kazuaki Matsui
Copywriter
Takeshi Okamoto
Creative Directors
Kazuaki Hashida
Junya Masuda

Designers
Goichi Nagakawa
Manabu Suzuki
Advertising Agency
Hakuhodo Kettle
Producer
Hiroo Suzuki
Agency Producers
Yoshitaka Akamatsu
Kinya Kawaguchi
Takaki Kobayashi
Kimiya Miakami

Sound Designers
Rinken Teruya
Hiroaki Tsukamoto
Environmental Consultant
Koji Kinjo
Marketing Managers
Keisuke Kuriyama
Natsuyo Shinchi

Brand Manager
Yoshitaka Tabata
Client
NTT Resonant
Brand
Goo Home

Digital

Hakuhodo Kettle
for NTT Resonant

Social Media Save the Earth
The aim of this execution is to involve members of Goo Home, a social networking site, in the launch of a new service. People select social networking sites for the quantity of members, because the value of such sites lies in connecting with others. The new value we created is 'the site where people can improve the environment by connecting to others'. For every 30 new members that join Goo Home, one real coral will be planted in Okinawa's sea. Thus, environmental action is now a direct motivation to join Goo Home, instead of just expanding your network.

balloonacy

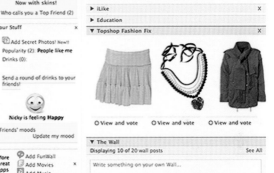

Art Directors
Marc Davies
Nicky Gibson
Copywriter
David Cadji-Newby
Creative Director
Iain Tait

Designers
Dickon Langdon
Andrew Zolty
Digital Agency
POKE
Agency Producer
Mike Pearson

Programmers
Nilesh Ashra
Mattias Gunneras
Greg Reed
Flash Programmer
Caroline
Butterworth
Developer
Derek McKenna

Technical Director
Igor Clark
Planner
Lise Lauritzen
Client
Orange

Digital

POKE
for Orange

Orange Balloonacy
We knew there were going to be lovely animal-shaped balloons around because they were in the TV ads. We can't see how we could have done anything other than set up a balloon race across the internet. The thing that got us really excited was creating a complex and mutually beneficial relationship between sites, players, and Orange, something fun for racers, yet rewarding for site-owners. We built a bespoke 'ad-serving' environment, managing relational data between each individual balloon and the sites. The reward: 40,000 balloons, 3,000 sites and 3.2million free exposures to Orange through the race itself.

Direct

Art Director
Yohey Adachi
Copywriter
Craig Howie
Creative Directors
Steve Elrick
Tadashi Tsujimoto
Director
Junpei Kojima

Producer
Kiyoshi Okumura
Production Company
Avex Hawaii
Advertising Agency
BBH Asia Pacific

Agency Producers
San Takashima
Hiroshi Tonomura
Music Composer
Yasuo Nakajima
Music Producer
Toru Midorikawa
Planner
Frank Reitgassl

Account Handlers
Hirotaka Kuki
Midori Watanabe
Client
Unilever Japan
Brand
AXE

 Digital

BBH Asia Pacific
for Unilever Japan

AXE Wake Up Edit
How do you get young guys in Japan to use AXE as part of their everyday routine? Have them wake up to a beautiful woman who reminds them! Make irresistible content for the modern alarm clock: the mobile phone. This integrated campaign was selected, the mobile phone execution was awarded a Nomination.

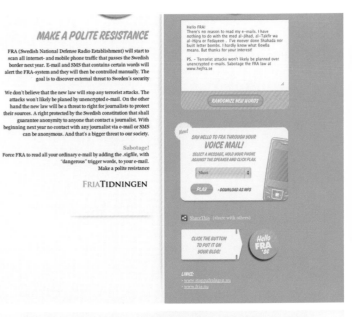

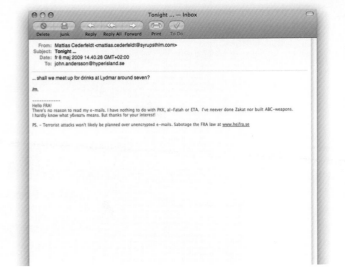

Art Director
Mattias Cederfeldt
Copywriter
Mia Robertsson

Creative Director
Fredrik Lundgren
Advertising Agency
Syrup Stockholm

Account Handler
Marlene Hernbrandt
Brand Manager
Jonas Sandström

Client
Fria Tidningen
Newspaper

Digital

Syrup Stockholm
for Fria Tidningen Newspaper

Hello FRA
The newspaper Fria Tidningen launched this campaign in response to a new surveillance law in Sweden, run by the FRA (Swedish National Defence Radio Establishment). We wanted people to stop talking and start acting. We wrote a standard text that people can put in their emails that will make FRA's computerised search programs react. The text can be changed randomly with different 'dangerous' trigger words.

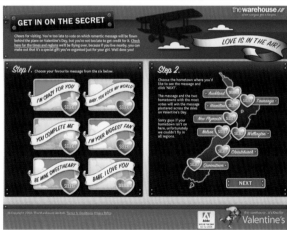

Art Directors
Dan Fastnedge
Jason Vertongen
Copywriters
Michelle
Rajalingham
Andrew Simpson
Digital Designer
Shanan Goldring

Creative Director
Dave King
Advertising Agency
AIM Proximity
Web Developer
Cameron Crosby

**Head of
Interactive Art**
Aaron Goldring
Planner
Jose Alomajan
Account Handlers
Matt Pickering
Alexia Walsh

Marketing Manager
Janine Hall
Brand Manager
Tui Flemming
Client
The Warehouse

Ambient

AIM Proximity
for The Warehouse

The Great Love Conspiracy
We wanted guys to know that The Warehouse could help them take care of all their Valentine's Day needs. It can be an expensive time of year for guys. So we appealed to them by telling them how they could impress their girlfriends without spending a cent. On our website, we told guys we were organising a plane to fly over various New Zealand cities with a romantic message trailing behind it. We then explained how the guys could take credit for it, and convince their loved one that they did it just for her. We then let them know exactly when and where it would appear, ensuring they would look like romantic heroes when their sweethearts looked up and saw the lengths each guy had gone to, to express his love.

Art Director
Attila Kiraly
Copywriters
Björn Persson
Mikael Ström

Creative Director
Björn Ståhl
Advertising Agency
Ogilvy Stockholm
Account Handler
Kristiina Mullersdorf

Marketing Manager
Maria Andersson
Brand Manager
Bonian
Golmohammadi

Client
United Nations
Sweden
Brand
United Nations

Print

Ogilvy Stockholm
for United Nations Sweden

True Evidence of War
Our assignment was to make people aware of the terrible civilian suffering in Georgia after the war, and raise donations for the refugees. We went to Georgia and collected personal belongings abandoned in the rubble. These items, accompanied by their stories, were placed into billboards, demonstrating that the war may have ended but the suffering had only just begun.

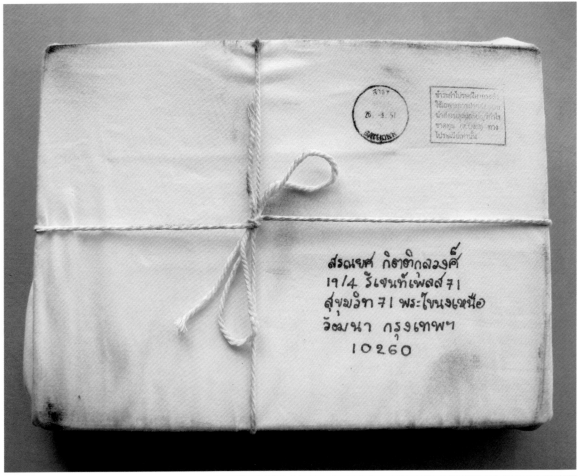

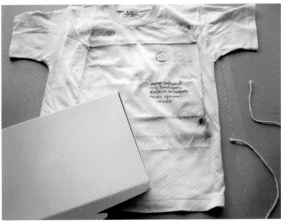

confidence to remove stains in 1 wash

Art Director
Dominic Stallard
Copywriter
Clinton Manson

Creative Directors
Clinton Manson
Dominic Stallard
Advertising Agency
Lowe Bangkok

Senior Vice
President Creative
Resources
Piyachat Cholasap

Brand Manager
Piyanut Panpiemras
Client
Unilever Thailand
Brand
Breeze Excel

▲ Addressed Direct Mail

Lowe Bangkok
for Unilever Thailand

Torture Test
The objective was to prove to sceptical consumers that Breeze Excel delivers on its promise: 'Confidence to remove stains in one wash'. We mailed a box (wrapped with a T-shirt) that contained a Breeze Excel sample to selected women's social groups across Thailand. As anticipated, the postal service ruined the T-shirts. If the recipients wanted their T-shirt to look new again, they had to wash it with the enclosed sample. This mailer allowed consumers to prove the efficacy of this product (and our claim) to themselves by interacting with it directly. Owing to increased sales and greater brand awareness, research is being done to use this mailer as part of a Unilever case study for successful integrated brand communications.

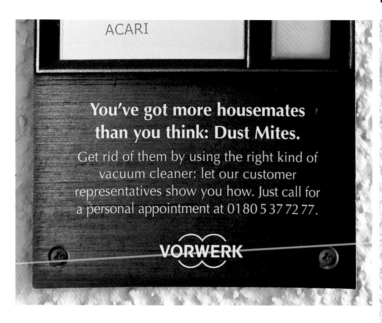

Art Director
Eva Stetefeld
Copywriter
Holger Gaubatz

Photographer
Per Schorn
Creative Directors
Simon Oppmann
Peter Römmelt

Advertising Agency
Ogilvy Frankfurt
Account Handler
Filiz Inan
Marketing Manager
Heike Langner

Client
Vorwerk Germany
Brand
Vorwerk

 Direct Mail Door Drop

Ogilvy Frankfurt
for Vorwerk Germany

Doorbell Panel Promotion
Vorwerk vacuum cleaners are sold by door-to-door sales people. But fewer consumers want to let a salesperson into their homes. So we attached sticky labels to front doors to show how many dust mites live in houses. The labels also told people how to get rid of them – book an appointment with a Vorwerk salesperson.

Digital

Clemenger BBDO
for New Zealand Transport Agency

Distracted Drivers
Driver distraction is a growing problem in New Zealand. Each year a staggering number of serious crashes are caused by drivers using their mobile phones behind the wheel. A recent study reported that two thirds of young people admitted to taking their eyes off the road to read and send text messages while driving. Our challenge was to inform people of the dangers, but our idea went one step further, and created a way to let them actually experience how something as simple as texting while driving can have fatal consequences.

Art Directors
Sarah Jackson
Lisa Scott
Copywriters
Tammy Keegan
Paul Nagy
Creative Director
Paul Nagy
Executive Creative Director
Philip Andrew

Advertising Agency
Clemenger BBDO
Agency Producers
Martin Gray
Lisa Scott
Editor
Jason Martin
Programmer
Marc Broad

Production Manager
Martin Gray
Head of Digital
Scott Sinclair
Mobile Technology
Run the Red
Account Manager
Linda Reuvecamp

Group Account Director
Sean Keaney
Business Director
Annabelle Wilkinson
Client
New Zealand Transport Agency

Digital

This is Real Art
for Royal Opera House

Who's Don?
Demystifying the subject for its audience, this short gritty drama begins with two friends sitting in a café. Akin to their streetwise appearances, they use strong urban language as one girl tells a harrowing story about a man called Don, someone they appear to know. Don has raped, committed murder and harassed a bride. In what seems to be a shocking recollection of contemporary life, a twist of narrative reveals that she's retelling the tale of an opera she's seen, 'Don Giovanni'. The aim was to move away from the elitist image of the Royal Opera House, promoting an accessible form of entertainment to a mainstream audience. The film has been shown globally in many media outlets.

Art Director
Paul Belford
Copywriters
Paul Belford
Susannah Hayes
Director
Susannah Hayes
Creative Director
Paul Belford

Advertising Agency
This is Real Art
Producer
Carlos Downie
Agency Producers
Chris Gorell Barnes
Kate Neilsen
Production Company
Ferocious Films

Editor
Julian Tranquille
Lighting
Cameraperson
Mark Emberton
Account Handler
Chris Gorell Barnes

Marketing Manager
Layla Amirshahi
Brand Managers
Sean Chapman
Rachel Coldicut
Client
Royal Opera House

Direct

Art Director
Nik Hodel
Copywriter
Martin Arnold

Creative Director
Pius Walker
Advertising Agency
walker

Marketing Manager
Stella Jegher

Client
Amnesty
International

Digital

walker
for Amnesty International

eBay Attack
Every year, an estimated two million women and young girls are victims of trafficking. Amnesty International's task is to bring to our attention this outrageous violation of human rights. In order to inform the public about modern slavery we created a direct campaign on the world's largest auction platform. With the help of 188 Amnesty activists, we launched an overnight offensive, planned to the last detail. We used eBay to get our message across: in hundreds of live auctions, we offered women for sale. The message was always put into the context of the respective product category. By taking a closer look, the consumer could discover the advert's true meaning, and realise how shockingly easy it is to buy a woman these days.

107

Direct

Art Directors
Magnus Thorne
Paul Turner
Copywriters
Magnus Thorne
Paul Turner

Director
Harry Dwyer
Producer
James Sorton
Post Production
Producers
Angela Lyttle
Beth Vander
Agency
Rapp London

Editor
Kevin Palmer
Sound Designer
Parv Thind

Brand Managers
Rosa Argent
Amanda Gent
Client
International Fund
for Animal Welfare
Brand
IFAW UK

Digital

Rapp London
for International Fund for Animal Welfare

Gorilla
This film was created to raise awareness of the International Fund for Animal Welfare and the work they do to protect critically endangered species like the gorilla. The idea was to re-make one of the most famous and best loved commercials of recent times, and put a very serious twist on it. To ensure even more cut-through, the viral was left virtually silent, giving the film a sombre and chilling mood that really dramatised the message. The film went viral in a big way, being uploaded, blogged, tagged and shared – gaining a huge amount of free media and PR. It reached an estimated 600,000 people in one form or another.

Art Directors
Lisa Fedyszyn
Jonathan McMahon
Copywriters
Lisa Fedyszyn
Jonathan McMahon
Creative Directors
Richard Maddocks
Nick Worthington

Designers
Ainsley Waite
Raffaella Wilson
Interactive Designers
Simon Koay
Phil Newman
Advertising Agency
Colenso BBDO

Agency Producer
Paul Courtney
Interactive Producer
Hamish Wanhill
Developer
Tim Smith
Account Director
Joanna Wealleans

Group Account
Director
Michael Redwood
Client
New Zealand Book
Council

Digital

Colenso BBDO
for New Zealand Book Council

Read a Book at Work
The New Zealand Book Council challenged us to find a fun new way to make books more accessible, and to encourage people to fall in love with reading again. These days, people spend far too much time working in front of their computers and not enough time reading books, so we figured that people would rather read books than do work. We disguised books as everyday office computer documents and released them online. You can now read Oscar Wilde through to DBC Pierre, anywhere, anytime, without anyone ever knowing. Even at work, where your boss and co-workers will be none the wiser. And all these books are housed in our online library, which is designed to look like a Windows desktop.

Art Director	Executive Director	Online Editor	Planner
Ben Green	Fiona Sharkie	Richard Lambert	Melanie Wiese
Copywriter	**Production Company**	**Lighting**	**Account Handlers**
Pat Lennox	Soma Films	**Cameraperson**	Georgette Mahoney
Director	**Advertising Agency**	Sean Meehan	Belinda Murray
Sean Meehan	The Campaign	**Sound Designer**	**Client**
Creative Director	Palace	Simon Lister	The Cancer Council
Tony Leishman	**Agency Producers**	**Music Composer &**	Victoria
Producer	Josh Armstrong	**Arranger**	**Brand**
Samantha McGarry	Fiona Gillies	Elliot Wheeler	Quit
	Editor	**Set Designer**	
	Drew Thompson	Arabella Lockhart	

Moving Image

The Campaign Palace
for The Cancer Council Victoria

Separation
Smoking kills around 3,000 Victorians each year, many of whom are loving and devoted parents. Our commercial aimed to convince these people that if they continued to smoke, they risked losing something just as precious as their health. Ultimately, we wanted to turn smokers into quitters. Research showed that while smokers easily dismiss the notion of self harm, they're not as comfortable with the effects that smoking can have on their children. Our creative execution forces smokers to confront the 'hidden cost' of their habit. Quitline calls increased by 92 per cent compared to the same time period the previous year.

Art Directors	Creative Director	Agency Producer	Planner
Lisa Fedyszyn	Nick Worthington	Jen Storey	Hayley Pardoe
Jonathan McMahon	**Producer**	**Editor**	**Account Director**
Copywriters	Susannah DiLallo	Suga Suppiah	Gemma Findlay
Lisa Fedyszyn	**Production Company**	**Director of**	**Client**
Jonathan McMahon	Plaza Films	**Photography**	Alzheimer's New
Director	**Advertising Agency**	Piet de Vries	Zealand
Dave Klaiber	Colenso BBDO	**Sound Design**	
		Sound Reservoir	

Moving Image

Colenso BBDO
for Alzheimer's New Zealand

Car
To raise awareness of Alzheimer's, we used the less than serious candid camera-style approach to show just how confusing and distressing life can be for a person living with this serious disease.

109

The Village Where Nothing Ever Happens   A Walk Through Miravete   Pebble   Tavern

Art Directors
Carlos Alvarez
Pablo González de
la Peña
Copywriters
Carlos Garcia Janini
Juan Nonzioli
Juan Silva
Direction
We are Pacheco

**General Creative
Director**
Juan Nonzioli
**Executive Creative
Director**
Juan Silva
Advertising Agency
Shackleton
Production Company
Mirinda Films

**Post Production
Company**
Molinare
Agency Producer
Cristina Cortizas
**Audiovisual
Production Manager**
Manuela Zamora
Sound & Music
Audioclip

Account Handler
Luz Gonzalez
Account Supervisor
Eva Galan
General Manager
Maite Rodriguez
Client
Conect (Specialized
Council of Pay TV
Thematic Channels)

Moving Image

Shackleton
for Conect

The Village Where Nothing Ever Happens / A Walk Through Miravete / Pebble / Tavern
Conect empirically demonstrated the advertising efficiency of Pay TV channels through a real exercise involving four steps: 1) Choose an unknown and never-advertised-on-TV product. 2) Launch an advertising campaign only on Pay TV, with a clear call to action to the product and its website. 3) Measure variables (knowledge, awareness, traffic, sales) before, during and after. 4) Accredit Pay TV for the experiment's efficiency and announce it to the market. We created an unusual tourism campaign by inviting people to do nothing: 'Here nothing ever happens. How long has it been since nothing happens to you? Come to Miravete. www.thevillagewherenothingeverhappens.com'. Four TV spots were broadcast exclusively on Pay TV channels, which invited viewers to the village and its website.

Art Director
Paul Bruce
Digital Art Director
Craig Bailey
Copywriters
Cleve Cameron
Richard Morgan
Creative Directors
Chris James
Simon Langley

Executive Creative Director
Warren Brown
Director
Joe Leonie
Producer
Anna Stewart
Production Company
Flying Fish
Advertising Agency
BMF

Agency Producer
Whitney Hawthorn
Planner
Gerry Cyron
Digital Planning Director
Aaron Michie
Account Handlers
Patrick Cahill
Esther Knox
Vicky Norton

Marketing Director
Neil Gordon
Client
Goodman Fielder
Baking
Brand
Wonder Performance

Integrated

BMF
for Goodman Fielder Baking

Not for Ducks
The task was to market new energy-enriched 'Wonder Performance' bread, designed especially for teens. Our creative leap was to launch with the idea that this new bread is great for teens, but too much for little ducks. We rolled the campaign out in three phases: firstly establishing a myth of ducks behaving in extraordinary ways using a series of unbranded virals and 'foreign news reports' seeded online; secondly, the bread company accepted responsibility via public announcements in mainstream media; thirdly, the public played along, filing thousands of documented 'sightings' of unusual duck behaviour. In total, some 29 forms of media were used to bring the idea to life.

111

Art Director	**Executive Creative**	**Agency Producer**	**Group Account**
Tom Martin	**Director**	Sevda Cemo	**Director**
Copywriter	James McGrath	**Editor**	Ricci Meldrum
Julian Schreiber	**Director**	Gene Hammond-Lewis	**Client**
Senior Graphic	Tony Rogers	**Sound Engineer**	Patties
Designer	**Producer**	Stevo Williams	**Brand**
Musonda Katongo	Jenny Livingston	**Production Manager**	Four'N Twenty Meat
Senior Interactive	**Interactive Producer**	Joanne Currie	Pies
Designer	Sam Hodgson	**Planner**	
Calvin Teoh	**Production Company**	Michael Hyde	
Creative Director	Renegade	**Account Manager**	
Ant Keogh	**Advertising Agency**	Sarah Galbraith	
	Clemenger BBDO		
	Melbourne		

Integrated

Clemenger BBDO Melbourne
for Patties

Magic Salad Plate
Instead of denying the Four'N Twenty Meat Pies' lack of health, as so many other brands do with their healthy choice meals, we decided to embrace it. To this end we created not an ad, but an idea that innovatively worked hand in hand with the pie to humorously say, 'For five minutes society, can you bugger off and let me eat what I want!' We created the Four'N Twenty Magic Salad Plate, a product that ridiculously lets pie eaters look like they're eating salad when, in truth, it's just part of the plate.

Art Director
Vince Lagana
Copywriter
Steve Jackson
Photographers
Tim Gibbs
Petrina Hicks
Sean Izzard
David Knight
Scott Newett
Daniel Smith

Creative Directors
Dave Bowman
David Nobay
Digital Creative Director
Brian Merrifield
Executive Creative Director
Steve Back
Director
Ralph van Dijk
Producer
Tom Eslinger

Advertising Agency
Saatchi & Saatchi
Australia
Agency Producer
Kate Whitfield
Sound Engineering
Sandcastle Studios
Mobile Designer
Christina Lock
Mobile Developer
Shaun O'Connor

Technical Direction
Dialect
Hyperfactory
Mobot
Project Manager
Paul Worboys
Account Handler
James Tracy Inglis
Marketing Manager
Abulah Mbamba
Brand Manager
Julia Dean
Client
United Nations

Print

Saatchi & Saatchi Australia
for United Nations

UN Voices Project
The UN Voices project was created to give everyone a voice. Really give them a voice. By using revolutionary mobile technology, we made posters and press ads talk for the very first time: after taking a mobile phone photo of the featured person's mouth, you send it to the number shown as a text message. Almost instantly your mobile will ring and you'll hear their story in a brief pre-recorded message. You are then directed to unvoices.org.au where you can hear other stories or add your own.

Art Directors	**Photographer**	**Advertising Agency**	**Client**
Jaideep Mahajan	Tarun Vishwa	Rediffusion Y&R	Bharti Airtel
Shameem	**Creative Directors**	**Senior Marketing**	**Brand**
Mohammad	Deepesh Jha	**Vice President**	Airtel Mobile Phone
Anunay Rai	Jaideep Mahajan	Chandrasekkar	Data Backup
Divya Sharma	**National Creative**	Radhakrisnan	
Copywriters	**Directors**		
Megha Dutta	Sagar		
Deepesh Jha	Mahabaleshwarkar		
	Ramanuj Shastry		

Print

Rediffusion Y&R
for Bharti Airtel

Airtel Mobile Phone Data Backup – Engineer / Housewife / Tourist
Replacing a handset is easy but replacing your data is not. With Airtel's Mobile Phone Data
Backup, if it's in your phone, it's safely stored on our servers. Since this is a service for existing
Airtel users, the challenge was to target them exclusively, with impact. In-shop posters were
put up at Airtel Relationship Centres (ARCs) as existing subscribers frequently visit ARCs to pay
their phone bills. In the first month of the campaign, 18 per cent of Airtel users subscribed to the
Airtel Mobile Phone Data Backup service.

Direct

Art Director
Sergio Lobo
Copywriter
Francisco Cassis

Creative Directors
Francisco Cassis
Rafa Antón

Advertising Agency
Vitruvio Leo Burnett

Client
Procter & Gamble
Brand
Herbal Essences

Print
Vitruvio Leo Burnett
for Procter & Gamble

Karaoke Shower Curtain
Leire Martínez, the face of Herbal Essences in Spain, became the new lead vocalist of La Oreja de Van Gogh, Spain's most famous pop band. So when they released their new album last summer, we saw a great opportunity to reinforce this endorsement and make the most out of this peak moment in Leire's popularity. We found the connection between shampoo and music in a simple insight – people like to sing in the shower. We created a 'karaoke shower curtain' of the band's first single. This idea outshone the usual promotions by giving away a useful, memorable gift that linked the brand and the band – shampoo and pop music – in a surprising way.

Art Director
Kerstin Eberbach
Copywriter
Lars Huvart
Photographer
Jo Bacherl
Designer
Kerstin Eberbach

Creative Directors
Thomas Hofbeck
Lars Huvart
Producer
Fabian Schrader
Advertising Agency
Ogilvy Frankfurt

Art Buyers
Martina Diederichs
Caroline Walczok
Account Handlers
Marco Bisello
Sascha Riedel

Marketing Manager
Jens Helfrich
Client
IKEA Germany
Brand
IKEA

Ambient
Ogilvy Frankfurt
for IKEA Germany

Bigger Storage Ideas
German flats and apartments are full of messy corners. That's why IKEA produces practical boxes and drawers in all shapes and sizes for all storage needs. Frankfurt IKEA asked us to promote their storage solutions, targeted particularly at people living in smaller apartments, with a big outdoor idea. The idea was to play with the widely recognisable shapes and designs of the IKEA storage range and to put them into a new and surprising context. By redesigning the front of an apartment building in a busy Frankfurt street with giant mock-ups of IKEA drawers and cardboard boxes, we generated the highest level of attention, and literally linked the product to where it belongs: in small flats and apartments.

115

Art Director
Fiona Parkin
Copywriters
Jane Drumm
Rebecca Kamm

Creative Director
Andy Blood

Advertising Agency
TBWA\WHYBIN\
TEQUILA

Marketing Manager
Mary Zefferelli
Client
Preventing Violence,
New Zealand

Ambient

TBWA\WHYBIN\TEQUILA
for Preventing Violence, New Zealand

Bar Code
How do you provide helpline details to a woman who will be beaten if these details are found? This has been a longstanding dilemma for organisations such as Preventing Violence, New Zealand. Thanks to a simple sticker device, there's a cheap and easily portable solution: adhesive, faux barcodes that disguise a helpline number as a code. They can be stuck onto any domestic object and go completely unnoticed by controlling partners. General practitioners and hospitals across New Zealand have adopted the barcode device, and international governmental and NGO agencies are following suit. Testimonials and requests for extra stickers demonstrate the success of the barcodes.

Art Director
Jan-Willem Smits

Copywriter
Edsard Schutte
Photographer
Arno Bosma

Designer
Pieter van der Meer

Advertising Agency
Ogilvy Amsterdam
Client
DHL

Ambient

Ogilvy Amsterdam
for DHL

Inlay Box
DHL wanted to inform its existing customers about the new improved Asia service. DHL customers use special DHL boxes for their shipments. Just phoning DHL is enough to get the boxes delivered within a day, totally free of charge and ready to use. Our solution was to provide DHL boxes with a very special inlay. The inlay, at the bottom of the box, shows another open box and together they make a long 'tunnel'. At the end of the 'tunnel' there is an Asian person handing over something. In the Hong Kong version the Asian person hands over a toy box, in the Shanghai version a laptop, and in the Beijing version a shoe. The text says, 'The fastest way to Hong Kong/Shanghai/Beijing. Take a look at www.dhl.nl to see our sharp prices'.

Ambient

Publicis Ambience
for Cancer Patients Aid Association

Spit Stain Graffiti
Gutka, an indigenous form of tobacco, has become a fixture in the mouths of millions of Indians, causing 80,000 cases of oral cancer every year. After Gutka is consumed, the leftover juice is usually spat onto a wall, causing an unsightly red stain that remains on the wall. These stains have become a part of the Indian landscape. When Cancer Patients Aid Association wanted to make the masses aware of the evils of Gutka, we used these stains to our advantage and created graffiti that looked as if the Gutka user was puking blood. Even with a minuscule budget of 100,000 Indian Rupees ($3,000) we could spread the message across 23 cities.

Art Directors
Siddhesh Khatavkar
Shantanu Suman
Copywriters
Nikhil Panjwani
Mayuresh Wagle

Photographers
MS Belliappa
Ashish Phatak
Creative Directors
Ashish Khazanchi
Prasanna Sankhe

Advertising Agency
Publicis Ambience
Production Manager
Shireesh Sabnis
Editor
Ganesh Dodmani

Marketing Manager
Anita Peter
Client
Cancer Patients Aid
Association

Ambient

BJL Manchester
for Versus Cancer

Lucky Balls
The task was to raise awareness of testicular cancer on an extremely tight budget. The piece was made to look like a UK lottery ticket in order to entice people to pick it up. It was placed in environments where men are likely to socialise.

Art Directors
Neil Boote
Andy Buchan
Copywriters
Neil Boote
Andy Buchan

Creative Directors
Pete Bastiman
Billy Mawhinney
Tom Richards

Advertising Agency
BJL Manchester
Account Handler
Kath Mainprize

Marketing Manager
James Ward
Client
Versus Cancer

Art Director	Creative Directors	Account Handler	Client
Simon Oppmann	Simon Oppmann	Marco Bisello	Deutsche Stiftung
Copywriter	Peter Römmelt	**Marketing Manager**	Denkmalschutz
Peter Römmelt	**Advertising Agency**	Dr Ursula Schirmer	
	Ogilvy Frankfurt		

Ambient

Ogilvy Frankfurt
for Deutsche Stiftung Denkmalschutz

Begging Sculptures
Germany's historical monuments can only be saved from disrepair at a great cost. Therefore, the Deutsche Stiftung Denkmalschutz (German Foundation for Monument Protection) urgently needed donations. We let those most affected by the dilapidation of the monuments beg for donations, i.e. the ancient sculptures of historical monuments themselves.

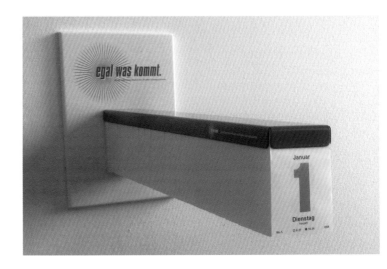

Art Directors	Creative Director	Advertising Agency	Account Handler
Ute Deyerling	Eberhard Kirchhoff	Saatchi & Saatchi	Petra Felgen
Dennis Kastner	**Chief Creative Officer**	Frankfurt	**Marketing Manager**
Copywriter	Burkhart von Scheven	**Agency Producer**	Sabine Reiner
Eberhard Kirchhoff		Amandus Platt	**Client**
			Schott Solar

Addressed Direct Mail Very Low Volume

Saatchi & Saatchi Frankfurt
for Schott Solar

20 Years Warranty
Schott Solar produces solar panels with 20 years' warranty. In order to present the Schott Solar brand in a distinctive and meaningful way to wholesale markets, we created a 20-year warranty calendar, which sticks out over 60cm from the wall. A message which can hardly be ignored.

Art Director	**Photographer**	**Advertising Agency**	**Brand Managers**
Susan Dearn	Penny Clay	M&C Saatchi/Mark	Peter Britton
Copywriter	**Creative Director**	**Agency Producer**	Debbie Mills
Mitch Alison	Gavin McLeod	Nick Lilley	**Client**
		Account Handler	Sydney Dogs & Cats
		Megan Wooding	Home

Direct Mail Door Drop Low Volume

M&C Saatchi/Mark
for Sydney Dogs & Cats Home

Find Me a Home
The Sydney Dogs & Cats Home briefed us to find a home for the 11 dogs that had been with them long-term, as these animals were seriously running out of time. Our secondary objective was to raise money for the home. We decided to remind people how good it feels to have a dog in their lives, so we brought the experience to life by placing cardboard cut-outs of dogs in car windows. We used photographs of the home's actual dogs and focused our activity on major car parks all over Sydney. In the weeks following the campaign, every one of the 11 dogs found a home. In addition, donations were up 20 per cent on the previous year.

Art Director	**Graphic Designer**	**Executive Creative**	**Account Supervisor**
Alexander Nagel	Anja Krumrein	**Director**	Annemarie Moeller
Copywriter	**Author**	Alex Schill	**Client**
Cosimo Moeller	Sasha Lord	**Advertising Agency**	Verlagsgruppe Lübbe
	Creative Director	Serviceplan	
	Christoph Everke		

Direct Mail Door Drop Low Volume

Serviceplan
for Verlagsgruppe Lübbe

Book on Paper Handkerchiefs
Her enthralling romantic adventure novels make Sasha Lord one of the most successful international bestselling authors of her genre. 'Across a Wild Sea', yet another promising title, was issued in German by the publisher Bastei Lübbe Verlag at the beginning of 2009. A special campaign was developed for the publisher to promote Sasha Lord's new novel. The first chapters of the tear-jerking book were printed as an exclusive preview on paper handkerchiefs and sent to the publisher's dealers and loyal readers as a 'pocket-handkerchief-book' in a tissue box.

119

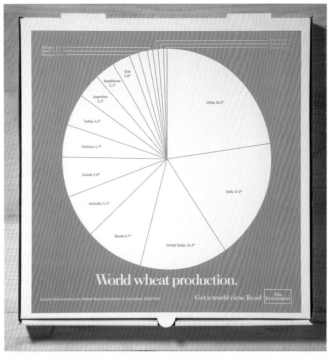

World wheat production.

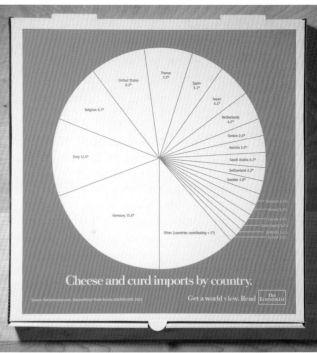

Cheese and curd imports by country.

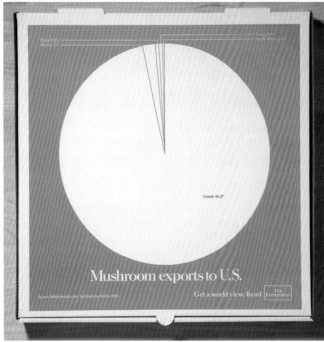

Mushroom exports to U.S.

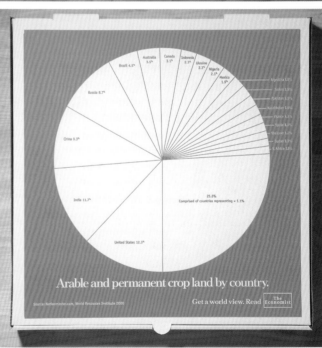

Arable and permanent crop land by country.

Art Director	Senior Creative	Advertising Agency	Account Director
James Clunie	**Director**	BBDO New York	Clayton Ruebensaal
Copywriter	Kara Goodrich	**Agency Producer**	**Account Associate**
Kara Goodrich	**Chief Creative**	Kathy Lando	Robin Quill
Creative Director	**Officers**	**Account Manager**	**Client**
James Clunie	David Lubars	Kate Houghton	The Economist
	Bill Bruce		

Direct Mail Door Drop Medium Volume

BBDO New York
for The Economist

Pizza Boxes
In September 2008, a print, online and outdoor advertising campaign was launched for 'The Economist' in Philadelphia, as one city in a cross-country promotional blitz. To reach college students, 80,000 Economist-branded pizza boxes emblazoned with Economist-inspired pie charts were distributed to pizzerias close to large college campuses in the Philadelphia area.

Direct

Creative Director
Roderick Fenske
Advertising Agency
Media Consulta TV &
Filmproduktion

Agency Producer
Till Dreier
Editor
Mark Hunt

Marketing Manager
Maria-Antonia
Jimenez-Nevado

Client
European Commission
DG Research
Brand
Marie Curie Actions

Media Consulta TV & Filmproduktion
for European Commission DG Research

Chemical Party
Marie Curie Actions is a European Union initiative that provides training, career development and mobility schemes for young researchers. To promote this programme, Media Consulta TV decided on an approach that would be at once educational and entertaining. The result was 'Chemical Party', a simple yet inventive spot that answers the question: what would happen if people meeting at a party reacted to each other like chemical elements? It both educated the viewer about the science of chemical reactions, and reflected the importance of networking and collaboration in the European research community. The visual simplicity of the spot emphasises the clarity and efficacy of the concept, while the irreverent humour appeals to a younger audience.

Art Directors
Frank van Rooyen
Chantelle dos Santos
Copywriter
Aviv Weil
Typographer
Chantelle dos Santos

Illustrator
Ben Crossman
Creative Director
Jonathan Deeb
**Executive Creative
Director**
Graham Warsop

Advertising Agency
The Jupiter Drawing
Room Johannesburg
Producer
Manuel Lopes
Account Handler
Greg Georgiades

**Client
Representatives**
Alison Hastings
Cailin Wandrag
Client
Absa Capital

Art Direction

The Jupiter Drawing Room Johannesburg
for Absa Capital

Cubism Manifesto Power of 3
The brief was to launch the Absa Capital brand in South Africa and cement Absa Capital as a key player in the local investment banking market. Coupled with an above-the-line campaign, a limited edition 99-page leather-bound book was created for key Absa Capital clients. Titled 'The Cubism Manifesto', each book showcased Absa Capital's distinctive 'power of 3' philosophy through a varied mix of design, storytelling, illustration, typography and photography. As a result, Absa Capital has entrenched its vision of becoming the leading investment bank in sub-Saharan Africa. One hundred books were used to convey one unique investment banking philosophy.

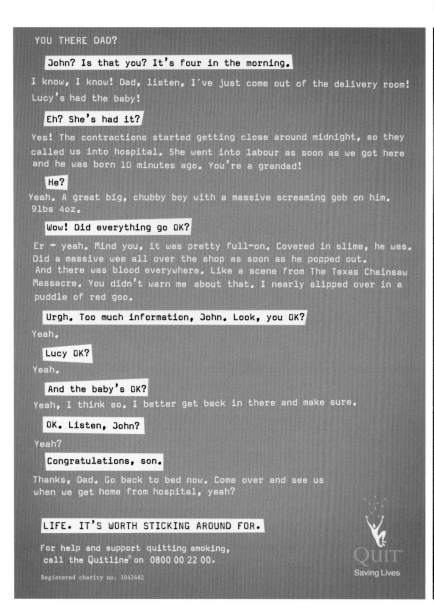

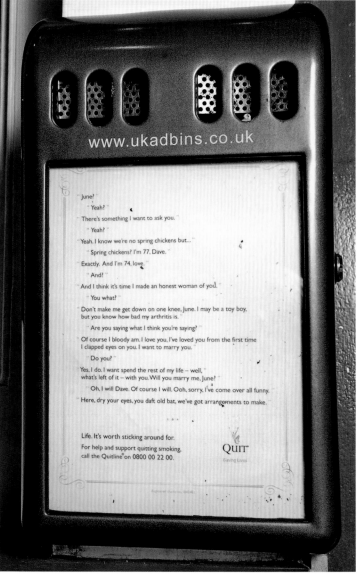

Copywriters
Ant Melder
Dan O'Bey
Art Director
Seamus Higgins

Typographers
Seamus Higgins
Roger Kennedy
Creative Director
Emma Perkins

Advertising Agency
Saatchi & Saatchi X
Marketing Manager
Kate Spicer

Brand Manager
Glyn McIntosh
Client
QUIT

Writing
Saatchi & Saatchi X
for QUIT

Grandad / Proposal
Most smokers are well aware of the dangers of smoking. Reiterating these has a limited effect. We realised that hope rather than fear could be a powerful message; by reminding smokers of the great things that can happen later in life, we could inspire them to quit rather than scare them into it. So we addressed them at 'point-of-puff' – on public ashtrays outside pubs, bars and cafés. Because they were smoking a cigarette, they had time to read the copy and, as many did, use their mobile phone to call the quitline.

IF YOU ARE A PARSEE,

ABOUT THIRTY VULTURES ARRIVE AT YOUR DEAD BODY EVEN AS THE LAST MAN FROM YOUR FUNERAL PROCESSION WALKS OUT OF THE TOWER OF SILENCE. VULTURES ARE INSTINCTIVELY FAMILIAR TO THE NATURE OF THE HUMAN BODY. THEY KNOW THAT YOUR EYES ARE THE MOST DELICATE PART OF YOU. IN AN INSTANT, THE BIRDS GATHER BY YOUR HEAD. RAVENOUSLY HUNGRY AND FIERCELY COMPETITIVE, THEY DON'T PECK AT YOUR EYES. THEY DIG INTO THEM. YOUR EYELIDS ARE TORN APART IN A MOMENT. AND YOUR EYEBALLS ARE PUNCTURED. THE AQUEOUS AND VITREOUS HUMOURS LEAK OUT. QUICKLY, BIT BY BIT, YOUR EYEBALLS ARE PICKED OUT OF THEIR SOCKETS. THE OPTIC NERVE AND ALL THE OTHER HUNDREDS OF BLOOD VESSELS ARE RIPPED OUT ALONG WITH THEM. YOUR CORNEA AND RETINA, OF COURSE, STAND NO CHANCE AS THE FEAST BEGINS.

- -

NO, I DON'T WANT TO PLEDGE MY EYES TO THE VULTURES. PLEASE GET IN TOUCH WITH ME.

MY NAME:_____
ADDRESS:_____
PHONE NO.:_____ E-MAIL ID:_____
PLEASE MAIL THIS COUPON TO:
EYE BANK ASSOCIATION KERALA, CBM OPTHALMIC INSTITUTE, LITTLE FLOWER HOSPITAL & RESEARCH CENTRE, ANGAMALY-683 573, KERALA.

IF YOU ARE A CHRISTIAN,

THE ORNATE WOODEN COFFIN FIRST DELAYS THE DECOMPOSITION PROCESS OF YOUR DEAD BODY, AND THEN HURRIES IT UP. BACTERIA BEGIN TO FORM AT ALL RELATIVELY SOFTER SPOTS IN YOUR BODY. YOUR EYES, WET AND DELICATE THAT THEY ARE, USUALLY ARE THE FIRST TARGETS. SOON, A STICKY CORNEAL FILM FORMS OVER YOUR EYES. AND UGLY BLACK SPOTS APPEAR ON THE WHITE TISSUE. INDIVIDUAL CELLS IN YOUR EYES BEGIN TO DIE, RELEASING ENZYMES THAT BREAK DOWN THE CELL MATERIAL AND CONNECTIONS TO OTHER CELLS. GASES ARE CONTINUOUSLY RELEASED AND MAKE YOUR EYES BULGE OUT AND FINALLY BURST OPEN. FLUIDS CONTINUE TO OOZE TILL YOUR EYES START SHRINKING, AND EVENTUALLY DECOMPOSE INTO A GOOEY MASS. IF THE SOIL AROUND YOUR COFFIN IS LOOSE AND HAS WORMS AND OTHER CREEPY CREATURES IN IT, THEN THE STORY GETS GORIER.

- -

NO, I DON'T WANT TO PLEDGE MY EYES TO BACTERIA AND WORMS. PLEASE GET IN TOUCH WITH ME.
MY NAME:_____
ADDRESS:_____
PHONE NO.:_____ E-MAIL ID:_____
PLEASE MAIL THIS COUPON TO:
EYE BANK ASSOCIATION KERALA, CBM OPTHALMIC INSTITUTE, LITTLE FLOWER HOSPITAL & RESEARCH CENTRE, ANGAMALY-683 573, KERALA.

IF YOU ARE A HINDU,

THE BLAZING FLAMES FROM YOUR FUNERAL PYRE INSTANTLY BURN UP THE EYEBROWS AND EYELASHES ON YOUR DEAD BODY. YOUR EYES POP OUT FOR A FEW SECONDS ONLY TO SINK IN MUCH DEEPER AS THE TEMPERATURE RISES. THANKS TO THE LIQUIDS INSIDE YOUR SKULL, YOUR EYES START BOILING. AND IN A FEW MINUTES, THEY ARE WELL COOKED. THE AQUEOUS HUMOUR IS THE FIRST TO DISAPPEAR. THE CORNEA, THE PUPIL AND THE LENS ARE SCALDED BEFORE THEY DISINTEGRATE TOTALLY. THE VITREOUS HUMOUR BOILS OVER AND EXPLODES. THE SHRIVELED UP RETINA EXPOSES ITSELF TO THE INTENSE HEAT FOR A BRIEF SECOND BEFORE TURNING INTO NOTHING. AND THE OPTIC NERVES SOON DISSOLVE IN THE BURNING MESS. WHEN YOUR WHOLE BODY IS TURNED INTO A COUPLE OF POUNDS OF ASH, THE EYES CONTRIBUTE ALMOST NOTHING TO THE WEIGHT.

- -

NO, I DON'T WANT TO PLEDGE MY EYES TO THE ASHES. PLEASE GET IN TOUCH WITH ME.
MY NAME:_____
ADDRESS:_____
PHONE NO.:_____ E-MAIL ID:_____
PLEASE MAIL THIS COUPON TO:
EYE BANK ASSOCIATION KERALA, CBM OPTHALMIC INSTITUTE, LITTLE FLOWER HOSPITAL & RESEARCH CENTRE, ANGAMALY-683 573, KERALA.

Copywriters
Anu Joseph
Sajan Raj Kurup
Art Director
Vikram Gaikwad

Typographer
Vikram Gaikwad
Creative Directors
Vikram Gaikwad
Anu Joseph
Sajan Raj Kurup

Advertising Agency
Creativeland Asia,
Mumbai
Account Handler
Sudheer Krishnan

Brand Manager
Fr (Dr) Sebestian
Vadakumpadan
Client
Eye Bank
Association Kerala

Writing
Creativeland Asia, Mumbai
for Eye Bank Association Kerala

Parsee / Christian / Hindu
The strategy was to evoke sentiment and encourage people to react strongly and immediately, by pledging their eyes for donation. Each of these small ads graphically described what happens to the eyes during the last rites of dead people in different religions. Examples included when a Hindu's body is cremated, when a Parsee's body is left for vultures to feed on, and when a Christian's body is buried. The campaign made a compelling argument in favour of eye donation; the cleverly worded coupons in these ads had a tremendous impact on the reader.

Copywriter
Prajato Guha
Art Director
Siddhi Yadav
Photographer
Kedar Malegaonkar
Typographer
Siddhi Yadav

Illustrator
Siddhi Yadav
Creative Directors
Prasoon Joshi
Denzil Machado

Advertising Agency
McCann Worldgroup
Mumbai
Account Handler
Shashank Lanjekar
Marketing Manager
Abbas Sikandar

General Manager
T S Rajan
Client
Prism Papyrus
Brand
Fedrigoni

Writing

McCann Worldgroup Mumbai
for Fedrigoni

Monsters, Ink
The brief was to create a direct mailer that would promote Fedrigoni's specially coated, non-blotting printing paper, and inform owners of printing presses and other print buyers across Mumbai that Prism Papyrus stocks it. Our ultimate aim was to solicit enquiries regarding paper samples. To show the perils of using non-coated paper (the ink blots and smudges that result during printing), we created 26 monsters out of ink blots, one for each letter of the English alphabet, and plonked them on the pages of a book that was then mailed to the target audience. 'Monsters, Ink' generated a monster of a response, in terms of enquiries regarding paper samples as well as traffic to the Prism Papyrus website.

The jury:
Mike O'Sullivan, Saatchi & Saatchi New Zealand
(Jury Foreman)
Matt Hardisty, AnalogFolk
Aidan Hawkes, Cunning
Vanessa Pearson, McCann Erickson South Africa
Tim Schierwater, Nordpol+ Hamburg Agentur für
Kommunikation
Chris Staples, Rethink Communications
Dave Woods, RMG Connect

Art Directors	Advertising Agency	Producer	Group Account
Calle Sjoenell	BBH New York	Dawn Rose	**Director**
Pelle Sjoenell	**Directors**	**Producer**	Chris Wollen
Creative Directors	The Malloys	Rebecca Skinner	**Clients**
Calle Sjoenell	**Director of**	**Senior Producer**	NYC & Company
Pelle Sjoenell	**Photography**	Julian Katz	Warner Brothers
Chief Creative	Sam Levy	**Production**	**Brand**
Officer	**Editor**	**Company**	Oasis 'Dig Out
Kevin Roddy	Tim Wheeler	HSI	Your Soul'
		Account Manager	
		Shane Chanstang	

Ambient

BBH New York
for Warner Brothers

Oasis 'Dig Out Your Soul' – in the Streets
We arranged for Oasis to teach over twenty New York City street-musicians new songs from their yet-to-be released album. Those musicians then took to the streets to perform the songs, weeks before the album was launched. News of the campaign was spread through PR, Oasis fan sites, the New York City website and people at the performances. The event received worldwide press coverage. The content captured by fans garnered 200,000 views on YouTube, Flickr and the NYC website. Then, the documentary premiered internationally on the MySpace network and received over 520,000 views and a second wave of global press coverage. Dig Out Your Soul became the first US top ten album for Oasis in ten years.

Art Director	Advertising Agency	Print Producer	Account Executives
Rob Omodiagbe	JWT New York	Lauren Eberhardt	Lauren Johnson
Copywriter	**Executive Creative**	**Digital Producer**	Lauren Rodwell
Chris Maiorino	**Directors**	Kathryn Leo	**Global Head of**
Creative Directors	Walt Connelly	**Account Director**	**Account**
Chris Maiorino	Kash Sree	Cristina Lilly	Richard Lennox
Rob Omodiagbe	**Chief Creative**	**Associate Account**	**Brand Manager**
Lisa Topol	**Officers**	**Director**	Janet Sussens
Digital Creative	Harvey Marco	Megan Frances	**Client**
Director	Ty Montague	Delage	DeBeers
Mason Hedgecoth	**Integrated Producer**		**Brand**
	Holly Otto		A diamond is forever

Ambient

JWT New York
for DeBeers

The Rose Campaign

DeBeers' line, 'A diamond is forever', was losing its meaning, relegated to a strapline on ads. In tough economic times, men were choosing flowers and chocolates as romantic gifts instead of diamonds. We decided to show the value of diamonds by demonstrating the temporary nature of other romantic gifts. We constructed an installation of 25,000 red roses spelling out 'A diamond is forever' in the middle of New York's Grand Central Station. Over the next ten days, the roses dried out, changed colour and died, poignantly driving home the message. Online, people could follow the roses' demise, hear interviews, and send rose emails that would wilt then die. Posters depicting other temporary gifts lined the walkways leading to the installation.

Art Directors	Creative Directors	Advertising Agency	Client
Basil Christensen	Basil Christensen	Ogilvy NZ	Jealous Lovers
Damon O'Leary	Damon O'Leary	**Producer**	Productions
Tom Paine	**Executive Creative**	Nick Barnes	**Brand**
Copywriters	**Director**		Jealous Lovers
Basil Christensen	Jeremy Taine		
Damon O'Leary			
Tom Paine			

Ogilvy NZ
for Jealous Lovers Productions

Jealous Lovers
To promote new production company Jealous Lovers, we targeted four of New Zealand's top creative directors. We found out which rival directors they'd used to shoot their most recent TVCs. We then located their vehicles. On the windscreens, we attached decals with personalised messages, relevant to their relationship with the 'other' director, and left magnetised pickaxes in their bonnets, branded with the Jealous Lovers web address. Insiders broke it to the directors that someone was trashing their vehicles. We covertly filmed their horrified reactions. Still shots were then seeded to industry blogsites along with a link to jealouslovers.tv, where creatives could view their reactions.

129

Art Director	**Producer**	**Planner**	**Client**
Paul Sharp	Oscar Birken	Nicole Milward	Lion Nathan
Digital Art Director	**Digital Producer**	**Account Handler**	**Brand**
Andy Cooke	Julia Prior	Simon Ludowyke	James Boag's
Copywriter	**Advertising Agency**	**Marketing Manager**	Draught
Mike Burdick	Publicis Mojo	Raniero Miccoli	
Creative Director	**Agency Producer**	**Brand Manager**	
Micah Walker	Penny Brown	Richard Spicer	

Ambient

Publicis Mojo
for Lion Nathan

The Great Tasmanian Pipeline
While James Boag's is a well-known and respected name in brewing, Boag's Draught was comparatively unknown outside its native Tasmania. To introduce it as a tap beer in mainland Australia, we exploited Tasmania's island status to create the Great Tasmanian Pipeline – a fictitious pipeline that supposedly pumped fresh Boag's Draught straight from the brewery to Australian pubs. The campaign involved ambient installations of the pipeline in bars and on the street, print executions, a mobile site, a Facebook fan page, rich online media and a microsite.

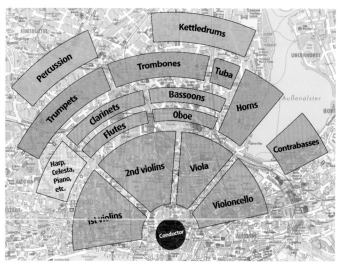

Jung von Matt Hamburg
for Philharmonic Orchestra of Hamburg

The Biggest Concert in the World
We created the biggest concert in the world, stationing 100 musicians in 50 locations throughout Hamburg, arranged as though they were in an orchestra pit. Each musician was able to follow the conductor, by watching a live transmission on the screens in front of them. They performed 'The Second Symphony' by Johannes Brahms simultaneously. In addition to the live event, the whole world was able to watch the concert online.

Art Directors	**Designer**	**Advertising Agency**	**Marketing Manager**
Simon Hiebl	Tobias Fritschen	Jung von Matt	Bettina Bermbach
Julia Ziegler	**Creative Directors**	Hamburg	**Brand Manager**
Copywriters	Fabian Frese	**Public Relations**	Milena Ivkovic
Fabian Bill	Götz Ulmer	**Executives**	**Client**
Jan-Florian Ege	**Chief Creative**	Joachim R Kortlepel	Philharmonic
Dr Stefan	**Officers**	Lutz Nebelin	Orchestra
Fockenberg	Armin Jochum	**Account Handlers**	of Hamburg
	Oliver Voss	Anke Göbber	
		Sandra Huckenbeck	

Ogilvy Toronto
for Unilever Canada

Body & Soul
In a groundbreaking way, we set out to smash the stereotypes that women over 45 face, connect with our Dove Pro-Age target and prove that 'Beauty has no age limit'. The result was 'Body & Soul', an original play we created, conceived and staged. Written and performed by 13 'real' women over 45, with no previous acting experience, it was directed by world-renowned, Order of Canada winning playwright Judith Thompson. The play opened to sold-out crowds in Toronto, set a box office record and generated over 127 million media impressions. Our documentary film, 'Finding Body & Soul', directed by Emmy award-winning documentarian Veronica Tennant, has aired twice on national TV. A second run of the play begins this summer.

Art Director	**Documentary**	**Costume Designer**	**Brand Manager**
Nadine Prada	**Director**	Dana Osborne	Margaret McKellar
Copywriter	Veronica Tennant	**Lighting**	**Assistant Brand**
Chris Dacyshyn	**Executive Producer**	Magi Oman	**Manager**
Photographer	Brenda Surminski	**Music Composer**	Andrea Stodart
Maude Arsenault	**Play Producer**	**& Arranger**	**Vice President Brand**
Creative Directors	Iris Nemani	Cathy Nosaty	**Development**
Janet Kestin	**Print Production**	**Account Handlers**	Geoff Craig
Nancy Vonk	**Producer**	Erin Gooderham	**Client**
Play Director	Chris Rozak	Aviva Groll	Unilever Canada
Judith Thompson	**Advertising Agency**	Patricia Paraventes	**Brand**
	Ogilvy Toronto	**Marketing Manager**	Dove Pro-Age
	Set Designer	Sharon MacLeod	
	Sue Lepage		

131

Ambient

TBWA\Germany (180/TBWA) Berlin
for adidas

Impossible Goalkeeper
Adidas wanted to be the number one football brand during the UEFA Euro 2008 championship in Austria and Switzerland, spreading their 'Impossible is nothing' philosophy far beyond the borders of the two countries. To rise above standard advertising chaos, we needed something as monumental and entertaining as the event itself. So we borrowed the 60m-high Ferris wheel in the Prater, the symbol of UEFA Euro 2008. We installed a 61m-tall version of the world's top goalkeeper, Petr Cech, with eight arms spinning along the Ferris wheel. A landmark and a tourist attraction were joined to make an unbeatable goalkeeper you could take a ride with. To complete the experience, we spread thousands of 3D postcards as souvenirs.

132

Art Director	**Advertising Agency**	**Management**	**Director Marketing**
Marco Bezerra	TBWA\ Germany	**Supervisor**	**Performance**
Copywriter	(180/TBWA) Berlin	Kerstin Gold	Martin Schindler
Emiliano Trierveiler	**Account Director**	**Production**	**Head of Brand**
Photographer	Falk Lungwitz	**Companies**	**Marketing**
Johann Sebastian	**Account Manager**	vertical vision &	Markus Rachals
Hänel	David Barton	Co.KG	**Group Brand**
Creative Director	**Agency Producer**	Limes	**Communication**
Stefan Schmidt	Katrin Dettmann	Vertriebsgesellschaft	**Manager**
Planner	**Art Buyer**	**Media Agency**	Sven Schindler
Moritz Kiechle	Martina Kersten	Carat Hamburg	**Client**
Retouching	**Project Managers**		adidas
24+7	Andreas Ebsen		
	Tanja Kurr		

Art Director
Simon Oppmann
Copywriter
Peter Römmelt

Creative Directors
Simon Oppmann
Peter Römmelt
Advertising Agency
Ogilvy Frankfurt

Account Handler
Marco Bisello
Marketing Manager
Dr Ursula Schirmer

Client
Deutsche Stiftung
Denkmalschutz
(German Foundation
for Monument
Protection)

Ambient

Ogilvy Frankfurt
for Deutsche Stiftung Denkmalschutz

Begging Sculptures
Germany's historical monuments can only be saved from disrepair at a great cost. Therefore, the Deutsche Stiftung Denkmalschutz (German Foundation for Monument Protection) urgently needed donations. We let those most affected by the dilapidation of the monuments beg for donations, i.e. the ancient sculptures of historical monuments themselves.

Art Directors
Frank Anselmo
Alfred S Park
Jeseok Yi

Copywriters
Francisco Hui
William Tran

Creative Director
Alfred S Park
Executive Creative Director
Richard Wilde

Advertising Agency
Big Ant International
Client
Global Coalition for Peace

Ambient

Big Ant International
for Global Coalition for Peace

What Goes Around Comes Around
With the election of a president opposed to the Iraq War, the Global Coalition for Peace wanted a campaign to reassert the importance of an immediate withdrawal from Iraq, while also raising awareness of the organisation. We came up with a simple and elegant outdoor campaign that focused on the spiralling cycle of war, reminding viewers that the violence perpetrated abroad will breed the hatred that fuels tomorrow's violence; that what goes around, comes around. To achieve peace, we must end the violence. With a limited budget, we selected locations in New York and San Francisco with sympathetic viewers who were most likely to respond. The result was a significant increase in donations of both time and money.

134

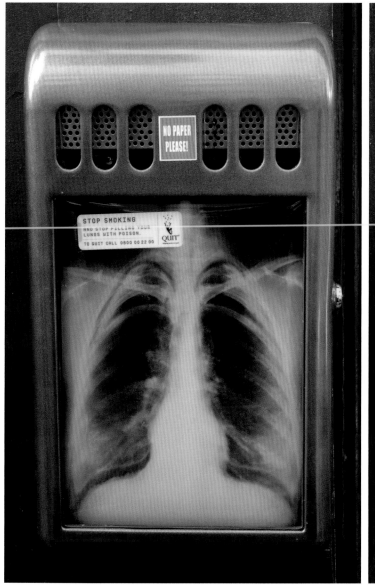 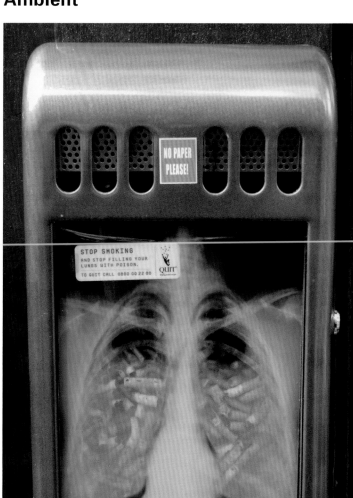

Art Directors
David Askwith
Rob Porteous
Copywriters
David Askwith
Rob Porteous

Typographers
Cris Jones
Scott Silvey
Creative Directors
Paul Silburn
Kate Stanners

Advertising Agency
Saatchi & Saatchi
London
Account Handler
Simon Ronchetti

Marketing Manager
Kate Spicer
Client
Quit

Ambient

Saatchi & Saatchi London
for Quit

Lungs
Since the introduction of the smoking ban throughout the UK, cigarette bins have appeared all over London. Our X-ray of the chest, gradually being filled with the smokers' own ash and cigarettes, served to shock smokers into realising the harm they were doing to their lungs.

Art Directors
Marina Caminal
Fernando Militerno
Copywriters
Ramiro Gamallo
Bernardo Wisky

Creative Directors
Pablo Capara
Fernando Militerno
Seto Olivieri
Advertising Agency
Leo Burnett
Argentina

Producers
Pedro Saleh
Federica Suarez
Santiago
Agency Producer
Nano Tidone

Account Handler
Andrea Prats
Marketing Manager
Diego Salamone
Client
Red Cross Argentina

Ambient

Leo Burnett Argentina
for Red Cross Argentina

Flooded House
The goal was to raise awareness and funds for the northern towns of Argentina that were affected by huge floods. A house was built inside a lake in the middle of the downtown area of Buenos Aires. The area is a nerve centre for urban movement and tourism, similar to Central Park in New York City. A sign read, 'The North of Argentina needs your help' with a telephone number for people to call to make donations. Thousands of people saw the house on their way to work. The whole country learned about it through the media. Over 60,000 donations were made, but most importantly, citizens became aware of the suffering experienced by part of the population 1,500km away.

The jury:

Mark Cridge, glue London (Jury Foreman)
Adriana Cury, Yan Elliott, WCRS
Graham Fink, M&C Saatchi London
Evan Fry, Crispin Porter + Bogusky
Roland Hafenrichter, Mather
Greg Hahn, BBDO New York
Steve McKenzie, Publicis Mojo Auckland
Dejan Rasic, Colman Rasic Carrasco
Kevin Roddy, BBH New York
Jon Williams, Grey London

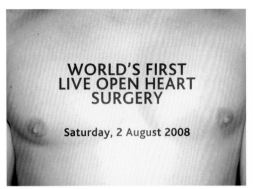

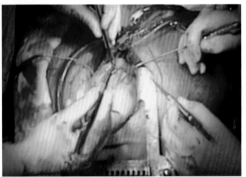

WORLD'S FIRST LIVE OPEN HEART SURGERY

Saturday, 2 August 2008

Wally bares his heart on TV

He agrees to first SA live telecast of open heart op

I ♥ TAKING THE STAIRS

I ♥ PARKING FAR FROM THE ENTRANCE

I ♥ FAST FOOD

I ♥ TAKING THE ESCALATOR

Art Director
Christopher Charoux
Copywriters
Lee Naidoo
Dominique Silva
Creative Director
Rui Alves

Producer
Juliet Curtis
Production Company
Urban Brew
Advertising Agency
Lowe Bull Gauteng

Digital Agency
Liquorice
Agency Producer
Juliet Curtis
Account Handlers
Claire du Plessis
Vanessa Vooslou

Brand Manager
Refilowe Maluleke
Client
Unilever SA
Brand
Flora

Integrated

Lowe Bull Gauteng
for Unilever SA

Meet Wally's Heart
Heart disease is a serious problem in South Africa. The brief was to raise awareness of heart disease and position Flora margarine as a way of lowering the risk of being affected by it. We used Wally, a person with a heart condition, to get the message across. The public was brought closer to Wally through a popular TV talk show. We then made history by broadcasting his open-heart surgery on television. During the rollout of this campaign, Flora margarine was present, delivering its 'Change your life. Love your heart' message on TV ads and other media.

Art Director
Jeff Anderson
Copywriter
Issac Silverglate
Writers
Sarah Silverman
Dan Sterling
Interactive Designer
Kenny Kim
Executive Creative Director
Ted Royer

Digital Creative Director
Scott Witt
Creative Chairman
David Droga
Director
Wayne McClammy
Executive Producer
Heidi Herzon
Production Company
Black Gold Films

Advertising Agency
Droga5
Digital Agency
Liberty Concepts
Agency Producer
Craig Batzofin
Head of Integrated Production
Sally-Ann Dale
Editor
Josh Reynolds

Director of Photography
Rhet Bear
Music Composer
Adam Berry
Client
Jewish Council of Education & Research
Brand
The Great Schlep

Integrated

Droga5
for Jewish Council of Education & Research

The Great Schlep
In Florida, elderly Jewish voters are a crucial voting block. In 2008, they were beginning to lean towards John McCain. To target them in a way they couldn't refuse, we encouraged their pro-Obama grandchildren to talk to them about Obama. We spread the word with a viral video featuring comedienne Sarah Silverman and a website that united and inspired a younger generation. Millions viewed the video and thousands of media outlets covered the campaign. For the first time in 12 years a Democratic nominee won Florida.

Art Directors
Danny Baarz
Kai Gerken
Copywriter
Susanne Düber
Designer
Lena Mahr
Creative Directors
Guido Heffels
Matthias Storath
Director
Ralf Schmerberg
Producer
Stephan Vens

Production Company
Trigger Happy
Productions
Advertising Agency
HEIMAT, Berlin
Design Director
Peter Weber
Agency Producer
Kerstin Breuer
Editor
Guido Heffels
Lighting
Cameraperson
Frank Griebe

Sound Designers
Christian Meyer
Rudolf Moser
Sound Design
Audioforce
Artists
(e.) twin Gabriel
Franz Hoefer
& Harry Sachs
Laura Kikauka
Mosermeyer
Plastique
Fantastique
Raumlabor

Christine Rebet
Manfred Reuter
Chiharu Shiota
Harald Smylka
souziehaas
Sissel Tolass
Planner
Matthias von
Bechtolsheim
Account Handlers
Sammy Bohneberg
Mark Hassan
Yves Krämer

Marketing Manager
Frank Sahler
Brand Manager
Jürgen Schröcker
Client
Hornbach Home
Improvement
Superstores
Brand
Hornbach

Integrated

HEIMAT, Berlin
for Hornbach

The House of Imagination
In August 2008, the Hornbach Home Improvement Superstores chain created a poetic promise that only a company of that size could possibly make good on: 'If you can imagine it you can build it'. After beginning with standard media, the idea became real by founding the 'House of Imagination', an empty apartment building in the middle of Berlin. International artists turned the rooms into amazing, bizarre, fantastic experiences. The location turned into the place to be with a strictly limited music club and restaurant. The event and exhibition were announced and documented with a billboard and TVC campaign. More than 2,000 people attended the official opening, and in total 24,000 people visited the 'House of Imagination'.

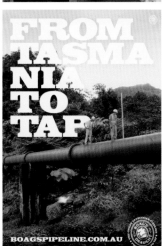

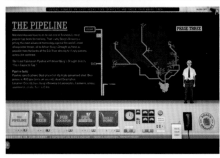

Art Director	**Producer**	**Planner**	**Brand Manager**
Paul Sharp	Oscar Birken	Nicole Milward	Richard Spicer
Digital Art Director	**Digital Producer**	**Account Handler**	**Client**
Andy Cooke	Julia Prior	Simon Ludowyke	Lion Nathan
Copywriter	**Advertising Agency**	**Marketing Manager**	**Brand**
Mike Burdick	Publicis Mojo	Raniero Miccoli	James Boag's
Creative Director	**Agency Producer**		Draught
Micah Walker	Penny Brown		

Integrated

Publicis Mojo
for Lion Nathan

The Great Tasmanian Pipeline
While James Boag's is a well-known and respected name in brewing, Boag's Draught was comparatively unknown outside its native Tasmania. To introduce it as a tap beer in mainland Australia, we exploited Tasmania's island status to create the Great Tasmanian Pipeline – a fictitious pipeline that supposedly pumped fresh Boag's Draught straight from the brewery to Australian pubs. The campaign involved ambient installations of the pipeline in bars and on the street, print executions, a mobile site, a Facebook fan page, rich online media and a microsite.

141

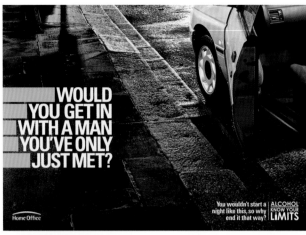

WOULD YOU GET IN WITH A MAN YOU'VE ONLY JUST MET?

You wouldn't start a night like this, so why end it that way? | ALCOHOL KNOW YOUR LIMITS

Home Office

WOULD YOU SMASH THIS IN SOMEONE'S FACE?

You wouldn't start a night like this, so why end it that way? | ALCOHOL KNOW YOUR LIMITS

Home Office

WOULD YOU PLUNGE IN FOR A DARE?

You wouldn't start a night like this, so why end it that way? | ALCOHOL KNOW YOUR LIMITS

Home Office

Art Directors Adam Lawrenson Dave Tokley **Copywriters** Matt Gilbert Benjamin Moreno **Designer** Darren Cox **Creative Directors** Mark Orbine Steve Vranakis **Directors** Matt Jerrett Vince Squibb	**Photographer** Jason Hindley **Producers** Spencer Dodd Jason Scanlon **Production Companies** Gorgeous Enterprises Independent **Advertising Agency** VCCP London **Agency Producers** Kitty Hackney Bradley Woodus	**Editors** Chris Morrish Paul Watts **Post Production Companies** Barnsley MPC **Directors of Photography** Alex Barber Ole Birkeland **Music Composers** Eight Legs Paloma Faith	**Sound Designer** Nick Angell **Sound Design** Wave **Art Buyer** Caroline Palmer **Planners** Dale Gall Cat Wiles **Account Handlers** Fleur Andrews Roly Poly Darby Michelle Gilson Tom Henton	**Marketing Manager** Lina El-Solh **Brand Managers** Lydia Fitzpatrick Matt Hines Graham Turner **Client** The Home Office **Brand** Know Your Limits

Integrated

VCCP London
for The Home Office

Binge Drinking

Getting drunk is a bonding experience that plays a central role in how young people socialise. It adds excitement and unpredictability for an age group who live for the moment. This campaign challenges 18 to 24-year-olds who drink excessively to consider the consequences of their actions on a night out. The core creative idea is a question which leaves the audience to decide whether their behaviour is acceptable or not, summarised in the line, 'You wouldn't start a night like this, so why end it that way?' It ran as a fully integrated campaign appearing in TV, radio, print, online and an installation.

Art Directors	Direction	Group Account	Content Brand
Calle Sjoenell	The Malloys	**Director**	**Partnership**
Pelle Sjoenell	**Producer**	Chris Wollen	Brad Gilford
Copywriters	Rebecca Skinner	**Account Manager**	**Client Chief**
Calle Sjoenell	**Senior Producer**	Shane Chastang	**Executive Officer**
Pelle Sjoenell	Julian Katz	**Marketing Director**	George Fertitta
Creative Directors	**Production Company**	Brant Weil	**Clients**
Calle Sjoenell	HSI	**Chief Marketing**	NYC & Company
Pelle Sjoenell	**Advertising Agency**	**Officer**	Warner Brothers
Chief Creative	BBH New York	Jane Reiss	**Brand**
Officer	**Editor**		Oasis 'Dig Out Your
Kevin Roddy	Tim Wheeler		Soul'

Integrated

BBH New York
for Warner Brothers

Oasis 'Dig Out Your Soul' – in the Streets
We arranged for Oasis to teach over twenty New York City street-musicians new songs from their yet-to-be-released album. Those musicians then took to the streets to perform the songs, weeks before the album was launched. News of the campaign was spread through PR, Oasis fan sites, the New York City website and people at the performances. The event received worldwide press coverage. The content captured by fans garnered 200,000 views on YouTube, Flickr and the NYC website. Then, the documentary premiered internationally on the MySpace network and received over 520,000 views and a second wave of global press coverage. 'Dig Out Your Soul' became the first US top ten album for Oasis in ten years.

143

Art Directors
Josh Gilman
Dino Spadavecchia
Copywriter
Rick Utzinger
Writer
Andre Ricciardi
Creative Directors
Alex Flint
Greg Wells
Executive Creative Director
Harvey Marco

Director
Tommy Means
Senior Producer
Rich Bendetti
Producer
Stef Smith
Interactive Producer
Sarah Milos
Production Company
Mekanism
Advertising Agency
Saatchi & Saatchi
Los Angeles

Editor
Lasse Jarvi
Directors of Photography
Richard Henkels
Malcolm Murray
Production Supervisor
Vieve Haag
Director of Broadcast Production
Damian Stevens

Interactive Account Supervisor
Andrew Corpman
National Account Supervisor
Erica Baker
Client
Toyota
Brand
Matrix

Integrated

Saatchi & Saatchi Los Angeles & Mekanism
for Toyota

Your Other You
Mekanism recently joined forces with Saatchi & Saatchi Los Angeles and Toyota for the innovative, elaborate and multi-platform 'Your Other You' project. The campaign uses web, print, viral and mobile media to play a week-long practical joke on a friend of the user.

Art Directors	Co-Executive Creative Directors	Integrated Producers	Advertising Agency	Interaction Director
Matt Denyer	Andrew Keller	Paul Aaron	Crispin Porter + Bogusky	Matt Walsh
Tim Eger	Rob Reilly	Amanda Ormerod		**Technical Director**
Ken Slater	**Associate Creative Director**	Sara Payne	**Director of Photography**	Scott Prindle
Copywriters		Ivan Perez-Armendariz		**Technical Lead**
Andrew Goldin	Omid Farhang	**Director of Interactive**	Max Malkin	Christian Spinillo
Craig Miller	**Interactive Designers**	Winston Binch	**Photographer**	**Development Partner**
Creative Directors	Brittany Bowden	**Group Executive Integrated Producer**	Martin Schoeller	Oddcast
Tony Calcao	Slava Morshch		**Director of Integrated Production**	**Client**
Scott Linnen	**Director**	Matt Bonin	David Rolfe	Volkswagen of America
Interactive Creative Director	Chris Smith	**Editing**	**Music Producer**	**Brand**
Jeff Benjamin	**Production Company** Smuggler	No6	Bill Meadows	Routan

Integrated

Crispin Porter + Bogusky
for Volkswagen of America

Routan Boom
The US birthrate is at its highest level in more than 35 years. This coincides with the launch of the first ever Volkswagen minivan: the Routan. Naturally Volkswagen grew concerned that people everywhere were making babies just to justify their selfish desire for German engineering. And where there's a cause, a celebrity crusade is sure to follow. So VW and actress/advocate Brooke Shields teamed up to bring the issue to light. Brooke also offers up a solution – The BabyMaker3000 – which allows online users to make a baby without actually 'making a baby'. Join Ms Shields as she campaigns to create widespread awareness about this troubling epidemic known as the Routan Boom.

145

Integrated

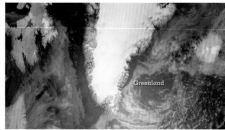

Interactive Art Director
Saman Rahmanian
Interactive Copywriter
Joel Kaplan
Senior Art Director
David Swartz
Senior Copywriter
Andrew Ure
Creative Directors
James Dawson-Hollis
Bill Wright

Associate Creative Directors
Paul Caiozzo
Nuno Ferreira
Ryan Kutscher
Co-Executive Creative Directors
Andrew Keller
Rob Reilly
Interactive Executive Creative Director
Jeff Benjamin
Director
Stacy Peralta

Producer
Nadine Brown
Executive Producers
Michael Degan
Loretta Jeneski
Integrated Producers
Rob Allen
Matt Bonin
Anthony Nelson
David Rolfe
Robert Valdes
Editors
Dan Aronin
Chan Hatcher

Jason MacDonald
Production Company
NonFiction
Advertising Agency
Crispin Porter + Bogusky
Music Composition
Amber Music
Photographer
Sterling Lorence
Programmers
Jim Alexander
Scott Prindle
Mat Ranauro

Interaction Director
Matt Walsh
Managing Director of Interactive
Winston Binch
Art Producer
Sheri Radel
Development Partners
Steady
WorkPlayWork
Client
Burger King

Integrated

Crispin Porter + Bogusky
for Burger King

Whopper Virgins
Which tastes better, Whopper or Big Mac? To answer the age-old question once and for all, Burger King travelled to some of the remotest parts of the globe to conduct the world's purest taste test. Only people who'd never eaten a burger could give an honest, unbiased opinion based on taste alone. Teaser TV ads, print and banners directed the curious to WhopperVirgins. com. Visitors saw just how far we were prepared to go to prove the universal appeal of the Whopper. Immediately, the internet and international media were buzzing with the news. After one week and countless blog comments and news stories, the online documentary disclosing the results debuted. New TV ads, print and banners announced its release.

The jury:
Mark Waites, Mother (Jury Foreman)
Olivier Altmann, Publicis Conseil
Chris Birch, Leo Burnett London
Danny Brooke-Taylor, Miles Calcraft Briginshaw Duffy
Richard Bullock, 180 Amsterdam
Andy Cheetham, Cheetham Bell/JWT Manchester
Mario D'Andrea, JWT Sao Paulo
Kit Dayaram, WCRS
Will Farquhar, McCann Erickson London
Andrew Keller, Crispin Porter + Bogusky
Eric Lynne, Partizan
Tomas Mankovsky, Fallon London
Ben Priest, Adam & Eve
Ian Reichenthal, Y&R New York
Björn Rühmann, The Vikings
Paul Shearer, Arnold UK
Craig Smith, BBH New York
Kate Stanners, Saatchi & Saatchi London
Feh Tarty, Wieden + Kennedy London
Dave Trott, CST
Nancy Vonk, Ogilvy & Mather Toronto
Sebastian Wilhelm, Santo

Director
Tom Kuntz
Copywriter
Eric Kallman
Art Director
Craig Allen
Creative Directors
Gerry Graf
Ian Reichenthal
Scott Vitrone
Producers
Jo Arghiris
Scott Kaplan

Production Company
MJZ
Advertising Agency
TBWA\Chiat\Day
New York
Agency Producer
Nathy Aviram
**Assistant Agency
Producer**
Laura Rosenshine
Editor
Gavin Cutler

Assistant Editor
Erik Laroi
Editing
Mackenzie Cutler
Editorial
Flame Artist
Angus Kneale
Colourist
Tim Masick
Telecine
Company 3 New
York

Visual Effects
The Mill New York
Planner
Lauren Hutter
Brand Manager
Osher Hoberman
Client
Mars
Brand
Skittles

TV Commercials 41-60 Seconds

TBWA\Chiat\Day New York
for Mars

Piñata
Our brief was to continue the Skittles 'Experience the Rainbow' campaign with a television execution for Chocolate Skittles, a variant in the Skittles portfolio, that would increase awareness and purchase frequency. The campaign is aimed at teens from 12 to 17, with a creative bulls-eye of 16 years of age. Our solution was to take another peek into the Skittles world with an everyday situation revolving around Chocolate Skittles, where the magical meets mundane reality in an unexpected way.

the Coke side of life

Director
Nicolai Fuglsig
Copywriter
Sheena Brady
Art Director
Hal Curtis
Creative Directors
Sheena Brady
Hal Curtis
Producer
Emma Wilcockson

Executive Producer
Eric Stern
Production Company
MJ2
Advertising Agency
Wieden + Kennedy
Los Angeles
Agency Producer
Matt Hunnicutt
Editor
Russell Icke

Special Effects
Angus Kneale
Andrew Proctor
Ben Smith
Music Arranger
Robert Miller
Sound Designer
Gus Koven
Planner
Britton Taylor
Account Handler
Ryan Peterson

Marketing Managers
Todd Arata
Pio Schunker
Client
The Coca-Cola
Company
Brand
Coca-Cola

TV Commercials 41-60 Seconds

Wieden + Kennedy Los Angeles
for Coca-Cola

It's Mine
Set against the backdrop of the Macy's Thanksgiving Day Parade in New York City, balloons Underdog and Stewie tussle over a giant Coke balloon, only to have the balloon of Charlie Brown pop up and claim the bottle.

Director
Noam Murro
Copywriter
Mike McKay
Art Director
Nick Spahr
Creative Director
Jamie Barrett
Advertising Agency
Goodby Silverstein
and Partners
Associate Creative Director
Nick Spahr

Group Creative Directors
Chris Ford
Mike McKay
Producer
Jay Veal
Senior Executive Producer
Shawn Lacy
Production Company
Biscuit Filmworks
Agency Producer
Tanya LeSieur

Agency Executive Producer
Tanya LeSieur
Editor
Avi Oron
Visual Effects
Animal Logic
Australia
Visual Effects Editor
Bruce Carter
Visual Effects Producer
Nerissa Kavanagh

Director of Photography
Jo Willems
Sound Designer
Brian Emrich
Sound Design
Trinitite
On-Line Company
Brickyard VFX
Telecine
Dave Hussey
Voice Over Mix
Rohan Young

Final Mix
Eben Carr
Graphics
Superfad
Client
Comcast

TV Commercials 41-60 Seconds

Goodby Silverstein and Partners
for Comcast

Rabbit
To make the point that Comcast never stops making the internet faster, 'Rabbit' opens on a rabbit. A rabbit that is then genetically modified and bred with a panther. A rabbit, that once genetically modified and bred with a panther, has turbines attached, is backed by an unusually strong tailwind and placed on ice. Continuing on, the rabbit panther thingy with turbines and tailwind on ice is then shaved with a cold-forged, high-glide surgical-grade razor, and driven by an over-caffeinated fighter pilot with a lead foot. The spot concludes with the whole rabbit panther turbine tailwind hairless razor pilot scenario travelling down a ski jump in Switzerland under better-than-ideal conditions.

Director
Paulo Gandra
Copywriter
Romero Cavalcanti

Creative Directors
Dulcídio Caldeira
Luiz Sanches
**Production
Company**
Cinema Centro

Advertising Agency
AlmapBBDO
Agency Producer
André Soares

Sound Design
Sonzeira
Client
Casa do Zezinho

TV Commercials 41-60 Seconds

AlmapBBDO
for Casa do Zezinho

Test
Without any speech, this commercial intends to show that people need to pay more attention to poor children. The movie is a test conducted in the centre of São Paulo. A young actor sat there in two situations: first, with expensive clothes; second, with clothes that made him look like a child from the streets. When the 'rich boy' sat on the sidewalk, people who were walking past stopped and talked to him, and asked him what was wrong and if they could help him. But when the same boy sat on the sidewalk with poor clothes, nobody stopped. The super inquires, 'Why are some children our problem and some aren't?'

Bulldozer

Lice

Pre-Nup

Director
Harold Einstein
Copywriter
Nathan Frank
Art Director
Dan Lucey
Creative Directors
Alison Gragnano
Kerry Keenan

Chief Creative Officer
Gerry Graf
Producer
Tom Rossano
Production Company
Station Films

Advertising Agency
Saatchi & Saatchi
New York
Agency Producers
Maura Hurley
Colin Pearsall
Editor
Ian Mackenzie

Music Arranger
Mark Healy
Client
Procter & Gamble
Brand
Crest

TV Commercials 41-60 Seconds

Saatchi & Saatchi New York
for Procter & Gamble

Bulldozer / Lice / Pre-Nup
Crest have between nine and 9,000 different brands, but it was clear we needed to find something to say that could speak for all of them. Luckily for us, Crest was already saying it, in their tagline, 'Healthy, beautiful smiles for life'. Smiles for life, that was it. Perfect. Life is full of difficult awkward situations and if you can smile through them, you'll probably do all right. We then needed a director to bring these stories to life. After talking with Harold Einstein we knew he was the guy. Nobody can smile through awkward conversations quite like he can. The commercial 'Bulldozer' was nominated by the jury, while Lice and Pre-Nup, as well as the campaign as a whole, were in the initial selection.

153

Thailand

Romania

Inuit Villagers

I like this one.

Kulusuk, Greenland

I like seal meat better.

Seal Meat

Director
Stacy Peralta
Senior Copywriter
Andrew Ure
Senior Art Director
David Swartz
Creative Directors
James Dawson-Hollis
Bill Wright
Co-Executive Creative Directors
Andrew Keller
Rob Reilly

Associate Creative Directors
Paul Caiozzo
Ryan Kutscher
Producer
Nadine Brown
Executive Producers
Michael Degan
Loretta Jeneski
Production Company
NonFiction
Advertising Agency
Crispin Porter + Bogusky

Editors
Dan Aronin
Chan Hatcher
Jason MacDonald
Editing
No6
Music Producer
Bill Meadows
Music
Amber Music
Still Photographer
Sterling Lorence
Flame Artist
Mark Dennison

Finishing
RIOT
Graphics
Blind
Audio Post
POP
Director of Integrated Production
David Rolfe

Senior Integrated Producer
Anthony Nelson
Integrated Head of Video
Matt Bonin
Client
Burger King

TV Commercial Campaigns

Crispin Porter + Bogusky
for Burger King

Whopper Virgins – Thailand / Romania / Seal Meat
Which tastes better, Whopper or Big Mac? To answer the age-old question once and for all, Burger King travelled to some of the remotest parts of the globe to conduct the world's purest taste test. Only people who'd never eaten a burger could give an honest, unbiased opinion based on taste alone. In the end, Hmong villagers preferred the Whopper, Transylvanian farmers preferred the Whopper, and Inuit fishermen preferred the Whopper. Although it turns out some of them would still rather eat seal meat.

Director
Tim Bullock
Copywriter
Richard Williams
Art Director
Ant Phillips
Creative Director
Ant Keogh
Executive Creative Director
James McGrath

Producers
Jonathan Samway
Kate Sawyer
Production Company
Prodigy
Advertising Agency
Clemenger BBDO
Melbourne
Agency Producer
Sevda Cemo
Editor
Adam Wills

Director of Photography
Keith Wagstaff
Music Supervisor
Karl Richter
Sound Engineer
Paul Le Couteur
Grading
Christine Trodd
Planner
Michael Derepas
Account Director
Phil Baker

Account Manager
Helen Fitzsimons
Group Account Director
Paul McMillan
Group Marketing Manager
Vince Ruiu
Senior Brand Manager
Richard Oppy
Assistant Brand Manager
Mim Orlando

General Manager
Peter Sinclair
Client
Foster's Group
Brand
Carlton Mid

TV Commercials 41-60 Seconds

Clemenger BBDO Melbourne
for Foster's Group

Woman Whisperer
The 'Woman Whisperer' communicates that Carlton MID (mid-strength beer) can give men 'mate time'; yes, that magical and often elusive time for one more beer. The end result is a commercial about men with extraordinary powers. Powers that won't save the planet, or even a life but maybe, just maybe, they can help a mate stay for one more beer.

Polo confidence

Director	Producers	Special Effects	Music Composer	Marketing Manager
Noam Murro	Richard Packer	Stephane Allender	Steve Winwood	Rod McLeod
Copywriters	Shishir Patel	**Editor**	**Music Arranger**	**Brand Manager**
Feargal Ballance	Jay Veal	Tim Thornton-Allan	Jakko	Sarah Luckcraft
Dylan Harrison	**Production Company**	**Lighting**	**Planner**	**Client**
Art Directors	Independent	**Cameraperson**	Kirsty Saddler	Volkswagen
Feargal Ballance	**Advertising Agency**	Matthew Libitique	**Account Handlers**	**Brand**
Dylan Harrison	DDB London	**Computer Graphics**	Jonathan Hill	Polo
Creative Director	**Agency Producer**	Diarmid Harrison-	Matt Ross	
Sam Oliver	Lucy Westmore	Murray		

TV Commercials 21-40 Seconds

DDB London
for Volkswagen

Dog
This is the story of a nervous dog who feels so confident when he rides in the VW Polo that he sings his heart out. It's the feeling you get when you're in the shower – you don't have a care in the world and, regardless of your ability, you can belt out any song that comes to mind. In the case of this nervous dog it's 'I'm a Man' by The Spencer Davis Group. This is how it feels to drive around in the safety of the Polo.

Director	Set Designer	Lighting	Account Handlers
Ulf Johansson	Jenny Burton-Akdag	**Cameraperson**	Diana Gonzalez
Copywriter	**Production Company**	Andrezej Sekula	Jessica Monsey
Mark Fitzloff	Smith & Jones Films	**Music**	**Marketing Manager**
Art Director	**Advertising Agency**	Beacon Street	Carl Stealey
Aaron Allen	Wieden + Kennedy	Studios	**Brand Manager**
Creative Directors	Portland	**Sound Design**	Gedioen Aloula
Mark Fitzloff	**Agency Producer**	Beacon Street	**Client**
Monica Taylor	Andrés Murillo	Studios	Procter & Gamble
Producer	**Editor**	**Planner**	**Brand**
Philippa Smith	Morgan Griswold	Britton Taylor	Old Spice

TV Commercials 21-40 Seconds

Wieden + Kennedy Portland
for Procter & Gamble

Is it Right for Me?
'Is it Right for Me' pokes fun at your stereotypical American pharmaceutical commercial. Men and boys of various ages and hair configurations express concern over their individual hair and body-hair combinations, and wonder whether Old Spice Hair and Body Wash might be right for them. And, of course, it always is.

Director	Producer	Agency Producer	Audio House
Tom DeCerchio	Bruce Dawson	Sue Bell	**Producer**
Copywriter	**Production Company**	**Editor**	Craig Zarazun
Jeff Galbraith	The Garden TV	John Devries	**Audio Company**
Art Director	**Post Production**	**Colourist**	Wave Productions
Daryl Gardiner	**Company**	Daniel Pruger	**Account Handler**
Creative Directors	School	**Lighting**	Brett MacFarlane
Dean Lee	**Advertising Agency**	**Cameraperson**	**Client**
Alan Russell	DDB Vancouver	Michael Bonvillain	Midas

TV Commercials 21-40 Seconds

DDB Vancouver
for Midas

Chase
This spot opens on news coverage of a police cruiser in hot pursuit of a getaway car on a winter day. Both cars get stuck in snow. An overhead shot reveals one of the villains leaving the passenger side of the car. Instead of fleeing the scene, he runs behind the car and begins to push. Rather than trying to apprehend the suspect, the officer runs behind the police cruiser and tries to push it. The payoff then reads, 'Is your car ready for winter? Trust the Midas Touch.'

Director	Advertising Agency	Telecine	Director of	Account Executive
Jim Jenkins	TBWA\Chiat\Day	Company 3	**Broadcast**	Lindsay Brown
Copywriter	New York	**Director of**	**Production**	**Managing Director**
Dan Giachetti	**Agency Producer**	**Photography**	Ozzie Spenningsby	Jamie Gallo
Art Director	Jason Souter	Manel Ruiz	**Planner**	**Senior Director of**
John Clement	**Agency Assistant**	**Sound Designer**	Jane Goodman	**Brand Marketing**
Creative Directors	**Producer**	Marc Healy	**Account Director**	Via Walia
Gerry Graf	Laura Rosenshine	**Mixer**	Andrew McCree	**Client**
Rob Smiley	**Editor**	Tom Jucarone	**Account Supervisor**	Hotels.com
Executive Producers	Ian MacKenzie	**Audio Mix**	Lisa Togami	
Ralph Laucella	**Assistant Editor**	Sound Lounge		
Melissa Miller	Charlotte Arnold	**Editing**		
Production Company	**Colourist**	MacKenzie Cutler		
O Positive	Tim Masick			

TV Commercials 21-40 Seconds

TBWA\Chiat\Day New York
for Hotels.com

Suitcase
The power of Hotels.com comes from the guests. Thanks to these users, there are nearly a million hotel reviews to study. They ensure that you never walk into a hotel room alone, because they eliminate the element of surprise. Hotels.com gives the hotel-staying community the biggest soapbox to speak from. And because of that power, maybe each Hotels.com user will be treated a little bit better.

Director
Vince Squibb
Copywriter
Matt Gilbert
Art Director
Dave Tokley
Creative Director
Mark Orbine
Producer
Spencer Dodd

Production Company
Gorgeous
Enterprises
**Post Production
Company**
Barnsley
Advertising Agency
VCCP
Agency Producers
Kitty Hackney
Bradley Woodus

Editor
Paul Watts
Music Composer
Paloma Faith
Sound Design
Wave
Planners
Dale Gall
Cat Wiles
Account Handlers
Fleur Andrews
Tom Henton

Marketing Manager
Lina El-Solh
Brand Managers
Lydia Fitzpatrick
Matt Hines
Client
The Home Office
Brand
Know Your Limits

TV Commercials 21-40 Seconds

VCCP
for The Home Office

Binge Drinking – Female
A young woman is at home getting ready for a night out with friends. Everything seems normal, and the mood is optimistic with music playing in the background. Then we see a series of increasingly dramatic scenes as the girl deliberately commits seemingly irrational and destructive acts of self sabotage as if they were part of the normal ritual of getting ready. We see her rip her tights, rub vomit into her hair and break the heel of her shoe. The advert culminates by asking the audience to make up their own mind about whether their behaviour is acceptable or not: 'You wouldn't start a night like this, so why end it that way?'

Director
Vince Squibb
Copywriter
Matt Gilbert
Art Director
Dave Tokley
Creative Director
Mark Orbine
Producer
Spencer Dodd
Production Company
Gorgeous
Enterprises

**Post Production
Company**
Barnsley
Advertising Agency
VCCP
Editor
Paul Watts
Agency Producers
Kitty Hackney
Bradley Woodus
**Director of
Photography**
Alex Barber

Music Composer
Eight Legs
Sound Design
Wave
Planners
Dale Gall
Cat Wiles
Account Handlers
Fleur Andrews
Tom Henton
Marketing Manager
Lina El-Solh

Brand Managers
Lydia Fitzpatrick
Matt Hines
Client
The Home Office
Brand
Know Your Limits

TV Commercials 21-40 Seconds

VCCP
for The Home Office

Binge Drinking – Male
A young man is at home getting ready for a night out with friends. Everything seems normal, and the mood is optimistic with music playing in the background. Then we see the young man deliberately committing seemingly irrational and destructive acts of self sabotage. The advert culminates by asking the audience to make up their own mind about whether their behaviour is acceptable or not: 'You wouldn't start a night like this, so why end it that way?'

Director
Sean Meehan
Copywriter
Pat Lennox
Art Director
Ben Green
Creative Director
Tony Leishman
Producer
Samantha McGarry
Set Designer
Arabella Lockhart

Production Company
Soma Films
Advertising Agency
The Campaign
Palace
Agency Producers
Josh Armstrong
Fiona Gillies
Editor
Drew Thompson

Lighting
Cameraperson
Sean Meehan
Music Composer
& Arranger
Elliot Wheeler
Sound Designer
Simon Lister
Online Editor
Richard Lambert
Planner
Melanie Wiese

Account Handlers
Georgette Mahoney
Belinda Murray
Client Executive
Director
Fiona Sharkie
Client
The Cancer Council
Victoria
Brand
Quit

TV Commercials 41-60 Seconds

The Campaign Palace
for The Cancer Council Victoria

Separation
Smoking kills around 3,000 Victorians each year, many of whom are loving and devoted parents. Our commercial aimed to convince these people that if they continued to smoke, they risked losing something just as precious as their health. Ultimately, we wanted to turn smokers into quitters. Research showed that while smokers easily dismiss the notion of self-harm, they're not as comfortable with the effects that smoking can have on their children. Our creative execution forces smokers to confront the 'hidden cost' of their habit. Quitline calls increased by 92 per cent compared to the same time period the previous year.

Director
Bart Timmer
Copywriter
Jeroen van de Sande
Art Directors
Cor den Boer
Jorn Kruijsen
Creative Directors
Cor den Boer
Jorn Kruijsen
Jeroen van de Sande

Producers
Robert Nan
Hein Scheffer
Set Designer
Genaro Rosato
Production Company
CZAR
Advertising Agency
TBWA\NEBOKO
Agency Producer
Wietske Hovingh

Editor
Annelien van
Wijnbergen
Lighting
Cameraperson
Alex Melman
Music Composer
Sebastiaan
Roestenburg
Music Arranger
Rens Pluym
Sound Designer
Rens Pluym

Account Handlers
Johan Jongkind
Machteld van
Woensel Kooy
Marketing Manager
Floris Cobelens
Brand Manager
Ilona van Wegen
Client
Heineken

TV Commercials 21-40 Seconds

TBWA\NEBOKO
for Heineken

Walk-in Fridge
Every woman's dream of a walk-in closet is surpassed by every man's dream: a walk-in fridge.

Director
Dave Klaiber
Copywriters
Lisa Fedyszyn
Jonathan McMahon
Art Directors
Lisa Fedyszyn
Jonathan McMahon

Creative Director
Nick Worthington
Producer
Susannah DiLallo
Production Company
Plaza Films

Advertising Agency
Colenso BBDO
Agency Producer
Jen Storey
Editor
Suga Suppiah

Director of Photography
Piet de Vries
Sound Design
Sound Reservoir
Planner
Hayley Pardoe

Account Director
Gemma Findlay
Client
Alzheimer's New Zealand

TV Commercials 41-60 Seconds
Colenso BBDO
for Alzheimer's New Zealand

Car
To raise awareness of Alzheimer's, we used the less than serious candid camera approach to show just how confusing and distressing life can be for a person living with this serious disease.

Director
Tom Kuntz
Copywriter
Mario Crudele
Art Director
Martin Ponce
Executive Creative Director
Hernán Ponce
Producers
Jeff Scruton
David Zander

Production Designer
Andy Reznik
Production Company
MJZ
Post Production Companies
Company 3LA
Final Cut
Advertising Agency
ponce buenos aires
Agency Producer
Jose Silva

Agency Production Director
Roberto Carsillo
Special Effects
The Mill
Editor
Carlos Arias
Cinematographer
Harris Savides
Colourist
Stefan Sonnenfeld

Music Performer
Allain Toussaint
Planner
Diego Luque
Account Handler
Nestor Ferreyro
Client Services Director
Vanina Rudaeff
Marketing Manager
Tomas Marcenaro

Marketing Vice President
Pablo Gazzera
Brand Manager
Hernan de Majo
Client
Unilever
Brand
AXE

TV Commercials 41-60 Seconds
ponce buenos aires
for Unilever

Chocolate Man
A guy sprays new AXE Dark Temptation all over his body and realises how fantastic and irresistible he is after turning himself into a chocolate man. Gorgeous women at the movie theatre, bus passengers, and hospital patients are all dying to try him. And he has no problem offering himself to them.

Director	Producers	Animation Company	Music Arranger	Client
Tom Kuntz	Jeff Scruton	Curious Pictures	Peter Lurye	American Legacy
Copywriter	Kate Sutherland	**Agency Producer**	**Account Handler**	Foundation
Will Chambliss	**Advertising**	Carron Pedonti	Paul Nelson	**Brand**
Art Director	**Agencies**	**Special Effects**	**Marketing Manager**	truth
Rob Kottkamp	Arnold	Brickyard VFX	Eric Asche	
Creative Directors	Crispin Porter +	**Editor**		
Alex Bogusky	Bogusky	Lawrence Young		
Pete Favat	**Production Company**	**Music Composer**		
John Kearse	MJZ	David Yazbek		
Tiffany Kosel				

TV Commercials 41-60 Seconds

Arnold & Crispin Porter + Bogusky
for American Legacy Foundation

Magical Amount
For years, Big Tobacco has denied that it has any control over how much nicotine finds its way into cigarettes. So imagine our surprise when, in 2006, a federal judge ruled that tobacco companies manipulated nicotine levels to keep smokers addicted. Now, before we go jumping down their throats, let's give them the benefit of the doubt. Maybe they were just looking for the magical amount. What would ever make us think this? An animated unicorn told us.

Director	Producer	Lighting	Group Marketing
Chris Palmer	Rupert Smythe	**Cameraperson**	**Communications**
Copywriters	**Production Company**	Ben Seresin	**Head**
Simon Aldridge	Gorgeous	**Sound Designer**	Chris MacLeod
Tom Spicer	Enterprises	Pav	**Group Marketing**
Art Directors	**Advertising Agency**	**Account Director**	**Manager**
Vince Chasteauneuf	WCRS	Jenny Bust	Nigel Hanlon
Kit Dayaram	**Agency Producer**	**Group Account**	**Client**
Creative Directors	James Lethem	**Director**	Transport for London
Yan Elliott	**Editor**	Fergus Adam	**Brand**
Luke Williamson	Paul Watts		THINK!

TV Commercials 41-60 Seconds

WCRS
for Transport for London

Awareness Test
To cut down on cycling fatalities, this ad allowed both drivers and cyclists to experience first hand how things that are seemingly obvious can become totally invisible to the human eye. One of the few virals that lived up to the name, it was viewed by over ten million people online in its first year. This advert was selected in both TV and Cinemas Commercials.

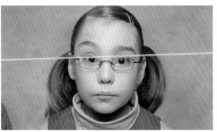 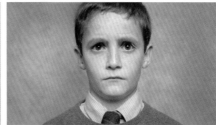

Director
Tom Kuntz
Copywriter
Nils-Petter Lovgren
Art Director
Nils-Petter Lovgren
Creative Directors
John Allison
Chris Bovill
Executive Creative

Director
Richard Flintham
Producer
Suza Horvat
Executive Producer
Debbie Turner
Set Designer
John Bramble
Production Company
MJZ

Advertising Agency
Fallon London
Agency Producer
Olivia Chalk
Editor
Steve Gandolfi
Lighting
Cameraperson
Mattias Montero

Music Composition
Baker/Smith/Butler
Sound Designer
Chris Turner
Planner
Rachel Barrie
Account Handler
Alex Best

Marketing Directors
Lee Rolston
Phil Rumbol
Client
Cadbury
Brand
Dairy Milk

TV Commercials 41-60 Seconds

Fallon London
for Cadbury

Eyebrows
This advert is about taking that moment of joy when you seize the opportunity to get away with your own little stunt, like making a funny face as your family portrait is being taken.

Director
Tim Bullock
Copywriter
Richard Williams
Art Director
Ant Phillips
Creative Director
Ant Keogh
Executive Creative Director
James McGrath

Producers
Jonathan Samway
Kate Sawyer
Production Company
Prodigy
Advertising Agency
Clemenger BBDO Melbourne
Agency Producer
Sevda Cemo
Editor
Adam Wills

Director of Photography
Keith Wagstaff
Sound Designer
Paul Le Couteur
Music Supervisor
Karl Richter
Grading
Christine Trodd
Planner
Michael Derepas
Account Director
Phil Baker

Account Manager
Helen Fitzsimons
Group Account Director
Paul McMillan
Group Marketing Manager
Vince Ruiu
Senior Brand Manager
Richard Oppy

Assistant Brand Manager
Mim Orlando
Client General Manager
Peter Sinclair
Client
Foster's Group
Brand
Carlton MID

TV Commercials 41-60 Seconds

Clemenger BBDO Melbourne
for Foster's Group

Speak Woman
'Speak Woman' communicates that Carlton MID (mid-strength beer) can give men 'mate time'; yes, that magical and often elusive time for one more beer. The end result is an advert about men with extraordinary powers. Powers that won't save the planet, or even a life but maybe, just maybe, they can help a mate stay for one more beer.

Director
Guy Ritchie
Copywriter
Jason Norcross
Art Director
Bryan Rowles
Production Company
Anonymous Content
Advertising Agency
72andSunny

Creative Directors
John Boiler
Glenn Cole
Jason Norcross
Bryan Rowles
Producers
Aris McGearyon
Dave Morrison
Editor
Robert Duffy

Agency Producers
Sam Baerwald
Angelo Ferrugia
Special Effects
Chris Badger
Giles Cheetham
Music Composer
Eagles of Death
Metal

Music Arrangement
Junkie JXL
Sound Designer
Matt Collinge
Account Handlers
Alex Schneider
Evin Shutt
Marketing Manager
Adam Collins

Senior Advertising Manager
Colin Leary
Client
Nike
Brand
Nike Football

TV Commercials 61-20 Seconds
72andSunny
for Nike

Next Level
The brief was to inspire footballers around the world to become better footballers. Our solution was to show what it takes at the highest level: successes, failures, hard work, knocked-out teeth, all of it. Viewers are directed to nikefootball.com where they can find products and training programmes to help them achieve their goals.

Director
Simon Ratigan
Copywriters
Samuel Akesson
Tomas Mankovsky
Art Directors
Samuel Akesson
Tomas Mankovsky
Executive Creative Director
Richard Flintham
Producer
Mike Wells

Set Designer
Jerry Blohm
Production Company
HLA
Advertising Agency
Fallon London
Agency Producer
Emma Gooding
Editors
Ted Guard
Bruce Townend

Lighting
Cameraperson
Bob Pendar-Hughes
Music Composer & Arranger
Warren Ellis
Sound Designer
Aaron Reynolds
Planner
Mark Sinnock
Account Director
Jonathan Pangu

Account Manager
Andy Fraser
Marketing Manager
James Kennedy
Client
SONY
Brands
SONY Cyber-shot
Handycam Alpha

TV Commercials 61-20 Seconds
Fallon London
for SONY

Foam City
Foam City was a project that took place in Miami in March 2008. The city was filled with 460 million litres of foam in order to create the ultimate photo opportunity. The ad documents this visual spectacle and people's reactions to it, resulting in images like no other.

Director
Garth Davis
Copywriter
Jim Ingram
Art Director
Ben Couzens
Producer
Karen Sproul

Creative Directors
Paul Catmur
Ben Coulson
Advertising Agency
George Patterson
Y&R
Agency Producer
Romanca Jasinski

Editor
Jack Hutchings
Planner
Keren Bester
Account Handlers
Mat Cummings
Kate Smither

Marketing Manager
Darryn Wallace
Brand Manager
Paul Donaldson
Client
Schweppes

TV Commercials 61-20 Seconds

George Patterson Y&R
for Schweppes

Burst
This campaign captures and brings to life the 'feeling of Schweppervescence' using super high speed photography of water balloons bursting in slowmotion.

Directors
Maureen Hufnagel
Claudio Prestia
Copywriter
Hernan Rebalderia
Art Director
Santiago Dulce
Creative Directors
Maximiliano
Anselmo
Sebastian Wilhelm

Producers
Jacqueline
Lijtenstein
Paula Mazzei
Production Company
Bendercine
Advertising Agency
Santo Buenos Aires

Agency Producers
Jose Bustos
Ezequiel Ortiz
Music Composer
Diane Warren
Music Production
Supercharango
Account Handlers
Guillermo Cicciari
Luciano Landajo

Marketing Manager
Viviana Conte
Brand Manager
Mariana Cordoba
Client
Arnet Broadband
Brand
Arnet

TV Commercials 61-20 Seconds

Santo Buenos Aires
for Arnet Broadband

Toby & Sheila
This is an ad to promote free local calls when you sign up to Arnet Broadband. Knowing that internet content makes conversation, we wrote and produced a film that could potentially spark conversation, and seeded it on YouTube. A few days later, we ran it on TV as an ad. It's the story of an old duck, Sheila, living on a ranch, who 'adopts' a puppy called Toby. Some time later, Sheila passes away. Knowing how tough that blow would be for Toby, the farmers decide to embalm her and keep her in the house. Maybe he won't notice, even if her beak is coming apart.

Airport

Phone

TV Commercial Campaigns

JWT New York
for MTV

Airport / Phone
Younger people have among the lowest turnout rates in elections, yet will be affected the most by the outcome. Our campaign sought to encourage young people to engage in the democratic process, and not allow other generations to make those decisions for them.

Director
Bryan Buckley
Copywriters
Scott Bell
Bee Reynolds
Art Directors
Hunter Fine
Armando Flores
Sara Worthington
Executive Creative Director
Jeff Bitsack

Chief Creative Officers
Harvey Marco
Ty Montague
Producers
Cindy Becker
Dan Duffy
Executive Producer
Kevin Byrne
Production Company
Hungry Man
Advertising Agency
JWT New York

Agency Producer
Owen Katz
Editor
Patrick Griffin
Assistant Editor
Luke McIntosh
Post Production Producer
Owen Katz
Lighting Cameraperson
Eric Lindley

Sound Designer
Andy Green
Line Producer
Mino Jarjoura
Account Manager
Angela Rebong
Account Supervisor
Claire Capeci
Client Supervisor
Armand Prisco
Client
MTV

Director
Ringan Ledwidge
Copywriter
Gavin Torrance
Art Director
Danny Hunt
Creative Director
Danny Brooke-Taylor

Advertising Agency
Miles Calcraft
Briginshaw Duffy
Producer
Sally Humphries
Production Company
Rattling Stick
Agency Producer
Lorraine Geoghegan
Editor
Rich Orrick

Lighting
Cameraperson
Alwin Kuchler
Music Composers
Ed Hulme
Phil Kay
Music Consultant
Abi Leland
Planner
Andy Nairn

Account Handler
Michael Pring
Marketing Manager
Jon Goldstone
Client
Premier Foods
Brand
Hovis

TV Commercials over 120 Seconds

Miles Calcraft Briginshaw Duffy
for Premier Foods

Go on Lad
This is a simple story of a boy running home with a loaf of bread under his arm. The twist is that his journey takes him through all the major events of the last century or so – from the suffragettes and the First World War to the Blitz and the 1980s Miners' Strike. It's a 122 second epic, covering the 122 years that Hovis has been baking its bread. And the moral of the story? That Hovis is 'As good today as it's always been'.

Director
Kim Gehrig
Copywriters
Kim Gehrig
Ed Warren
Art Director
Pablo Medina

Creative Directors
Kim Gehrig
Robert Saville
Mark Waites
Producer
Lucy Gossage
Production Company
Academy Films
Advertising Agency
Mother

Agency Producer
Ed Sayers
Special Effects
Framestore
Rushes
Smoke & Mirrors
Editor
Joe Guest
Lighting
Cameraperson
Matthias Montero

Music Composer
REM
Planner
Lucia Komeljon
Marketing Manager
Mathias Stock
Client
Amnesty
International

Cinema Commercials 61-120 Seconds

Mother
for Amnesty International

You Are Powerful
To illustrate how heroic differences are made by those who join Amnesty International, a series of clips has been cleverly adapted to make it look as though a timely intervention from an Amnesty member has made a direct contribution to someone's safety, and has led to the termination of abuse.

Director	**Production Company**	**Lighting**	**Account Handler**
Ringan Ledwidge	Rattling Stick	**Cameraperson**	Michael Pring
Copywriter	**Advertising Agency**	Alwin Kuchler	**Marketing Manager**
Gavin Torrance	Miles Calcraft	**Music Composers**	Jon Goldstone
Art Director	Briginshaw Duffy	Ed Hulme	**Client**
Danny Hunt	**Agency Producer**	Phil Kay	Premier Foods
Creative Director	Lorraine Geoghegan	**Music Consultant**	**Brand**
Danny Brooke-Taylor	**Editor**	Abi Leland	Hovis
Producer	Rich Orrick	**Planner**	
Sally Humphries		Andy Nairn	

Cinema Commercials 61-120 Seconds

Miles Calcraft Briginshaw Duffy
for Premier Foods

Go on Lad 90"
This is a simple story of a boy running home with a loaf of bread under his arm. The twist is that his journey takes him through all the major events of the last century – from the suffragettes and the First World War to the Blitz and the 1980s Miners' Strike. It's an epic covering the 122 years that Hovis has been baking its bread. And the moral of the story? That Hovis is 'As good today as it's always been'.

Director	**Art Directors**	**Production Company**	**Music Composer**
Bryan Buckley	Rob Doubal	Hungry Man	**& Arranger**
Copywriters	David Kolbusz	**Advertising Agency**	T Chung
Rob Doubal	Robert Saville	Mother	**Account Handler**
David Kolbusz	Augusto Sola	**Agency Producer**	Kerrianne Clem
Robert Saville	Mark Waites	Juliet Pearson	**Client**
Augusto Sola	**Creative Directors**	**Editor**	Orange
Mark Waites	Stephen Butler	John Smith	
	Robert Saville	**Lighting**	
	Mark Waites	**Cameraperson**	
	Producer	Scott Henrickson	
	Mino Jarjoura		

Cinema Commercials 61-120 Seconds

Mother
for Orange

Snoop Dogg
After five years in service, the Orange Film board campaign has gone through various developments, but at its core remains the desire to offer insights into the film-making industry in a humorous way, and remind cinema-goers to turn their mobile phones off during the movie. With his global popularity, famous cameo appearances and iconic status, Snoop Dogg was the perfect star to be sacrificed in front of the Orange board, and all the more vulnerable as the insensitive crew interrupt him on his own turf – during a recording session for the soundtrack to his film.

Poodles

Snail

Gymnast

Director
Neil Harris
Copywriters
Emer Stamp
Ben Tollett
Art Directors
Emer Stamp
Ben Tollett
Creative Directors
Sam Oliver
Shishir Patel

Advertising Agency
DDB London
Producer
Jess Aan de Wiel
Production Company
Stink
Agency Producer
Maggie Blundell
Special Effects
Glassworks

Editor
John Mayes
Lighting
Daniel Hill
Cameraperson
Olivier Cariou
Planner
Leo Rayman
Account Handler
Charlie Elliot

Marketing Director
Rod McLeod
Marketing Manager
Daniel Hill
Client
Volkswagen
Brand
Passat

TV Sponsorship Credits

DDB London
for Volkswagen

Poodles / Snail / Gymnast
This a series of idents that were shot and voiced like proper documentaries, to celebrate VW's sponsorship of documentaries on Channel 4. The subjects we set out to document were poodles with hazard warning lights implanted into their buttocks; a snail with headlights on its tentacles; and a gymnast on the asymmetric bars with an advanced braking system built into her hands.

Dusty

Malaria, Typhoo

China

Ruins

Ping Pong

Trekking

Alicante

Languages

Director	Creative Director	Advertising Agency	Planner
Tony Barry	Mark Roalfe	RKCR/Y&R	Angie Ma
Copywriters	**Producer**	**Agency Producer**	**Account Handler**
Joe Fitzgerald	Jacob Madsen	Katy Hampson	Cathy Powell
Kim Hutcheson	**Set Designer**	**Special Effects**	**National Advertising**
Art Directors	Tom Wales	MPC	**Manager**
Joe Fitzgerald	**Production Company**	**Editor**	Les Knight
Kim Hutcheson	Academy Films	Sam Gunn	**Client**
			Land Rover

TV Sponsorship Credits

RKCR/Y&R
for Land Rover

Land Rover Rough Guides – Dusty / Malaria, Typhoo / China / Ruins / Ping Pong / Trekking / Alicante / Languages
The brief was to utilise sponsorship to strengthen Land Rover's credentials as the best and most adventurous 4x4 brand. We tapped into the truth that Rough Guides and Land Rover believe in discovering new places, people and experiences.

The jury:
Grant Gilbert, Double G Studios (Jury Foreman)
Kyle Cooper, Prologue Films
Chris Dooley, National Television
Graeme Haig, Lambie-Nairn
Noah Harris, Freelance
Tom Tagholm, Channel 4
Alexander Turvey, Freelance
Dan Witchell, Proud

Director	**Producers**	**Sound Designer**	**Client**
Siri Bunford	Shananne Lane	Rich Martin	More4
Creative Directors	Louise Oliver	**Advertising Agency**	**Brand**
Siri Bunford	**Production Designer**	4Creative	Stanley Kubrick
Brett Foraker	Kate Quinn	**Director of**	Season
	Editor	**Photography**	
	Adam Rudd	Alex Barber	

TV Promotions, Stings & Programme Junctions

4Creative
for More4

Stanley Kubrick Season
The campaign was designed to promote a season of Stanley Kubrick films and a bespoke Channel 4 documentary about Kubrick on More4. It was important to us that the technique of shooting was faithful to Kubrick's – there could be no post production work, special effects or invisible edits. It needed to be shot entirely in camera with a steadicam, a technique Kubrick pioneered in 'The Shining'. Kubrick possessed a fearsome presence on set, and an obsessive-compulsive attention to detail. The objective of the trail was to convey those idiosyncrasies, while at the same time revering his genius.

Direction
Wilfred at Finish
Copywriters
Mina Patel
Tony Pipes
Art Directors
Bruce Hill
Mina Patel
Tony Pipes
Creative Director
Mina Patel

Executive Creative Director
Charlie Mawer
Client Group Creative Director
James Spence
Producer
Edel Erickson
Production Company
Red Bee Media

Post Production
Finish
Advertising Agency
Red Bee Media
Director of Photography
Frederico Alfonso
Production Manager
Steven Ryan

Account Handler
Elinor Jones
Marketing Manager
Anna Skelton
Head of Marketing
Lindsay Nuttall
Client
BBC Two

TV Promotions, Stings & Programme Junctions

Red Bee Media
for BBC Two

House of Saddam
Saddam and his family 'melt' before our eyes, representing the downfall of a dynasty. Having no access to the actors, we used various takes from the stills publicity shoot to create movement; we also used stand-ins for close-ups. The melting effect was not something we had seen before, and was created by merging a live shoot of paint dripping and post production techniques on the stills.

Director
Daniel Chase
Creative Director
Brett Foraker
Producer
Liz Arnott

Set Designer
Arne Knudsen
Special Effects
Marcus Dryden
Editor
Kel McKeown
Sound Designer
Rich Martin

Production Company
4Creative
Advertising Agency
4Creative

Director of Photography
Bill Pope
Client
Channel 4
Brand
Film 4

TV Brand Identities

4Creative
for Channel 4

Film 4 Ident – Cars
Film 4 wanted to add to its existing set of idents, using the same template of showing a cinematic scene, but shooting in a way that reflects the channel's considered approach to movie programming. The leaping car is familiar from countless car chases; shooting at high speed and from several angles shows viewers the consequenses of such a jump and a fresh perspective on what they expected to see.

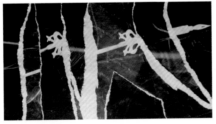

Designer
Carlos Bêla
Director
Luiz Fernando
Carvalho
Copywriters
Carlos Bêla
Roger Marmo
Mateus de Paula
Santos

Creative Directors
Carlos Bêla
Mateus de Paula
Santos
Producer
João Tenório
Head of Production
Loic Lima Dubois

Sound Designer
Tim Rescala
Production Company
Lobo
Animator
Carlos Bêla
Assistant Animator
Rachel Moraes

Computer Graphics Director
Luis Erlanger
Client
Globo
Brand
Capitu

TV Title Sequences

Lobo
for Globo

Capitu
'Capitu' is a TV series adaptation of 'Dom Casmurro', the masterpiece by 19th Century Brazilian novelist Machado de Assis. It features an ageing man writing his memoirs, trying to find proof that his childhood sweetheart and wife, Capitu, betrayed him with his best friend. To encapsulate these issues in the opening sequence and interstitials, Lobo relied on the animation technique and choice of imagery. Preliminary research started with the early 20th Century art movement Dada, following a suggestion by the series director Luiz Fernando Carvalho.

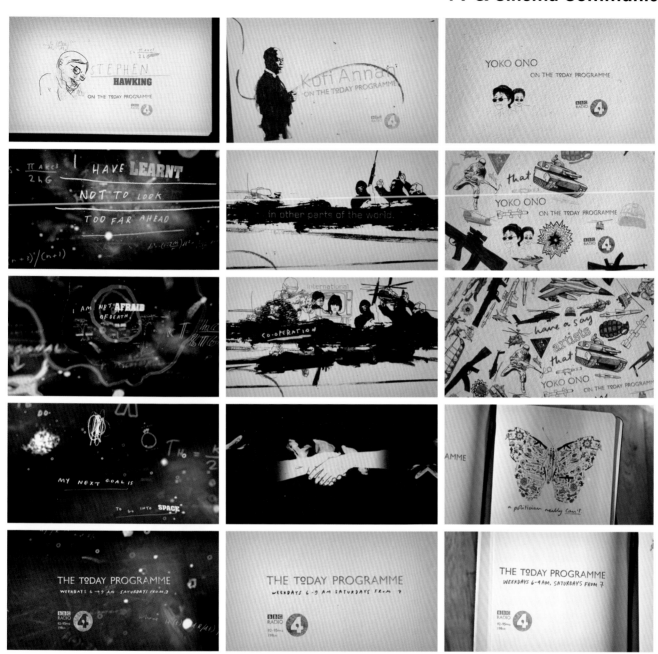

Stephen Hawking

Kofi Annan

Yoko Ono

Direction	Group Creative	Advertising Agency	Head of Account
Why Not Associates	**Director**	Red Bee Media	**Management**
Copywriters	Ruth Shabi	**Animation**	Michelle Marks
Anton Ezer	**Executive Creative**	Why Not Associates	**Account Director**
James de Zoete	**Director**	**Illustrators**	Elinor Jones
Art Directors	Charlie Mawer	Paul Davis	**Marketing Director**
Anton Ezer	**Producer**	Dave Foldvari	Chris Gottlieb
James de Zoete	Justin Cernis	Billie Jean	**Marketing Manager**
Creative Directors	**Production**	**Researchers**	Aiofe Lyanage
Sally Bowness	**Companies**	Samina Ahmed	**Client**
Anton Ezer	Great Guns	Katherine Knight	BBC News
	Red Bee Media	**Planner**	
		John Jones	

TV Promotions, Stings & Programme Junctions

Red Bee Media
for BBC News

Today Programme – Stephen Hawking / Kofi Annan / Yoko Ono
BBC Radio 4 wished to attract a new, younger audience to its world-famous flagship current affairs show, The Today Programme. To do this we decided to highlight the surprising line-up of guests that the show often attracts, and the stimulating nature of the topics they discuss. This would enable potential younger listeners to sample the show, while allowing current listeners to feel proud of their radio programme. To bring the revealing dialogue to life we used world-class illustrators and type animation.

Director	**Creative Director**	**Special Effects**	**Director of**
Neil Gorringe	Neil Gorringe	MPC	**Photography**
Art Directors	**Producer**	**Editor**	Tom Towend
Patrick Lyndon-	Selena Cunningham	James Rosen	**Client**
Stanford	**Production Designer**	**Sound Designer**	E4
Carl Sprague	Carl Sprague	Rich Martin	**Brand**
Alice Tonge	**Advertising Agency**		Skins
Adam Zoltowski	4Creative		

TV Promotions, Stings & Programme Junctions

4Creative
for E4

Skins, Series 2

While the trailer for the first series of Skins reflects its hedonistic, reckless tone, the aim of this trailer was to echo the more sombre, introspective tone of the second series of Skins, in which the lead character suffers brain damage, a main character dies, and another character is stalked. As the characters were now established, we hinted more at the journey they would be taking. The spot offers clues as to what will happen to each character.

Director	**Production**	**Animation Company**	**Media Company**
Vince Squibb	**Companies**	Passion Pictures	BBC Media Planning
Copywriter	Gorgeous	**Sound Designer**	**Account Director**
Paul Silburn	Red Bee Media	Parv Thind	Fiona Richards
Creative Director	**Post Production**	**Music Composer**	**Client**
Mark Roalfe	**Company**	Anne Dudley	BBC MC&A
Producer	The Mill	**Planner**	Future Media and
Sarah Caddy	**Advertising Agency**	Megan Thompson	Technology
Editor	RKCR/Y&R	**Media Planner**	**Brand**
Paul Watts	**Animation Director**	Helen Weeks	BBC iPlayer
	Darren Walsh		

TV Promotions, Stings & Programme Junctions

RKCR/Y&R
for BBC

Penguins

On 1 April 2008 the BBC created an amazing piece of footage designed to 'trick' the nation into believing penguins could fly. The incredible footage was the flagstone of an integrated campaign, which involved national press articles and coverage of the footage on BBC Breakfast. The trail was seeded on YouTube and other websites. Once the story had taken hold, the trail was released on BBC One. It demonstrated that when anything amazing happened on the BBC, you'd never have to miss it, thanks to BBC iPlayer, which allows you to catch up on BBC programmes.

176

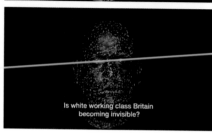

Director
Malcolm Venville
Copywriter
Mike Boles
Art Director
Jerry Hollens
Creative Director
Mark Roalfe
Producer
Louise Jones

Editor
Struan Clay
Sound Designer
Parv Thind
Production Company
Red Bee Media
Advertising Agency
RKCR/Y&R

Director of Photography
Ben Davis
Music Arranger
Billy Bragg
Planner
Megan Thompson
Account Handler
David Young

Marketing Manager
Ruairi Curran
Brand Manager
Lindsay Nuttall
Client
BBC
Brand
White Season

TV Promotions, Stings & Programme Junctions

RKCR/Y&R
for BBC

White
'White Season' is a series of BBC programmes about how Britain's white working class is becoming marginalised. In this trail, people from different cultures are writing 'I love Britain' and 'Britain is changing' on the face of a white working class man, while a poignant Billy Bragg version of the British anthem 'Jerusalem' is playing. The man's face becomes so covered in ink it eventually disappears into the background, reflecting his loss of identity.

Director
Jamie Hewlett
Copywriter
Ted Heath
Art Director
Paul Angus
Creative Director
Damon Collins

Producers
Cara Speller
Deborah Stewart
Editor
Seb Monk
Production Companies
Red Bee Media
Zombie Flesh Eaters

Animator
Jamie Hewlett
Animation Company
Passion Pictures
Music Composer
Damon Albarn
Advertising Agency
RKCR/Y&R
Marketing Manager
Karen Potterton

Head of Marketing & Communications
Louisa Fyans
Client
BBC
Brand
BBC Sport

TV Promotions, Stings & Programme Junctions

RKCR/Y&R
for BBC

Journey to the East
To promote the BBC's exclusive coverage of the 2008 Beijing Olympics, a campaign was created based on the ancient Chinese fables of 'Monkey'. The trailer featured three characters who used their Olympian prowess as they, like the athletes themselves, overcome obstacles on their journey to Beijing. The music and animation, by Damon Albarn and Jamie Hewlett from Gorillaz allowed the integration of PR, online content, programming and title sequences.

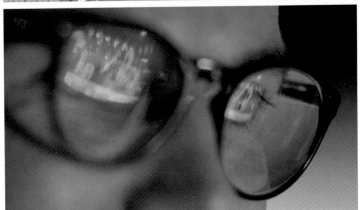

Director
Steve Reeves
Copywriter
Mike Boles
Art Director
Jerry Hollens
Creative Director
Mark Roalfe

Producer
Ella Littlewood
Editor
Scot Crane
Sound Designer
Parv Thind
Production Company
Red Bee Media

Advertising Agency
RKCR/Y&R
Director of Photography
Alex Melman
Music Composer
Gustavo Santaolalla
Music Performer
Kronos Quartet

Planner
Megan Thompson
Account Handler
Fiona Richards
Head of Marketing
Nicki Sheard
Client
BBC

TV Promotions, Stings & Programme Junctions

RKCR/Y&R
for BBC

Places
We all remember where we were when a significant news event happened, and through the decades, the BBC has been the place to go to for important news. Next time a significant event happens, find out with BBC News on your mobile. By using naturalistic filming, we recreated defining news moments. We wanted to make the viewer relive the experience, to make the hairs stand up on the back of their necks. This was achieved with the help of the music, a track called 'When our wings are cut, can we still fly?' by Kronos Quartet.

The jury:
Jon Kamen, @radical.media (Jury Foreman)
Olivier Apers, BETC Euro RSCG
Mike Boles, RKCR/Y&R
Mark Boyd, BBH London
Tom Hostler, Poke London
Carl Ratcliffe, Five

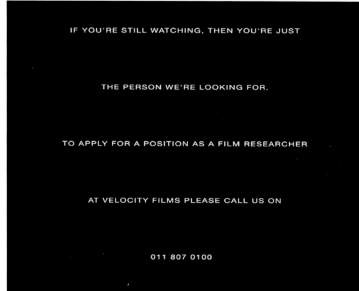

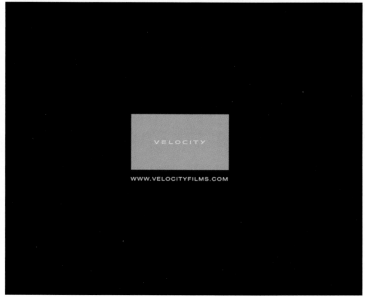

Copywriters
Conn Bertish
Stuart McCreadie
Art Director
Brenton Bubb

Creative Director
Conn Bertish
Advertising Agency
JWT Cape Town

Agency Producer
Rochelle April
**Production
Companies**
Condor
Velocity Films

Clients
Barry Munchick
Velocity Films

Broadcast Innovations

JWT Cape Town
for Velocity Films

Researchers Wanted
Velocity Films, one of South Africa's top production companies, was recruiting film researchers. Our job was to help them fill these positions with passionate people. We placed a recruitment message after the title sequences of movies playing in cinemas, so only true film buffs would be exposed to the message. Exactly the kind of people Velocity Films were looking for.

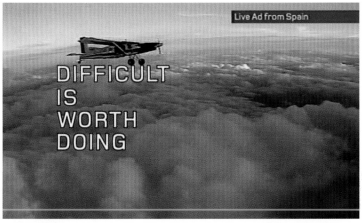

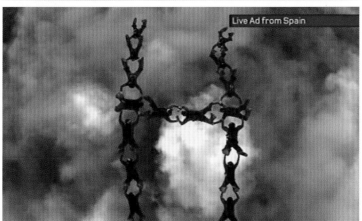

Director	Creative Director	Executive Producers	Directors of
Tim van Someren	Tom Tagholm	John Nolan	**Photography**
Copywriter	**Producers**	Charlie Read	Tony Danbury
James Springall	Sharon Guest	**Advertising Agency**	Gary Wainwright
Art Director	Dave Lewis	4Creative	**Client**
Craig Hanratty	**Senior Producer**	**Media Agency**	Honda
	Keeley Pratt	Starcom	

Broadcast Innovations

4Creative
for Honda

Honda Live
Honda wanted the launch of the new Honda Accord to break seemingly impossible boundaries, in keeping with the Honda proposition, 'If it's difficult, it's worth doing', so we decided to develop the first live (as opposed to as-live) TV commercial. We put together a specialist team to pull off one of the most daring launch events ever seen on TV: using 17 sky divers, seven cameras filming at 1400ft in rapidly changing weather conditions, live direction and audio mix, we produced one three-minute 21-second spot broadcast live on Channel 4. All in three weeks from green light to on air. The spot received unprecedented media coverage, in the UK and abroad, and grew audience share in the ad break itself by eight per cent.

Copywriter	**Designers**	**Editor**	**Account Executive**
Dagan Cohen	Eva Bodok	Steven van Hemmen	Sharoni van Hulzen
Art Director	Miriam de Kemp	**Photographer**	**Account Managers**
Dagan Cohen	**Animator**	Maurice Mikkers	Esther de Kok
Creative Director	Stefan van de Geer	**Music Composer**	Irene van Deijl
Dagan Cohen	**Advertising Agency**	Klaas Berings	**Client**
Interactive Designer	Lowe/Draftfcb	**Strategists**	De Uitkijk
Mark Vertegaal	Amsterdam	Dagan Cohen	**Brand**
		Barbara de Wijn	Upload Cinema

Broadcast Innovations

Lowe/Draftfcb Amsterdam
for De Uitkijk

Upload Cinema
How to find a new audience for De Uitkijk, the oldest film theatre in the Netherlands? The answer: Upload Cinema. A film club that brings the best videos on the web to the big screen. Every first Monday of the month, a fresh programme of internet shorts is screened in De Uitkijk in Amsterdam. Each month there's a new theme. The audience submits films through uploadcinema.nl; an editorial board selects the best and compiles a feature-length programme. Upload Cinema was silently launched in October 2008 and has developed the way many online communities do: without any form of traditional advertising, just by word of mouth and 'member get member'. The film club has been a great success right from the start.

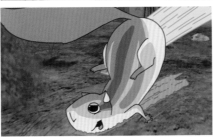

Copywriter	Producer	Agency Producer	Marketing Manager
Dieter Vanhoof	Patricia	Patricia	Peter Plaes
Art Director	Vandekerckhove	Vandekerckhove	**Brand Manager**
Paul Popelier	**Production Company**	**Planner**	Jan van Biesen
Creative Directors	Mortierbrigade	Patricia	**Client**
Joost Berends	**Advertising Agency**	Vandekerckhove	Studio Brussel
Philippe Deceuster	Mortierbrigade		
Jens Mortier			

Broadcast Innovations

Mortierbrigade
for Studio Brussel

Transformed Soap

Every year, Studio Brussel, the national Belgian radio station, runs a charity event called 'Music for Life'. This year it was all about mothers on the run. Millions of mothers and children are homeless because of violence and war. To promote the charity event and raise money, we used Belgium's most watched TV series, Thuis (Dutch for home). We replaced the actors in the opening sequence with Ugandan mothers, confronting viewers with real mothers on the run. The campaign was broadcast on only one channel but was picked up by many more. Three radio DJs also played listeners' favourite songs in exchange for a donation; in just six days, 3.5million was raised.

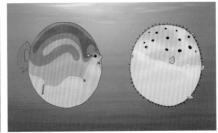

Director	Designer	Sound Designer	Head of Content	Mobile Director
Matthew Walker	Dominic Grant	Dougal Mcdiarmid	Mark Boyd	Peter Sells
Copywriter	**Production Company**	**Planner**	**Digital Project**	**Marketing Manager**
Claudia Southgate	Aardman	Dan Hauck	**Managers**	Alberto Bruno
Art Director	Animations	**Content Developer**	Azi Aramis	**Brand Manager**
Verity Fenner	**Advertising Agency**	Richard Adkins	Philip Dabrowski	Vincenzo Tortora
Creative Directors	BBH London	**Content Account**	**Account Handler**	**Client**
Mark Boyd	**Agency Producer**	**Director**	Michael Osbourn	Perfetti van Melle
Nick Gill	Ben Davies	Nic Gorini	**Business Director**	**Brand**
Producer	**Editor**	**Content Director**	Richard Lawson	Air Action Vigorsol
John Woolley	Matthew Walker	Richard Powell	**Group Business**	
			Director	
			Hugh Baillie	

Broadcast Innovations

BBH London & Aardman Animations
for Perfetti van Melle

The Adventures of Cippi

In 2007, Cippi blasted onto Italy's screens in an advert for Air Action Vigorsol. The flatulent chipmunk quickly became a star among Italian teenagers and the wider public. The 2008 challenge was to turn Cippi from advertising property into entertainment icon. The response was to treat Cippi like an entertainment brand and produce 12 cartoon episodes. Distribution came through editorial partnerships both on mobile – Vodafone enabled free access to 28 million people; and online – the films were placed on premium content portals. This led to seven million interactions, and the Cippi series even made it onto national TV.

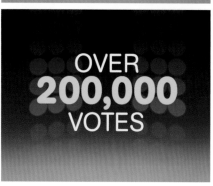

Copywriter
Lixaida Lorenzo
Art Director
Héctor Buscaglia
Creative Director
Jaime Rosado
Interactive Creative Director
Manuel Torres
Kortright

Interactive Designers
Juan Carlos Montes
Manuel Torres
Kortright
Production Company
Hocus Pocus
Advertising Agency
JWT San Juan
Agency Producer
Noro Sebastián

Editor
Mizael Morales
Sound Designer
Carlos Dávila
Account Handlers
Richard Pascual
Axel Ramos
Account Executive
Carlos Laureano

Media Directors
Kay Martínez
Norian Ocasio
Brand Managers
Carmen Corrada
Moira Tamayo
Client
Centennial PR

Broadcast Innovations

JWT San Juan & Hocus Pocus
for Centennial PR

Phone Star
Phone Star was the first vocal talent competition performed through a mobile phone. Thousands of hopefuls auditioned through their Centennial mobile phones. Judges from Sony BMG chose ten finalists. The audience voted for their favourite through text messaging. The faces of the contestants weren't seen; only their voices were heard. After five weeks and over 200,000 votes, we found our first Phone Star, who won a record deal with Sony BMG.

Copywriters
Mela Advincula
Alvin Tecson
Art Director
Mela Advincula

Creative Directors
Richard Irvine
Raoul Panes
Alvin Tecson
Advertising Agency
Leo Burnett Manila

Agency Producer
Lady Cajanding
Animator
Jojo Sacramento
Account Handlers
Sue Ann Nolido
Gela Pena

Marketing Vice President
Margot Torres
Client
McDonald's
Brand
McDonald's 24-Hour Delivery

Broadcast Innovations

Leo Burnett Manila
for McDonald's

Counting Sheep
Insomnia ads were created to tell nocturnal Filipinos that McDonald's now stays up late with them. This particular commercial, made specifically for McDonald's 24-hour delivery service, utilised TV stations' sign off time. TV stations were convinced to loop this animated spot after they had ended their broadcast day. Late-night channel surfers saw this looped ad instead of the usual static station IDs or colour bars.

THERE CAN ONLY BE ONE

Where amazing happens.

Director
Brett Foraker
Copywriter
Damon Troth
Art Director
Joanna Perry
Typographer
Mark Cakebread

Chief Creative Director
Jon Williams
Producer
Juliet Naylor
Advertising Agency
Grey London

Agency Producers
Andrew Blackburn
Rebecca Pople
Editor
Adam Rudd
Sound Designer
Rich Martin

Account Handler
Rhona Cairns
Brand Manager
Betty McBride
Client
British Heart Foundation

Grey London
for British Heart Foundation

Watch Your Own Heart Attack
One in three heart attack victims die before reaching hospital, mostly because they fail to recognise the symptoms and delay calling for medical assistance. 'Watch Your Own Heart Attack' allowed people to experience what those symptoms would feel like in the safety of their living rooms. The two-minute film, shot from the viewer's perspective, saw Steven Berkoff vividly take the viewer through the experience of a heart attack. This was appointment-to-view television, screened only once, backed by an integrated campaign to create national anticipation. Viewing figures actually went up in the commercial break as six million tuned in to have their own heart attack.

Direction
Dayton/Faris
Copywriters
Jamie Barrett
Craig Mangan
Ari Weiss
Art Directors
Stefan Copiz
Jack Woodworth
Creative Director
Jamie Barrett
Producer
Bart Lipton

Executive Producer
TK Knowles
Associate Creative Directors
Stefan Copiz
Ari Weiss
Production Company
Bob Industries
Advertising Agency
Goodby Silverstein and Partners
Agency Producer
Tod Puckett

Visual Effects Artists
Miles Essmiller
Geoff McAuliffe
Sean McLean
Patrick Poulatian
Jimi Simmons
Mandy Sorenson
Visual Effects Producers
Kirsten Andersen
Amy Appleton
Diana Young

Visual Effects Supervisor
Geoff McAuliffe
Visual Effects
Brickyard VFX
Editor
Geoff Hounsell
Lighting Cameraperson
Christophe Lanzenberg

Account Handler
Tanin Blumberg
Clients
National Basketball Association
ABC
ESPN
TNT
Brand
NBA

Goodby Silverstein and Partners & Bob Industries
for National Basketball Association

There Can Only Be One
In an effort to reconnect with disenfranchised NBA fans, we decided to strip the glitz and glamour from the game and have the players stare at a camera and speak from the heart. We filmed the 48 most famous players from 16 different teams. They all delivered the exact same script in the exact same cadence, repeating the words from a pre-recorded track they could hear on an invisible earpiece. Shooting over 48 players on green screen gave us the library of footage we needed to promote any game on any night.

Turn back time

Director	Executive Creative	Production Company	Multimedia
Trent O'Donnell	**Directors**	Jungleboys	**Developer**
Copywriters	Justin Drape	**Advertising Agency**	Christian Lee
Damian Fitzgerald	Scott Nowell	Three Drunk	**Account Handler**
Nick Morrissey	**Producer**	Monkeys	Andrew Stanley
Art Directors	Chloe Rickard	**Agency Producer**	**Clients**
Damian Fitzgerald	**Digital Producer**	Thea Carone	ABC
Nick Morrissey	Lisa Gray	**Editor**	Zapruder's Other
Creative Directors	**Digital Production**	Paul Swaine	Films
Adam Callen	**Company**	**System Architect**	**Brand**
Shane Gibson	The Feds Digital	Chris Jones	The Gruen Transfer

Three Drunk Monkeys & Jungleboys
for ABC

The Gruen Transfer
The Gruen Transfer was a new television show about advertising. To promote it we created fictional products all bearing the show's name – Gruen Beer, Gruen Bank, Gruen Beauty – and advertised them on ABC, Australia's only non-commercial network. What followed was outrage, intrigue, viewer engagement, invaluable press coverage and the highest rating debut show in ABC's history.

The jury:

Lizie Gower, Academy Films (Jury Foreman)
Ross Anderson, Polydor Records
Casper Balslev, LOVE
Zoë Bell, Mother
James Frost, Zoo Film Productions
Katie Griffiths, EMI Records
Andy Gulliman, Saatchi & Saatchi London

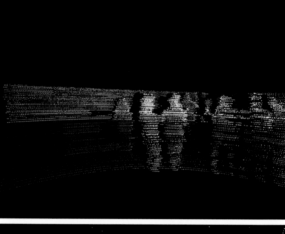

Director	Artist	Editor	Record Company
James Frost	Radiohead	Nicholas Wayman-	TBD Records
Producer	**Production Company**	Harris	
Dawn Fanning	Zoo Film Productions		

Music Videos

Zoo Film Productions
for TBD Records

Radiohead – House of Cards

Radiohead's 'House of Cards' is the first video to be shot with no cameras, using only lasers and scanners. Realising that one could scan moving images in real-time using 3D lasers, James Frost sought a way to use the technology to make a video. Radiohead seemed the only logical choice, given the band's previous ventures in forward thinking technology. Frost approached the band's managers directly with the concept; the idea could therefore be developed outside of the constraints of the corporate system. 'House of Cards' was the first music video premiered by Google, in July 2008.

Direction
Encyclopedia
Pictura
Associate Director
Daren Rabinovitch
Art Director
Isaiah Saxon
Producer
Mark de Pace

Executive Producer
Zachary Mortensen
Artist
Björk
**Production
Company**
Ghost Robot
**Post Production
Company**
UVPHACTORY

**Fabrication
Supervisor**
Tirsh Hunter
**Practical Effects
Supervisor**
Daren Rabinovitch
CGI Supervisor
Damijan Saccio

Record Company
One Little Indian
Records
**Video
Commissioner**
Paul McKee

Music Videos

Ghost Robot
for One Little Indian Records

Wanderlust
Björk is an archetypal nomad, shepherding giant yaks through the mountains. She uses hydromancy to decide whether to take them down a river or not. A second self, the Painbody Backpack, sprouts from her like a growth, then engages her in an action play which illustrates their relationship. The force that compelled Björk to go down river begins to manifest itself in Björk's head and in the physical world. This character, the River God, is a transcendental attractor who pulls her into the future. Shot in stereoscopic 3D, the video took nine months to complete. Also awarded Yellow Pencils in Art Direction and Special Effects.

Lighting
Cameraperson
Kasper Tuxen
Director
Martin de Thurah

Producer
Liz Kessler
Artist
Will Young
Production Company
Academy Films

Editor
Art Jones
Special Effects
David Payne
Set Designer
Catrin Meredydd

Record Company
SONY
Video Commissioner
James Hackett

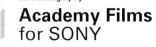

Cinematography

Academy Films
for SONY

Changes
Will Young was commissioned by James Hackett at SONY Music and shot on location in South East England last year. It was a particularly demanding shoot for Will as he was burnt, soaked, smoked, thrown to the ground and forced to run a mile as well as having to dodge a cow in a petrol station. Director Martin de Thurah shot over two days and one night on 16mm with long time collaborator, Kasper Tuxen. This was also selected in Music Videos.

					Animation
Animators	**Artist**	**Animation**	**Visual Effects**	**Lead Rigger**	**Radical Media**
Cesar Bravo	Gnarls Barkley	**Production**	**Producer**	Oleg	**for Atlantic Records**
Christian Brierley	**Production**	**Manager**	Maya Martinez	Alexander	
Randall Rose	**Company**	Peter Busch	**Visual Effects**	**Colourist**	**Who's Gonna Save my Soul**
Keith Sintay	Radical Media	**Animation**	**Supervisors**	Dave Hussey	This is the music video for Gnarls Barkley's 'Who's Gonna Save my Soul'. It's the story of a
Animation Director	**Editor**	**Associate Producer**	Thomas	**Record**	girl who dumps a boy who tears out his heart for her... literally. This was also selected in Music
Chris Milk	Livio Sanchez	Pampata Jutte	Tannenberger	**Company**	Videos.
Director	**Lighting**	**Blood Simulations**	Olcun Tan	Waxploitation	
Chris Milk	**Cameraperson**	Eric Ehemann	**ICG Supervisor**	**Video**	
Producer	Danny Hiele	**Flame Compositor**	Olcun Tan	**Commissioner**	
Anne Johnson	**Set Designer**	Simon Holden	**Motion Capture &**	Cathy Pellow	
Executive Producers	Zach Matthews		**Facial Scanning**	**Client**	
Jennifer Heath			Paul Debevec	Atlantic Records	
Frank Scherma					

Director
Dougal Wilson
Producer
Ciska Faukner
Artist
Goldfrapp

Production Company
Colonel Blimp
Editor
Amanda James
Special Effects
MPC

Lighting
Cameraperson
Mattias Montero
Set Designer
Clare Clarkson

Record Company
Mute Records
Video Commissioner
Carrie Sutton

Music Videos

Colonel Blimp
for Mute Records

Happiness
A man bounces down the street. Hilarity ensues. A respectful homage to Bobby Van's legendary performance in the 1953 László Kardos musical 'Small Town Girl'.

Director
Andrew Griffin
Producer
Andrew Griffin
Co-Producer
Sophia Pendar-Hughes

Artist
The Cinematic Orchestra
Production Company
Up The Resolution
Editor
Andrew Griffin

Director of Photography
Conor Connelly
Actors
Julia Ford
Peter Mullan
Gaffer
Billy Harron

Focus Puller
Jason Coop
Location Manager
Andy Bainbridge
Record Company
Ninja Tune
Video Commissioner
Vez

Music Videos

Up The Resolution
for Ninja Tune

To Build a Home
The budgets for two separate animated promos, 'To build a home' and 'Breathe', were combined to create one long-form live acion promo. Spanning both tracks, the film takes its cue from the shared lyrical themes of love and loss, the narrative following a couple fulfilling their dream of retirement to the remote hills of the countryside, albeit fleetingly and with tragic motivation. The hybrid format won the promo a special screening on Channel 4, as well as both a nomination at the UK Music Video Awards and screening among features at the Edinburgh Film Festival.

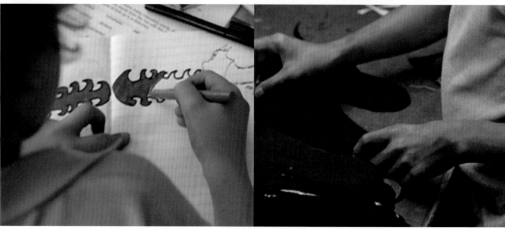

Editor	**Executive Producer**	**Lighting**	**Advertising Agency**
Alexandre de	Michael Ritchie	**Cameraperson**	Coleman Rasic
Franceschi	**Artist**	John Seale	Carrasco Sydney
Director	Radiohead	**Set Designer**	**Client**
Steve Rogers	**Production Company**	Lucinda Thompson	MTV Exit Asia
Producer	Revolver		
Georgina Wilson			

Editing

Revolver & Coleman Rasic Carrasco Sydney
for MTV Exit Asia

All I Need (MTV Exit Asia)
Agency Coleman Rasic Carrasco Sydney and Steve Rogers of Revolver created a music video for the single 'All I Need', from Radiohead's album 'In Rainbows'. The video clip was used to raise awareness of exploitation and human trafficking in developing countries. This was also selected in Music Videos.

Animation	Artist	Lighting	Video
Frater	Ladyhawke	**Cameraperson**	**Commissioner**
Direction	**Production Company**	Ross McLennan	Carmen Montanez-
Frater	Partizan Lab	**Record Companies**	Callan
Illustrator	**Editor**	Modular Records	
Sarah Larnach	Kate Owen	Universal Island	

Animation

Partizan Lab
for Modular Records/Universal Island

My Delirium
This is an animated music video by Frater for Ladyhawke's track 'My Delirium', featuring drawings by artist Sarah Larnach, who collaborated with animators Frater. The video was produced by Partizan UK's animation wing, Partizan Lab. The commissioning record label is Modular Records/Universal Island. The video was produced in late 2008.

Director
Thomas Jumin
Direction
So Me

Producer
Nathalie
Canguilehem

Artist
Justice
Production Company
Because Music

Special Effects
Machine Molle
Record Label
Ed Banger

Music Videos

Because Music
for Ed Banger

DVNO
After Justice's video 'Dance', So Me did it again with 'DVNO', in collaboration with Thomas Jumin from Machine Molle, who designed all the logos. The video features vintage motion logotypes and typography such as 20th Century Fox, HBO and Cannon Group, and at the end a piano part that refers to Stephen J Cannell Productions. Eight people worked on this project over a month and half, using Illustrator, Maya, RenderMan and Shake as software. This was also selected in the Art Direction category.

Director
Kim Gehrig
Producer
Dom Thomas
Artist
Wiley

Production Company
Academy Films
Editor
Ed Cheeseman

Lighting
Cameraperson
Ben Moulden
Set Designer
Gregg Shoulder

Record Company
Atlantic Records
Video Commissioner
Tim Nash

Music Videos

Academy Films
for Atlantic Records

Cash in my Pocket
Kim Gehrig shot Wiley's 'Cash in my Pocket' for Tim Nash at Atlantic Records in London in September 2008. Inspired by a craze for lip dub videos, Kim created a world where bankers were too busy having fun to notice that the financial world was literally crashing around them. Kim choreographed 60 extras, all street cast from the City of London, to perform the video in one take. No bank would allow her to shoot in their buildings as they were concerned about reprisals, so the Blue Fin Building doubled as a stockbroker firm.

Poolworldwide
for Kraak & Smaak

Squeeze Me
This is a music video in which a young man's seemingly boring routine is interrupted by tiny adventures in classic flip book animation.

Directors
Henk Loorbach
Andre Maat
Producer
William Griffioen

Artist
Kraak & Smaak
Production Company
Poolworldwide

Animators
Henk Loorbach
Andre Maat

Editors
Henk Loorbach
Andre Maat

Partizan
for Sub Pop Records

Ladies of the World
This is the Flight of the Conchords video for 'Ladies of the World' from their self-titled LP on Sub Pop Records, and the HBO series 'Flight of the Conchords', directed by Nima Nourizadeh and produced by Partizan.

Director
Nima Nourizadeh
Producer
Charles Spano
Artist
Flight of the
Conchords

Production Company
Partizan
Editor
Bill Yukich

Lighting
Cameraperson
Andrew Shulkind

Record Company
Sub Pop Records
Video Commissioner
Stuart Myers

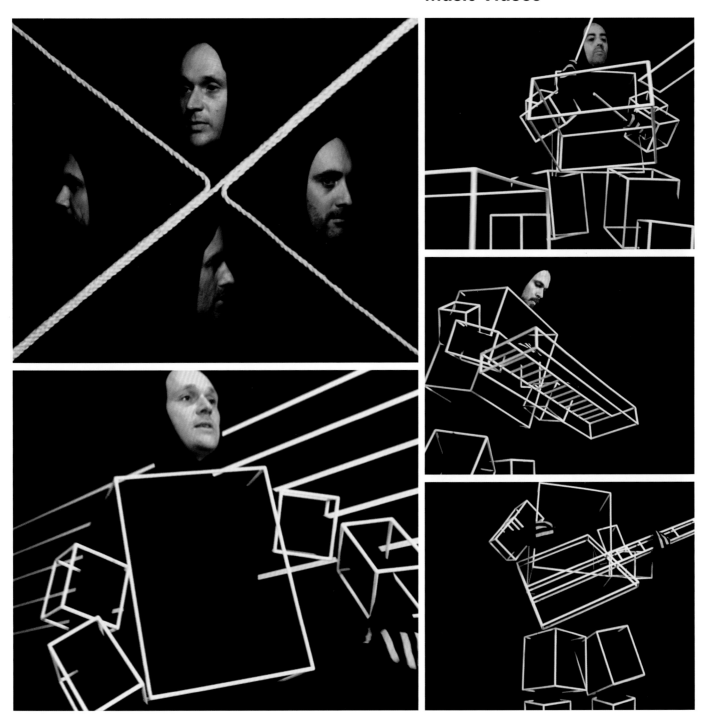

Director	**Artist**	**Editor**	**Lighting**
Wade Shotter	Fujiya Miyagi	Tom Lindsay	**Cameraperson**
Producer	**Production**	**Special Effects**	Steve Annis
Paul Carter	**Companies**	Dan Sollis	**Record Company**
Animator	Draw Pictures		Deaf Dumb & Blind
Dan Sollis	Joyrider		

Art Direction

Draw Pictures & Joyrider
for Deaf Dumb & Blind

Sore Thumb
The initial inspiration came from the idea of taking the simple visual language of early 80s wireframe/vector animation, and reinventing it with real physical wireframe structures. The challenge was to create this without any sort of 3D or stop motion animation or post-heavy effects. Every graphic and detail was made and shot in-camera, with the only post effects used being the overlaying or speed ramping of imagery. The final look was almost too realistic in places, so it was important to include a very human element to the project, which materialised in the form of purposefully bad puppetry. The tank miniatures were simply dragged across screen with black cotton in a deliberately inconsistent and jerky fashion.

Director
Nima Nourizadeh
Producer
Jon Adams
Executive Producer
Sasha Nixon

Artist
Hot Chip
Production Company
Partizan

Editor
Magnus
Lighting
Cameraperson
Tat Radcliffee

Set Designer
Gregg Shoulder
Record Company
EMI
Video Commissioner
Semera Kahn

Art Direction

Partizan
for EMI

Ready for the Floor
This is the third collaboration between Hot Chip and Partizan director Nima Nourizadeh, this time a homage to the Bat Dance video. The music video was commissioned by EMI Records for the release of the single 'Ready for the Floor'.

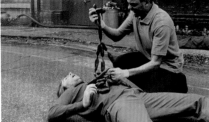

Director
Nima Nourizadeh
Producer
Grace Bodie
Executive Producer
Sasha Nixon

Artist
Santogold
Production Company
Partizan
Editing
Prime Focus

Special Effects
PPL
Lighting
Cameraperson
Adam Frisch

Record Company
Atlantic Records
Video Commissioner
Tim Nash

Art Direction

Partizan
for Atlantic Records

L.E.S Artistes
This music video was commissioned by Tim Nash at Atlantic Records for Santogold's first UK single 'L.E.S Artistes'.

Animator
Tobias Stretch
Director
Tobias Stretch

Producer
Tobias Stretch
Artist
Radiohead

Production Companies
Red Lion
Tobias Stretch Films

Editor
Tobias Stretch
Record Company
TBD Records
Client
Aniboom

Animation

Tobias Stretch Films
for TBD Records

Weird Fishes/Arpeggi
Tobias Stretch's amazing film for Radiohead's 'Weird Fishes/Arpeggi' is unusual to say the least. Not only did Tobias shoot and edit the film single handed, he also designed and built all the extraordinary life-size puppets, some of them over seven feet tall. These wildly surreal puppets soar over tranquil lakes, lush trees and at times, 60 feet in the air. Over 4,000 still images assemble to create this dramatic high-flying stop-motion fairytale. Sixty days of shooting, twelve hours a day in the transcendent wilderness of the Appalachian Mountains of northern Pennsylvania was what it took to make this psychotic dream a waking reality.

Radio

Mr Football Endzone Painter

Announcer   Bud Light presents, real men of genius.

Singer   Real men of genius!

Announcer   Today, we salute you, Mr Football Endzone Painter.

Singer   Mr Football Endzone Painter!

Announcer   Armed with a brush and bucket, you create pieces that will last forever, or at least, until they cut the grass.

Singer   Please don't mow in this area!

Announcer   Your art touches the heart, stimulates the mind, and taints the ground water in the entire tri-county area.

Singer   This water tastes funny!

Announcer   What do you get when you spray 480 metric tons of paint inside a dome? Diminished cognitive skills.

Singer   What's my name?

Announcer   So crack open an ice-cold Bud Light, oh Van Gogh of the Grid-iron. Because we know, you'll always be up for painting the town.

Singer   Mr Football Endzone Painter!

MVO   Bud Light beer, Anheuser-Busch, St Louis, Missouri.

Radio

Mr Football First Down Marker

Announcer Bud Light presents, real men of genius.

Singer Real men of genius!

Announcer Today we salute you, Mr Football First Down Marker guy.

Singer Mr Football First Down Marker guy!

Announcer Like a centurion guard protecting the Roman Empire, you stand ready to measure. To mark. Or, when needed, to pat a tight end's fanny.

Singer Can I touch you there?

Announcer You are blessed with poise, truthfulness and, most importantly, the ability to count to four.

Singer I know lots of numbers!

Announcer And how do you protect yourself from an out of control 300lb linebacker? A plastic yellow vest.

Singer It's also reflective!

Announcer So crack open an ice-cold Bud Light, oh, Guard of the Grid-iron. Because even no one measures up... to you.

Singer Mr Football First Down Marker guy.

MVO Bud Light beer, Anheuser-Busch, St Louis, Missouri.

Mr Golf Quiet Sign Holder

Announcer Bud Light presents, real men of genius.

Singer Real men of genius!

Announcer Today we salute you, Mr Golf Tournament Quiet Sign Holder Upper.

Singer Mr Golf Tournament Quiet Sign Holder Upper!

Announcer Boldly you patrol the line between order and anarchy, armed with only your wits, your resolve and your tiny cardboard sign stapled to a stick.

Singer Actually, I glued it on!

Announcer You protect professional golfers from what they fear most – idle chitchat 200 yards away.

Singer Stop breathing so loud now!

Announcer Because you know there's one thing this spectator sport could really do without – spectators.

Singer Get them out!

Announcer So crack open an ice-cold Bud Light, oh, Sultan of the Shush. We'll keep singing your praises, as long as you keep telling us, to shut up.

Singer Mr Golf Tournament Quiet Sign Holder Upper!

MVO Bud Light beer, Anheuser-Busch, St Louis, Missouri.

Copywriter
Jeb Quaid
Art Director
Aaron Pendleton
Creative Directors
Chuck Rachford
Chris Roe

Group Creative Director
Mark Gross
Associate Creative Directors
Pat Burke
Chris Carraway

Associate Producer
Patty Phassos
Executive Producer
Will St Clair
Executive Director of Integrated Production
Diane Jackson

Sound Mixer
Dave Gerbosi
Music Production
Scandal
Advertising Agency
DDB Chicago
Client
Anheuser-Busch
Brand
Bud Light

Radio Commercials
DDB Chicago
for Anheuser-Busch

Mr Football Endzone Painter / Mr Football First Down Marker / Mr Golf Quiet Sign Holder

Radio

Yoda Melvin

Man Admit, I do. Unsuccessful with women, I was. Figure out why I could not. Until in a spaceship convention bathroom, told me my friend, 'Melvin, dandruff you have!' Girls didn't mind I assumed. But unattractive, dandruff is. So Head & Shoulders I bought. No longer a problem dandruff is. Little black book, I acquired. Fill it with many phone numbers, I will.

MVO You've got bigger problems than dandruff. This message was brought to you by Head & Shoulders.

Statistic Spencer

Man I once had dandruff that covered eight to nine per cent of my scalp. Four out of five girls I dated noticed my flakes within an average of 2.3 days. After some evaluation in a ten times magnification mirror, I came to the conclusion that this matter required resolution. I purchased a 14.2 fluid ounce bottle of Head & Shoulders Pyrithione Zinc Dandruff Shampoo. I washed my hair daily for 72 seconds with an 18ml application of Head & Shoulders. Then I'd rinse, and repeat. Then I'd rinse, and repeat. Then I'd rinse. My scalp is now exponentially healthier. If I were to ask a woman at random out on a date, there's a 51.8 per cent chance she would respond affirmatively. Ah, give or take a two per cent margin of error.

MVO You've got bigger problems than dandruff. This message was brought to you by Head & Shoulders.

Ego Ed

Man I did not always looked this perfect, man. Uh uh. I once had dandruff. Yeah, I know. That must have been the reason that Vicki said no when I asked her out. Which is so sad, ya know, it's just so sad to me, 'cause she is just so superficial, ya know? But whatever, she was ugly. And then when that stupid chick Anna wouldn't go out with me, I realised it's got to be my flakes, 'cause it's not my looks and it's not my bank account. So I got Head & Shoulders. Picked up a couple of dozen bottles, I don't care. Stored some in the walk-in closet of my guestroom, next to my protein shake powders. 'Cause you know, I've got the room. I've got the disposable income. I just don't have the time right now. The dandruff was like ridiculously easy to get rid of. But now I cannot wait for Vicki and Anna to try to get back with me, you know, 'cause when they do, I'm just gonna have to laugh at them. I'm just gonna have to be like, 'Sorry ladies, that ship has sailed'.

MVO You've got bigger problems than dandruff. This message was brought to you by Head & Shoulders.

Copywriters
Aryan Aminzadeh
Kristin Graham
Julia Neumann
Michael Schachtner

Creative Directors
Paula Dombrow
Icaro Doria
Chief Creative Officer
Tony Granger

Agency Producer
Eric Korte
Recording Engineer
Rick Oakley
Planner
Frances Cook
Advertising Agency
Saatchi & Saatchi New York

Account Handler
Tara Allerton
Client
Procter & Gamble
Brand
Head & Shoulders

Radio Commercials

Saatchi & Saatchi New York
for Procter & Gamble

Yoda Melvin / Statistic Spencer / Ego Ed

Radio

Umbrella

(International hit song 'Umbrella' by Rihanna remixed to sound like South African Soweto gospel music)

When the sun shines, we'll shine together
Told you I'll be here forever
Said I'll always be a friend
Took an oath I'ma stick it out till the end
Now that it's raining more than ever
Know that we'll still have each other
You can stand under my umbrella
You can stand under my umbrella
(Ella ella eh eh eh)
Under my umbrella
(Ella ella eh eh eh)
Under my umbrella
(Ella ella eh eh eh)
Under my umbrella
(Ella ella eh eh eh eh eh eh)

Announcer Vodacom Passport allows you to take your South African call rate overseas. To activate, simply SMS 'Passport' to 45123. Vodacom Passport only from Vodacom. South Africa's leading cellular network.

Heartbreaker

(International hit song 'Heartbreaker' by Will.I.Am remixed to sound like South African Apostolic gospel music)

Where it's at
(Where it's at)
I know karma is gonna pay me back
(Pay me back)
I'm with the sweetest thing that's on the map
(That's on the map)
I broke her heart in 30 seconds flat
(In 30 seconds flat)
So so so sorry
(I'm so so so sorry)
Didn't mean to break your heart
(Didn't mean to break you heart)
Br – break your heart baby
I'm a heartbreaker

Announcer Vodacom Passport allows you to take your South African call rate overseas. To activate, simply SMS 'Passport' to 45123. Vodacom Passport only from Vodacom. South Africa's leading cellular network.

Drop It

(International hit song 'Drop it like it's hot' by Snoop Doggy Dogg remixed to sound like South African Mambazo music)

When a pimp's in the crib ma
(Drop it like it's hot)
Drop it
(Drop it like it's hot)
Drop it wena
(Drop it like it's hot)
Drop it
(Drop it like it's hot)
Drop it
(Drop it like it's hot)
Drop it
(Drop it like it's hot)
Drop it
(Drop it like it's hot)
Drop it
(Drop it like it's hot)
And if a nigga get a attitude
(Pop it like it's hot)
Pop it
(Pop it like it's hot)
Pop it wena
(Pop it like it's hot)
I got the rolly on my arm and I'm pouring Chandon
And I roll the best weed 'cause I got it going on

Announcer Vodacom Passport allows you to take your South African call rate overseas. To activate, simply SMS 'Passport' to 45123. Vodacom Passport only from Vodacom. South Africa's leading cellular network.

Music Arranger
Thabo Mduli
Copywriters
Mohlalifi Lentsoane
Neo Mashigo
Grant Sithole

Creative Director
Grant Jacobsen
Agency Producer
Karin Keylock
Recording Engineer
Kitso Moremi

Production Company
Sonovision &
Noiseroom
Advertising Agency
Draftfcb
Johannesburg
Account Handler
Heidi Nelson

Marketing Manager
Enzo Scarcella
Client
Vodacom
Brand
Passport

Use of Music
Draftfcb Johannesburg
for Vodacom

Umbrella / Heartbreaker / Drop It
The brief was to raise awareness of a new product from Vodacom called Vodacom Passport, which allows you to pay local call rates when travelling abroad. We re-recorded popular songs that topped world charts in music styles indigenous only to South Africa. The styles are popular Zionist gospel choir and Isicathamiya, made popular by Ladysmith Black Mambazo. This illustrated the fact that no matter where you travel, Vodacom Passport will always make you feel like you're back at home, because of the local tariff.

Eating Candy

MVO Eating candy compressed by Stuffit Deluxe.

FVO Mmhm

SFX Dentist's drill

MVO Stuffit Deluxe available for Mac or PC.
Download at stuffit.com.

Radio Commercials

Saatchi & Saatchi New York
for Smith Micro Software
Eating Candy

Copywriters	**Art Directors**	**Agency Producer**	**Client**
Icaro Doria	Menno Kluin	Eric Korte	Smith Micro
Menno Kluin	Grant Minnis	**Recording Engineer**	Software
Julia Neumann	Michael Schachtner	Rick Oakley	**Brand**
Laddie Peterson	**Chief Creative**	**Advertising Agency**	Stuffit Deluxe
	Officer	Saatchi & Saatchi	
	Tony Granger	New York	

New Year's Eve

MVO New Year's Eve compressed by Stuffit Deluxe.

Crowd 10, 9

SFX Vomiting

MVO Stuffit Deluxe available for Mac or PC.
Download at stuffit.com.

Radio Commercials

Saatchi & Saatchi New York
for Smith Micro Software
New Year's Eve

Copywriters	**Art Directors**	**Agency Producer**	**Client**
Icaro Doria	Menno Kluin	Eric Korte	Smith Micro
Julia Neumann	Grant Minnis	**Recording Engineer**	Software
Laddie Peterson	Michael Schachtner	Rick Oakley	**Brand**
	Chief Creative	**Advertising Agency**	Stuffit Deluxe
	Officer	Saatchi & Saatchi	
	Tony Granger	New York	

Radio

Black Capped Capuchin

Scene	High rise apartment, distant traffic
Interviewer	So, why the black hat all the time?
Man (30s, Brazilian)	You like the black hat, huh?
Interviewer	Yes, it's nice.
Man	Yeah, it's nice and sexy. I wear my black hat because I got a wide head. So it gives that slimming effect on my head.
Interviewer	Oh really? Right. So it's not because you're actually, secretly going bald?
Man	No no no, definitely I'm not bald.
Interviewer	It's because of the fatness of your upper head?
Man	Yes, exactly. Because of the fact that…
Interviewer	OK. Do you mind if I just have a look?
Man	No no no, ah no ah ah ah no… No… I might, catch a cold.
SFX	Scene fades
MVO	His animal? The black-capped capuchin. Find your animal at the Perth Zoo.

Small Clawed Otter

Scene	Small room
Interviewer	So, what's it like to have such abnormally small hands?
Man (20s, Chinese)	Well… Can't play sports. Can't play basketball, volley ball – any ball.
Interviewer (concerned)	Do people take advantage of you? Or…
Man	People like to slap you because they know that you can't slap them back.
Interviewer	But what's it like with the ladies?
Man	Ahh… The nice ones, some nice looking ones sometimes they just think – aww, small hands, must be small pe-
Interviewer gasps	
Man	Personality.
Interviewer	Oh, small personality – right.
SFX	Scene fades
MVO	His animal? The small clawed otter. Find your animal at the Perth Zoo.

Little Penguin

Scene	Small room
Interviewer	I couldn't help but notice how tiny you are!
Man (30s, little person, angry)	Tiny? I can't help but notice how much of a f***wit you are!
Interviewer (concerned)	Okay, ah… Do you think it's true that shorter people are angrier?
Man (annoyed)	Ahh! What do you f***ing think!?
Interviewer	Well it's just a question.
Man	It's a f***ing sh** question.
Interviewer	I've just got another couple of questions.
Man (cutting in)	Nah nah nah, no you don't – f*** off!
Interviewer	Well look…
Man	I've had enough. Take your skinny pants and your scarf and f***ing f*** off.
SFX	Man tipping over furniture, kicking the interviewer out of his house
Interviewer	Well I'm sorry I just…
Man	Aargh, f***ing hell. F*** off!
SFX	Door slams, scene fades
MVO	His animal? The little penguin.
Man	Na na na… Lanky c**t.
MVO	Find your animal at the Perth Zoo.

Copywriters
Kurt Beaudoin
Josh Edge
Director
Ralph van Dijk
Creative Director
Craig Buchanan

Recording Engineer
Scott Collins
Producers
Tanya Carswell
Elissa Loxton
Production Company
Eardrum

Advertising Agency
The Brand Agency
Planners
Meredith Simpson
Paul Yole
Account Handler
Sharon Chalwell

Brand Marketing Manager
Carol Shannon
Client
Perth Zoo

Radio Commercials

The Brand Agency
for Perth Zoo

Find Your Animal: Black Capped Capuchin / Small Clawed Otter / Little Penguin

Radio

Birds Dropping

MVO Did you notice, the pigeon dropping, on the wind vane, on the steeple of the church, on the marketplace, in the village?

SFX Click of a digital camera

MVO Samsung NV 10. 10 million pixels. For extra high definition.

SFX Samsung jingle

Blood Vessel

MVO Did you notice, the blood vessel, in the eye, of the rabbit, in the mouth, of the snake, on the rock, of the mountain, on the left?

SFX Click of a digital camera

MVO Samsung NV 10. 10 million pixels. For extra high definition.

SFX Samsung jingle

Copywriters
Alison Anselot
Rodrigo Aranda
Gregory Ginterdaele

Creative Directors
Michel de Lauw
Jean-Paul Lefebvre
Agency Producer
Monique
Sampermans

Production Company
Sonicville
Advertising Agency
Leo Burnett Brussels

Marketing Manager
Arnold Thirion
Client
Samsung Ortmans
Brand
NV10

Radio Commercials
Leo Burnett Brussels
for Samsung Ortmans
Birds Dropping / Blood Vessel

Radio

SFX   Lots of background noise. Sounds are muted
one after the other as the voiceover mentions
them.

Man   Silence the horn.
The jackhammer.
The alarm.
The pounding.
And that mobile.
Welder, peddler,
milling machines.
The noisy toddlers,
the loudmouth teens.
Stop the bike, the motorbike
And the honking, this instant!
The automobiles,
And that little van still
driving in the distance.
Turn off the music.
Guys?
Wind... Airplane.
Shut up spot!
The humming.
The clinking.
Sshhh. Sparrows, quiet please.
And seagulls, speak no more.
There you are zebra finch,
You are the bird I've been looking for.

Use Google Search Tips. Reduce the whole
world to a single result.

Copywriter
Ergin Binyildiz
Creative Directors
Tugbay Bilbay
Ergin Binyildiz
Engin Kafadar
Tevfik Naipoglu

Agency Producer
Murat Erman
Recording Engineer
Serdar Ongoren
Advertising Agency
Grey Istanbul

Account Handlers
Tugce Cengiz
Aylin Sonmezer
Marketing Manager
Mustafa Icil
Brand Managers
Esra Guler
Eren Kantarci

Client
Google Turkey
Brand
Google

Radio Commercials

Grey Istanbul
for Google Turkey

Google Search Tips
This radio spot aims to increase the awareness and usage of Google Search Tips. It is a simple
idea where a God-like voice cancels out the sounds of typical Istanbul city life one by one until
he finds the one sound he is searching for. The original work is in Turkish; this is the English
translation. Also selected in Sound Design.

Radio

Dancer

MVO Plain Insanity by Virgin Atlantic

SFX Cuckoo clock

MVO I don't often eat caviar for breakfast. Perhaps as rarely as twice a week. But it was only Wednesday. Or Dorisday. The lady in the tutu interrupted me mid-bite. She was licking a breakfast dog. 'I was born to dance', she sang as ketchup dribbled down her chin. Her wooden leg betrayed her. I quickly changed the subject to geography. 'What's the lay of the land?' I asked. She tapped her wooden leg with the heel of her red stiletto three times. Her balance was uncanny. 'I landed this evening', she said 'first class amenities for a business class fare', she said. 'Virgin Atlantic Upper Class', she screamed, as if she had won at bingo. It was plain insanity. So I stared at her leg. Teak. Or maybe mahogany.

Dog

MVO Plain Insanity by Virgin Atlantic

SFX Cuckoo clock

MVO A dog followed me home from the supermarket eight and three-quarter days ago. Not a big dog. But not a small one either. I let it in and made a pot of tea. It didn't care for the tea, but it ate all the digestives. I drew a picture of the dog in purple crayon and placed it at the supermarket. We watched the news every night and I became quite fond of him. I called him Derrick after a bully in my school. Yesterday there was a knock at the door. 'I'm here', the woman said. 'But where have you been?' I asked. 'I'm sorry, I'm married', she said 'my husband is in London', she said 'he flew first class for a business class fare. Virgin Atlantic Upper Class', she whispered. She was plainly insane. So I gave her the dog.

Ferret

MVO Plain Insanity by Virgin Atlantic

SFX Cuckoo clock

MVO I had seen him at supermarket the week before. He had been walking a blue iguana past the cleaning products. With sunglasses on. Today it was a ferret. I made my mind up to speak to him and approached with caution having seen a documentary on ferrets the night before. 'Is it acceptable to put salt on your cornflakes?' I asked the pale man. He removed his sunglasses and winked at me with his good eye. 'I thought so', I said. The ferret looked me up and down and I could tell he was drunk. The pale man then spoke slowly in a Northern Spangalese accent. 'I recently returned from London', he said 'I flew first class for a business class fare', he said, 'Virgin Atlantic Upper Class', he said. He was plainly insane, so I smiled and gave the ferret my business card.

Child

MVO Plain Insanity by Virgin Atlantic

SFX Cuckoo clock

MVO I can't have children of my own. I have a heart condition and there's no room for them. So when the small person approached, my guard was immediately up. It clutched a plastic budgie in its small hands. 'Plinky-plonky', I said. 'Where did the ducks go?' it asked sternly. This small person wasn't joking around, it meant business and I was against the ropes. 'Ducks fly from the dew', I gasped. 'Daddy flies first class for a business class fare', it said. 'Virgin Atlantic Upper Class', it shrieked. This small person had either cunningly baffled me with its double-speak, or was plainly insane. It skipped away whistling The Eye of the Tiger.

Copywriters
Brad Reilly
Brent Singer
Creative Director
Rob McLennan
Agency Producer
Tanja Rae

Sound Engineer
Bob Rolfe
Sound Studio
First Left
Editor
Bob Rolfe

Producer
Tanja Rae
Production Company
First Left
Advertising Agency
NetworkBBDO

Account Handler
Lynda Fiebiger
Client
Virgin Atlantic

Writing

NetworkBBDO
for Virgin Atlantic

Plain Insanity – Dancer / Dog / Ferret / Child
To explain how ridiculously low the fares on Virgin Atlantic Upper Class are, we wrote a radio campaign where the entire script is completely nonsensical except for the Virgin offer.

The jury:
Alan Dye, NB: Studio (Jury Foreman)
Kjell Ekhorn, Non-Format
Frith Kerr, Studio Frith
Dave Palmer, LOVE
Greg Quinton, The Partners
Gerard Saint, Big Active
Paula Scher, Pentagram Design New York

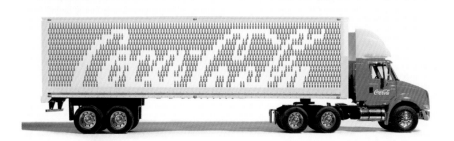

Designers
Chris Garvey
Josh Michels
Jonathan Warner
Rebecca Williams

Design Director
Sarah Moffat
Creative Directors
Bruce Duckworth
David Turner

Design Company
Turner Duckworth:
London and
San Francisco
**Senior Account
Director**
Jessica Rogers

Client
The Coca-Cola
Company
Brand
Coca-Cola

Integrated Graphics

Turner Duckworth
for Coca-Cola

The Coca-Cola Company
This redesigned packaging system returns simplicity and clarity to the Coca-Cola brand. Our design renews a spirit and aesthetic that celebrates Coke's core elements: the Spencerian script, dynamic ribbon device, and contour bottle shape. It also emphasises the positive and authentic qualities that make Coke a great brand. The new design expressed Coke's bygone imagery with a contemporary look.

Designer
Kerstin Eberbach
Art Director
Kerstin Eberbach
Creative Directors
Thomas Hofbeck
Lars Huvart

Photographer
Jo Bacherl
Copywriter
Lars Huvart
Producer
Fabian Schrader

Advertising Agency
Ogilvy Frankfurt
Art Buyers
Martina Diederichs
Caroline Walczok
Account Handlers
Marco Bisello
Sascha Riedel

Marketing Manager
Jens Helfrich
Client
IKEA Germany
Brand
IKEA

Environmental Graphics

Ogilvy Frankfurt
for IKEA Germany

Bigger Storage Ideas
German flats and apartments are full of messy corners. That's why IKEA produces practical boxes and drawers in all shapes and sizes for all storage needs. Frankfurt IKEA asked us to promote their storage solutions, targeted particularly at people living in smaller apartments, with a big outdoor idea. We played with the widely recognisable shapes and designs of the IKEA storage range and put them into a new and surprising context. By redesigning the front of an apartment building in a busy Frankfurt street with giant mock-ups of IKEA drawers and cardboard boxes, we generated the highest level of attention, and literally linked the product to where it belongs: in small flats and apartments.

Designers
Sharon Goh
Stanley Ho
Design Director
Theseus Chan

Illustrator
Joe Magee
Text & Interview
Alison Harley

**Printing &
Construction**
alsoDominie

Client
WORK
Brand
WERK Magazine

Catalogues & Brochures

Joe Magee
for WORK

WERK No.16: Joe Magee Special
A collaboration between Joe Magee and Theseus Chan, this issue presents a collection of
Magee's works. Joe Magee is an artist and film-maker who began his career making images
for newspapers, becoming a regular contributor to international publications such as The
Guardian, The New York Times and Newsweek. He has also developed a personal practice that
encompasses a range of traditional and electronic media, especially print making and moving
image works – experimenting with animation, video and interactive art.

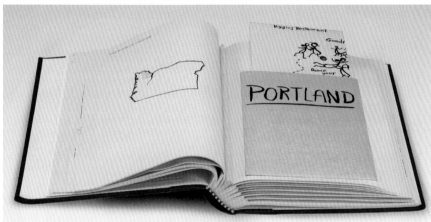

Designer
Kelly Wright
Art Director
Mira Kaddoura
Associate Creative Directors
Mira Kaddoura
Ginger Robinson

Illustrator
Justin 'Scrappers' Morrison
Photographer
Chris Mueller
Copywriters
Ginger Robinson
Alison Rusen
Image Manipulators
Frazer Goodbody
Sef McCullough

Design Group
Wieden + Kennedy Studio
Advertising Agency
Wieden + Kennedy Portland
Account Handler
Ken Smith
Brand Manager
Holly Macfee

Marketing Manager
Kevin Wright
Client
Oregon
Brand
Travel Oregon

Catalogues & Brochures

Wieden + Kennedy Portland
for Oregon

The Book of Oregon
The Book of Oregon is a limited edition hardbound book honouring the 20-year relationship between Travel Oregon and Wieden + Kennedy Portland. It is a whimsical travel guide, interweaving hand-illustrated maps of regional adventures and tales of unconventional Oregonians. Each book cover is hand silkscreened with an icon representing a natural wonder of Oregon. Inside, each chapter covers one of Oregon's regions, with portraits and stories about Oregon dreamers, from the kiteboarding daredevil of the Columbia River Gorge, to the Portland chef who led the slow food movement.

215

Graphic Design

Designers	Creative Directors	Photographers	Animation
Mark Denton	Mark Denton	Ben Moulden	A Large Evil
Dave Dye	Dave Dye	Sean de Sparengo	Corporation
Assistant Designer	Paul Silburn	**Copywriters**	**Design Company**
Oliver Carver	**Typographer**	Jonathan Benson	Coy! Communications
Art Directors	Andy Dymock	Adam Denton	**Advertising**
Chris Bowsher	**Hand Lettering**	Sean Doyle	**Agencies**
Stanley Cheung	**Artist**	Dave Dye	Dye Holloway
Daryl Corps	Alison Carmichael	Steve Howell	Murray
Mark Denton	**Illustrator**	Ben Kay	Saatchi & Saatchi
Rick Dodds	Steve Bright	Frances Leach	London
Dave Dye	**Illustration**	Dan Watts	**Client**
Rory McGaskill	A Large Evil		The Creative Circle
	Corporation		

Integrated Graphics

Coy! Communications
for The Creative Circle

The 2008 Bumper Creative Circle Campaign
The Creative Circle honours the longest running British Advertising Awards organisation.
The winning work was showcased in the 2008 annual but there was also a DVD, call for entries
material, certificates, promotional posters and other material that had to follow the same
theme. Given the importance of The Creative Circle's Britishness, it was decided to follow
the much-loved style of the traditional British comic annual.

216

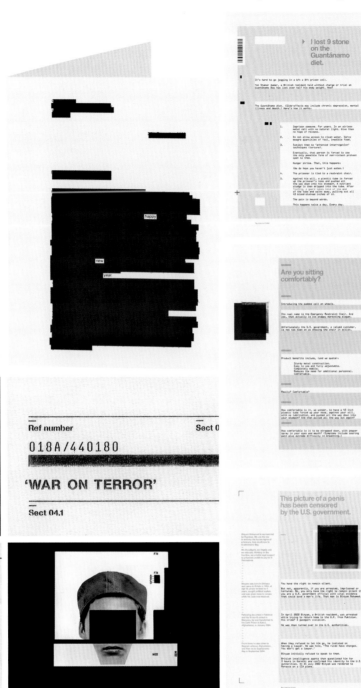

Designers
Paul Belford
Fred Birdsall
Sam Renwick
Creative Director
Paul Belford

Copywriters
Paul Belford
Pav
Thiruchelvarajah
Animator
Chris Perry

Design Group
This is Real Art
Account Handlers
George Lee
Kate Nielsen

Client Executive Director
Clare Algar
Client
Reprieve

Integrated Graphics

This is Real Art
for Reprieve

Business Cards / Diet / Censored Card / Chair / Scars / Form Film / Photofit Film
This is branding, advertising and moving image work for Reprieve, a global legal charity.

Art Director
Monika Steiner
Creative Directors
Christoph Everke
Matthias
Mittermueller
Tim Strathus

Executive Creative Director
Alex Schill
Copywriters
Tim Strathus
Mathias Woellm

Advertising Agency
Serviceplan
Account Supervisor
Alexander Monagas

Client
Das Hunger Projekt
Brand
Hungerproject

Annual Reports

Serviceplan
for Das Hunger Projekt

Ababa Banti
This business report of an African farmer – who is supported by not-for-profit organisation Hungerproject – is the perfect case study to illustrate how the project works. It was partly created to help raise more aid money.

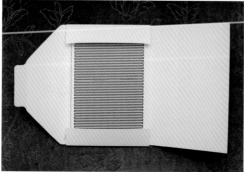

Designer
Dom Roberts
Photographer
Sam Roberts

Copywriter
Dom Roberts
Image Manipulator
Dom Roberts

Design Group
Mash
Client
Dom and Helena

Greeting Cards & Invitations

Mash
for Dom and Helena

Dom and Helena Wedding Invite
In October 2008, director of Mash, Dom Roberts, married the beautiful Helena. Dom took a week away from other projects to concentrate on creating an unusual and memorable piece for the wedding invitation. The theme: the notion of growing old together. Face shots were taken of the bride and groom which were used as a basis to create a chronological representation of their ageing faces into the future: 10, 20, 30 and 40 years into the future, growing old together. The scarily realistic results were printed in an A5 booklet on uncoated paper with thread stitching, packaged in a specially designed pack and printed with one-colour ink. Many a laugh was had by those invited to the big day.

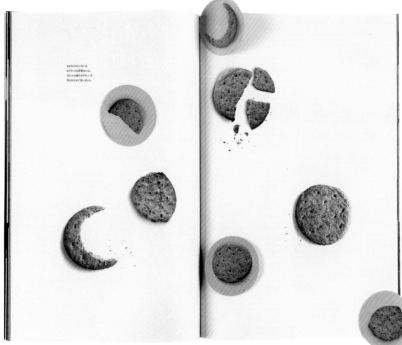

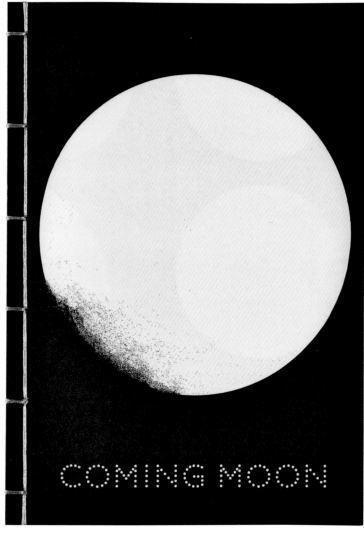

Designers	Illustrator	Advertising Agency	Clients
Yo Kimura	Chie Ichida	Dentsu Kansai	IDEE
Yoshihiro Yagi	**Copywriter**	**Account Handler**	Mitsubishi Estate
Art Director	Haruko Tsutsui	Kosaku Miyata	**Brand**
Yoshihiro Yagi	**Print Producer**		Marunouchi Cafe
	Takeshi Arimoto		

Catalogues & Brochures

Dentsu Kansai
for IDEE & Mitsubishi Estate

Coming Moon the Book

Young Japanese people are not very interested in traditional Japanese culture, such as moon viewing. Our aim was to increase the number of participants in the Coming Moon event and boost its appeal. We focused on making this traditional event, which takes place every mid-September when the moon looks most beautiful, more familiar to them. This book contains images and stories related to the moon to make the readers feel like they are moon viewing. It features 'Wolfman', who turns into a wolf when there is a full moon; 'Kaguya-hime', or the Moon Princess, a character from an old Japanese fairy tale; and 'The Space Rabbit'.

Art Director
Raj Kamble
Creative Directors
Stephen Lundberg
John Szalay
Mark Wnek

Illustrator
Lokesh Karekar
Copywriter
Raj Kamble

Advertising Agency
Lowe New York
Client
Museum of Sex

Greeting Cards & Invitations

Lowe New York
for Museum of Sex

Balloon
The brief was to create a low-budget flyer for an upcoming exhibition at the Museum of Sex called 'Exploring the Pleasure of Oral Sex'. Keeping the client's budget constraints in mind, we distributed balloons instead of flyers to promote the exhibition. After blowing into the balloon, you are able to read the address and details of the exhibition; it should also bring a smile to your face. Great curiosity was aroused when the balloons were handed out. When people blew into them, they were given a little taste of what the exhibition was all about.

Designers
Lizá Defossez
Ramalho
Artur Rebelo
Art Directors
Lizá Defossez
Ramalho
Artur Rebelo

Design Agency
R2 design
**Production
Controllers**
Pedro Ferreira
Rita João

Brand Manager
Dr Eduardo
Fernandes
Marketing Manager
Fábia Fernandes

Client
Ermida Nossa
Senhora da
Conceição

Environmental Graphics

R2 design
for Ermida Nossa Senhora da Conceição

Vai com Deus/Go with God

The Hermitage of Nossa Senhora da Conceição was built in Lisbon in 1707. Since reopening in 2008, the chapel has been used as a gallery for showcasing works by contemporary Portuguese artists. The gallery owner's aim was to make people aware of its reopening and its new purpose. What fascinated us was the chapel's original function as a place of worship. The dual presence of divinity and popular culture led us to play with idiomatic expressions that refer to God in Portuguese. The texts were read by passers-by at different rhythms over the course of the day. Composed with Knockout typeface, in the same colour and texture as their background, letters and words looked as if they were coming out from the chapel's wall.

222

Designer
Mari Kuno
Art Director
Manabu Mizuno

Creative Director
Manabu Mizuno
Photographer
Masaki Kusaka

Advertising Agency
good design
company

Client
.jp
Brand
MAMEW

Posters

good design company
for .jp

MAMEW Branding Poster Campaign
This is the campaign for a newly promoted cosmetics brand, MAMEW. The posters intend
to deliver the brand's concept: high quality cosmetics for all kinds of people regardless of
their age or style.

Designers	Creative Directors	Advertising Agency	Marketing Manager
Chris Fong	Chris Fong	McCann	Amy Wu
Nicky Sun	Nick Lim	Worldgroup Hong	**Client**
Cherry Yiu	Terry Tsang	Kong	Nike Hong Kong
Art Directors	Spencer Wong	**Account Handlers**	**Brand**
Chris Fong	**Photographer**	Calton Chu	Nike
Nicky Sun	U Hei Shing	Yen Lee	
Cherry Yiu	**Copywriters**	Penelope Yau	
	Terry Tsang	**Brand Managers**	
	Wong Wai	Mandy Liu	
		Jacqueline Tse	

Posters

McCann Worldgroup Hong Kong
for Nike Hong Kong

Paper Battlefield Campaign
Competing in and being a part of the most prestigious and competitive Nike League is the dream of every aspiring young basketball player. It is also an opportunity for the teens to show off their skills. So we took the spirit of competition and literally translated it into posters. Images of the top ten players with their individual skill were used as printing templates. The players were invited to our silkscreen workshop to print their image on top of each other. They handmade 350 posters. The posters became the battlefield; the random cross-printing, the battles. More importantly, the process conveyed our message.

225

Graphic Designer
Karla Kurz
Art Directors
Matthias Kracker
Stefan Roesinger

Creative Directors
Michael Ohanian
Jacques Pense
Copywriter
Lennart Frank

Advertising Agency
Jung von Matt
Stuttgart
Account Handlers
Ruben Ockenfels
Kerstin Stutzmann

Client
NBC Universal
Global Networks
Brand
13th Street

Integrated Graphics

Jung von Matt Stuttgart
for NBC Universal Global Networks

Horror
13th Street is Germany's most famous crime and horror channel. The brief was to design a new stationery range that goes along with 13th Street's positioning. We created bloodthirsty letterheads, envelopes, invoices and CD covers that proved 13th Street is the horror expert.

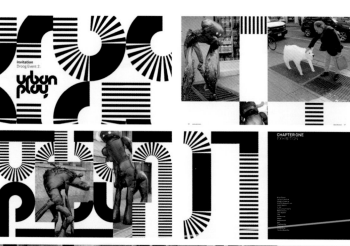

Design Thonik	**Brand Director** Renny Ramakers	**Client** Droog Design	**Brand** Urban Play

Integrated Graphics

Thonik
for Urban Play

Urban Play

Droog Design invited Thonik to structure the exhibition and design the visual communication for Urban Play, a post graffiti street art project aimed at inspiring city-dwellers to appropriate urban public space. We used the idea that typography can also be conceived as an urban game. Zebra crossings and bends can be translated into strokes and curves from which to construct an urban alphabet. This alphabet creates the visual identity of Urban Play. It links the cover and the artists' contributions in the catalogue, and fills the banners that mark the location of the art along Amsterdam's waterfront. Interpreted as three-dimensional blocks, the letters of this alphabet function as the carriers of the prints and the screens showing the exhibitors' interventions.

227

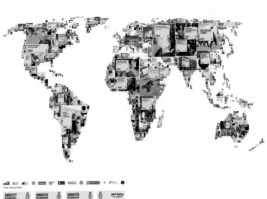

Designer	**Photography**	**Advertising Agency**	**Brand Manager**
Wolf Schneider	Flickr	Scholz & Friends	Anne-Catherine
Art Directors	Magnum Photos	Berlin	Paulisch
Vera Mueller	**Copywriter**	**Account Handler**	**Marketing Manager**
Olivier Nowak	Edgar Linscheid	Anna Kubitza	Markus N Beeko
Maria-Michaela Tonn	**Design Group**	**Brand Director**	**Client**
Kathrin Wetzel	Scholz & Friends	Penelope	Amnesty
Creative Director	Identify	Winterhager	International
Wolf Schneider	**Assisting Design**		
	Group		
	Wolf Ollins		

Integrated Graphics

Scholz & Friends Berlin
for Amnesty International

More Impact for Human Rights
The creative objective was to deliver more effectiveness in the battle for human rights through a new international visual profile for Amnesty International. The new visual identity is marked by a symbol of suppression and hope, a colour world that draws attention and expresses urgency, a documentary-style visual language, and a typeface that is suitable for conveying facts and for campaigns – promoting global identification and allowing easy applicability. During the launch process in Germany alone, all communication media were revised. All members (more than 20,000) received a simple toolkit with all the tools necessary for their day-to-day work – in the new international look.

228

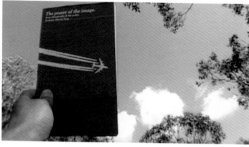

Designer
Julian Melhuish
Design Director
Julian Melhuish
Creative Director
Dave Bowman

Executive Creative Director
Steve Back
Copywriter
Julian Melhuish
Film Production
Saatchi Design

Post Production
Saatchi Design
Advertising Agency
Saatchi & Saatchi
Australia

Music Composer & Arranger
Cameron Bruce
Client
Sydney Writers'
Festival 2008

Moving Image

Saatchi & Saatchi Australia
for Sydney Writers' Festival 2008

The World, in Words
This is a trailer and ad for the Sydney Writers' Festival 2008. Writers from all over the world are invited to speak at the festival, bringing with them their individual cultural viewpoints. Book covers from other parts of the world were filmed at Sydney landmarks. This either shows an architectural parallel, or allows for a social/cultural comment. The two worlds are brought together through the medium of books.

Designers
Sharon Goh
Stanley Ho
Art Directors
Sharon Goh
Stanley Ho

Creative Director
Theseus Chan
Photographers
Clang
Lee Jen
Simon Larbalestier
Advertising Agency
WORK

Printing & Construction
alsoDominie
Marketing Manager
Valerie Chow

Client
Pedder Group
Hong Kong
Brand
Pedderzine Power

Catalogues & Brochuress

WORK
for Pedder Group Hong Kong

Pedderzine No.4: Worship Devotion Power
Pedderzine No.4: Worship Devotion Power is a tribute to what On Pedder envisions as future and cult classics. These 'artefacts' of timeless style are documented in an archaeological discovery of the past, present and future. Two different covers are dedicated to the same book; each cover reveals a different passage of time. This issue features the work of photographers Clang, Lee Jen and Simon Larbalestier.

Designers	Creative Directors	Design Group	Client
Alan Dye	Alan Dye	NB: Studio	National Portrait
Jodie Wightman	Nick Finney		Gallery
	Ben Stott		

Catalogues & Brochures

NB: Studio
for National Portrait Gallery

Wyndham Lewis Portraits

Wyndham Lewis was one of the European avant-garde's truly dynamic forces. Invited to design a promotional campaign for the exhibition 'Wyndham Lewis Portraits', we looked toward the opening salvo of the Vorticist movement, 'Blast', a publication edited and designed by Lewis. The campaign features a portrait by Lewis of his friend and champion TS Eliot, with bold, distressed wood type, and vertical and horizontal rules in homage to 'Blast'. This palette was applied across a range of promotional collateral including flyers, invites, press folders and posters. The catalogue features bold, uppercase 'wood' type, rules, punctuation and layout – evoking the striking visual aesthetic of 'Blast', while the colour palette echoes the hues found in the portraits themselves.

Designers	Copywriters	Design Group	Client
Henrik Kubel	Vesna Petresin	A2/SW/HK	Quad
Scott Williams	Robert		
	David Thorp		

Catalogues & Brochures

A2/SW/HK
for Quad

Jane and Louise Wilson

This is a publication produced to document Jane and Louise Wilson's opening show at the Quad Gallery in Derby. The cover features large type foil-blocked onto half-linen material. The 80-page hard cased, square back publication has two paper stocks, a throw-out, four-colour printing, gloss sealer and black thread stitching. Three bespoke typefaces were developed and employed throughout the design: Smith Clock Face for the essay folios; New Rail Alphabet Medium and Black for the main text and captions; and A2 Aveny-T Text for display setting.

Designers
Henrik Kubel
Scott Williams

Design Group
A2/SW/HK

Client
Danish Crafts

Catalogues & Brochures
A2/SW/HK
for Danish Crafts

CHNA TWN – LTD
This publication was produced to document the first stage of a research trip to Shanghai, Changxing and Hangzhou in China to explore craft and manufacturing. The cover features five photographs layered on top of each other as a reference to the number of participants. The 204-page publication has French folded pages, four-colour printing, a coloured foredge and Chinese binding. Three bespoke typefaces were developed and employed throughout the design: Rail Alphabet, Flavin and A2 Typewriter.

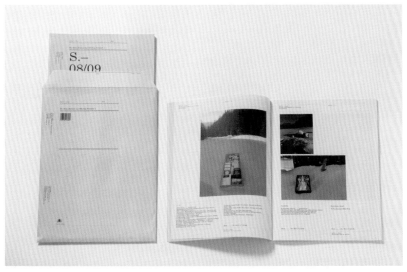

Designer
Sigi Mayer
Art Director
Sigi Mayer

Typographer
Sigi Mayer
Photographer
Horst Stasny

Copywriter
Rosa Haider-Merlicek
Brand Marketing Manager
Brigitta Zettl

Client
Brigitta Zettl

Catalogues & Brochures
Sigi Mayer
for Brigitta Zettl

SNEX
Brigitta Zettl is famous for exquisite and excellent gift boxes for fancy food. With this sales catalogue, clients order customised gift boxes which are sent by Brigitta Zettl individually to every address worldwide.

Designer	Photographer	Image Manipulator	Client
Guang Yu	Chen Man	Chen Man	adidas Originals
Art Director	**Copywriter**	**Marketing Manager**	China
Guang Yu	Chen Man	Judy Lu	**Brand**
			adidas Originals

Catalogues & Brochures

Guang Yu
for adidas Originals China

Sleek Series Limited Edition Catalogue
To me, limited edition means the possibility to create uniqueness in mass production.

Designer	Photographer	Client	Brand
Christopher Doyle	Ian Haigh	You, me and	Christopher Doyle
Creative Director	**Copywriter**	everyone I know	
Christopher Doyle	Christopher Doyle		

Catalogues & Brochures

Christopher Doyle

Christopher Doyle Identity Guidelines
Everybody defines themselves differently. My name is Christopher Doyle. I am a designer and a vegetarian. I have engaged with more identities than I can remember, but none more regularly or more intensely than my own. My identity is how I act, look, feel and sound as a person. It has taken 30 years to get to this solution. This is a guide to who I am today, and who I will be in the future. There are things I like about myself and things I hate. Things will happen to my identity that I'm not even aware of yet. I will continue to evolve. Hopefully.

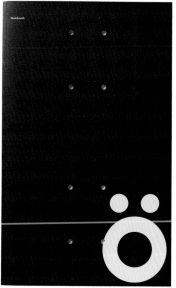

Art Director
Andreas Kittel
Creative Director
Anders Kornestedt

Photographer
Lisa Carlsson
Design Group
Happy Forsman
& Bodenfors

Account Handler
Linda Almström
Brand Marketing Manager
Ted Hesselblom

Client
Röhsska Museum

Catalogues & Brochures

Happy Forsman & Bodenfors
for Röhsska Museum

Skateboard
The Röhsska Museum's exhibition 'Skateboards' tells the story of what was once an underground lifestyle. The clean and simple catalogue is a contrasting complement to the multitude of colours and forms in the exhibition. Still, some design elements firmly anchor the catalogue in the world of skateboarding. The 'anti-slip' cover surface and eight unmistakable holes, together with an extra pair of wheels, turn the catalogue into a board for the extreme skater.

Designer
Qing Zhao

Client
Hanqingtang Design

Catalogues & Brochures

Qing Zhao
for Hanqingtang Design

07/70 Poster / 07/70 Posters Book
The 07/70 set of graphics was created for a poster exhibition. The range included the 07/70 logo, an invitation for the exhibition and the 07/70 poster album. The exhibition displayed 70 posters altogether, which is the meaning of this set of images. The invitation is a folded one; for the thread-stitched 07/70 poster album, the spine of the album is exposed to express a sense of clumsiness.

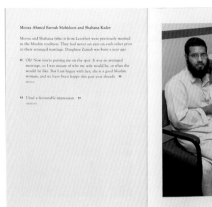

Designer
Garth Walker
Typographer
Garth Walker

Photographer
Garth Walker
Copywriter
Travis Lyle

Design Group
Mister Walker
Translator
Steven Kotze

Client
Henk and Wendy
Duys

Catalogues & Brochures
Mister Walker
for Henk and Wendy Duys

Home Affairs
This is a memento booklet narrating the various events on the day the designer/photographer and his wife were married at the offices of the Department of Home Affairs in Durban, South Africa. It features portraits and interviews with couples who were also married on Friday 15 August 2008 at the same place. The booklet was distributed to family and friends who attended the ceremony and to those who were unable to attend, both locally and in Europe.

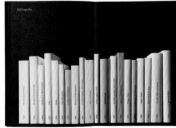

Designers
Ellen Diedrich
Astrid Stavro

Art Director
Astrid Stavro

Design Agency
Studio Astrid Stavro

Clients
Palau Robert
Generalitat de
Catalunya

Catalogues & Brochures
Studio Astrid Stavro
for Generalitat de Catalunya

Mercè Rodoreda, The Death of Innocence
The four major novels of celebrated Catalan novelist Mercè Rodoreda formed the theme of this exhibition. The exhibition was divided into four rooms, each dedicated to a novel. We assigned a colour to each novel/room, and used the number four as the basis for the graphic identity of the exhibition. The catalogues were in Catalan, Spanish, French and English. When placed together, the title of the exhibition can be read across the four covers. The catalogue had to inspire visitors to read Rodoreda's novels; we created models of her novels, photographed them and placed them inside the catalogue, so reading it would be like reading the novels.

234

Designer	Creative Director	Advertising Agency	Marketing Manager
Merle Schröder	Uli Gürtler	gürtlerbachmann	Prof Dr Björn
Art Director	**Copywriter**	Werbung	Bloching
Merle Schröder	Anke Gröner	**Account Handler**	**Client**
		Sharifa Hawari	Roland Berger
			Strategy Consultants

Catalogues & Brochures

gürtlerbachmann Werbung
for Roland Berger Strategy Consultants

Every Story Has a Beginning
Roland Berger Strategy Consultants is the biggest corporate and strategy consultant in Europe, and is always looking for new potential. But talents are often the target of many companies and can choose between various job offers. A convincing look as an employer brand was needed to recruit competent staff. A high-quality, meticulously designed book and slipcase were developed to assist in recruiting. Designed like old books, with the motto 'Every story has a beginning', first sentences of famous works are cited. After many first sentences, which resemble the beginnings of outstanding tales, the reader is invited to start his own story at Roland Berger.

Designer	Photographers	Design Group	Client
Michael C Place	Max Akkerman	Build	Generation Press
Art Director	Rick Guest	**Publisher**	**Brand**
Richard Bull	**Copywriters**	Generation Yacht	Not For Commercial
Creative Director	Nicola Place		Use
Michael C Place	Adrian Shaughnessy		

Catalogues & Brochures

Build
for Generation Press

Paste Catalogue
Not For Commercial Use is an ongoing promotional campaign by Build for the printers Generation Press. 'Paste' is the first part of the campaign; an exploration of the relationship of print and graphic design, and the response it can provoke from idle passers-by in the street. 'Paste' was disparate in its nature, including a series of postcards, posters, postings, pastings, mailouts and virals which were at best ephemeral and at worst unseen. Everything pointed to a website but nobody knew what notforcommercialuse.com was about. The 'Paste' catalogue was designed as the final revelation. Nothing in the series, including the catalogues, was sold, holding true to the project manifesto that everything should be 'Not For Commercial Use'.

Art Director
Yasemin Heimann
Creative Directors
Martin Breuer
Martin Venn

**Chief Creative
Officer**
Felix Glauner
Copywriter
Harald Linsenmeier

Advertising Agency
Euro RSCG
Duesseldorf
Account Handler
Harald Jaeger

Marketing Manager
Kathrin Kleinjung
Client
Quirin Bank

Catalogues & Brochures
Euro RSCG Duesseldorf
for Quirin Bank

Hide-and-Seek Booklet
Many banks keep their clients in the dark about their own allowances. They hide due charges and commissions in the fine print, or do not repay so-called kickbacks. To show that the Quirin Bank is different, the agency was asked to unveil questionable methods in the banking sector in an ironic and entertaining way. To explain the banks' common tricks to the clients, the agency created a booklet called 'The most popular hide-and-seek games in private banking' – complete with instructions for bankers and a request asking the client to become a spoilsport.

Designers
Emma Morton
Steve Owen
Adam Rix
Ravi Sohanpal
Art Director
Adam Rix
Creative Director
Phil Skegg
Creative Heads
Simon Griffin
Adam Rix

Typographers
Emma Morton
David Palmer
Phil Skegg
Rory Sutherland
Illustrators
Emma Morton
Tim Sinclair
Photographers
Mark Ingram
John Morrison
Tim Sinclair

Photographers
Jane Stockdale
Luke Watson
Ben Wedderburn
Copywriter
Simon Griffin
Artworker
Jonathan Robertson
Design Group
LOVE

Account Handlers
Sarah Benson
Ali Johnson
**Production
Managers**
Jason Munslow
Shelley Wood
Client
Silver Cross

Catalogues & Brochures
LOVE
for Silver Cross

It's a Boy/It's a Girl
This book was designed and written not only to showcase Silver Cross products, but also to reflect their ethos of 'passionate about parenting' by giving expectant parents a few lighthearted tips and advice.

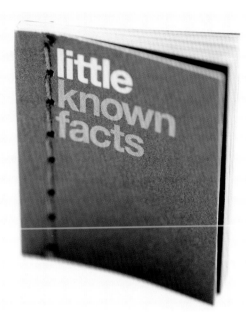

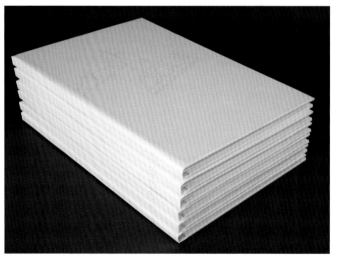

Designer	Creative Director	Copywriter	Client
Mark Lester	Mark Lester	Mark Lester	Wigan Little Theatre
Assistant Designer	**Illustrators**	**Design Group**	
Daniel Ingham	Daniel Ingham	MARK	
	Mark Lester		

Catalogues & Brochures

MARK
for Wigan Little Theatre

Wigan Little Theatre Brochure
Most organisations want communications that make them look bigger than they really are. Not this one. For one of Britain's best and longest established amateur theatres, thinking small was the obvious way to go.

Designer	Creative Director	Production	Client
Nicole Jacek	Ian Anderson	Darren Pascoe	Yorkshire Sculpture
Art Director	**Photographer**		Park
Nicole Jacek	Jonty Wilde		**Brand**
			Sarah Staton

Catalogues & Brochures

Nicole Jacek
for Sarah Staton

Shucks, Sucks, Sticks, Stacks
This book was designed to accompany Sarah Staton's exhibition 'Shucks, Sucks, Sticks, Stacks' at the Yorkshire Sculpture Park in Wakefield, UK; a representation of Staton's fluid approach. The 'Y' of 'CMYK' was replaced with a fluorescent yellow to pump up the intensity of the printed image – an expression of the ultramodernsupersurreal hypercolourful ambition of the art, combined with a conceptual and physical experience of the colour, book-ended with a clean palette. The Headline Font 'Line 433' was custom made for this book.

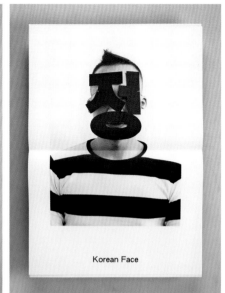

Type Faces

Japanese Face

Korean Face

Designers
Chiung-Hu Chiu
Ken-Tsai Lee
Creative Director
Ken-Tsai Lee

Illustrator
Ken-Tsai Lee
Photographer
Chiung-Hu Chiu

Copywriter
Ken-Tsai Lee
Design Group
ken-tsai lee design
studio

Client
Harvest
Brand
Ken-Tsai Lee

Catalogues & Brochures

ken-tsai lee design studio
for Harvest

Type Faces
This brochure accompanied my show, the theme was 'Type Faces'.

Designer
Mike Roberts
Art Director
Mike Roberts
Creative Directors
Ben Casey
Steve Royle

Typographer
Mike Roberts
Photographer
Guy Farrow
Copywriter
Lionel Hatch

Image Manipulator
Mike Roberts
Print Producer
Duarte Goncalves
Design Group
The Chase

Account Handler
Eileen O'Leary
Brand Manager
Steve Mapley
Client
The Manchester and
Cheshire Dogs'
Home

Catalogues & Brochures

The Chase
for The Manchester and
Cheshire Dogs' Home

Dogs Home
The Manchester and Cheshire Dogs' Home required a document that outlined the positive work the organisation had been doing. They had a new initiative that tackled not only the welfare of stray and abandoned dogs but also the causes of abandonment, through offering training, education and support, and working with owners to help keep dogs in a loving home. The report also needed to encourage people to support the charity. In order to strike a chord with the public and get them to relate to the plight of the dogs, we drew parallels with the suffering of human homelessness. The photographic stories give the dogs an almost human characteristic and, in turn, can be linked to the new initiatives.

238

Designers
David Simpson
Anthony Smith
Typographer
Jon Hatton

Producer
Matthew Beardsell
Design Group
Music

Brand Manager
Matt Lowery
Client
Manchester City
Football Club

Brand
City in the
Community

Catalogues & Brochures

Music
for Manchester City Football Club

City in the Community CSR Report
Manchester City Football Club has the best track record for community initiated projects in the premiership. The CSR report was an opportunity for the club to let stakeholders and supporters know what it has been up to. By scaling the report up to a broadsheet and using bold imagery we produced a document that was as accessible as it was engaging. What was initially a 'side project' was transformed into a flagship piece for the club.

Designer
Naomi Hirabayashi
Art Director
Naomi Hirabayashi

Photographer
Yasutomo Ebisu

Stylist
Miyoko Okao

Client
minä perphonen

Catalogues & Brochures

Naomi Hirabayashi
for minä perphonen

Monkicho
This is a mail-order catalogue for customers who cannot reach minä perphonen's shop.
To give customers an idea of the real thing, a selection of fabrics used for this season's products have been sewn onto the back of the cover. Also attached are the care instruction tags for the various fabrics. The book has been designed so that when it is closed, only the threads sewn in are visible.

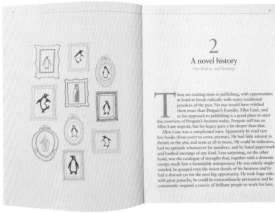

Designers
Heather Briggs
Robert Riche
Design Director
Robert Riche
Illustrators
Heather Briggs
Robert Riche

Copywriter
Duncan Campbell-Smith
Design Group
Radley Yeldar
Account Handler
Simon Hutley

Head of Corporate Communications
Rebecca Sinclair
Director of Marketing & Publicity
Joanna Prior

Client
Penguin Group
Brand
Penguin

Catalogues & Brochures
Radley Yeldar
for Penguin Group

The Book of Penguin
Founded in 1935, Penguin is one of the world's best-loved brands. To celebrate this, Penguin wanted to create a book that explains the international group, inspires employees, authors and partners, and encourages pride in the past and excitement about the future. The Book of Penguin is intentionally a book (not a website, blog or podcast). Its subtle, booky style uses gentle humour with simple, brand-based illustrations echoing the 'dignified, but flippant' character of the company. While it is a celebration, the calm tone reflects the aim to quietly inspire, not to lecture or boast.

Designers
Suck Zoo Han
Brian E Smith
Patrick Tobin

Art Director
Michael J Walsh
Creative Director
Anthony P Rhodes

Design Group
Visual Arts Press

Client
School of Visual Arts

Catalogues & Brochuress
Visual Arts Press
for School of Visual Arts

SVA Undergraduate Catalogue
The objective of the School of Visual Arts' undergraduate catalogue, 'Proof', is to show prospective students why SVA is the pre-eminent training ground for the next generation of artists. We wanted to prove that SVA, located in New York City, is the best art school to attend. Our solution was to present visual and factual evidence, first by giving dozens of facts about New York City, SVA and its students, then by presenting literally hundreds of examples of student work throughout the book, setting a new standard for publications of this kind.

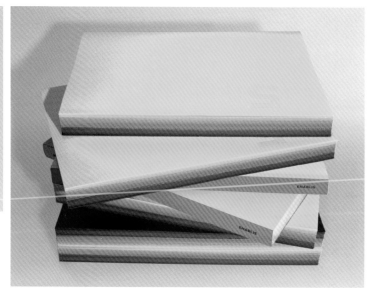

Designers
Isabelle Allard
Julie Brassard
Art Director
Julie Brassard
Creative Director
Barbara Jacques

Copywriter
Patrice Dancziger
Image Manipulator
Daniel Cartier
Producer
Louis Dorval

Design Group
Identica
Printing
Litho Acme

Client Chief
Executive Officer
Charles Sirois
Client
Enablis

Annual Reports

Identica
for Enablis

High 5
Enablis is a not-for-profit organisation that helps African entrepreneurs establish their projects in south and central Africa. The colour spectrum used in the annual report reflects the diversity of this exceptional part of the world.

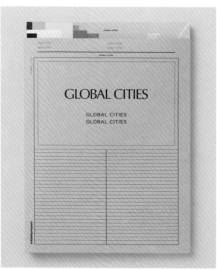

Art Directors
Oskar Andersson
Pascal Prosek
Creative Directors
Lisa Careborg
Anders Kornestedt

Photographers
Helene Binet
Oriana Elicabe
Design Agency
Happy Forsman &
Bodenfors

Account Handler
Robert Axner
Brand Marketing
Manager
Bitte Nygren

Client
The Swedish
Museum of
Architecture

Annual Reports

Happy Forsman & Bodenfors
for The Swedish Museum of Architecture

Global Cities
The Swedish Museum of Architecture invited 15 architects and journalists to write on the topic of global cities. Inspired by the modern, crowded city, the book branches out in different visual directions, yet the design is tightly held together by a strict grid.

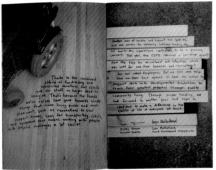

Annual Reports

WAX
for Calgary Society for Persons with Disabilites

Art Director
Jonathan Herman
Creative Directors
Monique Gamache
Joe Hospodarec

Photographer
Justen Lacoursiere
Copywriter
Saro Ghazarian

Design Group
WAX
Printing
Blanchette Press

Client
Calgary Society for
Persons
with Disabilites

CSPD 2008 Annual Report
To express the significance of fundraising on a human level, the entire annual report was written by hand on objects that were purchased from fundraising efforts to help people living with disabilities.

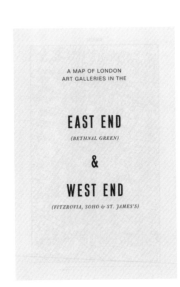

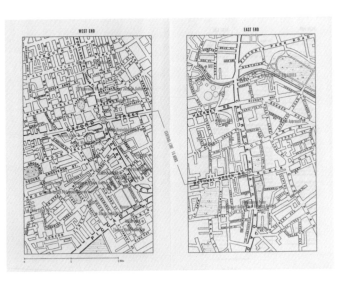

Leaflets

Fraser Muggeridge Studio
for London Art Galleries

Designer
Stephen Barrett

Art Director
Fraser Muggeridge

Design Group
Fraser Muggeridge
Studio

Clients
London Art Galleries

A Map of London Art Galleries
The map of London art galleries was designed to encourage gallery visitors to travel between the East End and West End of London. By visually linking the two walkable areas via the Central line they became directly connected, motivating people to travel between them. Coupled with the paring down of information is a sense of care and attention to detail that evokes value and integrity from a seemingly humble object.

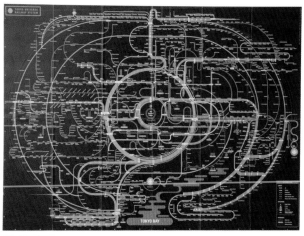

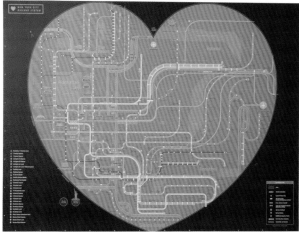

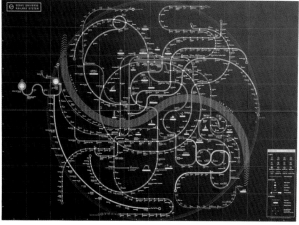

Designer
Sol Jin
Art Director
Ji-hwan Kim
Design Director
Ji-hwan Kim

Design Consultant
Yun-sung Kim
Creative Director
Ji-hwan Kim
Illustrator
Sol Jin

Copywriter
Da-hyung Han
Image Manipulator
Ji-hwan Kim

Design Group
ZERO PER ZERO
Supporting Design Group
Knock Creative

Leaflets

ZERO PER ZERO
for City Railway System

Tokyo Railway System / New York City Railway System / Seoul Railway System
CityRailway System is a new approach to projecting the identity of a city onto its subway map. Whereas standard subway maps aim to convey information as clearly and concisely as possible, City Railway System by ZERO PER ZERO is distinguished by grafting symbolic elements of each city onto the map, while also preserving clarity. We introduced the traditional heart shape from Milton Glaser's I LOVE NY logo as the symbol for New York City. For Seoul, we chose the representation of the Han River as the curvature in the Tae-Geuk mark of the national flag of Korea, and for Tokyo, the sun disc of the Japanese national flag. The railway map itself is also a good souvenir.

Calendars

Codesign
for Antalis Hong Kong

Antalis 2009 Calendar
This calendar is a cute miniature of a pallet of printed sheets – the most typical of what you can see in printing workshops. The wooden pallet was made with reference to the real thing. The page layout of the calendar mimics a magazine printed sheet; the 365 sheets contain 365 days of the year stacked up on three wooden pallet boards (four months in each pile), one arranged on top of another. A small batch of sticker notes is enclosed for users to attach to important dates. The notes will look exactly like a pile of printed sheets on which pressmen have marked advances.

Designer	**Photographer**	**Design Group**	**Client**
Christy Chen	Kwan Kai Wing	Codesign	Antalis Hong Kong
Design Directors	**Copywriters**	**Marketing Manager**	**Brand**
Hung Lam	Christy Chen	Miranda Hui	Antalis
Eddy Yu	Alice Lee		

Calendars

Eric Chan Design
for Polytrade Paper Corporation

Polytrade Diary 2009
The 'Love. Cover. Hong Kong' diary is a tribute to Hong Kong. The designer used various book covers to illustrate different people's individual stories. We witness the stories of the band maniacs, café owners and a young girl training hard to be a swimmer. We share the love between father and son, unity between school-master and his students. We sense the aroma of the fruit market, and hunger for the Chinese roast poultry, traditional bakeries and the wonton noodle. We also mourn for the closing of an 80-year-old grocery store. The designer aims to remind people about environmental protection, and the importance of preserving tradition and caring for people.

Designers	**Typographers**	**Image Manipulators**	**Client**
Eric Chan	Jim Wong	Jim Wong	Polytrade Paper
Jim Wong	Iris Yu	Iris Yu	Corporation
Art Directors	**Photographer**	**Design Group**	**Brand**
Eric Chan	Thomas Ng	Eric Chan Design	Polytrade Paper
Jim Wong	**Copywriters**	**Marketing Manager**	
Iris Yu	Cat Tyrell	Venus Ng	
Creative Director	Fiona Wan		
Eric Chan			

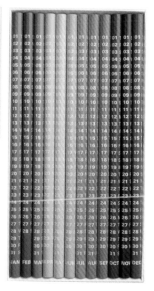

Designers
Keith Hancox
Matt Michaluk
Creative Director
Bob Mytton

Copywriter
Tom Chesher
Print Producer
Keith Lunt

Design Group
Mytton Williams
Paper Supplier
Naomi Lighter

Client
Mytton Williams

Calendars

Mytton Williams

Pencil Calendar
We wanted to create this year's calendar using the designer's most important tool: the pencil. From this initial idea, the concept of a tactile, interactive pencil calendar developed. The resulting calendar consists of 12 colour coded pencils indicating the seasons of the year. The close-fitting pencil box carries the message '12 pencils, 365 days. Infinite creative possibilities'. No further packaging is required for posting. Promotionally, the opportunity to sharpen off 365 days gives the Mytton Williams name maximum exposure.

Art Directors
Ivo Hlavac
Christian Sommer
Creative Directors
Florian Drahorad
Helmut Huber

Executive Creative Directors
Matthias Harbeck
Alex Schill
Photography
Layoutsatz 2000

Copywriter
Nicolas Becker
Advertising Agency
Serviceplan
Production Company
Pinsker Druck und
Medien

Account Supervisor
Lena Inderwiesen
Client
Wuesthof

Calendars

Serviceplan
for Wuesthof

Onion Calendar
Wuesthof knives are among the sharpest on the market. In fact, they're so sharp and cut so precisely that they can cut an onion into 365 slices. As it happens, that's exactly the same number as there are days in the year. The perfect product for a tear-off calendar.

245

Designers
Ben Christie
Jamie Ellul
Tommy Taylor
Creative Directors
David Azurdia
Ben Christie
Jamie Ellul

Photographer
Tommy Taylor
Photography
Fotolia

Copywriters
Ben Christie
Jamie Ellul
Tommy Taylor
Design Group
Magpie Studio

Brand Manager
Phil LeMonde
Client
Gavin Martin
Associates

Direct Mail
Magpie Studio
for Gavin Martin Associates

Gavin Martin Vegetable Ink Mailer
When award-winning printer Gavin Martin Associates introduced vegetable inks, they were keen to share the news – and reassure customers that their high standards wouldn't be compromised. Magpie Studio's solution consists of a giant vegetable complete with a first place rosette to carry all the details. And because it hit the market just before Halloween, they plumped for a giant pumpkin.

Designer
Leon Bahrani
Design Director
Robert Ball

Creative Director
Greg Quinton
Photographer
Louis Wilson

Copywriter
Robert Ball
Design Group
The Partners

Project Director
Hannah Kirkman
Client
Thrislington Cubicles

Direct Mail
The Partners
for Thrislington Cubicles

Physical Education
The brief was to promote a range of Thrislington toilet cubicles to busy headteachers, who are inundated with marketing material from other manufacturers. 15,000 blank schoolbooks were printed with Thrislington's no-nonsense manifesto and sent directly to headteachers. Unlike the competition, the books don't portray an idealised world, but empathise with real issues and illustrate how to solve them practically. The approach is humorous, gets to the point and cuts the crap.

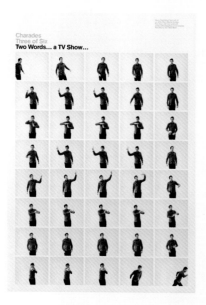

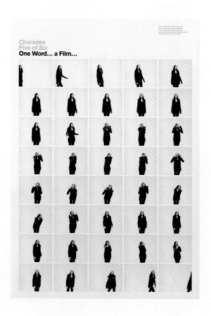

Designers
Graham Birch
Stuart Radford
Victoria Walmsley
Mark Wood

Creative Directors
Stuart Radford
Andrew Wallis
Typographer
Stuart Radford

Design Group
Radford Wallis
Client
Radford Wallis

Greeting Cards & Invitations
Radford Wallis

Radford Wallis Christmas Card 2008
For our 2008 Christmas card, we took inspiration from the traditional Christmas game of
charades. Members of the team acted out the title of a famous book, film or TV show. The
footage was broken down over 40 frames to create a series of posters. As in the conventional
game of charades, recipients were encouraged to guess the answers. A supporting webpage
featured clues, answers and the animations.

Art Directors
Charlie Thomas
Mia Wallenius
Creative Director
Alexander McQueen

Photographer
Gary Hulyer
Image Manipulator
James Hackworthy
Design Group
Gucci Group

Account Handler
James Fooks-Bale
Corporate Image Director
Annie Leonard

Brand Manager
Janet Fischgrund
Marketing Manager
Preia Narendra
Client
Alexander McQueen

Greeting Cards & Invitations

Gucci Group
for Alexander McQueen

Fashion Show Invite SS09
This is the invitation for Alexander McQueen's Spring/Summer 09 fashion show. A lenticular printed piece was utilised to morph two portraits, one of the designer and one of a mercury skull. The objective was to communicate the show's concept of 'evolution'.

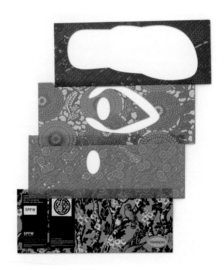

Art Director
Eric Benitez
Creative Director
Marcos Sulzbacher

Typographers
José Roberto
Bezerra
Marcos Souza
Advertising Agency
AlmapBBDO

Account Supervisor
Cristina Chacon
Marketing Manager
Carla Schmitzberger

Client
São Paulo
Alpargatas
Brand
Havaianas

Greeting Cards & Invitations

AlmapBBDO
for Havaianas

SPFW Invitation
The brief was to draw attention to Havaianas during São Paulo Fashion Week in a way that would fit with the theme. We designed an invitation to the Havaianas lounge, based on a tribute to the 100th anniversary of Japanese immigration, the theme of fashion week. The invitation was printed on Japanese paper. The use of the tattoo was mandatory to enter the lounge. Written on the envelope in Japanese was, 'São Paulo Fashion Week. Havaianas, we love you'.

Designers
Felipe Caldas
Ana Camargo
Claudia Niemeyer
Assistant Designer
Bruno Senise

Creative Director
Fred Gelli
Photographer
Guido Paternó
Castello
Artworker
Fabricio Menezes

Producer
Luciana Moletta
Production Manager
Anderson Marciano
Design Group
Tátil Design

Client
Tátil Design
Brand
Designing Naturally

Greeting Cards & Invitations

Tátil Design

Natural Medium
At Cannes Lions 2008, our agency presented the 'Designing Naturally' workshop, which discussed the role of design as a tool to transform the future. For our invitations, we asked our team to select images that, along with the time and date of our workshop, were laser printed on fallen leaves collected from the streets of Rio de Janeiro. Simple, different, meant to be looked at against sunlight – our invitation became a new medium, a flyer that is actually supposed to be thrown away on the ground. Paint free, borrowed from nature for a purpose then returned to it.

Designers	**Paper Engineer**	**Producers**	**Design Group**
David Simpson	Phil Skegg	Matthew Beardsell	Music
Anthony Smith		Jon Hatton	

Greeting Cards & Invitations

Music

Music Christmas Cards
Our objective was to create a Christmas card to keep Music in the minds of both clients and peers. We used the sleeves from recycled vinyl records to add a touch of sparkle and create an eco-friendly Christmas card.

Designers	Creative Directors	Illustrators	Design Group
Nick Finney	Alan Dye	Paul Bower	NB: Studio
Daniel Lock	Nick Finney	Anthony Burrill	**Client**
Ben Stott	Ben Stott	Billie Jean	NB: Studio
		James Joyce	

Greeting Cards & Invitations

NB: Studio

This Year... 2009
This is the second in the series 'This Year...' conceived as an annual New Year mailer from NB: Studio. We asked four illustrators to put a positive spin on the gloomy news surrounding the global economic meltdown. Each design was then lovingly screenprinted over the top of a real dollar bill to create a set of four limited edition prints signed by the artists. Each illustrator responded in a completely different way: James Joyce put a smile on George Washington's face; Billie Jean highlighted the biggest political event for over 40 years; Anthony Burrill gave an optimistic call to arms; and Paul Bower defaced the note with some irreverent playground humour.

Designer
Paul Pateman
Art Director
Paul Pateman
Creative Director
Paul Brazier

**Creative Group
Heads**
Mike Nicholson
Paul Pateman
Illustrator
Paul Pateman

Copywriter
Mike Nicholson
Advertising Agency
Abbott Mead Vickers
BBDO

Account Handler
James Drummond
Client
Museum of
Childhood

Greeting Cards & Invitations
Abbott Mead Vickers BBDO
for Museum of Childhood

Top to Toe
The brief was to get the public to visit the Museum of Childhood's 'Top to Toe: Fashion for Kids'
exhibition. We designed a traditional mix-and-match book, which was used as promotional DM
and invitations to the launch night. The book enabled recipients to mix and match historical
outfits featured in the Museum, before inviting them to visit the exhibition.

Designers
Miho Aishima
Michael Johnson

Design Director
Michael Johnson

Design Group
johnson banks

Client
johnson banks

Greeting Cards & Invitations
johnson banks

Recycled Christmas Cards
Every year the designer Christmas card is a design trial. Now we've set another challenge: how
green can we make it? For the second year running we've ram-punched the unused magazines
in the studio; this year we made angels from old copies of 'Mojo', 'Design Week', 'The
Economist' and anything else we had lying around.

Designer
Morag Myerscough
Furniture Designers
Luke Morgan
Morag Myerscough
Artist
Luke Morgan

Typographer
Morag Myerscough
Signwriter
Morag Myerscough
Assistant Signwriter
Charlotte Read

Project Director
Martyn Evans
Design Studio
Studio Myerscough

Client
The Cathedral Goup
Brand
The Deptford Project

Environmental Graphics

Studio Myerscough
for The Cathedral Group

The Deptford Project
In summer 2008, an old 60s 35-tonne commuter train carriage was converted into an unusual café installed in a derelict railway site in Deptford High Street, South London. Morag Myerscough was responsible for the creative concept and realisation of the graphics, interior, furniture and external platform garden. The carriage's hand-decorated exterior depicts playful images and words inspired by local history, trains and tea – denoting the ship building industry, marine rope-making and the livestock originally transported to Smithfield on the railway. The bespoke furniture was made from recycled laboratory tops and hand-painted stools with sitting-related slogans. The loo, by artist Luke Morgan, is a shrine to Elvis set in a garden shed.

Designer
Neil Hedger

Typographer
Neil Hedger

Production Manager
Gary Morris

Client
Mimi Hajime Ueoka

Stationery
Neil Hedger
for Mimi Hajime Ueoka

Mimi Hajime Ueoka Drum Tuition
Mimi Hajime Ueoka, a professional drum tutor from Japan, now has a business card that he can throw into the crowd. His details are laser cut into wooden chopsticks to create a memorable communication that prospective students can even practise with.

Designer
Mark Lester
Creative Director
Mark Lester

Typographers
Daniel Ingham
Mark Lester
Design Group
MARK

Brand Manager
Cathy Bolton
Marketing Manager
Jon Atkin

Client
Manchester
Literature Festival

Stationery
MARK
for Manchester Literature Festival

Manchester Literature Festival
Manchester Literature Festival is an annual and innovative celebration of new writing which takes place across the city every year. Manchester Literature Festival wanted an iconic identity that would raise brand awareness amongst potential new audiences and funders. Also selected in Logos & Typefaces.

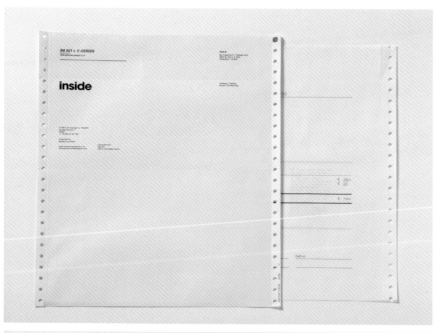

Designer	Copywriter	Client	Brand
Sigi Mayer	Sigi Mayer	Marcus Gruze	wine
Art Director	**Marketing Manager**		
Sigi Mayer	Carina Gruze		

Stationery

Sigi Mayer
for Marcus Gruze

inside
The brief was to create a new identity for a winemaker. The young owners are brother and sister; they started the business in Carinthia without any experience, against the advice of many in the area. They know the risks, but are determined to create the best wine on Earth.

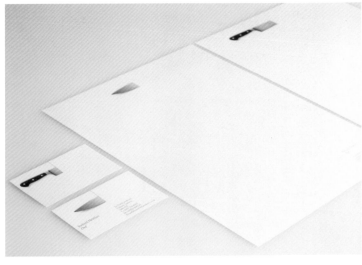

Designer
Mark Smith
Creative Director
Mark Smith

Photographer
Nahim Afzal

Design Group
Marksmith

Client
Richard McLellan

Stationery
Marksmith
for Richard McLellan

Chef
Chef Richard McLellan has worked for some of London's finest restaurateurs, including Marco Pierre White and Tom Aikens. Richard recently started to work as a consultant chef and asked us to come up with an identity for him. We used his knife to create a bold but witty stationery range.

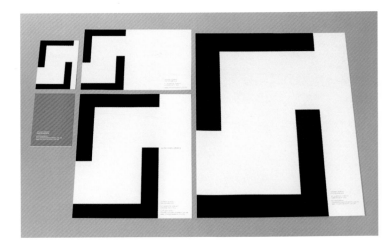

Designers
Kevin Lee
Matt Maurer

Creative Director
Ady Bibby
Photographer
Stuart Hendry

Design Group
True North
Producer
Frank Highlight

Production
APG Highlight
Client
Stuart Hendry

Stationery
True North
for Stuart Hendry

Stuart Hendry
After a number of years as a faithful assistant, Stuart Hendry was ready to offer the world his own photographic skills. But first he needed a bold, iconic identity to put his name on the map. A set of photographer's 'L's did the job in a quite unexpected way.

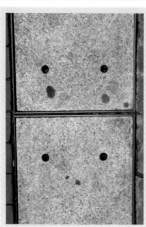

Henry Iddon
Photographer

14 Arrowsmith Gardens
Cleveleys
Lancashire
FY5 2RS
+44 (0) 7976 375013
hv.henryiddon.con
www.henryiddon.con

Designer
Mark Lester
Creative Director
Mark Lester

Photographer
Henry Iddon
Artworker
Daniel Ingham

Design Group
MARK

Client
Henry Iddon
Photography

Stationery

MARK
for Henry Iddon Photography

Henry Iddon
Henry Iddon is an internationally renowned photographer. Universally known as 'H', his
nickname proved to be the inspiration for the new identity.

Designer
Amresh Mondkar
Creative Director
Joby George

Chief Creative Officers
Vitthal Deshmukh
John Mani

Copywriter
John Mani
Advertising Agency
The Classic
Partnership
Advertising Dubai

Client
Prasad Karmarkar

Stationery

The Classic Partnership Advertising – Dubai
for Prasad Karmarkar

Tearproof
Our client, Mr Prasad Karmarkar, conducts anger management courses. We created this 'tearproof' business card to help him promote his services. On receiving the card, the recipient is urged to tear it, but is unable to. In failing to tear the card, he gets frustrated and angry.

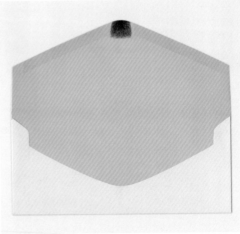

Art Director
Federico Callegari

Creative Directors
David Angelo
Colin Jeffery

Advertising Agency
David&Goliath

Client
Coco de Mer

Stationery

David&Goliath
for Coco de Mer

Coco de Mer
This envelope was created to extend the Coco de Mer brand personality and voice into its stationery. As a high-end erotic boutique known for being unabashedly provocative, is it any surprise that their envelopes are sexually suggestive? After all, Coco de Mer is in the business of turning people on.

Designers
David Simpson
Anthony Smith

Producer
Matthew Beardsell

Design Group
Music

Music

Music Business Cards
We wanted to produce a business card that would create an impression, no matter who the recipient was. The cards are laser cut from recycled vinyl, and each employee chose his or her top 12 tunes.

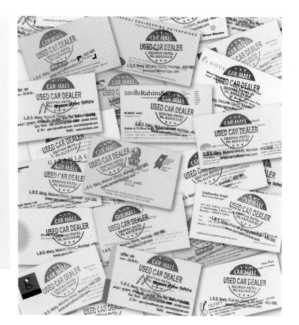

Designer
Bryan Elijah
Art Director
Bryan Elijah

Design Directors
Vikram Gaikwad
Sajan Raj Kurup
Creative Directors
Vikram Gaikwad
Anu Joseph
Sajan Raj Kurup

Copywriter
Sajan Raj Kurup
Advertising Agency
Creativeland Asia

Brand Manager
Deepak Patel
Client
Car Mall Used Cars

Creativeland Asia
for Car Mall Used Cars

Used Cards
The objective was to communicate the client's business of buying and selling used cars in an innovative and memorable way. Given the economic conditions, this had to be done in the most cost-effective way too. The card had to create a lot of buzz and word of mouth for the business. Since the client dealt with used cars, we decided to create used cards. The idea was to take the old visiting cards of random people and overwrite them with the Car Mall Used Cars seal. The cards were welcomed with surprise, and recall of the store went up by 40 per cent compared to other secondhand car stores in Mumbai. None of the card recipients forgot Car Mall.

Stationery

Creativeland Asia
for Indiana Motors

Spanner
Millions of cards are handed out every year. Most of them end up in trash cans or plastic folders, never to be looked at again. We wanted to design a card that a person would hold on to, and as such decided to give it a purpose other than just being a business card. Our idea was to create fabricated metal cards that doubled up as a spanner. Along with carrying the details of our client, they could be of use if you needed to change a tyre or tighten a loose nut.

Designer Vikram Gaikwad	**Creative Directors** Vikram Gaikwad	**Copywriters** Anu Joseph	**Brand Manager** Binal Makhija
Art Director Vikram Gaikwad	Anu Joseph	Sajan Raj Kurup	**Client** Indiana Motors
Design Director Sajan Raj Kurup	Sajan Raj Kurup	**Advertising Agency** Creativeland Asia	**Brand** Indiana Motors Auto Repair

CD, DVD & Record Sleeves

Non-Format
for Lo Recordings

Red Snapper – A Pale Blue Dot
To reinforce Red Snapper as a brand, we borrowed the visual language of fashion retail material. By diverting the usual print budget away from the digipak, the packaging became an exercise in minimalism, with emphasis on materials and production techniques. A collection of swing tags, each with its own visual and textural characteristics, became the core design elements of the packaging. A 'super embossed' PVC tag, a silkscreen printed grey board tag, and a litho printed white card tag are secured to the blank digipak with a thin plastic kimble tag, which also fastens the digipak closed. If the kimble tag is cut, the three swing tags can be stored in the pouch on the inside flap of the digipak.

Designers Kjell Ekhorn	**Art Directors** Kjell Ekhorn	**Design Studio** Non-Format	**Client** Lo Recordings
Jon Forss	Jon Forss	**Marketing Manager** Vincent Oliver	
	Gavin O'Shea		

260

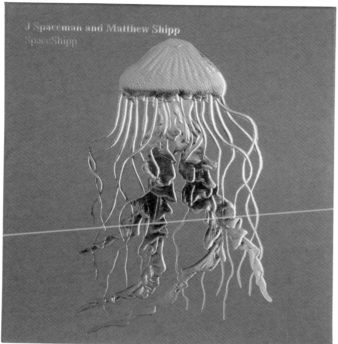

Graphic Designer
Frauke Stegmann

Client
Treader

CD, DVD & Record Sleeves

Frauke Stegmann
for Treader

Treader (Series IV 1 – 3)
These CD sleeves have been designed for independent music label Treader.

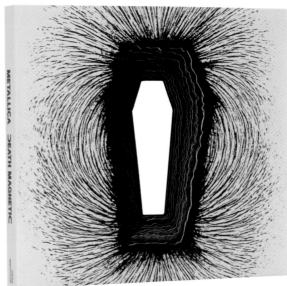

Designers
Emily Charette
Jamie McCathie
Marty O'Connor
Design Assistant
Brian Labus
Design Director
Sarah Moffat
Creative Directors
Bruce Duckworth
David Turner

Photographers
Anton Corbin
Robert Daly
Andy Grimshaw
Britt Hull
Gavin Hurrell
Mike Kemp
Harper Reed
Tom Schierlitz
Craig Snelgrove
David Turner

Photography
Missouri State
Highway Patrol
Artworker
Craig Snelgrove
Retouchers
Peter Ruane
Craig Snelgrove

Design Company
Turner Duckworth:
London and
San Francisco
Client
Metallica

CD, DVD & Record Sleeves

Turner Duckworth
for Metallica

Death Magnetic Digi CD
Challenged with creating an engaging packaging piece for Metallica's ninth studio album, 'Death Magnetic', Turner Duckworth developed an iconic, three-dimensional CD pack using a conspicuous, sunken grave image and an innovative, layered die cut. The end product shows dirt being sucked down towards a coffin, which lies low in a deepening pit. The classic Metallica logo was reworked and a signature, typographic style created.

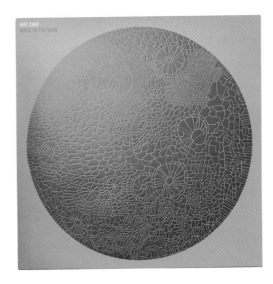

CD, DVD & Record Sleeves

Wallzo
for EMI Records

Designer
Darren Wall
Illustrator
Darren Wall

Design Group
Wallzo

Client
EMI Records

Brand
Hot Chip

Made in the Dark LP
We were briefed to produce artwork to build on the positive reaction to the last Hot Chip campaign for 'The Warning'. This album artwork features a deliberately obscure and mysterious icon which we named 'The Artefact'. This icon builds on the elusive nature of the album title ('Made in the Dark') but deliberately doesn't explain it. These illustrations are featured throughout the packaging on the gatefold sections, booklets and even the discs themselves. The idea was to avoid direct artistic references and produce something that is both confrontational and desirable. Each artefact is embossed and printed with a copper ink to heighten the sense of it being a piece of packaging and not purely a flat artwork.

CD, DVD & Record Sleeves

Farrow
for Spaceman Recordings

Songs in A&E
'Songs in A&E' is the seventh album we have worked on with Jason Pierce from Spiritualized. The main format of this CD cover is a hardback book containing photographs of intravenous administration equipment, which looks much more beautiful than it sounds, and alludes to a prolonged period of hospitalisation for the musician.

Designers	**Photographers**	**Client**	**Brand**
Mark Farrow	Juliette Larthe	Spaceman	Spiritualized
Sabine Fasching	John Ross	Recordings	
J Spaceman	**Design Group**		
Gary Stillwell	Farrow		

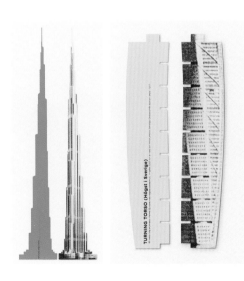

Applied Print Graphics

Happy Forsman & Bodenfors
for The Swedish Museum of Architecture

Skyscraping Bookmarks
These skyscraping bookmarks depict the three tallest buildings in Sweden (in 1:1000 scale). Each image has been heavily rasterised to appear sharper when viewed from a distance. To put the three buildings in an international context, there is also a bookmark of the world's tallest building, the Burj Dubai. The bookmarks are sold in the Swedish Museum of Architecture in Stockholm.

Art Director	**Design Agency**	**Brand Manager**	**Client**
Oskar Andersson	Happy Forsman &	Bitte Nygren	The Swedish
Creative Directors	Bodenfors	**Marketing Manager**	Museum
Lisa Careborg	**Account Handlers**	Bitte Nygren	of Architecture
Anders Kornestedt	Robert Axner		
	Madeliene Sikström		

263

Applied Print Graphics

Happy Forsman & Bodenfors

Happy Wrapping
What does a design agency give clients and friends for Christmas? Something useful and creative, which lets the client be the designer for once. Wrapping paper in three different colours (or skin tones) was given to the recipients along with 61 stickers, to help them create unusual looking gifts to go under the Christmas tree. Each gift literally cries out for attention: grumpy, pleased, surprised, mad or flirtatious.

Art Direction
Happy Forsman
& Bodenfors

Client
Happy Forsman
& Bodenfors

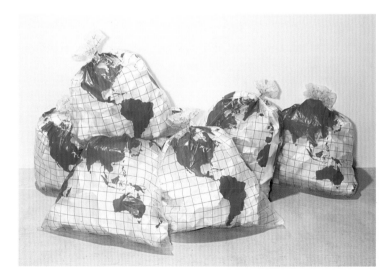

Applied Print Graphics

MR_DESIGN
for Earth Garbage Bag

Earth Garbage Bag
Earth Garbage Bag is a bag with a world map on its surface. Put rubbish into it, and it takes the shape of a globe.

Designer
Yuko Endo
Art Director
Kenjiro Sano
Typographer
Kenjiro Sano

Photographer
Mikiya Takimoto
Copywriter
Kenjiro Sano

Design Group
MR_DESIGN
Account Handler
Keiko Sano

Brand Marketing Manager
Keiko Sano
Brand
Earth Garbage Bag

Designers
Jonathan Ellery
Stephen McGilvray
Creative Director
Jonathan Ellery

Design Group
Browns
Account Handler
Joel Todd

Group Marketing Manager
Martin Webster
Client
Howard Smith Paper Group

Brand
Howard Smith Paper Graphic Design & Print Awards

Posters

Browns
for Howard Smith Paper Group

Howard Smith Paper Graphic Design & Print Awards Posters
This poster campaign was devised to promote the second Howard Smith Paper Graphic Design and Print Awards. The posters were mailed at intervals throughout the year to maintain brand profile and stimulate interest. The posters were A0 in size but mailed as A4.

Posters

Leo Lin Design
for NTNU & TDC, Taipei

Taipei – Tokyo Typography Exhibition
The English characters of the word 'Tokyo' are used to create the Chinese letters for the word 'Taipei'. The poster thereby connects two different writing systems and tries to communicate the characteristics of the oriental culture. A two-directional arrow is embedded in the letter 'O' in order to communicate the typographic relation of the two cities, as well as the basic concept of the design exhibition.

Designer	Art Director	Advertising Agency	Clients
Leo Lin	Leo Lin	Leo Lin Design	NTNU
			TDC, Taipei

Posters

Graflex Directions
for 'Piece Together for Peace' Project

War and Peace: War
This is the third instalment of my 'Piece Together for Peace' project – 'War and Peace'. In riding out this once-in-a-lifetime economic crisis, in which direction will humanity choose to head? 'War' expresses concern for the future of the human race: will humans once again plunge the world into a catastrophic war?

Designer	Design Group	Client	Brand
Kentaro Nagai	Graflex Directions	Graflex Directions	'Piece Together for
Art Director			Peace' Project
Kentaro Nagai			

Designers
Yo Kimura
Yoshihiro Yagi
Art Director
Yoshihiro Yagi

Copywriter
Haruko Tsutsui
Advertising Agency
Dentsu Kansai

Printer
Nao Morimi
Account Handler
Kosaku Miyata

Clients
Idee
Mitsubishi Estate
Brand
Marunouchi Cafe

Posters

Dentsu Kansai
for Marunouchi Cafe

Coming Moon
Moon viewing is a Japanese tradition, with moon viewing events usually taking place in mid-September, when the moon looks most beautiful. A haiku reading event called Coming Moon was held in 2008 in Tokyo, bringing together the writing of haiku poems with praising the beauty of the moon. Haiku is a form of Japanese poetry consisting of short poems of 17 syllables. The essence of haiku is to share an observation by using words with great economy. We adopted this idea to design posters for Coming Moon, showing dots with missing parts or in distorted forms that gradually begin to look like the moon. The simple use of black and white in the visuals is intended to allude to the moon's light and dark sides.

267

Designers
Jasphine Chew
Gigi Lee
Art Directors
Jasphine Chew
Gigi Lee
Design Director
Gigi Lee

Creative Director
Adrian Miller
Illustrator
Jasphine Chew
Photographer
Edmund Leong

Copywriter
Primus Nair
Advertising Agency
Saatchi & Saatchi
Malaysia
Account Handler
Melissa Gonsalvez

Client
Amnesty International
Malaysia
Brand
Letter Writing
Campaign

Posters
Saatchi & Saatchi Malaysia
for Amnesty International Malaysia

Fountain Pen
This ad was designed to graphically demonstrate how anyone can help free prisoners of conscience just by picking up a pen.

Designers
Li Junrong
Hei Yiyang

Art Director
Hei Yiyang
Creative Director
Hei Yiyang

Design Agency
SenseTeam

Client
HuaSen Architecture
Brand
HSArchitecture

Posters
SenseTeam
for HuaSen Architecture

Seeds of the Cities
These are the exhibition tour posters for HuaSen Architecture. The slotting letters come from the LED indicator system in the exhibition. The pattern on the poster can be related to the other poster, indicating its unlimited meaning.

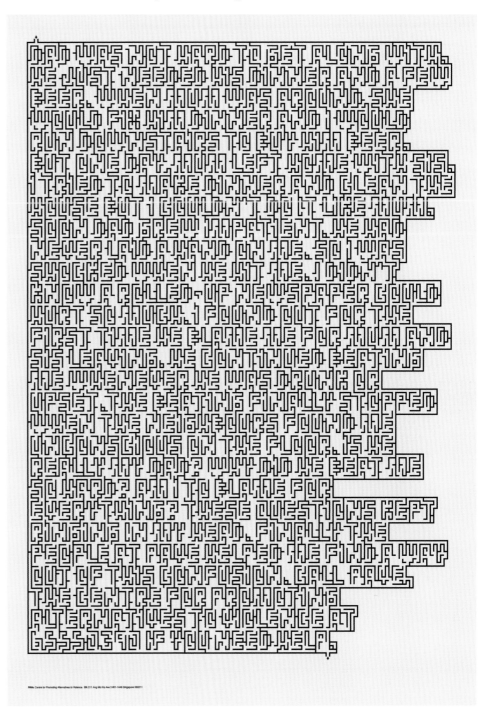

Designer
Jonathan Yuen
Art Directors
Pann Lim
Jonathan Yuen

Creative Director
Pann Lim
Typographer
Jonathan Yuen
Copywriter
Eugene Tan

Advertising Agency
Kinetic Singapore
Account Handlers
Pann Lim
Eugene Tan
Jonathan Yuen

Brand Manager
Pang Kee Tai
Client
PAVe

Posters

Kinetic Singapore
for PAVe

Lost Child
While enduring emotional and physical abuse, victims are often robbed of their ability to think clearly or make sound decisions about their situation. They are confused and lost. Every step they take is like walking through a maze. The role of PAVe (Centre for Promoting Alternatives to Violence) is to help victims, through counselling and guidance, find a way out of their pain and their predicament.

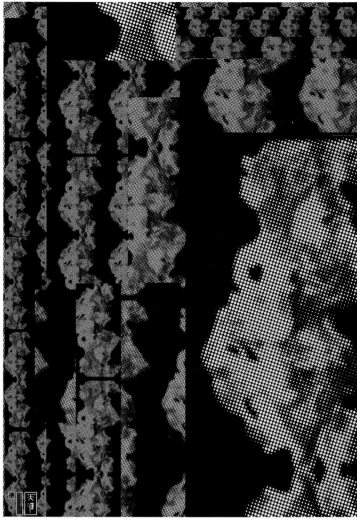

| **Designer** | **Art Director** | **Creative Director** | **Client** |
| Han Jiaying | Han Jiaying | Han Jiaying | Frontiers Magazine |

Posters

Han Jiaying
for Frontiers Magazine

2008 Frontiers Series Posters
To most painters, these traditional images in ink are symbols with traditional meanings. To me, these characters are purely formal icons with oriental features; one does not expect the original meanings of these symbols to become the actual content. In other words, a voice is raised against any expression with rational meaning.

Designer
Helmut Meyer
Art Directors
Albert S Chan
Ina Thedens
Creative Director
Helmut Meyer

Illustrators
Daniel Cojocaru
Martin Popp
Copywriters
Alexander Haase
Dr Stephan Vogel

Advertising Agency
Ogilvy Frankfurt
Art Buyers
Christina Hufgard
Caroline Walczok
Account Handler
Michael Fucks

Marketing Managers
Claudia Fix
Detlef Stueber
Client
Action World
Solidarity

Posters

Ogilvy Frankfurt
for Action World Solidarity

Women's Rights Campaign
The wolf in sheep's clothing? This campaign takes advantage of the current India hype, using popular ethno-visuals to publicise shocking facts about women's rights in India. In its authentic look and feel, the campaign reflects the style of Indian advertising posters.

Designer	Design Group	Client	Brand
Eduardo del Fraile	Eduardo del Fraile	ADG-FAD	LAUS 2009

Posters

Eduardo del Fraile
for ADG-FAD

LAUS Rub-on Poster
The LAUS prizes are the most prestigious among graphic designers in Spain. To advertise the opening of the submission period, we used a real rub-on with typography as the only graphic element. This transferable typography reticle uses a system that was the key working tool of our profession for many years, taking us back to a world in which the project was firmly based on professional know-how and divested of all non-natural elements.

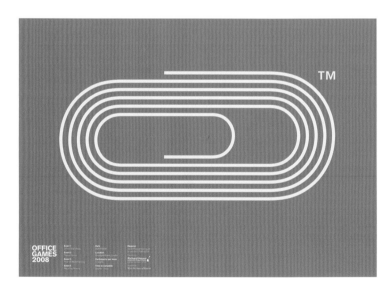

Designers	Creative Director	Design Group	Brand
Samuel Hall	Jack Renwick	The Partners	Office Games
Neil Southwell	**Illustrator**	**Client**	
Alex Woolley	Alex Woolley	Richard House	
		Children's Hospice	

Posters

The Partners
for Richard House Children's Hospice

Office Games
Richard House Children's Hospice needed a promotional poster for their inaugural fundraising event, Office Games. The humble paperclip became the heart of the design, creating the main running track graphic.

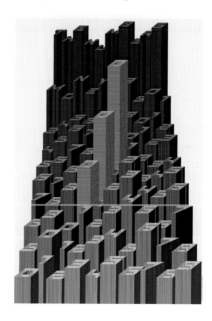

Posters

702 Design Works
for 3.14 CREATIVE & NYTDC

Money: The Numbers/Coexistence
This poster was produced for 'Money: The Numbers', a project by the Type Directors Club, to advertise the policy of 3.14 CREATIVE. High buildings symbolise the competition to get more money, which leads to economic growth. But we can also use 'Money: The Numbers' as a tool to help us coexist with the beautiful natural world.

Designer
Mika Shinozaki
Art Director
Gaku Ohsugi

Design Director
Gaku Ohsugi

Design Group
702 Design Works

Clients
3.14 CREATIVE
NYTDC

Posters

Hat-trick Design Consultants
for Darwin200

Darwin
Darwin200 is a national programme of events celebrating Charles Darwin's scientific ideas and their impact around his 200th birthday on 12 February 2009. We were asked to design a poster promoting the programme for schools, colleges, universities and partner museums around the country. The iconic image of Darwin was created using his travels, discoveries, theories and observations in one continuous lifeline. The poster was released in September 2008.

Designers
Gareth Howat
Jim Sutherland

Creative Directors
Gareth Howat
David Kimpton
Jim Sutherland

Illustrator
Ken Miki
Design Group
Hat-trick Design
Consultants

Marketing Manager
Bob Bloomfield
Client
Darwin200

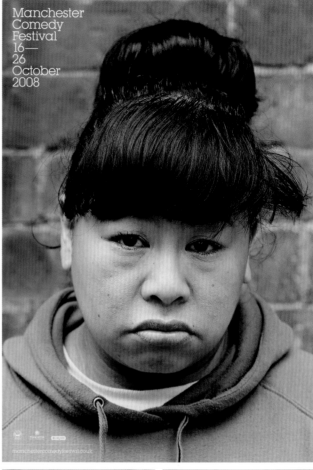

Designer	Photographer	Design Group	Marketing Manager
Mark Lester	Richard Moran	MARK	Anna Greenwood
Creative Director	**Image Manipulator**	**Brand Manager**	**Client**
Mark Lester	Daniel Ingham	Don Ward	The Comedy Store

Posters

MARK
for The Comedy Store

Manchester Comedy Festival 2008
So how do you sell comedy? Easy: you show wacky and zany images of people laughing their heads off, rolling in the aisles, splitting their sides. Except that would be incredibly boring, because it's exactly what you'd expect, isn't it? So... how about showing people in need of a good laugh?

Senior Designer
Jess Andersen

Strategic Design Agency
e-Types

Senior Strategist
Michael Thouber
Theatre Director
Martin Tulinius

Client
Kaleidoskop Theatre

Posters

e-Types
for Kaleidoskop Theatre

Kaleidoskop Theatre Seasonal Posters
These posters mark the beginning of a new season at Kaleidoskop Theatre. With e-Types, Kaleidoskop set out to establish a newfound pertinence for the theatrical arts, wanting to communicate a modern and relevant theatre, with an aesthetic that can fathom the very contemporary themes dealt with in modern drama, to a dynamic urban audience. E-Types focused on a visual style that referenced pop art and punk, keeping the underground theatre's vibe and energy intact. They also created a recognisable and powerful visual statement that stood out in the streets of Copenhagen, setting new standards for how theatres communicate in the process.

275

Posters

Grafica
for Centre de Fotografia
Documental de Barcelona

La Resistencia
Last year the subject of photography festival Trafic was La Resistencia (The Resistance).
We created a free newspaper which was distributed in the streets of Barcelona. The newspaper, besides containing the festival programme, was conceived and laid out so that people could create two posters with it.

Designer
Meri Iannuzzi
Art Director
Pablo Martin

Design Director
Pablo Martin
Design Group
Grafica

Client
Centre de Fotografia
Documental
de Barcelona

Brand
Trafic

Posters

good design company
for Laforet

Laforet Private Party Poster
This poster was enclosed in the invitation to a private party held at a popular shopping mall, called Laforet, in Tokyo.

Art Director
Manabu Mizuno

Design Director
Manabu Mizuno

Advertising Agency
good design
company

Client
Laforet

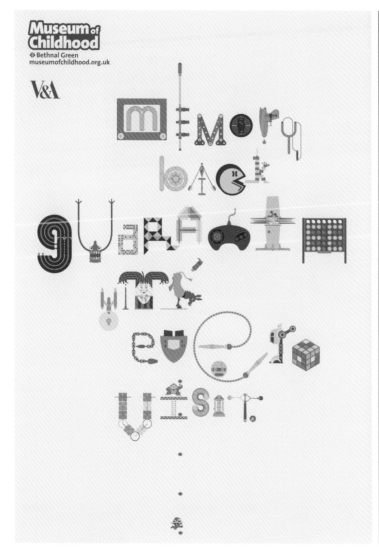

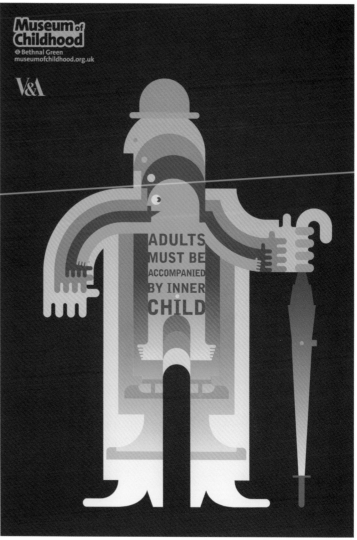

Designer
Paul Pateman
Art Director
Paul Pateman
Creative Director
Paul Brazier

Creative Group Heads
Mike Nicholson
Paul Pateman
Copywriter
Mike Nicholson

Print Producer
Linda Carlos
Advertising Agency
Abbot Mead Vickers
BBDO

Account Handler
James Drummond
Client
Museum of
Childhood

Posters

Abbott Mead Vickers BBDO
for Museum of Childhood

Memory Back Guarantee / Inner Child
The brief was to get the public to visit the Museum of Childhood. Our insight was that the museum really takes you back to your youth. To dramatise this, we devised posters that literally encouraged you to relive your childhood.

Art Director	**Photographer**	**Account Handler**	**Client**
Andreas Kittel	Lisa Carlsson	Linda Almström	Röhsska Museum
Creative Director	**Design Group**	**Brand Marketing**	
Anders Kornestedt	Happy Forsman &	**Manager**	
	Bodenfors	Ted Hesselblom	

Posters

Happy Forsman & Bodenfors
for Röhsska Museum

Skateboards Posters
The Röhsska Museum's exhibition 'Skateboards' tells the story of what was once an underground lifestyle. The exhibition posters play on the magic of skateboarding: it is all about finding that perfect spot. Even without visible skateboards or skaters, the photos still send a clear message.

Typographer	**Creative Directors**	**Design Group**	**Client**
David Azurdia	David Azurdia	Magpie Studio	Morton & Peplow
Designer	Ben Christie	**Proprietor**	
David Azurdia	Jamie Ellul	Rebecca Morton	

Logos & Typefaces

Magpie Studio
for Morton & Peplow

Morton & Peplow
Morton & Peplow is a Munich delicatessen that specialises in British cuisine. Our identity combines two classic icons of Britishness – the bowler hat and the domed silver service platter – to create a logo that oozes heritage. A classic Gill Sanstype serves to reinforce this quintessential British feel.

Designers
Garry Blackburn
Gary Martyniak

Creative Director
Garry Blackburn

Design Group
Rose

Client
St Mary's Church

Rose
for St Mary's Church

St Mary's Church Restoration Identity
This logo was designed for the restoration of St Mary's Church in Rotherhithe, London. The committee required a single mark to symbolise the 300-year-old church and the repair work. The solution was simple: an illustration of the church, rotated to become a drill to represent the restoration work. The identity was designed to help raise funds and draw attention to the restoration of the church to its former glory, while also reflecting the industry and labour.

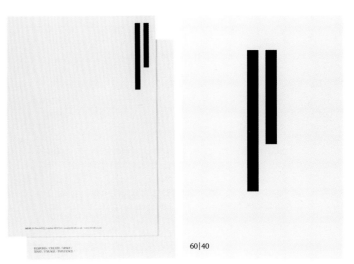

Designer
Robin Howie
Design Director
Justin Davies

Creative Directors
Rob Howsam
Stuart Youngs
Design Group
Purpose

Account Handlers
Louisa Phillips
Alice Reynolds

Brand Managers
David Clarke
Tracey Rowledge
Clare Twomey
Client
60|40

Purpose
for 60|40

60|40 Logo
60|40 consists of three independent artists committed to bringing the applied arts into the 21st Century. They aim to expand the environment for experimental applied arts through their work and writing, as well as make public a passionate commitment to the future of craft practice in the UK. 60|40 approached Purpose to create a bold identity for the newly launched group. The new identity had to challenge current perceptions of contemporary crafts, which are perceived by many as stuffy and old fashioned. 60|40 needed a logo that could work as a stamp of ownership. Our response was to create a confident identity rooted in the balance and ambiguity of the 60|40 name.

Designers
Andy Hills
Rob Sherwood
2D Animation
Designer
Kyli John

Senior Designer
Ross Shaw
Design Director
Ian Styles

Copywriter
Linda Vaux
Design Group
Roundel
Project Director
Linda Vaux

Client
Oxford Oratory
Brand
Reaffirmation &
Renewal Campaign

Logos & Typefaces

Roundel
for Oxford Oratory

Oxford Oratory
The Reaffirmation & Renewal campaign was launched to raise funds for a development programme at the Oxford Oratory which includes the redecoration of the Church of St Aloysius, built in 1875. Much of the original Victorian design was concealed by later generations. Roundel's logotype branding, designed for the Oxford Oratory campaign, references the detailed stenciling and architectural features that are being rediscovered as the church is restored to its former glory.

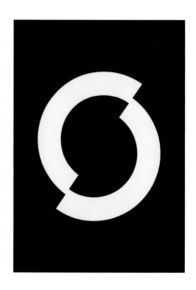

Typographer
Charles Stewart
Designer
Adam Giles

Design Directors
Gareth Howat
David Kimpton
Jim Sutherland

Design Group
Hat-trick Design
Consultants

Brand Manager
Helen Ireland
Client
Scottish Opera

Logos & Typefaces

Hat-trick Design Consultants
for Scottish Opera

Scottish Opera Identity
Scottish Opera is Scotland's national opera company and the largest performing arts organisation in Scotland. The company needed an identity that would challenge the perception of opera as the preserve of rich people, aesthetes and corporate freeloaders, and make it more accessible to a wider audience. The brief was to 'open up opera'. The solution is based on taking the 'O' of opera and opening it up to form the 's' of Scotland. The resulting mark is also reminiscent of opera singers shattering glasses with their voices. The angle created in the mark was then used in Scottish Opera typography and imagery to make collateral ownable.

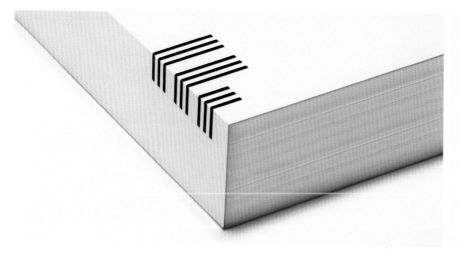

Designers
Mark Farrow
Sabine Fasching
Gary Stillwell

Design Group
Farrow

Publishers
Charlotte Fiell
Peter Fiell

Client
Fiell Publishing

Logos & Typefaces

Farrow
for Fiell Publishing

Fiell
This identity for a publisher is designed to work in two different ways. On books we have used both the spine and cover to create a highly visible three-dimensional logo. This three-dimensional form is then echoed in the alternative version of the mark created for use on stationery and in print.

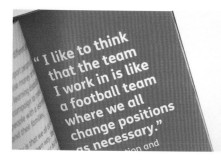

Type Designers
Phil Garnham
Jason Smith

Design Studio
Fontsmith

Brand Manager
Nina Clarke

Client
Mencap

Logos & Typefaces

Fontsmith
for Mencap

FS Me Typeface
FS Me has been designed to exceed government standards for typeface accessibility. Its simple, elegant feel and extensive character set provide freedom for scale and creativity. Every character shape and its set of character combinations have been considered and tested for their appeal and legibility. FS Me has been designed to support people with a learning disability to access written information. It widens the reach of any piece of type-based design work.

Point of Sale

Ogilvy & Mather Hong Kong
for The Hong Kong Jockey Club

Diamond / Mansion / Rolls Royce
The Hong Kong Jockey Club Mark Six Lotteries is a weekly draw where players pick numbers in the hope they'll win the jackpot. Jackpots often reach millions of dollars, making winners instant millionaires and able to afford the things they could only ever dream of before. The campaign utilises the methods ticket players use to pick their lucky numbers.

Art Directors	**Illustrator**	**Advertising Agency**	**Client**
Eugene Tsoh	Frank Lau	Ogilvy & Mather	The Hong Kong
Chow Wai Man	**Copywriters**	Hong Kong	Jockey Club
Creative Director	Andrew Crocker	**Account Handlers**	**Brand**
Gavin Simpson	Gavin Simpson	Sandy Ling	Mark Six
	Thomas Tsang	Kitty Wong	
		Joanne Yu	

Designers	Creative Director	Copywriter	Account Handler
Driv Loo	Pann Lim	Eugene Tan	Carolyn Teo
Jonathan Yuen	**Illustrator**	**Image Manipulator**	**Brand Manager**
Art Directors	Driv Loo	Gillianne Chen	Joy Koh
Pann Lim	**Illustration**	**Advertising Agency**	**Client**
Driv Loo	Kinetic Singapore	Kinetic Singapore	Hasbro Singapore
Jonathan Yuen	**Photographer**		**Brand**
	Jeremy Wong		Play-Doh

Point of Sale

Kinetic Singapore
for Hasbro Singapore

Astronaut / Chef / Fairies
While imagination sets the mind free, Play-Doh has always been helping children's imagination take shape. Posters featuring children's faces were placed in toy stores and toy sections of major department stores. These posters could be unfolded to reveal what goes on in children's heads. Children and parents alike were able to discover why Play-Doh makes the perfect playmate for those who explore the depths of their mind and free their imagination.

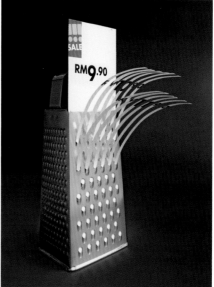

Designers
Joseph Lee
Lim Ken Peng
Khor Kok Yang
Art Directors
Joseph Lee
Ng Heok Seong
Khor Kok Yang

Design Director
Ng Heok Seong
Creative Director
Ng Heok Seong
Photographer
Hoch
Copywriter
Mohan Prabhakar

Advertising Agency
Lowe & Partners
Malaysia
Account Handlers
Ong Bee Lin
Nicole Wong
Brand Manager
Yeong Tze Kuen

Marketing Manager
Yap Poh Choo
Client
IKEA Malaysia
Brand
IKEA

Point of Sale
Lowe & Partners Malaysia
for IKEA Malaysia

IKEA Sale – Fruit Peeler / Potato Peeler / Grater
IKEA is known for finding ways to keep lowering the prices of its items. The task was to find an arresting way to highlight the company's price reductions in the store environment during the sale. The solution was ambient communication that uses Ikea kitchen items that appear to slice, peel and shred their price tags, indicating progressively lower prices.

Designer
Marco Bezerra
Art Director
Marco Bezerra
Illustrator
Marco Bezerra

Copywriter
Emiliano Trierveiler
Retoucher
Andreas Pilz
Advertising Agency
TBWA\ Germany,
Berlin

Agency Producer
Katrin Dettmann
Brand Managers
Yumi Choi
Kiduk Reus

Client
Kiduk Reus & Yumi
Choi GbR
Brand
Bonanza Coffee
Heroes

Point of Sale
TBWA\Germany, Berlin
for Kiduk Reus & Yumi Choi GbR

Coffee Heroes
Celebrate your heroes at Bonanza Coffee Heroes! This is a small gourmet coffee house in the trendiest area of Berlin. Its goal was to build up a relationship with this very alternative audience, known to reject mass media, and to stand out from the competition. Berlin is the mecca of street art, and the target audience are the Coffee Heroes. So we just united street art and heroes. With a series of stencils, the coffee was used to print the faces of cool, alternative heroes, like Muhammed Ali, Obama and Marlon Brando, allowing the audience to 'drink' their idols. Three days before the American elections, Barack Obama's face was printed on hundreds of cups of coffee, which were served to customers.

284

Point of Sale

The Chase
for The Royal Mail

Royal Yearpack Vinyls
Each year, Royal Mail produces a Yearpack with all the stamps issued that year. The brief was to develop a photographic solution for the stamp themes within the Yearpack. Finding a photographic solution that visually captured the scale and range of content for the 14 different subjects was key to answering the brief. Our solution uses the iconic white frame of the Royal Mail stamps which is common to all sets. To raise awareness of the Yearpack's release, we produced white vinyl frames, which were positioned on glass counters of Post Offices. These framed the tellers so that they appeared to be part of the stamp.

Designers	**Photographer**	**Brand Manager**	**Brand**
Chris Challinor	Maria Moore	Alastair Pether	Yearpack
Oliver Maltby	**Design Group**	**Client**	
Creative Director	The Chase	The Royal Mail	
Oliver Maltby			

Point of Sale

Net#work BBDO Cape Town
for Associated Magazines

Burka
One of the cover stories in the January 2009 issue of Marie Claire South Africa explored what life is like for Western expatriates living in Dubai, a society which, despite its liberal reputation, is nonetheless governed by strict Islamic rules. To draw attention to the article, we persuaded the magazine to add an extra cover – with a die-cut – revealing only the eyes of the cover model beneath; an image which resembles the veiled headgear of a woman wearing a burka. The copy reads, 'Dubai: Expats under Sharia law'.

Art Director	**Copywriter**	**Account Handler**	**Client**
Alexis Beckett	Kyle Cockeran	Natasja Madinda	Associated
Design Director	**Advertising Agency**	**Brand Manager**	Magazines
Mike Schalit	Net#work BBDO	Kate Wilson	**Brand**
Creative Director	Cape Town	**Marketing Manager**	Marie Claire
Ivan Johnson		Vanessa Marks	

Designers
Ian Cartlidge
Melissa Price

Design Group
Cartlidge Levene

Client
Guardian News
& Media

Signage & Information Graphics
Cartlidge Levene
for Guardian News & Media

New Guardian News & Media Office
Guardian News and Media's new 150,000 sq ft offices in London's Kings Place are arranged over four floors. A key part of the brief was to develop a solution with low environmental impact. Our response was to make the directional signage out of cardboard. We designed a system of boxes which are screenprinted in vibrant colours and arranged to create dynamic asymmetric shapes. The use of the material is made apparent by leaving the fluted cardboard edges exposed. Entrance branding consists of 3D letters which appear to be aligned when approaching the building from King's Cross, but break up to become abstract when nearing the entrance. Manifestations consist of word pairings which express 'plurality of opinion'.

Design Company
De Designpolitie

Brand Manager
Julius Vermeulen

Client
TNT

Stamps
De Designpolitie
for TNT

Green Stamps
TNT contracted De Designpolitie for the largest stamp issue of 2008: the 'green' stamps. The idea was to come up with ten themes for ten stamps which were translated into optimistic designs for a better world. Our main concern was that the stamps did not come across as being sanctimonious. How do you ensure that you don't rap people on the knuckles, you aren't negative, but you still manage to create some awareness? We also did the research ourselves, so it really became our project. The only thing we didn't manage to push through was a stamp about CO2 compensation for air travel, as TNT did not want any connotations of its recently acquired Boeings.

The jury:

Andy Cowles, IPC Media (Jury Foreman)
Mirko Borsche, Bureau Mirko Borsche
Stephen Coates, Freelance
Scott Dadich, Wired Magazine
Richard Spencer Powell, Winkreative London
Suzanne Sykes, Marie Claire
Matt Willey, Studio8 Design

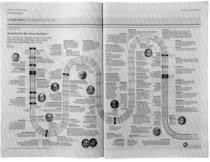

Art Director
Sónia Matos

Editor in Chief
José Manuel
Fernandes

Entire Newspapers

Público

Público
Público is one of the most influential daily newspapers in Portugal. Its graphic structure is solidly designed around a game of multi-thematic and mono-thematic pages or flat planes, in which photography and infographics play an important role. In addition to the main body of the newspaper, composed of hard news, there is a daily supplement called P2. P2 is different editorially and graphically; photography and typography are enhanced. We think of it as a different rhythm of reading within the newspaper. Público also has a range of weekly supplements: Ípsilon, covering arts and leisure; Fugas, covering travel and lifestyle; and Pública, the Sunday magazine.

Art Director
Chris Dixon
Deputy Art Director
Randy Minor

Design Director
Chris Dixon
Designer
Chris Dixon
Publisher
Larry Burstein

Illustrator
Barbara Kruger
Photographer
Henry Leutwyler

Photography Director
Jody Quon
Editor in Chief
Adam Moss

Magazine Front Covers
New York Magazine

Brain
The week of the breaking news of Governor Spitzer's prostitute scandal, we provided several fine artists and graphic designers with a number of carefully chosen photographs of Spitzer and asked them for their visual interpretation of the event. We hoped that one of these art contributions would make a memorable and exciting cover. Barbara Kruger's simple response was brilliant. She cleverly summarised the essence of the shocking scandal by adding her signature iconic red text box saying 'BRAIN' with an arrow pointing to the crotch on a photograph of Spitzer. The news dailies had flooded the market the week before with daily coverage, allowing us to publish a cover with virtually no type, and create something iconic.

Art Director
Chris Dixon
Deputy Art Director
Randy Minor

Designers
Hilary Fitzgibbons
Jeff Glendenning
Carol Hayes
Hitomi Sato
Design Director
Chris Dixon

Publisher
Larry Burstein
Illustrator
Riccardo Vecchio
Photographer
Dan Winters

Photography Director
Jody Quon
Editor in Chief
Adam Moss

Entire Magazines

New York Magazine

40th Anniversary Issue

For New York Magazine's 40th anniversary, we created an issue that was a celebration of the city of New York and the people who have influenced it over the past 40 years. The cover photograph of the skyline was the same one on the first cover of New York Magazine in 1968, this time rendered in metallic black and white. All of the display typography inside the issue is in the original Egyptienne typeface, a nod to the history of the magazine. The issue is filled with photographic and illustrative portraits and stories of famous and infamous New Yorkers.

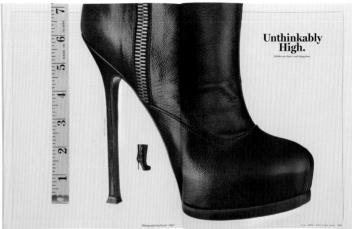

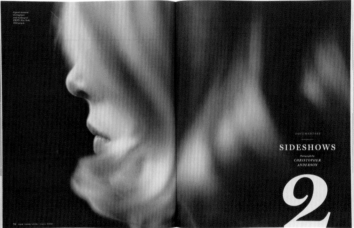

Art Director
Chris Dixon
Deputy Art Director
Randy Minor
Design Director
Chris Dixon

Designer
Caroline Jackson
Crafton
Publisher
Larry Burstein

Photographer
Christopher
Anderson
Photo Editor
Nadia LaChance

**Photography
Director**
Jody Quon
Editor in Chief
Adam Moss

Entire Magazines

New York Look

New York Look: Fall Fashion 2008
New York Look is New York Magazine's special fashion issue that is published twice a year.
Each issue is a visual and written summary of the trends and ideas from that season's fashion
shows in Paris, Milan and New York. The magazine also contains an extensive photo portfolio
by one documentary photographer who spent time at the shows in all three cities.

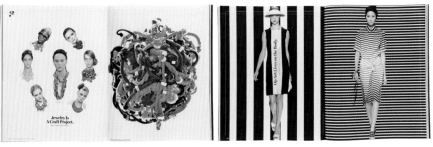

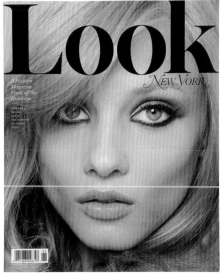

Entire Magazines

New York Look

New York Look: Spring Fashion 2009

Art Director
Chris Dixon
Deputy Art Director
Randy Minor

Design Director
Chris Dixon
Publisher
Larry Burstein

Photographer
Benjamin Lowy
Photo Editor
Nadia LaChance

Photography Director
Jody Quon
Editor in Chief
Adam Moss

Entire Magazines

Swallow Magazine

Swallow Magazine
Swallow Magazine is a hardbound food and travel publication with a unique sideways glance. Taking cues from outside the realms of foodie faddism, it is a magazine for those who like their dinner dirtier and a whole lot more exciting. The inaugural issue digests the Nordic countries, a region often overlooked in terms of gustatory delights. Swallow Magazine is published annually in New York City, and distributed to select locations worldwide.

Creative Director
James Casey
Illustrators
Jared Buckhiester
Jenny Mörtsell
Editor in Chief
James Casey

Photographers
Corey Arnold
Peter Beste
Immaculada Diaz
Nick Haymes
Alex Hoerner
Gustav Karlsson
Frost

Jouko Lehtola
Mark Likosky
Horacio Salinas
John Short
Ebbe Stub Wittrup

Prop Stylists
Victoria Granof
Chrissie MacDonald
Publishers
Swallow
Publications

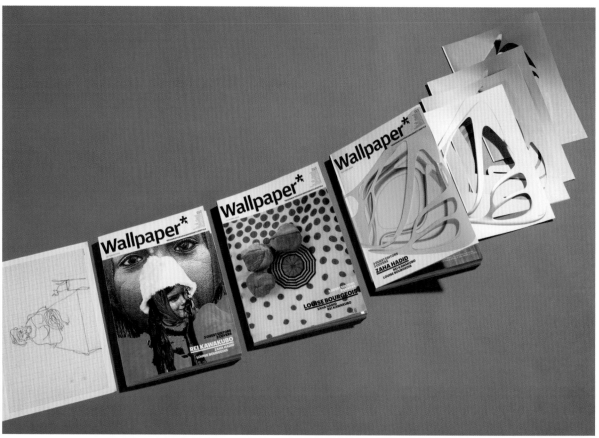

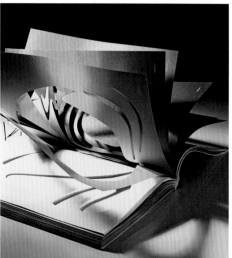

Art Director
Meirion Pritchard

Editor in Chief
Tony Chambers

Entire Magazines

Wallpaper*

Wallpaper* Guest Editors Issue
For the October issue of Wallpaper* we entrusted three sections of the magazine to three of the world's leading figures in art, architecture and design: Louise Bourgeois, Zaha Hadid and Rei Kawakubo. Bourgeois collaborated with fellow artists and friends Helmut Lang, Roni Horn and Peter Zumthor. Her section also included a specially commissioned bound-in portrait by Tracey Emin. Hadid literally carved a sculptural representation of a new work into the pages of Wallpaper*. Her vision: Carving, layering, the void, space: it needs a big hole in the magazine. And Kawakubo's visual feast using graphics, photography and art summons up COMME des GARÇONS' maverick spirit.

Art Directors
Claudia de Almeida
Robert Vargas

Designers
Claudia de Almeida
Dirk Barnett
Robert Vargas

Creative Director
Dirk Barnett

Editor in Chief
Joe Levy

Entire Magazines

Blender Magazine

Blender Magazine Redesign
Blender speaks to contemporary music fans with a distinctive voice that combines critical authority with the irreverence of the music it covers. Our redesign goal was a modern magazine that – through a striking new look – delivers service and information with the ease that readers now expect in the technological age. We engineered a cohesive, graphic design approach to reflect the flow of organic and mechanical sounds the magazine covers. Playing off custom-built gigantic geometric type used for section heads, drop caps and display, we took fat rules, rounded the corners and used them as ratings keys, abstract accents, and chart lines. The result is a vibrant, lasting visual impact that will draw the readers in deeper.

Design Director
Scott Stowell

Designers
Gary Fogelson
Robert A Di Ieso Jr
Serifcan Ozcan
Ryan Thacker

Design Group
Open

Client
Good Worldwide

Entire Magazines

Open
for Good Worldwide

Good Issues
Good is all about getting things done and changing the world at the same time, or in the words of Ben Franklin (and Ben Goldhirsh, the founder of Good), 'doing well by doing good'. Every issue has an editorial theme: issues 008 through 013 were called 'Big Ideas!', 'All You Can Eat', 'The China Issue', 'Get Lost', 'New School', and 'Why Vote?'. Many magazines have a point of view about the world, but with Good we preach to the non-converted, to get the message out to as many people as possible. Additionally, Good is printed on paper manufactured using biogas energy and 30 per cent post-consumer waste. And 100 per cent of your subscription payment goes to the charity of your choice.

Art Director
Francesco Franchi
Designer
Ilaria Tomat
Creative Director
Luca Pitoni
Photo Editor
Raffaele Vertaldi

Fashion Editor
Elisa Furlan
Fashion Assistant
Alessandro Cardini
Writers
Sara Deganello
Saverio Fossati

Picture Researcher
Giulia Soave
Editors in Chief
Walter Mariotti
Gianni Riotta

Editorial Consultant
Paolo Martini
Deputy Managing Editor
Guido Furbesco

Entire Magazines

IL

IL – Intelligence in Lifestyle
IL is a new high-end monthly magazine for men, dedicated to contemporary passions and consumptions, and which uses current events as a key to interpret changes in lifestyles. Sold together with the newspaper Il Sole 24 Ore, IL provides news, interviews, and reports about the latest lifestyle trends around the world. The idea is to talk about 'soft' news as if it were 'hard' news; in a serious, journalistic way which is also informative and elegant. As a result, the magazine design is influenced by weekly news magazines and fashion style magazines. It also takes great care over typography and headline design, drawing inspiration from the strong and simple design of popular 70s magazines.

Art Director
Albert Handler
Designer
Anouk Rehorek
Creative Director
Ulrike Tschabitzer-Handler
Publishers
Unit F büro für mode

Photographer
Joachim Baldauf
Image Manipulator
Mario Rott
Design Agency
moodley brand identity

Editors
Harald Weiler
Judith Zwanzger
Editor in Chief
Ulrike Tschabitzer-Handler

Proofreader
Hubert Kapaun
Client
Unit F büro für mode
Brand
8 Magazine

Entire Magazines

moodley brand identity
for Unit F büro für mode

8 Magazine

This is a professionally designed high-class magazine with a double use: it announces a festival for fashion and photography; and it is a special-interest magazine for Austrian fashion design and fashion photography. The challenge was to create a medium for three genres: fashion magazine, programme information and special interest magazine. The outcome was a 56-page journal, based on an elaborate graphic concept, that merges the genres by providing each of them with a specific area for presentation. By following the structure the reader is led through the festival magazine – without mistaking it for a standard programme brochure.

Art Director
Katja Kollmann
Creative Director
Mirko Borsche

Designers
Nina Bengtson
Jasmin Müller-Stoy

Photographer
Mark Borthwick
Editor in Chief
Christoph Amend

Client
ZEITmagazin
Brand
DIE ZEIT

Entire Magazines

ZEITmagazin

Special Edition Fashion – Die Neuen Hippies

The New Hippies is the special fashion issue of ZEITmagazin, the German weekly DIE ZEIT's magazine supplement (circulation 500,000). An entire issue, seemingly based on a retro phenomenon, was made to look the opposite of retro: fresh, up-to-date, and capturing the spirit of the year 2008. The theme for the magazine was 'fashion gets colourful'. Features included: Hip, Hipper, Hippies; Marc Jacob's Universe; and The Big Showdown. Translation of cover one: The new hippies – their home is, once again, California. Translation of cover two: But this time around, they are dressed decently. A fashion issue.

Designer
Matt Willey
Publisher
Wojciech Ponikowski

Design Group
Studio8 Design

Editor in Chief
Martyna Bednarska-
Cwiek

Client
Publishing & Design
Group

Entire Magazines

Studio8 Design
for Publishing & Design Group

FUTU Magazine
This is the guest art direction and design of Polish magazine FUTU by Studio8 Design.

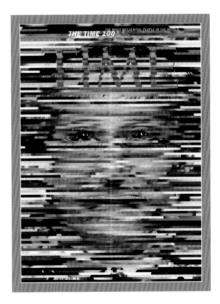

Art Director
Ben Thoma
Designer
Patrik Bolecek

Copywriter
Katie Ann Naylon
**Executive Creative
Director**
Hal Wolverton

**Chief Creative
Officer**
Jose Cabaco
Design Group
Euro RSCG New York

Client
Time Magazine

Magazine Front Covers

Euro RSCG New York
for Time Magazine

Time Magazine
Time Magazine approached us with an opportunity to create a cover for their special issue, '100 Most Influential People'. We decided to use all 100 influential people in the composite of this one face.

ELLE

JULY 2008
£3.50

OH SIENNA! OH SIENNA! HOW MUM DO WE LOVE YOU? ☆

9 770269 259174

Creative Director
Marissa Bourke

Photographer
Jan Welters

Editor in Chief
Lorraine Candy

Magazine Front Covers

Elle

July 2008 Sienna Cover

The July 2008 subscriber's cover of 'Elle' was a first for a commercial magazine. A full-length black-and-white image is usually anathema to a glossy title, but Creative Director Marissa Bourke allowed for the image of Sienna Miller to make the impact, rather than a jumble of cover lines. This cover proves to readers that 'Elle' is an edgy, modern magazine, unafraid to take sartorial risks – exactly what the fashion-buying audience want from this style bible. Subscriber covers, which relate to the newsstand version but demonstrate further fashion focus, are a resounding success: 99.9 per cent of subscribers elect to receive them rather than the newsstand version.

Art Director	Designer	Photographer	Editor in Chief
Chris Dixon	Chris Dixon	Bert Stern	Adam Moss
Deputy Art Director	**Publisher**	**Photography Director**	
Randy Minor	Larry Burstein	Jody Quon	

Magazine Front Covers

New York Magazine

Spring Fashion 2008
For the spring fashion issue cover of New York Magazine, we were incredibly fortunate. We had the opportunity to work with photographer Bert Stern as he recreated his well-known 'Last Sitting' photos of Marilyn Monroe, but with today's contemporary actress Lindsay Lohan. Stern duplicated the original 1962 set, right down to the lighting. Lohan was unafraid of some of the eerier parallels between herself and Monroe, and she embraced every aspect of the shoot. Seven hours and hundreds of frames later, the pictures were made. The image chosen for the cover best represented the spirit of this fascinating project.

Art Director
Meirion Pritchard

Illustrator
Anthony Burrill

Editor in Chief
Tony Chambers

Magazine Front Covers
Wallpaper*

Wallpaper* Work Issue Front Covers
Four covers were produced for Wallpaper* magazine's first ever work-themed issue, using bold, striking type, with their own slogans: 'Work is Play'; 'Work More Live More';'Work Hard and Be Nice to People'; and 'Play and Work and Play'. Typical of Burrill's style, the covers were an apt continuation of his cult 'Work Hard' poster. The four collectable covers also used an experimental matt printing technique to further the tactility and individuality of each issue.

Art Directors
Johannes von Gross
David Henne

Creative Director
Mirko Borsche
Editor in Chief
Dennis Buchmann

Photographers
Manfred Jarisch
Peter Langer
Heji Shin
Armin Smailovic

Illustrators
Nadine Schemmann
Daniel Stolle
Client
Axel Springer Verlag

Magazine Front Covers
Axel Springer Verlag

Humanglobaler Zufall
Humanglobal Coincidence, or Humanglobaler Zufall, is a magazine about what the title means: people from all over the world and how they are connected by coincidence. Every issue contains six reportages, which are connected by a leitmotiv of people that know each other. Humanglobal Coincidence is the first magazine that gives room to the fascination of coincidence. Also selected in Entire Magazines.

302

Book Design

The jury:

Damon Murray, FUEL (Jury Foreman)
Simon Elliott, Rose
John Gall, Random House
Jonathan Gray, Gray 318
Julian Humphries, Harper Collins
Jamie Keenan, Keenan Design
Sascha Lobe, L2M3 Kommunikations Design

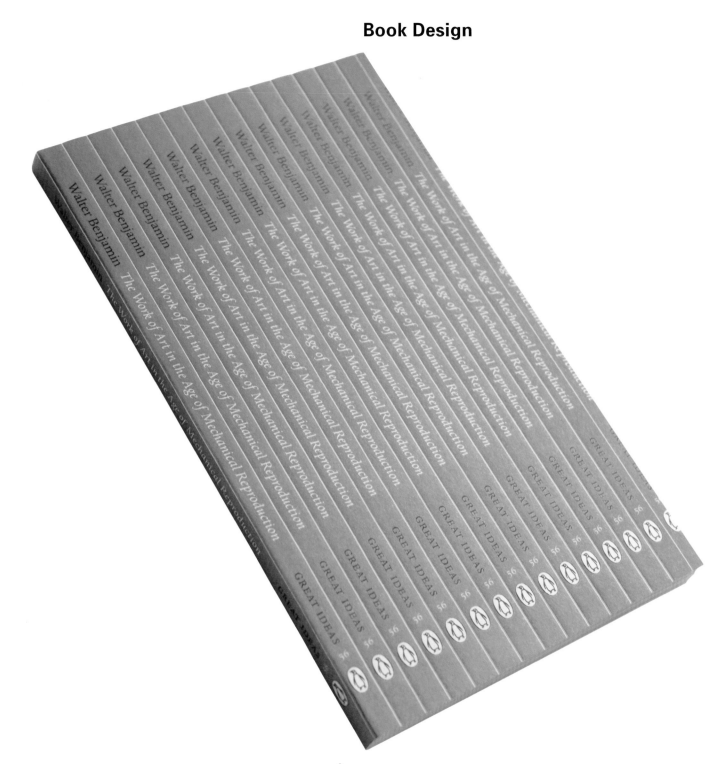

Design Directors	Designer	Design Group	Client
David Pearson	David Pearson	David Pearson	Penguin Books
Jim Stoddart		Design	

Book Front Covers

David Pearson Design
for Penguin Books

The Work of Art in the Age of Mechanical Reproduction
Our aim was to produce a book cover for Walter Benjamin's 'The Work of Art in the Age of Mechanical Reproduction' that adhered to the fixed parameters of Penguin's Great Ideas series. We used type as image and only two colours. We have also incorporated a debossed element.

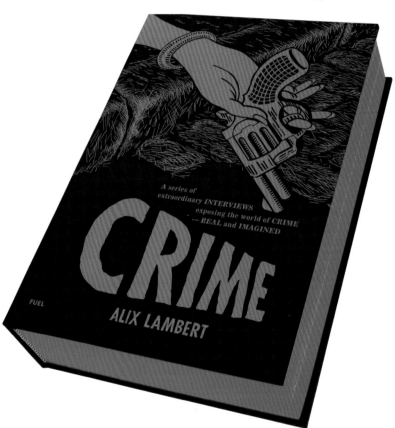

Designers
Damon Murray
Stephen Sorrell
Photographer
Alix Lambert

Editors
Damon Murray
Stephen Sorrell

Design Group
Murray & Sorrell
FUEL

Author
Alix Lambert
Client
FUEL Publishing

Entire Books

Murray & Sorrell FUEL
for FUEL Publishing

Crime
Through a series of extraordinary interviews, this book explores the gap and overlap between real crime and its representation in the arts. It includes authors, actors and directors, plus bank robbers, prisoners, victims of crime and the police. David Cronenberg, Viggo Mortensen, Samantha Morton and Ice-T are all featured. The screenprinted cover – a scene from an unknown crime – refers to 50s thrillers, drawn using scraperboard to give a gritty immediacy. The paper is similar to a pulp-fiction novel, and the headlines inspired by American newspapers of the 40s. Red gilded edges give the book a hardboiled but seductive feel.

305

Book Design

Art Director
Masashi Kawamura

Designer
Masashi Kawamura

Client
Utrecht

Entire Books

Masashi Kawamura
for Utrecht

Rainbow in Your Hand
This book started as a personal design experiment, and was published by the Japanese bookstore Utrecht in 2008. I wanted to introduce a new dimension to flipbooks, which have always been about creating animations by flipping through consecutively illustrated pages. In this book, I created a 3D rainbow using the arch-shaped afterimage that appears in between the pages when the flipbook is flipped.

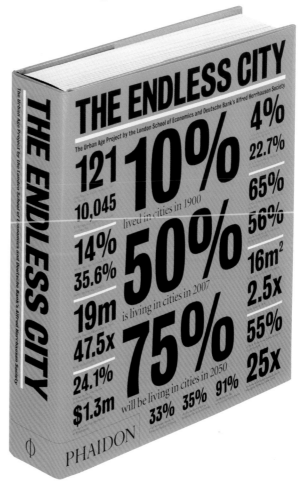

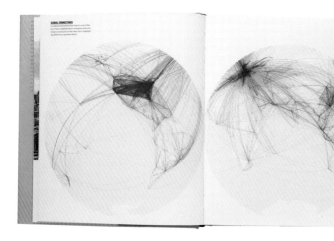

Design Director
Quentin Newark
Designer
Paola Faoro

Publisher
Emilia Terragni
Publishing
Phaidon Press
Cartographer
Bruno Moser

Design Studio
Atelier Works
Editors in Chief
Ricky Burdett
Deyan Sudjic

Client
London School of
Economics,
The Urban Age
Project

Entire Books

Atelier Works
for London School of Economics

The Endless City
This book catalogues six years of research into how cities function, why some are successful and others not. The design had to orchestrate prose, photographs, diagrams, maps and statistics into a coherent narrative.

Book Design

Designer
Paul Belford
Creative Director
Paul Belford

Photographers
Paul Belford
Charlie Crane
Laurie Haskell
Xiaofei Zhang

Design Group
This is Real Art
Print Producer
Neil Gibson

Print Production
TAG London
Client
The Creative Circle

Entire Books

This is Real Art
for The Creative Circle

Creative Circle Annual 2007
A creative circle is a square. So this awards annual for the Creative Circle is square (which is also a good shape to show both portrait and landscape format work). And the target on the cover is a square. The bullet holes drilled into this target relate to gold, silver, bronze and inbook winners. Next to the winning work inside, we see special gold, silver and bronze ink swatches in the shape of the holes in the cover. The number and type of swatches relates to the number and type of awards won. Every piece of work featured has its own page. And all the winning work is shown in situ.

308

Design Directors
Gareth Howat
David Kimpton
Jim Sutherland

Designer
Jessica Sutherland
Copywriter
Jim Sutherland

Illustrators
Jessica Sutherland
Jim Sutherland

Design Group
Hat-trick Design
Consultants

 Entire Books

Hat-trick Design Consultants

Garage Book
This is a self-initiated, promotional book based on observations made in my dad's garage. We wanted to produce a book that celebrated the amazing collection of ironmongery in dusty drawers and cabinets. We wanted people to see magic in the everyday. We photographed everything we liked the look of, and that looked like other things. We wanted to turn the mundane into a magical world full of spiders, robots and rockets. A limited run of 500 editions was printed and distributed in small bookshops in London.

Art Director
Masami Takahashi
Designer
Masami Takahashi

Copywriter
Masami Takahashi
Design Group
MASAMI DESIGN

Clients
All Japan Federation
Printing Industry
Associations

Ministry of Economy,
Trade and Industry

Entire Books

MASAMI DESIGN
for All Japan Federation Printing Industry Associations

Book on Dress
The request by the ministry of economy, trade and industry to create the future of off-set printing in Japan led to this book. What I developed is not a future image of the printing industry, but new work for that industry in the long-term, supporting people's livelihoods. I created the idea of future clothes and proposed a way of producing these clothes. The objective of the book is to help people in the future. I hope the content will be improved and the clothes, by using the printing process, will become more attractive.

310

Art Director
John Fulbrook
Designer
Chip Kidd

Copywriter
Chip Kidd
Publisher
Scribner

Typographer
Chris Ware
Illustrator
Charles Burns

Editor
Colin Harrison

Entire Books
Chip Kidd

The Learners
'The Learners' takes the concept of 'designer as author' to a literal extreme. This is my second novel and the publisher indulged and enabled my various design quirks. For the most part though, it's pretty straight-forward. I wanted the story to be the most important thing; how it looks is secondary and intended to strictly serve the prose.

311

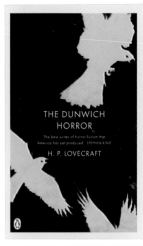

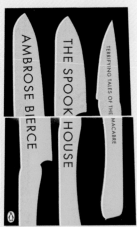

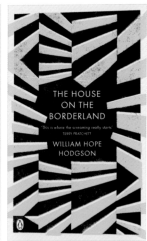

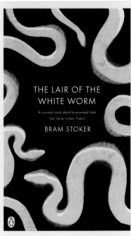

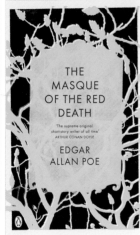

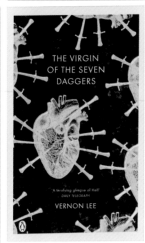

Art Director
Jim Stoddart
Designer
Coralie Bickford-Smith

Illustrator
Coralie Bickford-Smith

Design Group
Penguin Group UK

Client
Penguin
Brand
Penguin Classics

Book Front Covers

Penguin Group UK
for Penguin Classics

The Dunwich Horror / The Beetle / The Haunted Dolls' House / The Spook House / The House on the Borderland / The Lair of the White Worm / Lois the Witch / The Virgin of the Seven Daggers / The Masque of the Red Death / The Haunted Hotel
In this series of ten 'A' format paperbacks, each cover features an illustration created using the cyanotype process. This early photographic technique produced the ethereal texture ideal for these ghostly tales, complemented by the choice of uncoated stock. The process, along with the use of bold graphic elements and a two-tone palette, references Romek Marber's iconic photogram-based 60s crime fiction covers. Simple, understated type defy genre convention without sacrificing the visual impact appropriate to a horror series.

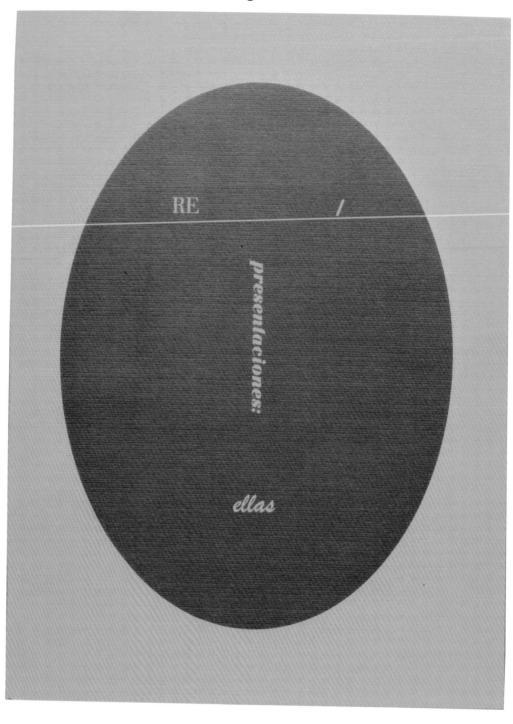

Designer
Ena Cardenal de la
Nuez

Editing
Casa África
Pre-Press
Cromotex

Printing Company
Tf Artes Gráficas

Client
Casa África

Book Front Covers

Ena Cardenal de la Nuez
for Casa África

Re/Presenting: Them

This is a catalogue published by Casa África for the homonymous show. It presents the work of four female African artists whose work revolves around the female condition and women's role in Africa. Not wanting to favour one piece over the rest, we opted for a typographic solution. With the words that make up the title we created a face: eyes, nose and mouth, elements present in any human face. 'RE/presenting:' is set in Bodoni to give it a neutral feel. 'them' is set in Brushscript, an almost handwritten typeface. The oval portrays an anonymous face resembling an African mask, a face that could belong to any member of those African communities in which women play such a fundamental role.

Art Director
Chie Morimoto

Illustrator
Ichio Otsuka

Client
Iwanami Shoten

Book Front Covers

Chie Morimoto
for Iwanami Shoten

IKU IKU JITEN
This is a new design for the long-selling book on child care from Iwanami Shoten. Raising a child takes up a huge part of our lives, and unexpected troubles can occur every minute. We wanted this book to be always at hand for parents, so before starting work on the design, we analysed their daily behaviour.

Art Director
Jim Stoddart
Designer
Coralie Bickford-Smith

Illustrator
Coralie Bickford-Smith

Design Group
Penguin Group UK

Client
Penguin
Brand
Penguin Classics

Book Front Covers

Penguin Group UK
for Penguin Classics

Madame Bovary / Great Expectations / Wuthering Heights / Sense and Sensibility / Cranford / Tess of the D'Urbervilles / Pride and Prejudice / Crime and Punishment / Jane Eyre / The Picture of Dorian Gray
These cloth-bound, jacketless hardbacks have a single matt foil stamped into the cover. The series uses a unifying grid system: each title has its own colour combination and repeating pattern. 'The Picture of Dorian Gray', for example, features a peacock feather design that picks up the book's themes of ego and superficiality. These sumptuous, tactile books evoke a rich heritage of bookbinding, while retaining a fresh appeal to modern readers; they both stand out in bookshops and have a longevity appropriate to their contents.

Art Director
Roberto Beretta
Designer
Roberto Beretta

Photographers
Roberto Beretta
Andreu Llorens

Publishers
Edizioni Corraini

Author
Roberto Beretta
Client
Edizioni Corraini

Entire Books

Roberto Beretta
for Edizioni Corraini

The Quick Brown Fox Jumps Over a Lazy Dog
Hidden in buildings, road markings and street furniture are 26 letters. They're subtle, still and don't shout to be heard, but they're everywhere. They're fonts of urban life, a continuous and silent stream of typography, an A to Z entirely realised in London by Roberto Beretta in collaboration with Andreu Llorens. The 26 letters are also hidden in the most famous English pangram, 'The quick brown fox jumps over a lazy dog', which gives this book its title.

Designers
Damon Murray
Stephen Sorrell

Photographer
Hugo Glendinning
Editor
Honey Luard

Design Group
Murray & Sorrell
FUEL
Client
White Cube

Brand
Jake & Dinos
Chapman

Entire Books

Murray & Sorrell FUEL
for White Cube

Fucking Hell
This book is a catalogue for an exhibition by Jake and Dinos Chapman at White Cube gallery. The artwork 'Fucking Hell' took the artists four years to make, and the book was an important document for the work beyond the lifespan of the exhibition. As well as showing the epic scale of the work, it highlights some of the detail and narrative in the scenes. Each book was individually burnt – as well as the obvious reference to the fires of Hell, this refers to the first Hell sculpture destroyed in a warehouse fire, plus the book burning that took place during the Nazi era. The fonts used are from this period and the endpapers are made from reversed swastikas.

Design Director
Marcel de Quervain
Designers
James Cuddy
Katie Homes
Darren Perry
Jamie Young

Creative Director
Joshua Blackburn
Copywriters
Joshua Blackburn
JB Miller
Publisher
John Bond

Image Manipulator
Johnie Clayton
Editor
John Bond
Design Group
Provokateur
Project Manager
Eve Conboy

Producers
Lisa Bretherick
Matthew Glover
Client
Provokateur
Brand
Acme Climate Action

Entire Books

Provokateur

Acme Climate Action
Most books on climate change endlessly recycle the same facts and advice. 'Acme Climate Action' is a novel approach engaging people in new ways. It is all about action; not telling people what to do, but giving them the tools to do it. The result is a book that one doesn't so much read as use – to destruction. Every page has a purpose: to be torn out, stuck up, shared, posted, made and activated. Even the cover is designed to be made into a picture frame.

Art Director
Guang Yu
Designer
Guang Yu

Typographer
Guang Yu

Photographer
Gu Xiaobo
Editor
Ji Wang

Client
Lv Shanchuan

Entire Books

Guang Yu
for Lv Shanchuan

Event 2008 – Lv Shanchuan

Book Design

Creative Director
Anthony Hodgson
Copywriter
Andrew Pern

Photographers
Sam Bailey
Antonio Olmos

Publisher
Face
Design Goup
Face

Client
The Star Inn

Entire Books
Face
for The Star Inn

Black Pudding & Foie Gras
This book tells the story of Michelin-star chef Andrew Pern's life growing up in Yorkshire. It is part autobiographical and part cookbook, revealing the secrets of one of the UK's brightest young chefs. The aim was to create a tactile and intriguing book aimed at foodies and also those who can't and won't cook. The Star Inn is a 15th Century thatched inn stooped in tradition and history; the book has been produced to take its place on the bookshelves in the restaurant.

Designers
Declan Stone
Garech Stone
Creative Directors
Declan Stone
Garech Stone

Publishers
ADCN
Typographer
Declan Stone
Photographer
Arie Kievit
Image Manipulation
Magic Group

Design Group
The Stone Twins
Editor in Chief
Marion Laman
Pre-Press
Straight Premedia
Print Studio
Spinhex & Industrie

Marketing Managers
Minou Adami
Myrthe Franke
Client
ADCN (Art Directors
Club Nederland)

Entire Books
The Stone Twins
for Art Directors Club Nederland

ADCN Annual 2008
The Art Directors Club of the Netherlands (ADCN) Annual 2008 is a record of the year's most significant work in Dutch advertising and design. The goal of The Stone Twins was to develop an unusual concept to set it apart from earlier editions, and to generate a buzz in the advertising industry. Not content with merely creating a dazzling fluorescent pink cover and divider pages with targets, the duo commissioned the Dutch Army to fire live ammunition at each book, resulting in a one-off bullet-hole. The concept seeks to metaphorically suggest creative (and sales) targets, as well as comment on the self-aggrandising ad world.

Design Director
Jane Pirone
Creative Director
Jane Pirone

Publisher
Jane Pirone
Publishing Company
Not For Tourists

Editors
Craig Nelson
Rob Tallia

Client
Not For Tourists

Entire Books
Not For Tourists

Not For Tourists Guide to London 2009
Not For Tourists was created to enhance people's experiences of urban areas. Unlike a tourist guide that covers limited ground, it has a greater area of coverage as well as more useful and comprehensive content. It combines point of interest and destination information with maps for navigation. From NFT's conception, it's been a major endeavour to fit that amount of content into a small, portable book while making it intuitive to use. The challenge in expanding to London has been to maintain a cohesive, consistent design, while taking the city's characteristics and culture into consideration.

Art Director
Koji Iyama
Designer
Yoshiko Akado

Publisher
Koji Iyama
Typographer
Koji Iyama

Photographer
Sachie Abiko
Design Group
iyamadesign

Brand Manager
Hiroshi Suganuma
Client
Guardian Garden

Entire Books
iyamadesign
for Guardian Garden

Typescape
This is an experimental book to consider the meaning and shape of the Chinese characters Kanjis. I disjointed Kanjis and extracted the smallest elements, then placed them in a common scene to link them. These continuing scenes with Kanji elements enable you to think about the origins of these characters. Kanji characters are ideograms developed from hieroglyphics; the shapes and combinations of the elements have their own meaning. By placing the elements in a suitable situation, I aimed to visually explain the origin of Kanji.

Art Directors	Copywriter	Design Group	Marketing Managers
Pann Lim	Eugene Tan	Kinetic Singapore	Louis Lim
Gen Tan	**Publishing Group**	**Editors in Chief**	Father Thomas
Designers	Church of St Peter &	Pann Lim	**Client**
Pann Lim	St Paul	Eugene Tan	Church of St Peter
Gen Tan	**Photographer**	Gen Tan	& St Paul
Creative Director	Stefan Khoo	**Advertising Agency**	
Pann Lim		Kinetic Singapore	

Entire Books

Kinetic Singapore
for Church of St Peter & St Paul

Reverse
True to its title, the back of this book is its cover. Each page features a poor person, viewed only from the back. The perforated edge of each French fold encourages the reader to tear it open for a closer look into the world of the poor and underprivileged. At the end of the book (or start of the book, so to speak), the reader discovers that the words encountered throughout the book form the introduction to the book.

Designers	Creative Directors	Copywriter	Editors
Erwin K Bauer	Erwin K Bauer	Erwin K Bauer	Erwin K Bauer
Dieter Mayer	Dieter Mayer	**Photographer**	Dieter Mayer
		Dieter Mayer	**Client**
			SpringerWienNewYork

Entire Books

Erwin K Bauer & Dieter Mayer
for SpringerWienNewYork

Orientation & Identity
The young discipline of signage offers an exciting view of two and three-dimensional design projects that give individual places their specific character, make orientation easier and give us a structured overview of the respective contents. The 17 different projects discussed in this book show the potential this new field harbours for clients, urban planners, entrepreneurs and politicians. The individual designers' backgrounds are as different as the backgrounds of the various clients. Artists, logistics experts, classical communication designers and architects share their views here. All of them give the reader an insight into their multi-faceted design approaches and offer us a glimpse behind the scenes.

319

Book Design

Art Director
Merle Schröder
Designer
Merle Schröder
Creative Director
Uli Gürtler

Copywriter
Anke Gröner
Advertising Agency
gürtlerbachmann
Werbung

Account Handler
Sharifa Hawari
Marketing Manager
Prof Dr Björn
Bloching

Client
Roland Berger
Strategy Consultants
Holding

Entire Books

gürtlerbachmann Werbung
for Roland Berger Strategy Consultants

Every Story Has a Beginning
Roland Berger Strategy Consultants is the biggest corporate and strategy consultant in Europe, and is always looking for new potential. But these talents are often the target of many other companies as well. A convincing look as an employer brand was needed to recruit competent staff. A high-quality, meticulously designed book and slipcase were developed to assist in recruiting. This intelligent, high-end approach aims to stimulate interest in a career at Roland Berger. Designed like old books, with the motto 'Every story has a beginning', first sentences of famous works are cited. After many first sentences, which resemble the beginnings of an outstanding tale, the reader is invited to start his own story at Roland Berger.

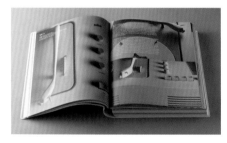

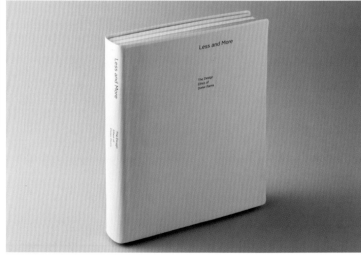

Designers
Miyuki Amemiya
Yusuke Fujisawa
Naofumi Ishida
Nobuhiko Omata
Yasunori Sanai
Yosuke Shibata
Tamotsu Shimada

Art Director
Tamotsu Shimada
Creative Director
Keiko Ueki
Copywriter
Shinya Kamimura

Photographers
Toshihiko Murakami
Koichi Okuwaki
Sebastian Struch

Design Group
Shimada Design
Client
Suntory Museum,
Osaka

Entire Books

Shimada Design
for Suntory Museum, Osaka

Less and More – The Design Ethos of Dieter Rams
Dieter Rams, who was at the vanguard of the increasingly complex industrial design of the 20th Century, held onto his principle of 'less but better'. Controlling the appetite for decoration that designers are often eager to satisfy, Rams always wanted to be faithful to the entity of products. It is Rams' ideal and ideas that this poster's design aims to express. The pure form of Rams' product is extracted by effacing its 'skin' to the limit and highlighting its 'bones', while the details about which Rams has been particular are enhanced by a strong lightness contrast. The border between appearance and disappearance or the limit of existence; this is what had to be discerned to visualise 'less but better'.

Art Director
Barrie Tullett

Editor
Ken Cockburn

Design Group
The Caseroom

Client
The Caseroom Press

The Caseroom
For The Caseroom press

The Ghost in the Fog
'The Ghost in the Fog: XXV The Corrections' is the ghost of a book. It documents corrections made by the editors, translators and contributors to 'How to Address the Fog: XXV Finnish Poems 1978-2002'. Published in 2005, the original went through five sets of amendments. This book reveals those changes. Only the corrected text, the marginal notes and the proof-readers' marks remain, forming a different kind of poetry – one of an accidental, concrete kind. It is a book of absences. Brought to light by Barrie Tullett from the corrections, observations and alterations of Ken Cockburn, Anni Sumari, Robin Fulton, David McDuff, Donald Adamson and Robyn Marsack.

Design Director
Robert Riche
Designers
Heather Briggs
Robert Riche
Copywriter
Duncan Campbell-Smith

Illustrators
Heather Briggs
Robert Riche
Design Group
Radley Yeldar
Account Handler
Simon Hutley

Director of Marketing & Publicity
Joanna Prior
Head of Corporate Communications
Rebecca Sinclair

Client
Penguin Group
Brand
Penguin

Radley Yeldar
for Penguin Group

The Book of Penguin
Founded in 1935, Penguin is one of the world's best-loved brands. To celebrate this, Penguin wanted to create a book that explains the international group, inspires employees, authors and partners, and encourages pride in the past and excitement about the future. Many thanks to the whole host of people at Penguin for all their help and support on the project. 'The Book of Penguin' is intentionally a book, not a website, blog or podcast. Its subtle, booky style uses gentle humour with simple, brand-based illustrations echoing the 'dignified, but flippant' character of the company. While it is a celebration, the calm tone reflects the aim to quietly inspire, not to lecture or boast.

Art Director
Michael J Walsh

Designers
Suck Zoo Han
Brian E Smith
Patrick Tobin

Creative Director
Anthony P Rhodes
Design Group
Visual Arts Press

Client
School of Visual Arts

Entire Books

Visual Arts Press
for School of Visual Arts

SVA Undergraduate Catalog
The objective of the School of Visual Arts' undergraduate catalogue, 'Proof', is to show prospective students why SVA is the pre-eminent training ground for the next generations of artists. We wanted to prove that SVA, located in New York City, is the best art school to attend. Our solution to that aim was to present visual and factual evidence, first by giving dozens of facts about New York City, SVA and its students, then by presenting literally hundreds of examples of student work throughout the book, setting a new standard for publications of this kind.

The jury:

Glenn Tutssel, The Brand Union (Jury Foreman)
Nikki Austen, The Body Shop International
Mark Bonner, GBH
Stephen Doyle, Doyle Partners
Gary Holt, SomeOne
Stuart Jane, Venturethree
Richard van der Laken, Designpolitie
Martin Lawless, 300million
Jim Sutherland, Hat-trick Design Consultants

STYLE?   FORM?

SUBSTANCE?   FUNCTION?

Art Directors
Shane Bradnick
Johnny Brian
Copywriter
Michael Canning
Creative Directors
Chris James
Simon Langley
Artists
DMOTE
Luca Ionescu
Studio Number One

Executive Creative Director
Warren Brown
Production Manager
Clinton Bell
Advertising Agency
BMF
Art Buyer
Sarah Thompson
Strategic Planning Director
Simon McCrudden

Digital Producer
Sora Nobari
Flash Developer
Ed Stuckey
Account Manager
Michelle Bradfield
Account Director
Fleur Kennedy
Group Account Director
Nick Garrett

Brand Manager
Piers Halleen
Client
Lion Nathan Australia
Brand
Tooheys Extra Dry 696ml

Brand Applications: Printed Material

BMF
for Lion Nathan Australia

TED696 Project
Many Australian beer brands also sell their product in a larger-size 'longneck' bottle. To grow their market and give their current customers this option, Tooheys Extra Dry (TED) wanted to launch their own longneck beer bottle: the TED 696ml. In Australia, longneck beer bottles are always sold in brown paper bags. If we could own this bag, we would in effect own the category. So we launched the TED696 Project – a collaboration between TED and some of the world's best street artists to design brown paper bags. We then opened it up to the public. These designs were printed and distributed nationally throughout liquor stores, claiming the medium in which all longneck beer bottles are sold.

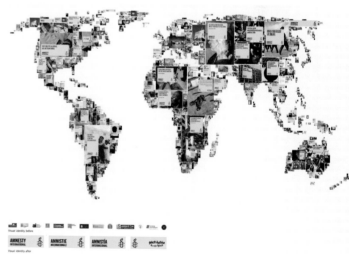

Designer
Wolf Schneider
Art Directors
Vera Mueller
Olivier Nowak
Maria-Michaela
Tonn
Kathrin Wetzel

Copywriter
Edgar Linscheid
Creative Director
Wolf Schneider
Photography
Flickr
Magnum Photos
Design Group
Scholz & Friends
Identify

**Assisting Design
Group**
Wolff Olins
Advertising Agency
Scholz & Friends
Berlin
Account Handler
Anna Kubitza
Marketing Manager
Markus N Beeko

Brand Manager
Anne-Catherine
Paulisch
Brand Director
Penelope
Winterhager
Client
Amnesty International

Existing Brand Schemes: Large Business

Scholz & Friends Berlin
for Amnesty International

More Impact for Human Rights
The creative objective was to deliver more effectiveness in the battle for human rights through a new international visual profile for Amnesty International. The new visual identity is marked by a symbol of suppression and hope, a colour world that draws attention and expresses urgency, a documentary-style visual language, and a typeface that is suitable for conveying facts and for campaigns – promoting global identification and allowing easy applicability. During the launch process in Germany alone, all communication media were revised. All members (more than 20,000) received a simple toolkit with all the tools necessary for their day-to-day work – in the new international look.

325

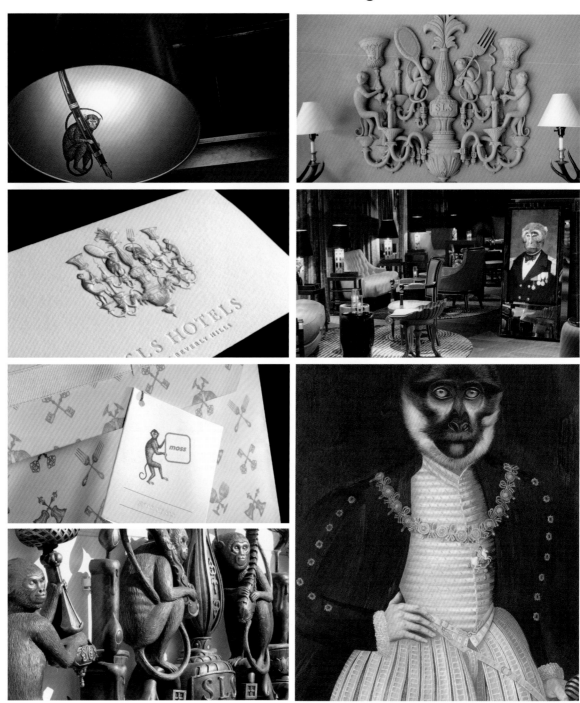

Designers
Ross Goulden
Jason Gregory
Peter Hale
Sophie Paynter

Design Directors
Jason Gregory
Peter Hale

Creative Directors
Mark Bonner
Jason Gregory
Peter Hale
Design Group
GBH

Marketing Manager
Theresa Fatino
Client
SBE Entertainment

New Branding Schemes: Large Business

GBH
for SBE Entertainment

SLS Hotels

SLS is an international luxury hotel brand that combines elegance and excellence with creativity and playful wit. The brief emphasised the need for a logo which felt traditional and authentic while embodying the brand's subversive difference. The graphic solution draws on traditional European heraldry. At first glance, the logo looks like a crest adorned by beasts. On closer inspection, it is revealed as a chandelier being vandalised by mischievous monkeys. Additional graphic language, essential for the huge range of applications and communications required by the hotel, was created including a library of monkey related engravings and paintings.

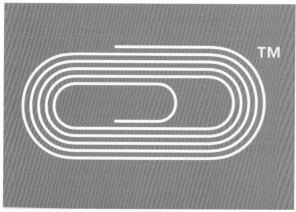

Designers
Samuel Hall
Neil Southwell
Alex Woolley

Creative Director
Jack Renwick
Photographers
Samuel Hall
Dave Wood

Illustrator
Alex Woolley
Design Group
The Partners

Client
Richard House
Children's Hospice
Brand
Office Games

New Branding Schemes: Small Business

The Partners
for Richard House Children's Hospice

Office Games

The Richard House Children's Hospice needed an identity for its inaugural fundraising event Office Games, a charity event that brings together the office and sport. Events include Floppy Discus, Office Chair Relay, and Post-it Note Fencing. The company didn't want it to appear too charity-like and use guilt to make people take part; it wanted the focus to be on the fun and enjoyment of the event. The humble paperclip became the heart of the identity, creating the main running track logo and a set of icons depicting each sporting event. Marketing communications included banners, flyers, animations, posters, T-shirts and trophies. Bold use of the core red gave us a cost effective way of achieving maximum impact.

327

Designer
Mark Lester
Creative Director
Mark Lester

Photographer
Richard Moran
Image Manipulator
Daniel Ingham

Design Group
MARK
Marketing Manager
Anna Greenwood

Brand Manager
Don Ward
Client
The Comedy Store

New Branding Schemes: Small Business

MARK
for The Comedy Store

Manchester Comedy Festival
So how do you sell comedy? Easy: you show wacky and zany images of people laughing their heads off, rolling in the aisles and splitting their sides. Except that would be incredibly boring, because it's exactly what you'd expect, isn't it? So... how about showing people in need of a good laugh?

Designers
Fiona Curran
Sam Lachlan
Creative Director
Garrick Hamm
Illustrators
Fiona Curran
Sam Lachlan
Vanessa Wright

Typographer
Fiona Curran
Design Group
Williams Murray
Hamm

Client Services Director
Panna Patel
Marketing Manager
Jonathan Jackson
Brand Director
Simon Cochrane

Client
Jamie Oliver
Enterprises
Brand
Recipease

New Branding Schemes: Medium Business

Williams Murray Hamm
for Jamie Oliver Enterprises

Jamie Oliver Kit Food
Jamie Oliver launched Recipease as a new food and kitchen shop where customers can learn to cook. The brief was to create a new retail concept to get customers excited and involved in food preparation and by learning how to put meals together on site, building a growing passion for food. We communicated the sense of 'meal assembly' through the simple idea of an airfix kit. The illustrations and their various combinations create witty language that talks about good food and the ease of cooking.

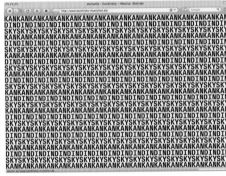

Designer
Thomas Mayfried
Art Directors
Swantje Grundler
Thomas Mayfried

Design Group
Thomas
Mayfried Visual
Communication

Clients
E.ON Energi Munich
Städtische Galerie
im Lenbachhaus

Brand
Kandinsky

New Branding Schemes: Medium Business

Thomas Mayfried Visual Communication
for Städtische Galerie im Lenbachhaus

Identity for Vasily Kandinsky Retrospective, Munich
The Lenbachhaus museum in Munich conceived a Kandinsky retrospective in cooperation
with the Centre Pompidou and Guggenheim. For the Munich venue, a sponsor supported all
communications. The brief was to create new communications to attract a broad German-speaking
audience. Most people have heard the name Kandinsky, but fewer are as familiar with the painter's
work. We began by using his name as a 'luxury' brand, without mentioning occasion, place or date.
The new brand was presented to the public in September 2008 with a press advertisement and
outdoor poster campaign. The URL was the only clue to identifying the exhibition. Later on, basic
information was provided by attaching neon-coloured stickers to posters, billboards and press ads.

330

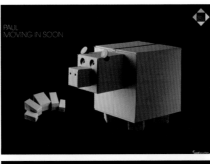

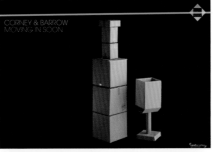

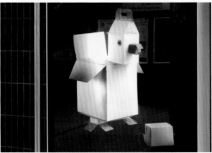

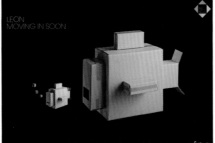

Designers
Ian McLean
Alex Swatridge
Art Directors
Gareth Howat
David Kimpton
Jim Sutherland

Copywriter
Alex Swatridge
Photographer
John Ross
Illustrator
Beanie Brownjohn

Design Group
Hat-trick Design
Consultants
Marketing Manager
Kristi O'Connell

Client
Land Securities
Brand
New Street Square

New Branding Schemes: Medium Business

Hat-trick Design Consultants
for Land Securities

New Street Square
New Street Square is a Land Securities mixed-use scheme, a £300million project in central London. They needed a distinctive, adaptable campaign to inform the public which tenants were occupying the retail spaces. Once the retailers were open and trading, phase two of the campaign was to build public awareness of the development. For phase one, cardboard boxes were used as a metaphor for moving in. They were arranged to represent the variety of retail on offer, and photographed to become the shop window vinyls. 3D spotlit installations were created in the doorways of units. In phase two, brown boxes became coloured gift boxes, bringing to life the quality of the retail. These were then animated for the website.

331

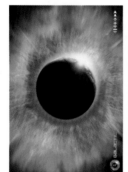

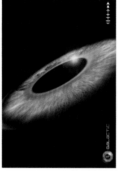

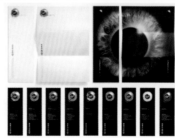

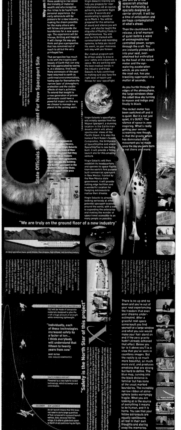

Designers
Piers Komlosy
Mark Wheatcroft
Senior Designers
Mark Bonner
Russell Saunders
Creative Directors
Mark Bonner
Jason Gregory
Peter Hale

Illustrator
Toby Tinsley
Typographers
Mark Bonner
Bruno Maag
Marc Weyman
Livery Application
Start Design

Design Group
GBH
Brand Marketing Managers
Susan Newsam
Ned RocknRoll

Client
Stephen
Attenborough
Brand
Virgin Galactic

New Branding Schemes: Large Business

GBH
for Virgin Galactic

Virgin Galactic
Virgin Galactic is the world's first spaceline, turning civilians into astronauts. The vision of mankind is represented by the human iris and signifies an opportunity to look back at earth with our own eyes. This identity grows with each new 'astronaut', creating multiple versions. An epic book for full ticket holders contrasts the 'noise' of the media with the tranquillity of the experience. Stationery features each individual's iris. Print explains the flight in detail and a display typeface unites all materials. The livery incorporates the 'Branson' iris under the fuselage, looking back at Earth as SS2 begins its descent.

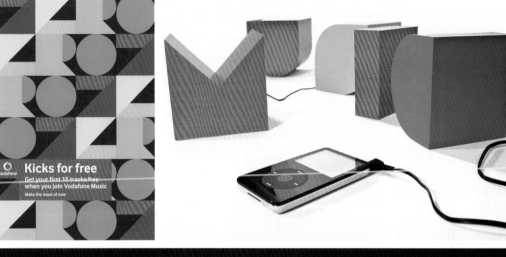

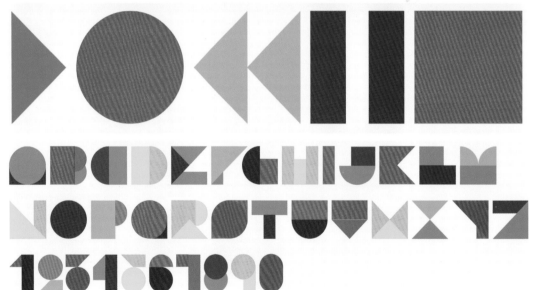

Designers
Chris Blaydes
Martin Cadwallader
Stephan Charbit
Mark Chatelier
Richard Holt
Sean Rees
Design Director
Lisa Carrana

Copywriter
Sarah Brownrigg
Creative Directors
Ewan Ferrier
Gianni Tozzi
Executive Creative Director
Glenn Tutssel

Senior Artworker
Alex Mesher-Smith
Design Group
The Brand Union
Client Director
Christina Futcher

Head of New Media & Branded Entertainment
Charlie Carrington
Director of Brand Strategy
David Erixon
Client
Vodafone

New Branding Schemes: Large Business

The Brand Union
for Vodafone

Vodafone Music
International mobile telecommunications company Vodafone operates in more than 25 countries. It wanted a global identity that would allow it to connect with existing customers and a wider music-loving audience. The Brand Union created a set of symbols, alphabet and rules from the contemporary shapes of music, needing no translation. The distinctly Vodafone visual language builds an emotional relationship with consumers in an overcrowded music market. It is playful, colourful and interactive, and provides unlimited ways of expression using the universal symbols for stop, play, record, rewind and pause. The language crosses borders, enabling Vodafone to build an emotional relationship with their consumers globally.

333

Designers	Photographer	Brand Manager	Client
Miho Aishima	Alex Kent	Debbie Bannigan	Swanswell Trust
Michael Johnson	**Design Group**	**Brand Consultant**	**Brand**
Design Director	johnson banks	Johnathan Mercer	Swanswell
Michael Johnson			

Existing Brand Schemes: Medium Business

johnson banks
for Swanswell Trust

Swanswell

Swanswell Trust is a drug and alcohol rehabilitation service based across the Midlands. We decided to use the 'well' at the end of the name; various typographic experiments followed, before the discovery that a piece of paper, crumpled at one end, could act as a metaphor for someone's life smoothing itself out. Each employee receives a small book of cards; when they want to give out a card, they remove it from the pad and scrunch one end to create a physical demonstration of their logo (and service) firsthand. We also developed a family of useful words and phrases that can be used as headlines and copy for posters and leaflets, and a suite of photos of crumpled family situations.

LONDON
VISION
CLINIC

LONDON
VISION
CLINIC

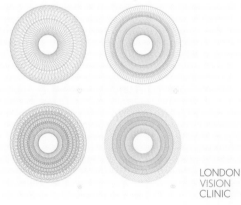

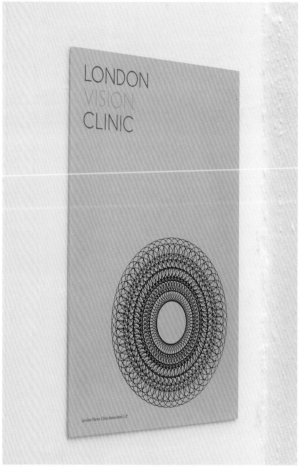

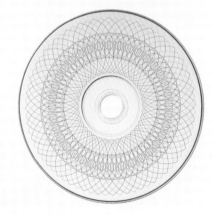

Designers	Art Directors	Design Group	Marketing Manager
Gareth Howat	Gareth Howat	Hat-trick Design	Craig Engelfried
Mark Wheatcroft	David Kimpton	Consultants	**Client**
	Jim Sutherland		London Vision Clinic

Existing Brand Schemes: Medium Business

Hat-trick Design Consultants
for London Vision Clinic

London Vision Clinic
Launched in August 2008, Harley Street based London Vision Clinic is the UK's leading practice for laser eye surgery. Surgeons use the latest technology to treat prescription strength and refractive eye conditions that exceed the norm for laser eye surgery in the UK. The identity programme needed to reflect the intricate, delicate and precise nature of their surgery. Five guilloché 'eye' patterns were employed, each created using a single icon repeated to form an eye. Each icon represents a key stage in the process: screening, service, treatment, results, aftercare. Intricate lineweights were maintained even on large scale applications. Applications included signage, stationery, print, moving image and the web.

335

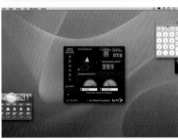

Art Director
Aaron Dietz
Copywriter
Mandy Dietz
Creative Director
Christian Haas
Flash Programmer
Mike Kellogg

Developer
Mike Kellogg
Chief Digital Officer
Mike Geiger
Advertising Agency
Goodby Silverstein
and Partners

Agency Producer
Tena Goy
Senior Producer
Margaret
McLaughlin
Account Handler
Jen Fox

Account Manager
Zoe Kretzschmar
Client
Sprint

Brand Applications: Digital/Interactive

Goodby Silverstein and Partners
for Sprint

NOW Widget
The internet is right now, it's happening as you read this. Sprint's mobile broadband site displays what NOW actually looks like. A digital curator of live feeds, cams and streaming data constitutes the world's most elaborate widget. A downloadable version allows people to take the site with them. In the absence of a single dollar spent on media, it was picked up by over 100,000 blogs, with people spending an average of five minutes on it.

Designers
Ennio Franco
Rasmus Knutsson
Design Director
Virgilio Santos
Senior Copywriter
Neil Starr
Creative Director
Carla Echevarria
Interactive Designer
Kathrin Hoffmann
**Interaction Design
Director**
Claudia Bernett

Technical Director
Kevin Sutherland
**Executive Technical
Director**
Will Turnage
**Associate Creative
Director**
Nathalie Huni
**Executive Creative
Director**
James Temple

Flash Developers
Ben Doran
Neil Duggan
Nicolas Le Pallec
Tomas Vorobjov
**Presentation Code
Developer**
Michael Potts
Senior Producer
Dylan Connerton
Associate Producer
Krystal-Joy Williams

Advertising Agency
R/GA London
Planning Director
Darren Savage
**Director of Brand
Design**
Marc Shillum
Client
Nokia

Brand Applications: Digital/Interactive

R/GA London
for Nokia

Nokia viNe
Nokia viNe is a breakthrough mobile application that records photos, videos, songs, text, and voice while geotagging them to a multimedia map of the user's life. To create it, we joined several applications in the ultimate travelogue tool. It's an easy way to relive, search and share the user's experiences as they happen. Nokia viNe also represents a new way of approaching branding, in which name, design, and functional interface are seamlessly combined – the first time intuitive brand design has served both as the branding and the interface of an application. And, while users are documenting their lives, they are sharing the Nokia brand.

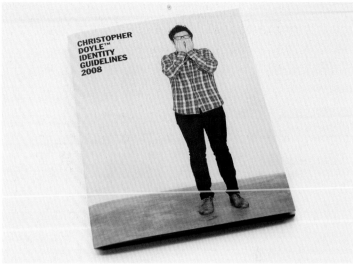

Designer
Christopher Doyle
Copywriter
Christopher Doyle

Creative Director
Christopher Doyle
Photographer
Ian Haigh

Client
You, me and
everyone I know

Brand
Christopher Doyle

Brand Applications: Printed Material

Christopher Doyle

Christopher Doyle Identity Guidelines
Everybody defines themselves differently. My name is Christopher Doyle. I am a designer and a vegetarian. I have engaged with more identities than I can remember, but none more regularly or more intensely than my own. My identity is how I act, look, feel and sound as a person. It has taken 30 years to get to this solution. This is a guide to who I am today, and who I will be in the future. There are things I like about myself and things I hate. Things will happen to my identity that I'm not even aware of yet. I will continue to evolve. Hopefully.

Designer
Mark Lester
Copywriter
Mark Lester

Creative Director
Mark Lester

Illustrator
Daniel Ingham
Typographer
Daniel Ingham

Design Group
MARK
Client
Wigan Little Theatre

Brand Applications: Printed Material

MARK
for Wigan Little Theatre

Wigan Little Theatre Brand Identity
Most organisations want communications that make them look bigger than they really are. Not this one. For one of Britain's best and longest established amateur theatres, thinking small was the obvious way to go.

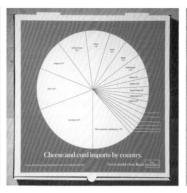

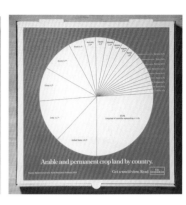

Art Director
James Clunie
Copywriter
Kara Goodrich
Creative Director
James Clunie
Senior Creative Director
Kara Goodrich

Chief Creative Officers
David Lubars
Bill Bruce
Advertising Agency
BBDO New York
Agency Producer
Kathy Lando

Account Manager
Kate Houghton
Account Director
Clayton Ruebensaal
Account Associate
Robin Quill

Senior Vice President
Clayton Ruebensaal
Client
The Economist

Brand Applications: Printed Material

BBDO New York
for The Economist

Pizza Boxes
In September 2008, a print, online and outdoor advertising campaign was launched for 'The Economist' in Philadelphia, as one city in a cross-country promotional blitz. To reach college students, 80,000 Economist-branded pizza boxes emblazoned with Economist-inspired pie charts were distributed to pizzerias close to large college campuses in the Philadelphia area.

Design Directors
Brian Fraser
Simon Learman
Art Director
Brian Fraser

Copywriter
Simon Learman
Executive Creative Directors
Brian Fraser
Simon Learman

Illustrator
Harry Malt
Advertising Agency
McCann Erickson
London

Client
McCann Erickson
London

Branded Environments

McCann Erickson London

Agency Branding
We wanted to demonstrate how McCann Erickson London has changed. And that the real beauty is to be found inside our Art Deco building, inside the heads of the people that work there. So we created a new identity that formed a physical connection between the brilliant minds of our employees and the building. In doing so, we transformed a traditional office space into a thought-inspiring environment that fosters freethinking. When you pass through our building, you'll find that it's crammed full of wonderful ideas, thousands of them. Our drawings are constantly evolving too, as they help to define our brand philosophy and culture. It's all about making people feel good when they come to work. Feel free to drop in.

Brand Applications: Branded Environments

johnson banks
for Glenfiddich Single Malt

Glenfiddich Barrel Art
These pieces were designed to show the amount of time it takes to prepare this famous whisky. The 'job' of each item is explained, so for 15 years the staves of the barrel stand guard, and for 12 years the flavour simply grows and grows. All of the artwork is made from whisky barrels, which are then etched or sand-blasted with type. The pieces were on temporary display and are now used as talking points at whisky events and at the distillery's own gallery.

Designers	**Design Director**	**Photographer**	**Client**
Owen Evans	Michael Johnson	Kevin Summers	Glenfiddich Single
Michael Johnson	**Model Maker**	**Design Group**	Malt
Pali Palavathanan	Wesley West	johnson banks	**Brand**
			Glenfiddich

Brand Applications: Branded Environments

GBH
for PUMA International

PUMA Il Mostro
In 2008, PUMA became a competitor in, and official supplier of the 2008 Volvo Ocean Race. GBH were briefed to create all branding and design for PUMA's involvement, which included creating the livery of the race boat itself. It was key that the PUMA philosophy of doing things its own way was on display in the usually corporate world of sailing. Named 'Il Mostro' (Italian for monster) after PUMA's biggest selling shoe, the boat was designed to look just like the shoe. In addition, GBH designed a 'boating' typeface, which was used for the 'Il Mostro' logotype and formed the basis of the overall branding for PUMA ocean racing, the team, advertising and merchandise.

Designers	**Design Directors**	**Design Group**	**Global Brand**
Jason Gregory	Jason Gregory	GBH	**Manager**
Peter Hale	Peter Hale	**Creative Directors**	Antonio Bertone
Russell Saunders		Mark Bonner	**Client**
Jacob Vanderkar		Jason Gregory	PUMA International
		Peter Hale	

339

Designers
Adam Giles
Mark Wheatcroft
Architect
Nicola Osborn

Design Directors
Gareth Howat
David Kimpton
Jim Sutherland
Illustrator
Adam Giles

Design Group
Hat-trick Design
Consultants
Marketing Manager
Kristi O'Connell

Client
Land Securities
Brand
Cardinal Café

Brand Applications: Branded Environments

Hat-trick Design Consultants
for Land Securities

Cardinal Café
A café for estate workers was built in the reception area of Cardinal Place, a large commercial development in Victoria, London. To create the name and branding for the café, we devised a character inspired by the cardinal bird – a title affiliated with the area. Using a character enabled us to create vibrancy in the café area, keeping it distinct from the corporate reception area. Graphics were applied using vinyl, which is updatable, allowing for the birds to 'move' around the area over time.

Typography
Thonik
Design Agency
Thonik

Brand Director
Aaron Betsky

Client
The International
Architecture
Biennale Venice

Brand
The 11th International
Architecture Biennale
Venice

Brand Applications: Branded Environments

Thonik
for The International Architecture
Biennale Venice

Out There: Architecture Beyond Building
Thonik provided all the graphics for the 11th International Architecture Biennale in Venice. The agency, in close collaboration with curator Aaron Betsky, was also responsible for the scenography of the Corderia, which featured 3D graphic walls related to the visual identity. Thonik's 2D and 3D design was based on a chain of globes, alternating with universally recognisable angular house shapes, which provided opportunities for endless configurations and series in reference to the ornamentation and beauty of Venice itself.

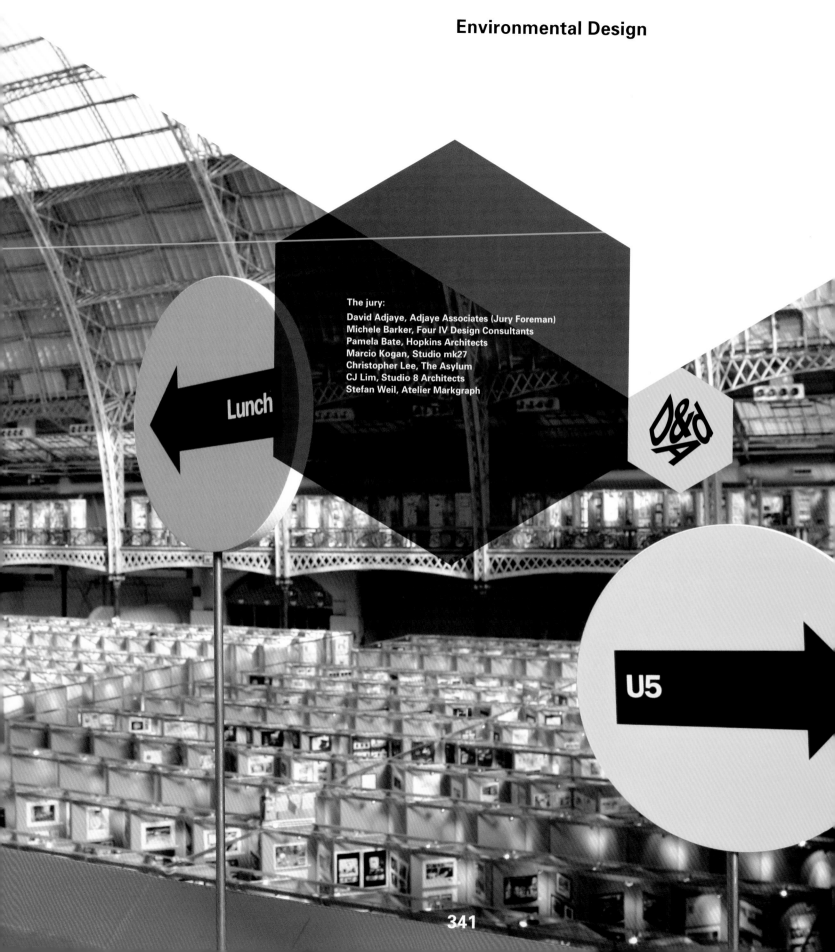

The jury:
David Adjaye, Adjaye Associates (Jury Foreman)
Michele Barker, Four IV Design Consultants
Pamela Bate, Hopkins Architects
Marcio Kogan, Studio mk27
Christopher Lee, The Asylum
CJ Lim, Studio 8 Architects
Stefan Weil, Atelier Markgraph

Lunch

U5

Designer	Manufacturer	Design Studio	Client
Ante Rasic	Graditeljstvo	Studio Rasic	Mediterranean
Creative Director	Jakovljevic		Sculptors'
Ante Rasic			Symposium
			Brand
			White Road

Public Space & Community

Studio Rasic
for Mediterranean Sculptors' Symposium

Bijela Cesta 'U iscekivanju kise' – White Road 'Waiting for the Rain'
'Waiting for the Rain' is part of an art project entitled 'White Road' within the Mediterranean Sculptors' Symposium in the Park of Sculptures in Labin, Croatia. The aim was to realise a multidimensional project in relation to nature, sculpture and man. The project then became a space of public awareness for a community and its visitors. The road itself is 352m long, consisting in 13 sections by 13 different artists. Each section is 25m long and 5m wide. The work has a multi-dimensional meaning, and includes nature and weather as an integral part of its look and form. One extra dimension is the text 'White Road', which is formed by the cut-out plates.

Architects
Alan Dempsey
Alvin Huang
Photographer
James Brittain

Assembly
Design Research
Lab Rieder
Project
Coordinators
Yusuke Obuchi
Patrik Schumacher

Architectural Firm
Nex Architecture
Manufacturer
Rieder
Structural
Engineering
Adams Kara Taylor

Client
Design Research Lab
Brand
Architectural
Association School

Public Space & Community

Nex Architecture
for Design Research Lab

[C]space DRL10 Pavilion
This pavilion is the winning entry to a design competition held by the Architectural Association School to celebrate the tenth anniversary of the Design Research Lab. The structure was put together by merging many flat concrete and steel elements into a single continuous curved form, with a thickened ground that accommodates multiple different uses and modes of occupation. The design and construction of the pavilion made radical use of digital modelling and fabrication techniques to manage over 850 uniquely shaped pieces and 3,000 joints of varying angles. The realisation of this project was generously supported by Rieder, Adams Kara Taylor, Buro Happold, Zaha Hadid Architects, and Innova Construction.

Architect
David Kohn
Illustrator
Rory Crichton

Architectural Practice
David Kohn
Architects

Art Directors
Pablo Flack
David Waddington

Client
Bistrotheque
Brand
Flash

Leisure & Tourism

David Kohn Architects
for Bistrotheque

Flash

Flash was a temporary restaurant at the Royal Academy of Arts open from November 2008 to January 2009. As part of the GSK Contemporary season of arts events, the restaurant was conceived as an installation within a gallery space, where the dining experience had the theatricality and provisional nature of a performance. The dining room interior was constructed of art packing crates inlaid with mirrors and trompe l'oeil scenes from an anarchic garden: swirling plantlife, dining underwater creatures and flocks of parakeets, inspired both by the history of the site as the gardens of Burlington House and imaginary worlds beyond Mayfair.

344

Designers	Art Directors	Advertising Agency	Client
Yuya Kawamura	Hideo Kambara	Dentsu Tokyo	KDDI
Yasunari Mori	Yasunari Mori	**Account Handler**	CORPORATION
Kenichi Togashi	Kenichi Togashi	Takeshi Miayakawa	**Brands**
Copywriter	**Creative Directors**		Au
Takanori Inoue	Hideo Kambara		Ply
	Hirotoshi Seki		

Temporary Exhibitions

Dentsu Tokyo
for KDDI CORPORATION

Ply Exhibition

Au is the second largest mobile carrier in Japan, and is facing increasing competition. Our goal was to introduce the product's new design-focused functionality in a market where there are more function-oriented designs. We used the idea of 'ply – layers' to incorporate new functions by keeping the same design. This resulted in Ply, a six-layered mobile phone with a totally new look, as each layer had a different colour and function. We presented the product at a paper craft exhibition to showcase it in an emotional manner, rather than as a new technology. Of the 291,675 exhibition visitors, 84 per cent gave the design quality a good rating, and 82.5 per cent answered that their impression of the company had improved.

345

Architectural Author	Interior Designers	Suzana Glogowski	Photographer
Marcio Kogan	Carolina Castroviejo	Eduardo Glycério	Nelson Kon
Architectural	Diana Radomysler	Gabriel Kogan	**Design Group**
Co-authors	**Architect**	Maria Cristina Motta	Studio mk27
Samanta Cafardo	**Collaborators**	Oswaldo Pessano	**General Contractors**
Carolina Castroviejo	Renata Furlanetto	Lair Reis	Fairbanks & Pilnik
Diana Radomysler		Mariana Simas	
		Landscape Architect	
		Renata Tilli	

Residential

Studio mk27
for Fairbanks & Pilnik

Casa Panamá
The site of Casa Panamá, a house built for private clients, is located just some blocks from Paulista, the financial centre of São Paulo. The client has an important art collection, featuring modern Brazilian art, and the property was designed to house this collection. The works of art are scattered throughout the residence, from the bedrooms to the gardens. The stone and wood, materials that refer to traditional Brazilian buildings, are mixed with modern materials, such as reinforced concrete and plastic, which creates an architectural language.

Architect	Architectural	Structural	Cost Consultant
Alex de Rijke	Company	Engineers	Ross Russell
Architectural	dRMM	Michael Hadi	**Client**
Assistant	**Mechanical**	Rutger Snoek	Ross Russell
Joana Pestana	**Engineering**	**Project Manager**	
Gonçalves Lages	DJW Consulting	Ross Russell	

Residential

dRMM
for Ross Russell

Sliding House

The brief was to design a self-built house to retire to in order to grow food and enjoy the landscape, on a site that was a combination of rolling England and agricultural Holland, with stringent planning parameters for rural development. An appreciation of vernacular farm buildings led to a manipulation of the local timber framed and clad 'shed' idiom. The resulting linear building is sliced into three parts: house, annexe and garage, pulled off axis to create a courtyard. A 20 ton mobile roof/wall structure creates combinations of enclosure, open-air living and views according to position. This house offers radically variable spaces, shelter, sunlight and insulation according to season, weather, or a desire to delight.

Designer
Janet Wardley

Head of Visual Display
Janet Wardley

Technical Design
Harvey Nichols Display Production Team

Client
Harvey Nichols & Company

Retail & Services

Harvey Nichols & Company

Coat Hanger Skeletons
Two gigantic dinosaur skeletons appeared across the front windows of the Harvey Nichols Knightsbridge store in September 2008. The skeletons, one of a dinosaur and the other of a prehistoric fish, were designed and created in-house by Harvey Nichols' visual display team. These skeletal forms created a powerful sculpture that on closer inspection could be seen to have been made entirely out of wooden coat hangers. To highlight this fact, items of clothing were displayed occasionally, hung from a coat hanger 'bone'. Over 11,000 wooden coat hangers were cut, manipulated and suspended within the windows to form this structure which was in place for six weeks.

348

Designers
Cherin Tan
Ng Chee Yong

Design Director
Cara Ang

Creative Director
Chris Lee
Design Group
Asylum Creative

Client
Artisan Cellars

Retail & Services

Asylum Creative
for Artisan Cellars

Artisan Cellars
This cellar is as much a conversation piece as the wine it stores: 400 bottles of luxury cuvée wines are contained in a 3m x 6m cement block, extruding from the shop into the public space. The focus is the dramatic angular tunnel and its top-rate gems. The design of Artisan Cellars, a high-end wine retail space specialising in small production vineyards, stands in contrast to other cookie-cutter cellar spaces. Wine-worthy quotes by renowned writers are etched into understated white-washed walls. The simplicity and crispness of the surroundings give emphasis to the ten-seater tasting room, which will play host to a series of cosy wine tasting sessions for discerning groups.

349

Principal Architects	**Architectural**	**Creative Directors**	**Global Brand**
Giuseppe Lignano	**Company**	Mark Bonner	**Manager**
Ada Tolla	LOT-EK	Jason Gregory	Antonio Bertone
Project Architects	**Designers**	Peter Hale	**Client**
Koki Hashimoto	Mark Bonner	**Design Group**	PUMA International
Keisuke Nibe	Harry Edmonds	GBH	**Brand**
	Jason Gregory		PUMA
	Peter Hale		
	Adam Mileusnic		
	Jacob Vanderkar		

Leisure & Tourism

GBH & LOT-EK
for PUMA International

PUMA City
Aiming to shake up the stuffy world of sailing, PUMA became a competitor and official supplier of the 2008 Volvo Ocean Race. PUMA commissioned LOT-EK and GBH for the architecture and branding of its corporate hospitality venue for the event. The result was the creation of a flat pack structure made of 24 regular shipping containers which, when bolted together, housed three PUMA stores, two offices, a bar and hospitality terraces, all over three floors. The structure, called PUMA City, was designed to be disassembled, shipped as regular containers and reassembled at each port it visited during the race.

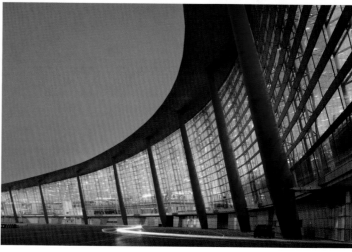

Architectural Firm	Structural	Client	Brand
Foster + Partners	Engineering	Beijing Capital	Beijing Capital
Airport Consultants	Arup	International Airport	International Airport
NACO		Company	

Leisure & Tourism

Foster + Partners
for Beijing Capital International Airport

Beijing Capital International Airport Terminal 3
Beijing's new international terminal is the world's largest and most advanced airport building, not only technologically, but also in terms of passenger experience, operational efficiency and sustainability. Completed as the gateway to the city for athletes participating in the 29th Olympiad, it is designed to be welcoming and uplifting. A symbol of place, its soaring aerodynamic roof and dragon-like form celebrate the thrill and poetry of flight, and evoke traditional Chinese colours and symbols.

Architectural Firm	Plaza Architectural	Structural & Facade	Clients
Perkins Eastman	**Firm**	**Engineering**	City of New York
Concept	PKSB Architects	Dewhurst	Coalition for Father
Architectural Firm		MacFarlane and	Duffy Theatre
Choi Ropiha		Partners	Development Fund
			Times Square
			Alliance
			Brand
			TKTS

Public Space & Community

Choi Ropiha
for The City of New York

TKTS Booth & Redevelopment of Father Duffy Square
The project stems from an international design competition held to re-create New York's iconic TKTS booth in Father Duffy Square, the northern triangle of Times Square. While the brief simply requested a new booth, our design expanded the booth's function to also be a public gathering point and viewing platform for Times Square. The design has two parts: translucent red steps that terrace upwards from the ground inviting the public onboard for a new perspective of Times Square; and the booth itself which is neatly tucked beneath. With analogies to the 'red carpet' of Broadway, the red steps give the booth a memorable and fitting presence in Times Square, which strengthens the position of TKTS as a New York cultural institution.

352

Architects
Casey Jones
Reed Kroloff
David Rockwell
Designers
Keetra Dixon
Zach Gage
Thomas Haggerty
Casey Jones

Reed Kroloff
Craig Negoescu
David Rockwell
James Tichenor
Tucker Viemeister
Joshua Walton
Design Groups
Jones I Kroloff
Rockwell Group

Researchers
Mira Burak
Thomas Gardner
Virginia Harper
Kelli Harris
Delphine Mauroit

**Supporting
Researchers**
Dana Karwas
Jenny Kim
Client
Fondazione La
Biennale di Venezia

Temporary Exhibitions

Jones I Kroloff & Rockwell Group
for Fondazione La Biennale di Venezia

Hall of Fragments at the 11th International Venice Architecture Biennale
When visitors enter the Corderie dell'Arsenale, they are confronted with the 4,624 square foot Hall of Fragments, with a glowing hourglass-shaped passage of moving imagery in its centre. This is created by two giant convex screens (60 x 14.5 square foot each) onto which geometric distortions of film clips are projected. The exhibit transforms the relationship between people and their architectural environment so that the size, speed and number of visitors will determine the visuals projected on the screens, resulting in a different and new visual every time. Our firm and Jones I Kroloff chose a diverse array of clips from classic and contemporary American and foreign films, all of which exhibit remarkable architectural visions or alter our perception of known environments.

353

Designers
Cherin Tan
Ng Chee Yong

Design Director
Cara Ang
Creative Director
Chris Lee

Design Group
Asylum Creative

Client
Chocolate Research
Facility

Retail & Services

Asylum Creative
for Chocolate Research Facility

Chocolate Research Facility
Consider it a world first: chocolate bars offered in 100 different flavours. Delve into the myriad colours of the designer packaging and multitude of flavours that the concept boutique has to offer as it draws attention to chocolate, both in taste and design. Each bar comes in an understated monochromatic box. But that's only on the surface. Turn it around and things take a patterned and printed twist. The retail space sports clinical white interiors and a shop window containing rows of LED numbers, akin to the running numbers in a laboratory.

Architect
Asif Khan
Furniture Designer
Asif Khan

Steelwork Fabricator
Brian Deighton
Sash Window Joiner
Chris Reid

General Contractor
Jack O'Durdle
Structural Engineering
Adams Kara Taylor

Clients
Sophie Murray
Jane Wood
Brand
Brownfield Catering

Leisure & Tourism

Asif Khan
for Sophie Murray & Jane Wood

West Beach Café, Littlehampton
Asif Khan's first project was commissioned on his graduation from the Architectural Association. It is the product of local craftsmanship, technical innovation, a spectacular site, and a remarkable client. This traditional seaside fish and chip shop was re-imagined as a doll's house and designed to embrace English weather. Equipped to adjust its configuration seasonally, in summer the entire facade can be swung open to fill the dining space with sea air, create a room outside on the beach, or turn the café into a stage for concerts. During winter and high winds, the façade is closed and full height sash windows provide extraordinary views across the English Channel.

Designers	Creative Directors	Manufacturer	Client
Eduard Cehovin	Eduard Cehovin	Andrej Canzelj	City Council of
Tanja Devetak	Tanja Devetak	**Design Group**	Ljubljana, Slovenia
		Design Center	

Public Space & Community
Design Center
for City Council of Ljubljana, Slovenia

Zebra Crossing
Urban centres contain ordinary spaces which connect people, where people meet and travel from one point to another. To visual artists, on the other hand, they represent a place for free expression and critical reflection on the environment into which they are integrated. The Zebra project redefines the visual image of road markings, where their functionality and choice of colour remain the same. In this sense it gives design a public character that expresses good codes of practice in an innovative way. The project's goal is to change the existing image of the pedestrian crossing using a new design dimension.

Designer	Assistant Signwriter	Artist	Client
Morag Myerscough	Charlotte Read	Luke Morgan	Cathedral Group
Typographer	**Furniture Designers**	**Design Studio**	**Brand**
Morag Myerscough	Luke Morgan	Studio Myerscough	The Deptford Project
Signwriter	Morag Myerscough	**Project Director**	
Morag Myerscough		Martyn Evans	

Public Space & Community
Studio Myerscough
for Cathedral Group

The Deptford Project
In summer 2008, an old 60s 35-tonne commuter train carriage was converted into an unusual café installed in a derelict railway site in Deptford High Street, South London. Morag Myerscough was responsible for the creative concept and realisation of the graphics, interior, furniture and external platform garden. The carriage's hand-decorated exterior depicts playful images and words inspired by local history, trains and tea – denoting the ship building industry, marine rope-making and the livestock originally transported to Smithfield on the railway. The bespoke furniture was made from recycled laboratory tops and hand-painted stools with sitting-related slogans. The loo, by artist Luke Morgan, is a shrine to Elvis set in a garden shed.

355

Architects	Environmental	Structural Engineers	Liturgical Metalwork	Screens & Chairs
Keith Boswell	**Graphic Designers**	Peter Lee	**Fabricator**	**Fabrication**
Raymond Kuca	Lonny Israel	Eric Long	Marirose Jelicich	Mare Island
Design Architects	Alan Sinclair	Mark Sarkisian	**Omega Window**	Woodworks
Craig W Hartman	**Sacred Art &**	**Liturgical Consultant**	**Fabrication**	**Doors & Door Pulls**
Gene Schnair	**Designs**	Br William Woeger	Enclos Corp	**Fabrication**
Architects of Record	Rev Paul D Minnihan	**Design Firm**	Pohl	Tice Industries
Kendall/Heaton	Rev Ron Schmidt	Skidmore, Owings &	**Inscriptions**	**Client**
Associates	**Technology**	Merrill LLP	**Fabrication**	Roman Catholic
Product Designers	**Specialist**	**Project Management**	Thomas Swan Sign	Diocese of Oakland
Lonny Israel	Neil Katz	Conversion	Company	
Alan Sinclair		Management	**Ambry Screens**	
		Associates	**Fabrication**	
			Tortorelli Creations	

Public Space & Community

Skidmore, Owings & Merrill LLP
for Roman Catholic Diocese of Oakland

The Cathedral of Christ the Light

The Cathedral of Christ the Light's design of sacred elements includes product and furniture design, typography, and environmental graphic design. Our objective was to celebrate the 2,000-year-old liturgical traditions of the Catholic faith, but position the symbolic meaning of these elements within contemporary culture. The design implements technology to create continuity from the past to the 21st Century. A 12th Century image of Christ is transformed through 94,000 perforations lasercut into a dia-grid of panels. The great doors are inscribed with adjoining circles forming the ancient vesica piscis symbol. The surface texture on custom door-pulls forms a topographic map of the spiralling 13th Century Fibonacci sequence.

Architectural Author	Architectural Co-	Architect	Design Group
Marcio Kogan	**authors**	**Collaborators**	Studio mk27
Landscape Architect	Renata Furlanetto	Carolina Castroviejo	**General Contractor**
Renata Tilli	Suzana Glogowski	Maria Cristina Motta	Mantra Engenharia
	Oswaldo Pessano	**Interior Designer**	
	Diana Radomysler	Diana Radomysler	

Residential

Studio mk27
for Mantra Engenharia

Casa Corten

Casa Corten is an urban house near São Paulo's largest park. The site is long and narrow, and its residents make use of the rooftop and, especially, the park itself for leisure. The front facade is made of Corten weathering steel. There is a dialogue between the rusty texture on the outside and the stone, wood, white mortar and glass that build the space. On the ground floor, there is an ample room with a ceiling height of 5.2m and four folding doors that completely open out to the deck and external fireplace. In the living room, a free wooden volume houses the kitchen and utilities. The three bedrooms are located on the second floor.

Architectural Studio
Jump Studios

Creative Director
Shaun Fernandes

Client
Bloomberg

Jump Studios
for Bloomberg

Bloomberg Installation
A tree 'grows' through three consecutive floors of Bloomberg's London headquarters, offering meeting and socialising opportunities at each constituent part. The trunk becomes an enclosure, the branches become benches and the canopy a series of soft recliners to relax on.

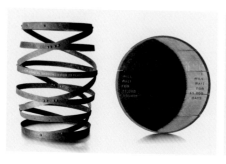

Designers
Owen Evans
Michael Johnson
Pali Palavathanan

Design Director
Michael Johnson
Model Maker
Wesley West

Photographer
Kevin Summers
Design Group
johnson banks

Client
Genfiddich Single
Malt
Brand
Glenfiddich

johnson banks
for Glenfiddich Single Malt

Glenfidich Barrel Art
These pieces were designed to show the amount of time it takes to prepare this famous whisky. The 'job' of each item is explained, so for 15 years the staves of the barrel stand guard, and for 12 years the flavour simply grows and grows. All of the artwork is made from whisky barrels, which are then etched or sand-blasted with type. The pieces were on temporary display and are now used as talking points at whisky events and at the distillery's own gallery.

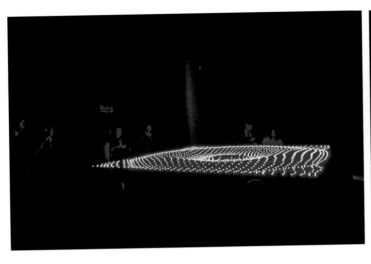

Design Group
Héctor Serrano
Studio

Client
Roca

Héctor Serrano Studio
for Roca

Waterdrop
'Waterdrop' is a homage to water; a spectacular and engaging installation capturing the beauty of water. It represents the experience of a drop falling into water, creating hypnotic movement and ripples. The project invites us to enjoy and explore water without using a drop, reflecting Roca's fundamental belief that innovation and sustainability can go hand in hand. The installation uses innovative and sophisticated technology in an unexpected and inventive way to capture this natural phenomenon. Now permanently housed in Roca's showroom in Madrid, the project has also been exhibited in London and Frankfurt.

Designer
Adam Giles
Manufacturer
Richard Smart

Creative Directors
Gareth Howat
David Kimpton
Jim Sutherland

Design Group
Hat-trick Design
Consultants
Marketing Manager
Richard Glassborow

Client
Land Securities
Brand
Piccadilly Lights

Installations

Hat-trick Design Consultants
for Land Securities

Piccadilly Lights Switch
Land Securities commissioned a temporary hoarding for one of their premises at Piccadilly Lights, before it was occupied by new tenants. The hoarding was designed to celebrate the company's ownership of this prestigious London location. The copy on the hoarding reads: 'Piccadilly Lights, owned, managed and illuminated by Land Securities'.

The jury:
Bruce Duckworth, Turner Duckworth (Jury Foreman)
Perry Haydn Taylor, Big Fish Design
Neil Hedger, Freelance
Mårten Knutsson, Family Business
Allison Miguel, Freelance
Katja Thielen, Together Design
Grant Willis, Williams Murray Hamm

Packaging Design

Designers
Yo Kimura
Yoshihiro Yagi
Art Director
Yoshihiro Yagi

Copywriter
Haruko Tsutsui
Printer
Nao Morimi

Advertising Agency
Dentsu Tokyo
Account Handler
Kosaku Miyata

Brand Manager
Chie Ichida
Client
Ichida Garden

Packaging

Dentsu Tokyo
for Ichida Garden

Newspaper to New Paper Project
We designed a piece of packaging for the street vendor that sells farm-grown fruit and vegetables, based on the old newspaper used to wrap vegetables. A newspaper has two benefits: its ability to retain moisture and keep vegetables fresh for longer; and the fact that it is being reused. Under the 'Newspaper to New Paper' project, we used newspapers that had been thrown away and added an element of playful and engaging design, for both those selling the produce and those buying it. As a result, the project was eco-friendly as well as budget-friendly. By simply adding dots and stripes to the old newspaper, we created a completely new packaging design.

360

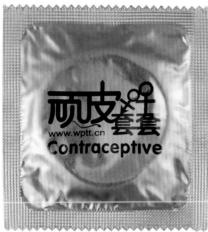

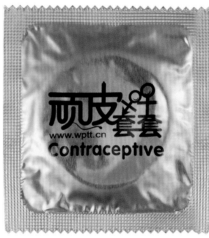

Designer	Copywriter	Design Studio	Marketing Manager
Matin Ma	Eric Shang	HanTang	Perry Ma
Design Director	**Creative Directors**	Communications	**Client**
Wayne Huang	Eden Cheng	Group	Quzhou Seezo
Art Directors	Wayne Huang	**Account Handler**	Trading
Joy Huang	**Illustrators**	Tommy Tao	**Brand**
Wayne Huang	Nunu Wang	**Brand Manager**	Wptt Contraceptive
So Kayan	Ru Zhang	Jack Tan	
Jing Wang	**Photographer**		
	Eric ShangGuo Kui		

Packaging

HanTang Communications Group
for Quzhou Seezo Trading

Trouble Maker Condoms
Wptt Contraceptive wanted to create new packaging with visual impact. The objective was to emphasise the effectiveness of Wptt Contraceptive products by indicating the painful consequences of having sex without a condom. More than 100,000 people have used the condoms, and sales have increased by 12 per cent.

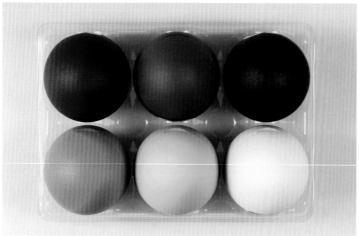

Physical Shape

Dfraile
for Soso

Designers	Art Director	Design Studio	Client
Eduardo del Fraile	Eduardo del Fraile	Dfraile	SosoFactory
Aurelia Gonzalez	**Copywriter**	**Industrial**	**Brand**
Industrial Designers	Eduardo del Fraile	**Development**	Soso
Eduardo del Fraile		Grupo Idea	
Aurelia Gonzalez			

Soso

Soso is a brand of high quality salts, which come from a salt mine located in a natural reserve in the south of Spain. The client was looking for a distinguishing container that could be used both to store salts and as a salt cellar. An egg is the perfect container, as its own shell is the packaging, so it was decided that an egg shape would be reproduced. The project and the brand were named Soso, which means 'lacking salt' or 'short of salt' in Spanish. Also selected in Packaging.

Designer
Ivana Martinovic
Retoucher
Dylan Morgan

Design Studio
War Design Studios
Account Handlers
Kate Jensen
Melissa Walker

Marketing Manager
Hannah Logan

Client
Logan Wines
Brand
Logan

Packaging

War Design Studios
for Logan Wines

Signature
Peter Logan's very particular approach to his winemaking inspired this choice of dimensional embroidery for the redesign of the Logan wine label. This was a fitting metaphor for the patience, care and love that goes into every bottle. By illustrating fruits, berries, leaves and flowers, each label visually indicates the textures and flavours inside.

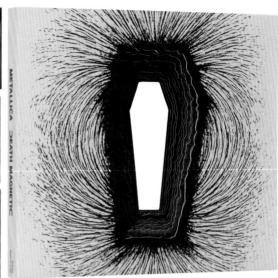

Designers
Emily Charette
Jamie McCathie
Marty O'Connor
Design Director
Sarah Moffat
Design Assistant
Brian Labus
Creative Directors
Bruce Duckworth
David Turner

Photographers
Anton Corbin
Robert Daly
Andy Grimshaw
Britt Hull
Gavin Hurrell
Mike Kemp
Harper Reed
Tom Schierlitz
Craig Snelgrove
David Turner

Photography
Missouri State
Highway Patrol
Artworker
Craig Snelgrove
Retouchers
Peter Ruane
Craig Snelgrove

Design Company
Turner Duckworth:
London and San
Francisco
Client
Metallica

Packaging

Turner Duckworth: London and San Francisco
for Metallica

Death Magnetic Digi CD
For Metallica's ninth studio album, 'Death Magnetic', Turner Duckworth developed an iconic, three-dimensional CD package using a conspicuous, sunken grave image and an innovative, layered die cut. The end product shows dirt being sucked down towards a coffin, which lies low in a deepening pit. The classic Metallica logo was reworked and a signature, typographic style created.

Designer
Clem Devine

Creative Director
Dean Poole

Design Studio
Alt Group

Client
Xero

Packaging

Alt Group
for Xero

Xero Wine Bottle
Xero is an online accounting system designed for small businesses and their advisors. The brief was to develop a direct mail piece to act as a general promotional gift that supported the company's product and positioning. The solution was a bottle of wine with the bottom line in mind.

Designers
Eszter Clark
Ryan Meis

Copywriter
Vinnie Chieco
Creative Directors
Katie Jain
Joel Templin

Illustrator
Paul Hoffman
Design Studio
Hatch Design

Client
JAQK Cellars

Packaging

Hatch Design
for JAQK Cellars

JAQK Cellars Full House
JAQK Cellars is a new fine wine brand that wraps one thing people love, wine, inside another, gaming. This lifestyle approach to branding wine is virtually unheard of in the industry, creating a huge opportunity to stand out in a hopelessly crowded category. Collaborating with a colleague who named the iPod, we named the company, as well as each wine, and positioned it under the tag line, 'Play a little'. We did all the design work and sourced all materials, going as far as finding a specialty glass boutique in Milan to create the customised bottle for the flagship Cabernet.

Designer	Creative Directors	Art Buyer	Client
Daniel Schweinzer	Helmut Meyer	Christina Hufgard	Friedrich Wilhelm
Art Director	Gregor Seitz	**Account Handler**	und Karin Reller
Daniel Schweinzer	**Photographer**	Carina Hadasch	OHG
Copywriter	Jo Bacherl	**Marketing Manager**	**Brand**
Lukas Liske	**Advertising Agency**	Karin Reller	Rellana Hair
	Ogilvy Frankfurt		

Packaging

Ogilvy Frankfurt
for Rellana Hair

Woolly Heads
The objective was to promote Rellana Hair, a range of fringed yarn, to wool buyers who are looking for something special in the upcoming winter season. In order to demonstrate the typical character of the wool at first sight, faces were printed on the labels around the balls of wool. As a result, the packaging communicated the main use of the yarn: it is perfect for hats and scarves.

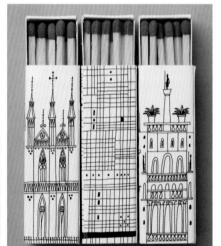

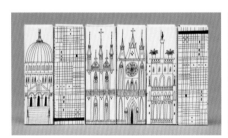

Art Director	Design Agency	Brand Marketing	Client
Lisa Careborg	Happy Forsman &	**Manager**	The Swedish
Creative Director	Bodenfors	Bitte Nygren	Museum
Anders Kornestedt	**Account Handler**		of Architecture
Illustrator	Madeliene Sikström		
Klas Fahlén			

Packaging

Happy Forsman & Bodenfors
for The Swedish Museum of Architecture

Matchbox City
With illustrations of different architectural styles – Renaissance, international and gothic – together the match boxes create a small city block. The boxes are sold in the Swedish Museum of Architecture in Stockholm.

Designer
Santosh Padhi
Art Director
Santosh Padhi

Advertising Agency
Leo Burnett Mumbai
Account Handler
Mona Mehra

Marketing Manager
Subash Panigrahi
Client
Lokart

Brand
Lokart Paint Thinner

Packaging

Leo Burnett Mumbai
for Lokart

Splash – Blue / Green / Orange /Yellow
The purpose of a thinner is to make paint thinner. To highlight the product's benefit, we decided to place it upfront on the packaging in an eye-catching way: in the form of colour splatters. What sets this range apart is that each bottle of thinner has a different form of splatter on it.

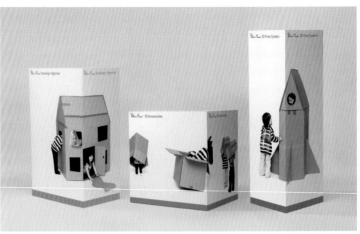

Designer	Creative Heads	Photographer	Account Handlers
Emma Morton	Simon Griffin	Ben Wedderburn	Sarah Benson
Art Director	Adam Rix	**Artworker**	Ali Johnson
Emma Morton	**Typographer**	Jonathan Robertson	**Client**
Creative Director	Emma Morton	**Design Studio**	Silver Cross
Phil Skegg		LOVE	

Packaging

LOVE
for Silver Cross

Small Kids, Big Boxes
Prams, pushchairs and strollers aren't the most fun things for kids to play with, but the boxes are much more interesting. Rather than chuck out the old boxes for recycling, we wanted people to re-use them as houses, boats or even space rockets.

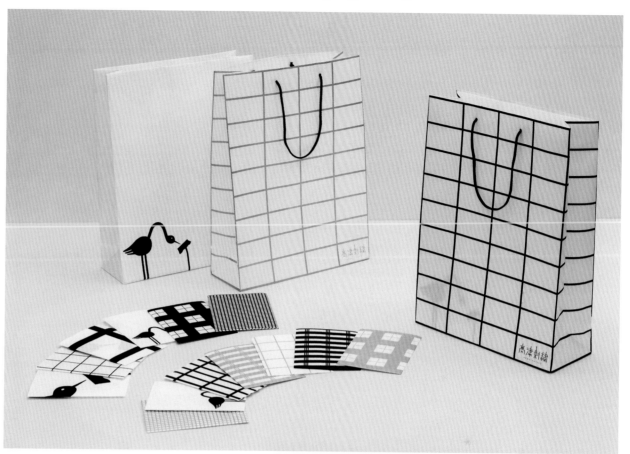

Designers
Yo Kimura
Yoshihiro Yagi
Art Director
Yoshihiro Yagi

Copywriter
Haruko Tsutsui
Illustrator
Chie Ichida

Print Producer
Takeshi Arimoto
Advertising Agency
Dentsu Kansai

Account Handler
Kosaku Miyata
Client
Kouzu Embroidery

Packaging

Dentsu Kansai
for Kouzu Embroidery

Silhouette of Crane
The image and the theme for this packaging is the Japanese fairy tale, 'The Grateful Crane', in which a crane does fine embroidery in return for a Japanese man's kindness. We chose this story for the embroidery theme, and because the crane is the symbol of Japan. Different forms of packaging – shopping bags, envelopes and wrapping paper – are exquisitely designed. Each package has two parts: one for the inside; the other for the outside. The inside part portrays the crane, while the outside is made with semi-transparent paper to show the silhouette of the crane inside, as the scene of the original story. We also prepared different patterns for the outside and the inside for customisable packaging.

Designer	Client	Brand
Allison Murray	Bob Parkinson	Made by Bob

Packaging

Allison Murray
for Made by Bob

Made by Bob
Made by Bob is a restaurant and delicatessen in the heart of the Cotswolds. Bob Parkinson, a trained London chef, devises, prepares, and sells all his own products within his establishment. Everything has his idiosyncratic mark and his total involvement, hence the idea behind the brand name. The packaging focuses on a chef's blue-and-white striped tied apron to emphasise real cooking and chef credentials. The brand language and tone of voice is direct and uncomplicated. The packaging is clean, modern, and restrained. The carrier bags are designed to look like a real apron.

Designers
Natalie Chung
Sarah Pidgeon
Copywriter
Sylvie Saunders
Creative Director
Shaun Bowen

Digital Artworker
Lucy Milne
**Senior Digital
Artworker**
Henry Preston
Realisation Manager
Tracy Sutton

Design Agency
Pearlfisher
Account Handlers
Beth Marcall
Nic Robson
Erin Tucker

Head of Buying
Zoe Jackson
Client
Jamie Oliver
Brand
Jme

Packaging

Pearlfisher
for Jamie Oliver

Jme Food Range
Jme is a stand-alone brand that moves Jamie Oliver from the kitchen into the home, retaining the chef's values, while bringing together experienced designers, producers and growers to form a collaborative lifestyle brand. The Jme identity reflects this collective spirit. Jme larder products are practical yet creative, referencing the artisan traditions of market stall markers and handwritten labels. Each item is given the freedom to reflect its function and personality through design, with the striking logo used to link the eclectic ranges. Ranges are segmented according to how we use our homes, celebrating individuality rather than dictating a lifestyle ideal. Flexible, fresh and fun, it's the future of lifestyle branding.

Designer	Creative Group Head	Account Handler	Client
Joe Holt	Aaron Hinchion	Kevin Smith	Henrietta Morrison
Art Director	**Illustrator**	**Client Services**	**Brand**
Aaron Hinchion	Petra Borner	**Manager**	Lily's Kitchen
Copywriters	**Producer**	Liz Wilson	
Aaron Hinchion	Eve Price		
Natalie Ranger	**Creative Agency**		
Creative Director	Albion		
Nick Darken			

Packaging

Albion
for Lily's Kitchen

Lily's Kitchen: Proper Pet Food

Entrepreneur Henrietta Morrison came to Albion with a new idea: pet food that is actually made from good cuts of meat and nice healthy veggies. All stuff that makes dogs and cats smell better and live longer. No more slurry, ash or bits of carcass. We told Henrietta it was only natural to name her brand after her own dog Lily. And we told her that her brand proposition should simply be 'Proper Dog Food', because that was what she was passionate about. We wanted Lily's Kitchen to feel modern but have a timelessness to it. Something that says, 'The food in this tin is quality', without resorting to the usual pictures of big dog faces.

372

Art Director
Reginald Wagner
Copywriters
Madelen Gwosdz
Katharina Trumbach
Creative Director
Katrin Oeding

Illustrators
Santa Gustina
Jan Simmerl
Advertising Agency
Kolle Rebbe/KOREFE

Account Handlers
Carolin Meyer
Kristina Wulf
Marketing Manager
Anthony Hammond

Client
Anthony's Garage
Winery
Brand
Anthony's
Honeytube

Packaging

Kolle Rebbe/KOREFE
for Anthony's Garage Winery

Honeytube
Winemaker Anthony Hammond produces his delicatessen foods in a former tractor repair shop. As such, all his products need an industrial look and feel. This honey comes in packaging similar to that found in garages; in this case, in tubes. Different illustrations for each type of honey let consumers peek 'behind the scenes'. In comic book style, the illustrations show bees working in a factory, on the nectar and its special ingredients.

Graphic Designer
Jan Simmerl
Art Director
Reginald Wagner
Copywriter
Katharina Trumbach

Creative Director
Katrin Oeding
Illustrator
Reginald Wagner
Advertising Agency
Kolle Rebbe/KOREFE

Account Handlers
Carolin Meyer
Kristina Wulf
Marketing Manager
Anthony Hammond

Client
Anthony's Garage
Winery
Brand
Anthony's Oil Change

Packaging

Kolle Rebbe/KOREFE
for Anthony's Garage Winery

Oil Change
Both the name of the oil and its packaging match the industrial look and feel of the brand. Called Oil Change, based on what garages often do, the oil is packaged in high-quality oil cans with a different illustration for each type of oil. The illustrations depict tiny monsters hidden in the oil stains, which emerge when you look through the bottles. The monsters represent the three different ingredients, lemon, rosemary and chilli, and what happens to them when you combine them with olive oil.

Packaging

Family Business
for The Absolut Company

Absolut Colors
In an Absolut world, all people have the right to be who they are and be proud of it. The Absolut Colors packaging was created in collaboration with Gilbert Baker, the man behind the Pride flag, to hold up that belief. It was launched with a cocktail collection and numerous parties all over the world, and will be used for many years to support all kinds of proud people.

Designers	**Copywriters**	**Project Manager**	**Client**
Gilbert Baker	Mårten Knutsson	Melker Ström	The Absolut
Fredrik Lindquist	Fredrik Skärheden	**Account Handler**	Company
Design Director	**Creative Director**	Frederika Curry-	**Brand**
Jesper Klarin	Mårten Knutsson	Ohlson	Absolut Vodka
Art Director	**Advertising Agency**	**Marketing Director**	
Jesper Klarin	Family Business	Cecilia Falk	

Packaging

Happy
for VF Arvind Brands

Skinny Jeans
With the Lee Skinny campaign generating a mad rush at all Lee stores, we decided to take it one step further. Lee wanted to be the brand for skinny jeans. So we created a packaging design that matched the season's hottest trend – skinny. Needless to say, the packaging received just as many compliments as the ladies wearing the jeans themselves. In no time, people were spotted with skinny bags; everybody knew what they had just purchased and from where. The packaging also added to the visual merchandising of Lee stores.

Designer	**Creative Directors**	**Advertising Agency**	**Client**
Praveen Das	Praveen Das	Happy	VF Arvind Brands
Art Director	Kartik Iyer	**Brand Manager**	**Brand**
Praveen Das	**Illustrator**	Vipul Mathur	Lee
Copywriter	Ramkrishna R		
Kartik Iyer			

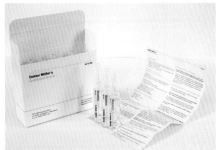

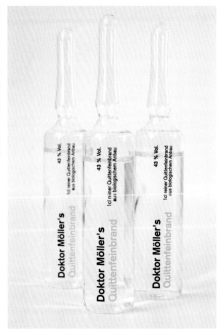

Graphic Designer
Adrian Jaeschke
Art Director
Alexander Nagel
Copywriter
Cosimo Möller

Creative Director
Christoph Everke
Executive Creative Director
Alex Schill

Advertising Agency
Serviceplan
Account Supervisor
Anne Jordan

Client
Schnapsbrennerei
Doktor
Thorsten Möller
Brand
Doktor Möller's
Quince Brandy

Packaging

Serviceplan
for Doktor Möller's Quince Brandy

Doktor Möller's Quince
The objective was to feature a non-medical product with the peculiarity that it could be used as medicine. But only when prescribed by a doctor!

Designer
Santosh Padhi
Art Director
Santosh Padhi

Production Manager
Nitin Dighe
Advertising Agency
Leo Burnett India

Account Handler
Mona Mehra
Marketing Manager
Dipen Doshi

Client
Fudkor India
Brand
Fudkor Lemon
Flavoured Tea

Packaging

Leo Burnett India
for Fudkor Lemon Flavoured Tea

String
There are plenty of tea bags available on the market; to stand out on the shelf, we designed packaging that didn't carry a logo on the front of the tin. The tin was an olive colour, with an actual size tea bag string coming out of the lid, on which the logo was printed. This made the contents of the tin very clear.

Packaging Design

Physical Shape

Stranger & Stranger
for Solerno

Solerno

The orange liqueur market is dominated by two old French brands whose dark bottles and syrupy liquids are enjoyed mainly by older women at Christmas. Solerno's lighter, brighter liqueur is aimed at the 'Sex and the City' generation and needed packaging that would inspire a younger audience to experiment with a blood orange liqueur. Although the orange squeezer punt idea was arrived at early on, it took over two years to develop the bottle production and define the provenance of the product. The famous glassmakers of Murano in Italy were the main inspiration for the bottle shape and smoked colouration.

Designers	Creative Director	Design Agency	Client
Guy Pratt	Kevin Shaw	Stranger & Stranger	William Grant & Sons
Kevin Shaw	**Illustrator**	**Brand Manager**	**Brand**
	Alex Machin	Ann Ho	Solerno

Physical Shape

Turner Duckworth: London and San Francisco
for Metallica

Death Magnetic Special Edition Coffin

When asked to create a special edition box set to celebrate the release of Metallica's ninth studio album 'Death Magnetic', Turner Duckworth drew inspiration directly from the album name, creating a sleek, smooth, unadulterated coffin. The disconcerting package contains a limited edition CD, flag, T-shirt and plectrums, all designed by Turner Duckworth. A dark yet irresistible piece of memorabilia.

Designers	Design Director	Creative Directors	Design Company
Emily Charette	Sarah Moffat	Bruce Duckworth	Turner Duckworth:
Marty O'Connor	**Design Assistant**	David Turner	London and San
Jamie McCathie	Brian Labus	**Artworker**	Francisco
		Craig Snelgrove	**Client**
			Metallica

376

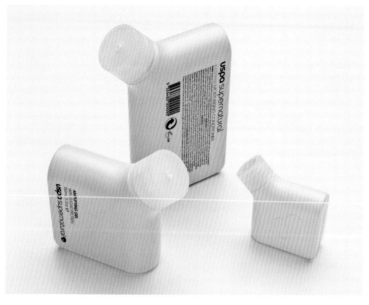

Designer
Mark Evans

Design Directors
Todd Gill
Brenan Liston
Jonnie Vigar

Design Studio
Container

Client
U Corporation
Brand
USPA

Physical Shape

Container
for U Corporation

USPA Supernatural Haircare
For USPA's Supernatural haircare range, the packaging design needed to express their philosophy – the combination of age-old botanical wisdom with the latest chemistry. The twist-cap extending up and out of the bottles represents nature and growth, while the translucency reveals the technology of the mechanism. A rich colour palette, combined with bottles that orientate in a variety of configurations, allows strong merchandising options.

Designer
Mark Evans

Design Directors
Todd Gill
Brenan Liston
Jonnie Vigar

Design Studio
Container

Client
Original & Mineral
Brand
O&M

Physical Shape

Container
for Original & Mineral

Original & Mineral Haircare
O&M is a pioneer of ammonia free hair colour technology. To help the brand distinguish itself, Container were commissioned to produce a new identity and deliver packaging that reflected O&M's offer of salon professional results without harsh chemicals. The forms developed for the wet range are reminiscent of milk bottles, giving a visual cue to the formulations within: they are clean, natural and nourishing. The styling products make a bold statement that helps to create visual tension when merchandised with O&M's other products on the shelf.

Designers
Tiziana Haug
Sung Kim

Copywriters
Carmine Montalto
Mary Ellen
Muckerman

Creative Director
Todd Simmons
Design Studio
Wolff Olins

Client
Living Proof™
Brand
No Frizz

Physical Shape

Wolff Olins
for Living Proof™

Living Proof
The design challenge was to create a brand that stands apart from all other beauty brands. As each one of Living Proof's products is completely individual and solution-specific, we developed a packaging system that would mimic that; each form is exclusive to a particular solution, and the system will expand with the addition of future product lines. These forms will grow into a diverse collection of shapes and sizes as the company adds new products, but always stay rooted by material selection and colour palette. In addition to creating the brand and the packaging, we also named the product and created messaging to express product benefits and increase shopability.

378

The jury:

Sebastian Conran, Conran & Partners (Jury Foreman)
Sebastian Bergne, Sebastian Bergne Ltd
Kenya Hara, Hara Design Institute
Dan Harden, Whipsaw
Luke Miles, LG Electronics Design Europe
Luke Pearson, PearsonLloyd
Pontus Wahlgren, IDEO

Designers
Jody Akana
Bart Andre
Daniel Coster
Evans Hankey
Richard Howarth
Daniele De Iuliis

Jonathan Ive
Steve Jobs
Duncan Kerr
Shin Nishibori
Matthew Rohrbach
Peter Russell-Clarke
Douglas Satzger

Christopher Stringer
Eugene Whang
Rico Zörkendörfer
Manufacturer
Apple

Design Group
Apple Industrial
Design Team

Work & Industry
Apple Industrial Design Team

MacBook Air
The MacBook Air is a full-size 3lb notebook encased in 0.16 inches to 0.76 inches of sleek, sturdy anodised aluminium. The 13.3-inch widescreen LED backlit display is mercury and arsenic-free, making it more power efficient. The keyboard is full-size and has backlit key illumination with a built-in ambient light sensor to automatically adjust keyboard and display brightness for optimal visibility. The MacBook Air also includes a built-in iSight camera and an oversized trackpad with multi-touch technology.

Design Director	**Technical Designers**
Dick Powell	Colin Jaggard
Designers	Dan Walker
Richard Seymour	**Manufacturer**
Richard Smith	Quantum Saddle
Nick Talbot	Company
Dan Walker	

Design Group
Seymourpowell
Brand Marketing Manager
Matthew Stockford

Client
Quantum Saddle
Company
Brand
Quantum

Leisure

Seymourpowell
for Quantum Saddle Company

Quantum AMS Saddle
The Quantum AMS Saddle has been in design and development for ten years, and is set to turn the saddle market on its head. Underneath the traditional saddle exterior lies Formula One technology, which brings true innovation to a market that has remained unchanged for 200 years. Finished in the best quality calfskin, the Quantum looks like a traditional saddle, but is different in most other respects, thanks to the use of modern materials and aerospace technology. Key to the design is a unique chassis, which enables the best possible fit to the horse. This chassis comprises of two padded carbon-fibre fins, contoured to fit the back, joined at the front by a strong structure, the bridge.

381

Design Director
Omer Arbel

Manufacturer
BOCCI

Client
BOCCI

Home
Omer Arbel
for BOCCI

22
The 22 series is a complete suite of Canadian Standards Association approved interior wall accessories that challenge the traditional, tired and ubiquitous cover plate concept. Designed by Omer Arbel to 'mud in' directly on drywall, millwork or any wall surface without a visible coverplate or trim, the 22 series is an extremely subtle and minimal alternative to the currently available options.

Design Agencies
PearsonLloyd
Steelcase Design
Studio

Manufacturer
Steelcase

Client
Steelcase

Work & Industry

PearsonLloyd & Steelcase Design Studio
for Steelcase

cobi™ chair
The cobi™ chair is a response to collaborative environments and new working methods, which involve team meetings and periods of concentrated sitting on shared chairs. A flexible platform supporting a wide demographic range through self-adjusting features was paramount, as chairs were being shared regularly. As a solution to this problem, Steelcase have designed a revolutionary rocking mechanism which adjusts to users' centre of gravity, not weight. A fluted co-moulded back has fingers that flex like a second rib cage, adjusting to back shape vertically and laterally as well as tortional twisting. An elastomeric band controls spread and provides a pliable edge for side sitting.

383

Product Design

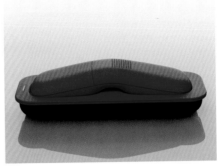

Designers
Sachin Chauhan
Tej Chauhan

Manufacturer
SGW Global
Design Group
ChauhanStudio.

Marketing Manager
Lesley Taylor

Client
SGW

Home

ChauhanStudio.
for SGW

Colombo Two

The objective was to design an enduring and emotive telephone that would appeal to a broad audience. It had to suit a range of environments and be easy to relate to and use, efficient to manufacture and have a competitive retail price to make it as accessible as possible. The design was kept modern but also friendly by trying to create an essence of familiarity. Being a landline telephone, a visual distinction was created between the earpiece and mouthpiece areas, a light reference to traditional telephone receivers. The shape of the handset is designed for comfort and ease of use. It is available from Corso Como 10 in Milan to mainstream high street retailers.

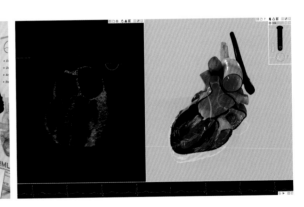

Design Directors
Adam Cubitt
Peter Reilly
Designers
Bruce Martin
Andrew Smith
Sue Wright

Technical Designers
Adam Cubitt
Peter Reilly
Manufacturer
Glassworks

Producer
Alenka Abraham
Design Group
Glassworks
Marketing Manager
Philip Brading

Client
Inventive Medical
Brand
HeartWorks

Health & Medical

Glassworks
for Inventive Medical

HeartWorks

Inventive Medical presents HeartWorks, a teaching tool for clinicians treating patients with heart disease. This original computer generated model of the heart presents intracardiac structures with an unprecedented degree of detail and accuracy, and the custom software produces real-time simulation of ultrasound images. The system was developed by three anaesthesiologists from the Heart Hospital in London, to facilitate teaching of the practical skill of transesophageal echocardiography during cardiac surgery. Doctors Sue Wright, Andrew Smith and Bruce Martin enlisted the help of a large number of eminent cardiac clinicians and morphologists to create this innovative virtual heart. Work with Glassworks, a leading computer graphics company, has seen the model and echocardiography simulator evolve into a remarkable training instrument.

Product Design

Design Director
Dr Vincent Forte
Technical Designer
Nick Shelley

Design Group
Maddison Product
Design Group

Manufacturer
Jeremy Keable
Managing Director
Giovanna Forte

Client
Funnelly Enough
Brand
Peezy

Health & Medical

Maddison Product Design Group
for Funnelly Enough

Peezy
Peezy is a revolutionary, single-use, hygienic and elegant mid-stream urine collection device for women. It brings dignity to the act of giving a urine sample, and it is quick, easy and clean. Most importantly, Peezy delivers a pure urine sample. By eliminating mess on the patient and environment, it is a valuable tool in the fight against hospital acquired infection. This elegantly simple device can make a major contribution to improved patient care and the health and safety of doctors, nurses, laboratory technicians, cleaning staff and many others in the NHS. In reducing the number of contaminated samples, Peezy provides substantial savings on expensive retests, estimated by NHS PASA to cost up to £2 per patient.

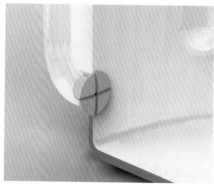

Design Director
Michael Siu
Designers
Wai-lun Chan
Frankie Fu
Paul Lo
Michael Siu
Pak-hong Wan
Design Groups
The Hong Kong
Polytechnic
University School of
Design
MIT (KAF) Project
Team

**Assisting Design
Groups**
CNC Workshop
Digital Output Centre
**KAF Principal
Investigator**
Susan Murcott
KAF Researcher
Tommy Ngai

Filtainer Researchers
Wai-lun Chan
Frankie Fu
Paul Lo
Pak-hong Wan
Logistics Assistant
Florence Lam

Client
Environment &
Public Health
Organization, Nepal
Brand
Filtainer: Clean
Water for All

Health & Medical

The Hong Kong Polytechnic University
School of Design
for Environment & Public Health
Organization, Nepal

Filtainer
Filtainer is the latest filter for KAF (the Kantian Arsenic Filter), a household drinking water treatment device used in developing countries. It removes arsenic, pathogens, iron, turbidity, odour, and contaminants from drinking water. All of these unfavourable substances, in particular arsenic, commonly exist in the ground-water of many countries. Filtainer was developed with the Massachusetts Institute of Technology (MIT) and the ENPHO. It is user-friendly for a population that is poor and with little or no education. All parts can be produced locally in developing countries via simple and low cost methods; all filtration substances can be found locally. Important design breakthroughs ensure safe and efficient water filtering, including clog-free performance by the patented Clogfree Flow Regulator.

385

Product Design

Apple Industrial Design Team

iPhone 3G
The iPhone 3G has all the features of the first generation iPhone, with 3G networking that is twice as fast. It has built-in GPS, as well as iPhone 2.0 software, which runs hundreds of third party applications. With its single sculpted polycarbonate back surface, it feels even better in your hand. A stainless steel band surrounds the optical-quality glass with superior clarity and scratch resistance. The 3.5 inch multi-touch display allows users to control iPhone with just a tap, flick or pinch of their fingers.

Designers			Manufacturer
Jody Akana	Daniele De Iuliis	Peter Russell-Clarke	Apple
Bart Andre	Jonathan Ive	Douglas Satzger	**Design Group**
Daniel Coster	Steve Jobs	Christopher Stringer	Apple Industrial
Evans Hankey	Duncan Kerr	Eugene Whang	Design Team
Richard Howarth	Shin Nishibori	Rico Zörkendörfer	
	Matthew Rohrbach		

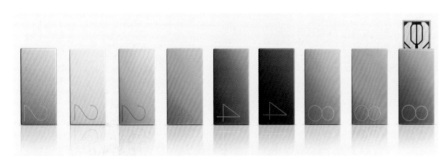

iriver

Domino
Many students and office workers don't leave home without their USB memory stick; Domino is designed for those to whom the USB stick has become an everyday object. It can be attached to a mobile phone, or another object the user carries with him or her on a daily basis. It doesn't look like an ordinary memory stick: inspired by a domino piece, the Domino is tiny in form and light in weight. To eliminate any visual distraction from the product's exterior such as a product logo or the product specifications, Domino bears only a numerical graphic as a visual cue to its capacity.

Design Director	Designers	Technical Designer	Marketing Manager
YeongKyu Yoo	Semin Jun	HyunWang Cho	Michael Sung
Design Group	Dowon Kim	**Manufacturer**	**Brand Manager**
iriver	YeongKyu Yoo	OhSeok Kwon	YeongKyu Yoo

The jury:
Grant Parker, DDB London (Jury Foreman)
Brian Connolly, Spark London
Dave Dye, Dye Holloway Murray
Harvey Marco, JWT New York
Ewan Paterson, CHI & Partners
Gary Todd, McCann Erickson London
Erik Vervroegen, TBWA\ PARIS

Art Directors
Eric Hor
Willeon Leong
Gary Lim
MUN
Designers
Willeon Leong
Gary Lim
MUN

Copywriters
Kevin Le
Ronald Ng
Illustrators
Willeon Leong
Gary Lim
Print Producer
Dickson Teh

Creative Directors
MUN
Ronald Ng
Advertising Agency
BBDO/Proximity
Malaysia
Account Handlers
Tieh Pui Yen
Dong Hyun Yoo

Brand Manager
Sally Hong
Client
Chrysler Korea
Brand
Jeep

Poster Advertising
BBDO/Proximity Malaysia
for Chrysler Korea

Bushman & Eskimo / Husky & Camel / Mountain Goat & Crocodile
To promote Jeep's superior all-terrain capability, we overlapped two images of objects that
are polar opposites to form the outline of the car, creating the impression that Jeep can go
anywhere. As for applying a clean design style to the concept, well, we hope that it will make
Jeep stand out from all the advertising in the car galaxy. Also selected in Press Advertising.

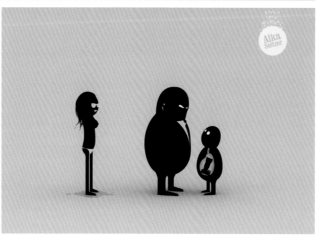

Art Director
Paul Kreitmann
Copywriter
Alexis Benoit
Illustrator
Paul Kreitmann

Creative Directors
Gilles Fichteberg
Jean-François Sacco
Art Buyer
Sylvie Etchémaïté

Advertising Agency
CLM BBDO
Account Handlers
Séverine Autret
Claire Roy-Thermes

Marketing Manager
Clotilde Masson
Client
Bayer
Brand
Alka-Seltzer

Press Advertising
CLM BBDO
for Bayer

Bear / Mafia / Magician / Paparazzi /Prison
The campaign features characters that swallow awkward objects to get out of embarrassing situations. With this twist on the classic stomach ache, the Alka- Seltzer brand stands out in a sector that can often be a little conventional. The campaign offers a way to 'dissolve' your psychological as well as physical (digestive) problems.

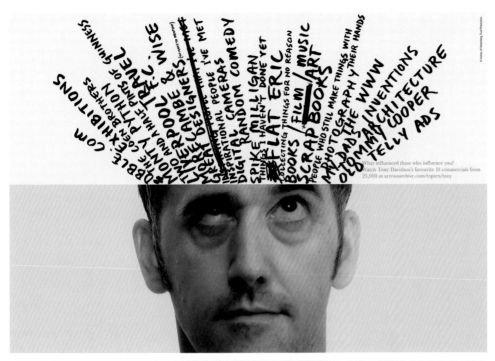

Press Advertising

Dye Holloway Murray
for The History of Advertising Trust

Davidson / Gill / Ledwidge / Silburn
To give the advertising community a reason to visit arrowsarchive.co.uk, we featured the most admired people in the business endorsing the fact that they had been influenced by its content: 24,000 'old telly ads'.

one colour leads to another m&m's

Art Director	Typographer	Advertising Agency	Marketing Manager
KC Chung	KC Chung	TBWA\Tequila	Sibylle Geisert
Designer	**Print Producer**	Singapore	**Client**
KC Chung	Sam Tan	**Account Handler**	Mars
Copywriter	**Creative Director**	Eunice Tan	**Brand**
Eddie Azadi	Graham Kelly		M&M's

Poster Advertising

TBWA\Tequila Singapore
for Mars

Wow / Yummy / Mmmm
Can the point-of-sale be a point of interesting discussion? M&M's certainly hoped so. As a chocolate candy synonymous with colour, its appeal had started to fade among young adults who felt they had outgrown the brand. Staying true to its playful and colourful nature, a change was made without changing what the brand stood for. Using an M&M at the heart of every design, evocative eye candy was created to arouse interest. What seemed like elaborate modern art actually conveyed two simple messages about M&M's: it's astoundingly colourful, and addictively delicious.

393

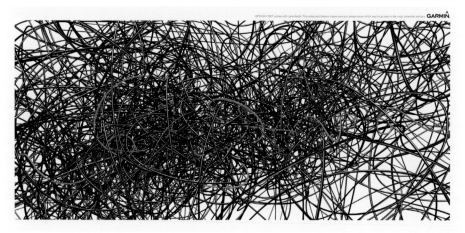

Art Directors
Kevin Lee
Kelvin Leong
Robin Wu
Tianhong Zhou
Designers
Jordan Dong
Minsheng Zhang
Tianhong Zhou

Copywriters
Weina Ha
Kit Ong
Illustrators
Jordan Dong
Robin Wu
Minsheng Zhang
Tianhong Zhou

Typographer
Kevin Lee
Creative Directors
Kevin Lee
Kelvin Leong
Kit Ong
Advertising Agency
Ogilvy Shanghai

Account Handler
Shining Gao
Marketing Manager
Yizheng Zhou
Client
Garmin
Brand
Lane Assist

Poster Advertising

Ogilvy Shanghai
for Garmin

Weave / Zigzag / Loop
Garmin wanted to inform consumers of its most advanced GPS feature yet: Lane Assist. People are aware of GPS systems and they think they are all the same. Garmin wanted to challenge that perception. We know unfamiliar roads can be as confusing as a maze, however Garmin can easily point the way to road users. After the launch of this campaign, consumers started to ask specifically for the Lane Assist GPS model. Sales shot up by more than 13 per cent within five months.

394

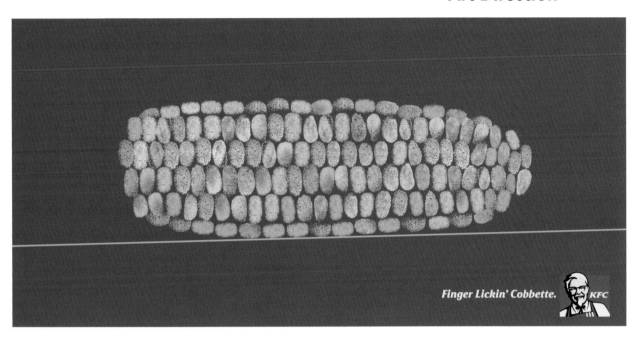

Art Director
Kevin Stark
Copywriter
Nick Kidney
Illustration
The Augurs

Typographer
Ali Augur
Creative Director
Marc Hatfield
Advertising Agency
BBH London

Planner
Ed Booty
Account Handler
Sylvia Pelzer
Marketing Manager
Jennelle Tilling

Client
Yum! Restaurants
International
Brand
KFC

Poster Advertising

BBH London
for KFC

Cobbette
The campaign was created to relaunch KFC's endline 'Finger lickin' good'. We wanted to connect this famous endline to the pleasure of eating KFC and the unique finger lickin' experience.

Art Director
Paul Pateman
Designer
Paul Pateman
Copywriter
Mike Nicholson

Illustrator
Paul Pateman
Print Producer
Linda Carlos
Creative Director
Paul Brazier

**Creative Group
Heads**
Mike Nicholson
Paul Pateman
Advertising Agency
Abbott Mead Vickers
BBDO

Account Handler
James Drummond
Client
Museum of
Childhood

Poster Advertising

Abbott Mead Vickers BBDO
for Museum of Childhood

Inner Child
Our brief was to encourage the public to visit the Museum of Childhood. The museum really takes you back to your youth. To dramatise this, we devised this poster as part of an integrated campaign to promote the museum and encourage people to relive their childhood. Also selected in Press Advertising.

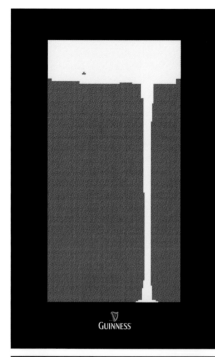

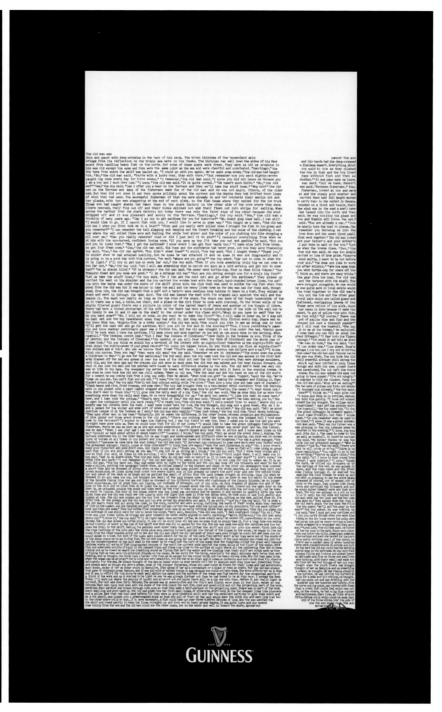

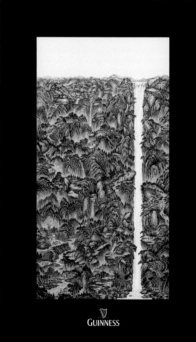

Art Directors	Copywriters	Creative Director	Client
Shi Yuan He	Shi Yuan He	Chee Guan Yue	Durty Nellies Irish
Johnnie Tey	Johnnie Tey	**Advertising Agency**	Pub Beijing
	Illustrator	Grey Beijing	**Brand**
	Zhi Ping Wang		Guinness

Poster Advertising

Grey Beijing
for Guinness

Guinness – Tetris / Chinese Painting / Novel

Whether you are busy at work or at play, a pint of Guinness is always what you look for at the end of the day.

Art Director
Dave Masterman
Designer
Kylie McLean
Copywriter
Ed Edwards
Illustrator
Kylie McLean

Image Manipulator
Kylie McLean
Print Producer
Ben Etheridge
Creative Director
Ewan Paterson
Advertising Agency
CHI & Partners

Planners
Ben Southgate
David Yates
Account Handlers
Jo Clays
Katy Emson
Sarah Gold

Marketing Managers
Lorraine Crowe
Emily Oldridge
Brand Manager
Danny Micklethwaite
Client
Arla Foods
Brand
Anchor Butter

Poster Advertising

CHI & Partners
for Arla Foods

Anchor – Free to Roam / Cows in Space / Roam
In 2007, a powerful new concept was identified for Anchor: to position it as a free-range butter.
While consumers had been used to free-range eggs, they had never thought about how their
butter was made. Anchor cows are different: they graze outside all year round and, unlike
other cows, are never crowded into concrete floored sheds. Anchor's free-range cows produce
delicious free-range milk to make their distinctive butter, hence our creative idea, 'Anchor,
the free-range butter company'. This identity has been at the heart of everything that Anchor
has done. In keeping with a natural and simple brand ethos, all creative executions have
a handmade feel, crafted from fuzzy felt.

397

Art Directors
Shashank Jha
Ashish Pathak
Designers
Shashank Jha
Ashish Pathak
Photographer
Israr Qureshi
Illustrators
Shashank Jha
Ashish Pathak

Textile Designer
Binal Shah
Creative Directors
Shamik Sengupta
Ferzad Variyava
Executive Creative Director
Tista Sen
Chief Creative Officer
Agnello Dias

Producers
Deepak Jadhav
Purushottam Joshi
Mukund Kapote
Chandrakant Matal
Vivek Warang
Advertising Agency
JWT India
Account Handler
Anuja Arora

General Manager
Suranjan Das
Marketing Manager
Sushil Chhugani
Client
MW.com India
Brand
Rolling Stone

Poster Advertising

JWT India
for MW.com India

Bob Marley / Jim Morrison / Madonna
Rolling Stone, the unattainable bible of music journalism, was coming to India. Is it possible to make the iconic look familiar? And still iconic? The refrain came from the heartland of the Indian cultural pot pourri. Hidden deep in its bosom were some of the oldest surviving traditional textile and embroidery art forms. Batik, Kantha, Madhubani and Zardozi were chosen to recast iconic Rolling Stone covers as posters in their new likeness. Gnarled hands and weather-beaten eyes worked their centuries-old magic on poster designs that had become folklore in modern iconography. And slowly, Rolling Stone opened its soul to India.

398

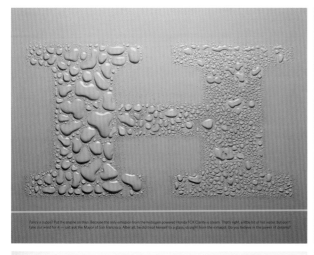

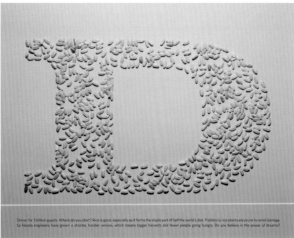

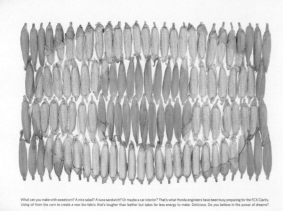

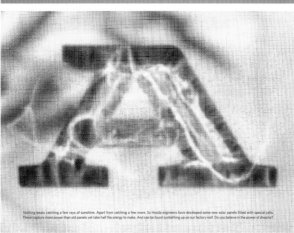

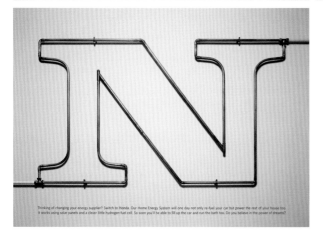

Art Directors	**Model Maker**	**Project Manager**	**Client**
Guy Featherstone	Gaël Langevin	Mark D'Abreo	Honda
Chris Groom	**Retouchers**	**Advertising Agency**	**Brand**
Copywriter	Danny Holden	Wieden + Kennedy	Honda Environment
Stuart Harkness	Dan Richardson	London	
Photographer	**Creative Directors**	**Account Handlers**	
Guido Mocafico	Tony Davidson	Ryan Fisher	
Typographer	Kim Papworth	Jonathan Tapper	
Guy Featherstone			

Press Advertising

Wieden + Kennedy London
for Honda

H / O / N / D / A
Honda has always been aware of its impact on the environment. The company wanted to show the measures it has taken to reduce this impact, so we ran a campaign that used the letters of the car manufacturer to represent the technologies and initiatives that Honda has invested in. The Honda typeface is very iconic and recognisable. Using letters on their own as well as showing them in sequence helped to get the messages across to people. Honda sponsored a series of environmental supplements in the Daily Telegraph where this work ran. The supplements covered aspects of design, manufacturing and architecture, and the developments that are taking place to ensure things are more environmentally friendly.

399

Art Director
Johnnie Tey
Copywriter
Albion Li

Illustrators
Andrew Tan
Johnnie Tey
Harimau Yusof
Di Zhang

Creative Directors
Chee Guan Yue
Adrian Zhu
Advertising Agency
Grey Beijing

Client
GSK
Brand
Panadol

Press Advertising

Grey Beijing
for GSK

Bush / Britney / Milkman
In order to demonstrate how indiscriminate a virus is, this campaign reproduces the chains of infection caused by people from different walks of life. The concept reinforces how one can 'save the day' by putting a stop to a virus.

Art Directors
Albert S Chan
Ina Thedens
Designer
Helmut Meyer
Copywriters
Alexander Haase
Dr Stephan Vogel

Illustrators
Daniel Cojocaru
Martin Popp
Creative Director
Helmut Meyer

Art Buyers
Christina Hufgard
Caroline Walczok
Advertising Agency
Ogilvy Frankfurt
Account Handler
Michael Fucks

Marketing Managers
Claudia Fix
Detlef Stueber
Client
Action World
Solidarity

Press Advertising

Ogilvy Frankfurt
for Action World Solidarity

Women's Rights Campaign
The wolf in sheep's clothing? This campaign takes advantage of the current India hype, using popular ethno-visuals to reveal shocking facts and background information about women's rights in India. In its authentic look and feel, the campaign reflects the style of Indian advertising posters.

Art Director
Dave Dye
Designer
Dave Dye
Advertising Agency
Dye Holloway
Murray

Copywriter
Tony Barry
Illustrator
Kin Pro
Creative Director
Dave Dye

Planner
Justin Holloway
Account Handler
Jorian Murray

Brand Marketing Manager
Dave Hieatt
Client
howies

Press Advertising

Dye Holloway Murray
for howies

Wash / Hat / Owner
We advertised howies Merino wool products in a way that doesn't feel like advertising.

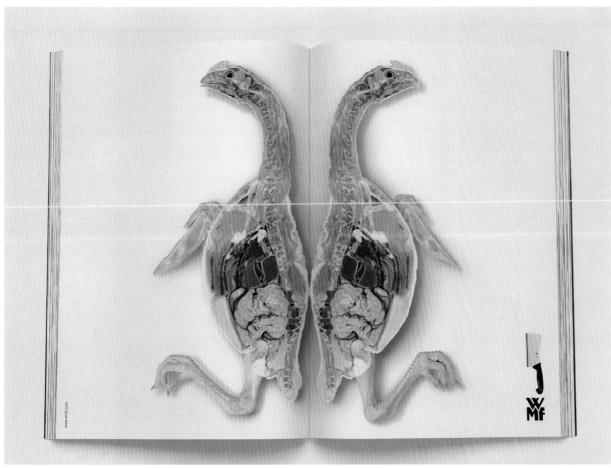

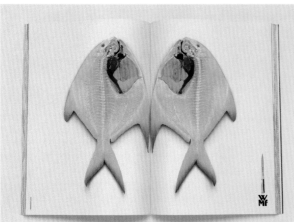

Art Directors
Supachai
Toemtechatpong
Sompat Trisadikun
Copywriter
Kittisak
Prechapanich
Photographer
Stapun Chuntaketta

Retoucher
Saranuwat
Thamniroth
Creative Director
Chanyutt
Boonyagate

**Executive Creative
Directors**
Keeratie
Chaimoungkalo
Sompat Trisadikun
**Advertising
Agencies**
Arc Worldwide
Thailand
Leo Burnett Thailand

Account Handler
Veevit Teotrakoon
Sales Manager
Somruetai
Hengsatanakul
Client
Italasia Thailand
Brand
WMF

Press Advertising

Arc Worldwide & Leo Burnett Thailand
for Italasia Thailand

Chicken / Fish / Lobster
The WMF knife is a piece of kitchenware designed especially for the modern housewife who loves cooking. Their main difficulty lies in preparing thick meat, ribs, and other food with a thick skin or shell. We demonstrated that the knife is sharp and increases the level of professionalism in preparing food.

Art Director
Paulo Areas

Copywriter
Tomas Correa
Creative Director
Ruy Lindenberg

Advertising Agency
Leo Burnett Brazil

Client
Fiat
Brand
Stilo

Press Advertising
Leo Burnett Brazil
for Fiat

Sky Window – Balloon / Bird / Plane
The 'Sky Window' campaign for Fiat Stilo is all about the car's sunroof. With a strong visual appeal, the adverts depict visual pollution in the city as a prison to the stressed driver. This dramatises the use of the Sky Window, which is the driver's escape route.

Press Advertising

Grey London
for Channel 5 Broadcasting

Keyhole
This is a press ad for 'Banged Up', a social experiment television show exploring the UK prison system.

Art Director
Nils Leonard
Copywriter
Nils Leonard
Typographer
Mark Cakebread
Creative Director
Nils Leonard

Chief Creative Officer
Jon Williams
Advertising Agency
Grey London
Art Buyer
Patrick Dickinson

Advertising Supervisor
Carl Ratcliff
Account Handler
Lisa Buckley

Client
Channel 5 Broadcasting
Brand
Banged Up

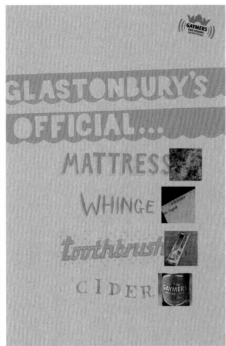

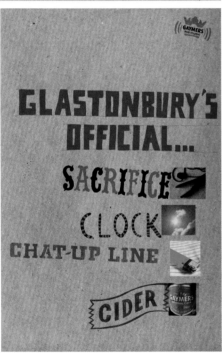

Press Advertising

Dye Holloway Murray
for Gaymer Cider Company

Fantasy / Mattress / Sacrifice / Schoolboy
Gaymers is the official cider of Glastonbury Festival. We needed to tell people in a way that showed Gaymers understood Glastonbury and all its quirks.

Art Director David Goss	**Illustrators** Paul Bower	**Planner** Justin Holloway	**Client** Gaymer Cider
Designer David Goss	David Goss	**Account Handler** Jorian Murray	Company
Copywriter Phoebe Coulton	**Print Producers** David Goss	**Brand Marketing**	**Brand** Gaymers Original
Photographer Laurence Haskell	Kieran Ward	**Manager** Fiona Chinn	
	Creative Director Dave Dye		
	Advertising Agency Dye Holloway Murray		

Illustrator
Harry Malt
Art Director
Brian Fraser

Design Directors
Brian Fraser
Simon Learman
Copywriter
Simon Learman

Executive Creative Directors
Brian Fraser
Simon Learman

Advertising Agency
McCann Erickson
London

Graphic Design
McCann Erickson London

Agency Branding
We wanted to demonstrate how McCann Erickson London has changed. And that the real beauty is to be found inside our Art Deco building, inside the heads of the people that work there. So we created a new identity that formed a physical connection between the brilliant minds of our employees and the building. In doing so, we transformed a traditional office space into a thought-inspiring environment that fosters freethinking. When you pass through our building, you'll find that it's crammed full of wonderful ideas, thousands of them. Our drawings are constantly evolving too, as they help to define our brand philosophy and culture. It's all about making people feel good when they come to work. Feel free to drop in.

409

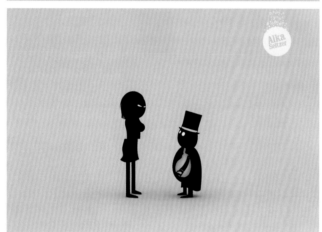
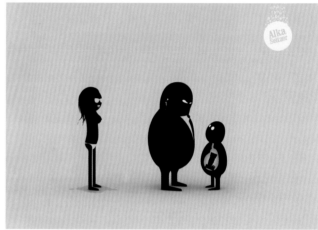

Illustrator
Paul Kreitmann
Art Director
Paul Kreitmann
Copywriter
Alexis Benoit

Creative Directors
Gilles Fichteberg
Jean-François Sacco
Advertising Agency
CLM BBDO
Art Buyer
Sylvie Etchémaïté

Account Handlers
Séverine Autret
Claire Roy-Thermes
Marketing Manager
Clotilde Masson

Client
Bayer
Brand
Alka-Seltzer

Press Advertising

CLM BBDO
for Bayer

Bear / Mafia / Magician / Paparazzi / Prison
This campaign features characters that swallow awkward objects to get out of embarrassing situations. With this twist on the classic stomach ache, the Alka-Seltzer brand stands out in a sector that can often be a little conventional. The campaign offers a way to 'dissolve' your psychological as well as physical (digestive) problems.

Illustrator
Yang Yong Liang
Artist
Yang Yong Liang
Art Directors
Yang Yong Liang
Lillie Zhong

Designer
Sean Tang
Copywriters
Rafael Freire
Jacqueline Ye
Photographer
Yang Yong Liang

Print Producers
Liza Law
Tao Shen
Joseph Yu
Creative Director
Yang Yeo

Advertising Agency
JWT Shanghai
Account Handler
Betty Tsai
Client
CEPF

 Poster Advertising

JWT Shanghai
for CEPF

Shan Shui
This campaign is the result of a collaboration with famous Shanghai artist Yang Yong Liang. Posters look like a beautiful landscape painting, but when zoomed in, there are neither mountain nor stream, but factory buildings and cars. The China Environment Protection Foundation wanted to warn people with these striking images that if we don't take any more action to reduce pollution of the environment, there will come a day when all the beautiful landscapes will have disappeared.

411

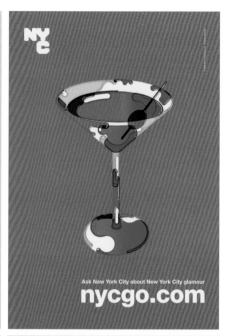

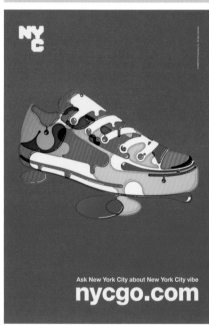

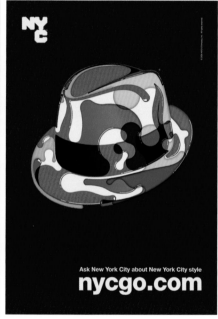

Illustrator Steven Wilson	**Print Producer** Stephanie Friese	**Illutration Agency** Breed London	**Client** NYC & Company
Art Director Nick Klinkert	**Digital Producer** Kenna Takahashi	**Advertising Agency** BBH New York	**Brand** nycgo.com
Creative Director Pelle Sjoenell	**Art Buyer** Travis Quinn		

Poster Advertising

Breed London
for NYC & Company

NYCGO – Bicycle / Hotdog / Martini / Sneaker / Taxi / Fedora
NYC & Company needed to support the launch of its new website, nycgo.com. The website would be the ultimate resource for all New York City information; it needed a campaign that was simple, visually arresting and depicted the type of information you could find on the site. Steven Wilson was commissioned by BBH New York to create a series of iconic illustrated images. Each image represented an aspect of New York City that you can find on the website. BBH New York wrote the line 'Ask New York City about New York City' to highlight that the site is the most authentic and reliable source of New York City information. The posters ran in Italy, Spain and the UK as bus shelters. The outdoor media presence in those markets was valued at nearly $5 million.

Illustrator	Copywriters	Advertising Agency	Account Planner
Jianfeng Pan	Carol Ong	BBH China	Philip Man
Art Directors	Leo Zhang	**Account Handlers**	**Marketing Manager**
Yinbo Ma	**Creative Director**	Joyce Hong	Jing Hui
Carol Ong	Johnny Tan	Jasmine Huang	**Client**
Typographer	**Design Group**		WWF China
Yinbo Ma	ALT Design		

Poster Advertising

BBH China
for WWF China

Panda Series – Antelope / Forest / Water
In China, there's a misconception that WWF only protects pandas, because of its iconic logo.
The challenge was to debunk the misconception by showcasing WWF China's success in wetlands, forestry and wildlife programmes.

Illustrator	Copywriters	Print Producer	Marketing Manager
Yuko Shimuzo	Matt Collier	Frank Blackwell	Steven Greaves
Art Directors	Wayne Robinson	**Advertising Agency**	**Brand Manager**
Matt Collier	**Typographer**	CHI & Partners	Gemma Adams
Wayne Robinson	Kylie McLean	**Account Handlers**	**Client**
Designer	**Creative Directors**	Danny Josephs	Tiger Beer
Kylie McLean	Ed Edwards	Holly Maguire	
	Dave Masterman	Brendon McLean	

Poster Advertising

CHI & Partners
for Tiger Beer

Anti-Climb / Overnight / Keys
The aim was to raise awareness of Tiger as a premium beer by reinforcing its genuine Far Eastern heritage, promoting reappraisal and trial amongst discerning 21 to 30-year-old 'early majority' urban male beer drinkers. The creative solution demonstrates Tiger's desirability by conveying the lengths to which people would go to intercept the beer while in transit. The executional style of a traditional Asian woodblock illustration reinforces Tiger's genuine Far Eastern export credentials. Posters ran in major city centres, strategically positioned to disrupt drinkers while on a night out, for example on London underground cross tracks, and as 6-sheets outside bars and in central city locations. Cities included London, Manchester, Liverpool, Birmingham, Leeds and Brighton.

Poster Advertising

Saatchi & Saatchi Los Angeles
for Toyota Motor Sales USA

Sky Psycho Jamboree Event Poster
To leverage Toyota's sponsorship of the 2008 Summer Dew Action Sports Tour, we were tasked with developing a creative to generate high rates of youth participation and spectatorship from the collective target of the Generation Y audience (ages 12–29) through a minimum of 200,000 brand interactions and 6,000 hand-raisers. Drawing inspiration from a vintage air show look and feel, Sky Psycho Jamboree successfully reinterpreted action sports by employing the illustration style of Tavis Coburn. Creatively, the campaign stood head and shoulders above the typically overdone youth sports design clutter. Sky Psycho Jamboree presented Toyota as a credible, authentic and relevant brand to a young, aesthetically savvy audience.

Illustrator
Tavis Coburn
Art Director
Peter Vattanatham
Copywriter
Napper Tandy

Creative Director
Dino Spadavecchia
Print Producer
Rachel Dallas-Noble

Advertising Agency
Saatchi & Saatchi
Los Angeles
Account Handler
Marisstella
Marinkovic

Marketing Manager
Paul Czaplicki
Client
Toyota Motor Sales
USA

Poster Advertising

BBH London
for English National Opera

Cavalleria Rusticana & Pagliacci
Our brief was to create a new visual identity to separate the English National Opera, or ENO, from the general cultural clutter of other arts institutions, and to showcase the diversity of individual productions and celebrate the eclectic nature of all the disciplines involved within the ENO. We used the circle as the dominant motif, which gave meaning to the existing logo, at the same time creating a distinct and ownable visual identity. This production of 'Cavalleria Rusticana' and 'Pagliacci' (Cav & Pag) has been updated from the original Comedie del Arte style to a 70s northern working men's club. It is a tale of deception and subterfuge, which is reflected in the illustration.

Illustrator
Paul Slater
Art Director
Mark Reddy
Designer
Chris Chapman

Creative Director
Mark Reddy
Advertising Agency
BBH London
Art Buyer
Sarah Pascoe

Account Handler
Jane Roach
Marketing Manager
Caroline Priest

Client
English National
Opera
Brand
Cavalleria Rusticana
& Pagliacci

415

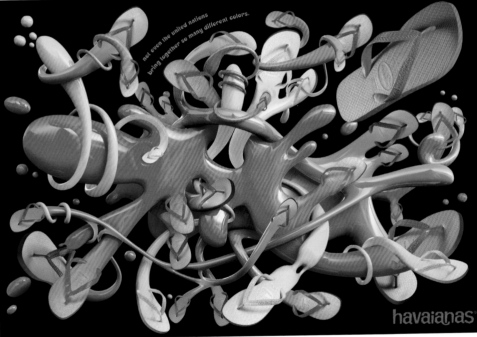

Poster Advertising

AlmapBBDO
for Havaianas

Havaianas Ink Campaign

We needed to revive Havaianas sandals in the US market. The best way to do this was to highlight the vast choice of colours, casual style and fun of these sandals. We created colourful, vibrant and organic graphics, which mimic the composition of the inks that make the different coloured sandals. The campaign highlights the variety of colours and the casual style of the sandals.

Illustrators
Rodrigo Gelmi
M.sampaio
Art Director
Danilo Boer
Copywriter
Tales Bahu

Typographer
José Roberto
Bezerra
Creative Directors
Marcello Serpa
Marcus Sulzbacher

**Executive Creative
Director**
Marcello Serpa
Advertising Agency
AlmapBBDO
Marketing Manager
Carla Schmitzberger

Client
São Paulo
Alpargatas
Brand
Havaianas

Illustrators
Adelmo Barrero
Junior Cortizo
Marcos Kotlhar
Art Directors
Marcos Kotlhar
Marcus Sulzbacher

Copywriter
Cassio Zanatta
Photographers
Fernando Nalon
Daishi Pais

Typographer
José Roberto
Bezerra
Creative Director
Marcello Serpa
Advertising Agency
AlmapBBDO

Marketing Manager
Carla Schmitzberger
Client
São Paulo
Alpargatas
Brand
Havaianas

Poster Advertising

AlmapBBDO
for Havaianas

Havaianas Window Campaign
Havaianas needed to communicate Brazilian values and show that every time you put on a pair of flip-flops, you are wearing a small piece of Brazilian life and popular culture. Using the flip-flop shape we created windows showing spectacular views of Brazilian cities, beaches and jungles, inviting viewers into the homeland of Havaianas.

Illustrator
Shailesh
Khandeparkar
Art Director
Shailesh
Khandeparkar

Designer
Shailesh
Khandeparkar
Copywriter
Shailesh
Khandeparkar

Creative Directors
Abhijit Avasthi
Piyush Pandey
Advertising Agency
Ogilvy & Mather
Mumbai

Marketing Manager
Madhur Das
Client
WWF India
Brand
WWF

Poster Advertising
Ogilvy & Mather Mumbai
for WWF India

Save Ourselves – Tree
We wanted to create posters that graphically show the interdependence of nature and man, and the danger we pose to ourselves by harming the environment; that by saving nature, we are actually saving ourselves.

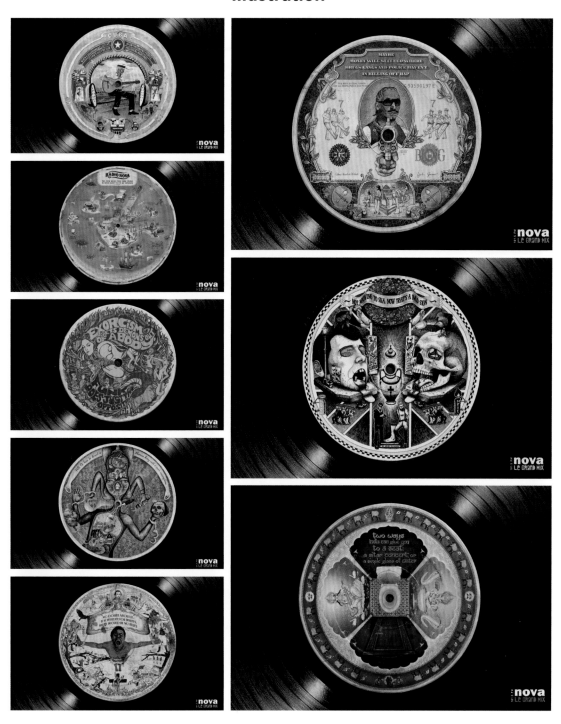

Illustrators
Jean-François
Bouchet
Jessica Gerard-Huet
Richard Mongenet
Jean Spezial
François Valla
Illustration
Am I Collective
Production Plein
Soleil

Art Director
Jessica Gerard-Huet
Copywriter
Jean-François
Bouchet
Photographer
Roger Turqueti
Retoucher
Grazielle @ Asile

Creative Direction
Les Six
Advertising Agency
Young & Rubicam
France
Account Handlers
Geraldine Hincelin
Claire Nicaise-
Schindler

Brand Managers
Bruno Delport
Marc H'Limi
Eric Karnbauer
Client
Nova Radio
Brand
Le Grand Mix

Press Advertising

Young & Rubicam France
for Nova Radio

Cuba / Electro / Funk / Folk / Blues / Rap / Ska / India
Nova is not your usual radio station. No one plays as many different styles of music as it does.
The station started in 1981, and helped rap, world music and electro emerge in France. It is truly
different. Very open. However, Nova had not run any ad campaigns for ten years. Fortunately, it
liked ours because it was not trying to sell anything. It was not about the station itself, but about
music. And (pleasant surprise!) Nova even asked for more ads, in order to make the campaign
as 'musically wide' as possible, and to express its identity, well summed up by 'Le Grand Mix'.

Illustrator	Copywriters	Advertising Agency	Client
Mark Khaisman	Lennart Frank	Jung von Matt	tesa®
Art Director	Tassilo Gutscher	Stuttgart	**Brand**
Stefan Roesinger	**Creative Directors**	**Account Handler**	tesapack® ultra strong
Graphic Designer	Mark Khaisman	Harald Isenmann	
Dominic Stuebler	Michael Ohanian	**Marketing Manager**	
	Joachim Silber	Achim Franck	

Press Advertising

Jung von Matt Stuttgart
for tesa®

Tesa Tape Art
The goal was to create an attention-grabbing consumer campaign for tesapack® ultra strong that plainly illustrates the product's benefit. The communication focusedon generating awareness of the product and its strength. To demonstrate the performance of tesapack® ultra strong we developed analogies for power and strength. The visuals were made entirely of adhesive tape. For the execution we booked Mark Khaisman, an American illustrator, who helped us make this campaign a big success.

420

Illustration

Packaging

Kolle Rebbe/KOREFE
for The Deli Garage

Powerfuel

The Deli Garage is a cooperative that supports small, local manufacturers of deli goods with aesthetic packaging, imaginative designs and inspired ideas for successful market entry. The garage theme runs through every product launched by The Deli Garage; the packaging is always a mix between high-end design and garage connotations. Powerfuel is a range of flavoured vodkas: espresso; ginger and coriander; and melon and mint. Stored in handy, lovingly illustrated pocket flasks, they fit easily into boilersuits and taste best right after knocking-off time.

Illustrator Heiko Windisch	**Copywriter** Katharina Trumbach	**Advertising Agency** Kolle Rebbe/KOREFE	**Marketing Manager** Anthony Hammond
Art Director Reginald Wagner	**Print Producer** Stephan Gerlach	**Account Handlers** Carolin Meyer	**Client** The Deli Garage
Graphic Designer Jan Simmerl	**Creative Director** Katrin Oeding	Kristina Wulf	**Brand** Powerfuel

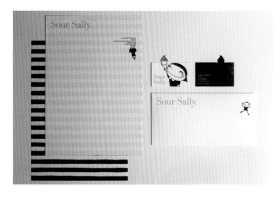

Graphic Design

Kinetic Singapore
for Sour Sally

Sour Sally

Yoghurt is sour, hence the name Sour Sally. It became the name of the yoghurt boutique and the unique character behind the whimsical make-believe world. She's not an everyday comic figure but a unique character with funny oddities. She is entirely hand-drawn, right down to the tiniest detail. The character interacts with the environment and everything about the frozen yoghurt boutique oozes Sour Sally.

Illustrator Leng Soh	**Designers** Pann Lim	**Creative Director** Pann Lim	**Marketing Manager** Donny
Art Directors Pann Lim	Leng Soh	**Advertising Agency** Kinetic Singapore	**Client** Sour Sally
Leng Soh	**Copywriter** Michelle Lin	**Account Handler** Alicia Tan	
	Typographer Leng Soh		

421

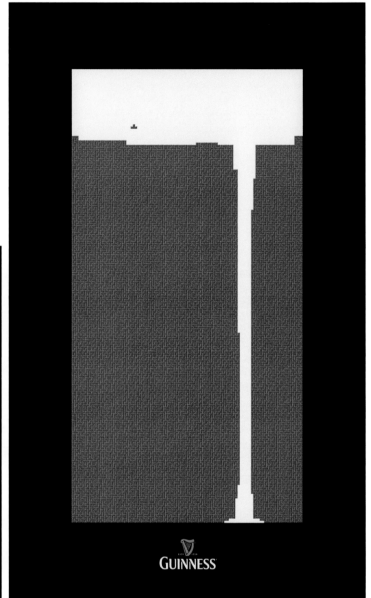

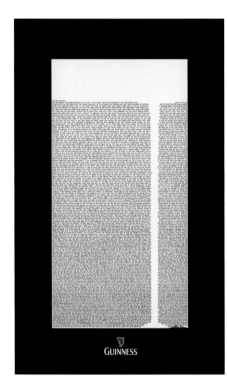

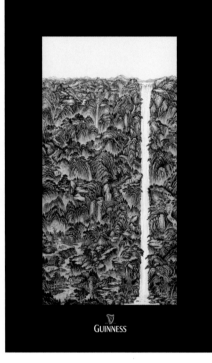

Illustrator	Copywriters	Creative Director	Client
Shi Yuan He	Shi Yuan He	Chee Guan Yue	Durty Nellies Irish
Art Directors	Johnnie Tey	**Advertising Agency**	Pub Beijing
Shi Yuan He		Grey Beijing	**Brand**
Johnnie Tey			Guinness

Graphic Design

Grey Beijing
for Guinness

Guinness – Novel / Chinese Painting / Tetris
Whether you are busy at work or at play, a pint of Guinness is always what you look for at the end of the day.

Illustration	Copywriters	Creative Director	Marketing Manager
Am I Collective	Prabashan	Christopher Gotz	Baskaran Jayaraman
Art Directors	Gopalakrishnan	**Advertising Agency**	**Client**
Prabashan	Pather	Ogilvy Cape Town	Castrol
Gopalakrishnan	Sanjiv Mistry	**Account Handlers**	**Brand**
Pather	**Print Producer**	Dane Hamer	Magnatec
Sanjiv Mistry	Thabied Hendricks	Wouter Lombard	

Graphic Design

Ogilvy Cape Town
for Castrol

Oil Journey
Castrol Magnatec is an intelligent motor oil that seeks out the engine parts that need it most. On this 70m-long billboard – the longest in South Africa – we depicted an engine as a surreal illustrated world through which the Magnatec oil navigates a path to reach its destination. Along its epic journey, the oil encounters a fantastical array of personified engine parts that either lure the oil in or chase it away. The intricate illustration gave passing rush-hour motorists something new to look at every time they drove past.

Illustrator
Noma Bar
Designers
Victoria Walmsley
Mark Wood

Typographers
Victoria Walmsley
Mark Wood

Creative Directors
Stuart Radford
Andrew Wallis
Design Group
Radford Wallis

Fundraising Officer
Martina Borosova
Client
Sense International

Graphic Design

Radford Wallis
for Sense International

Sense International Annual Review
Sense International wanted an annual review that would begin to demonstrate some of the challenges and difficulties that deaf-blind people face on a daily basis, and explain how the organisation helps relatives, friends and communities solve these issues. A series of narrative portraits were created to reflect each person's story and to show how Sense International has had a positive impact on their lives. The illustrations incorporate objects that explain how they are now able to communicate and interact with the people around them.

Illustrators
Paul Bower
Anthony Burrill
Billie Jean
James Joyce

Designers
Nick Finney
Daniel Lock
Ben Stott

Creative Directors
Alan Dye
Nick Finney
Ben Stott

Design Group
NB: Studio
Client
NB: Studio

Graphic Design

NB: Studio

This Year... 2009
This is the second in the series 'This Year...' conceived as an annual New Year mailer from NB: Studio. We asked four illustrators to put a positive spin on the gloomy news surrounding the global economic meltdown. Each design was then lovingly screenprinted over the top of a real dollar bill to create a set of four limited edition prints signed by the artists. Each illustrator responded in a completely different way: James Joyce put a smile on George Washington's face; Billie Jean highlighted the biggest political event for over 40 years; Anthony Burrill gave an optimistic call to arms; and Paul Bower defaced the note with some irreverent playground humour.

Graphic Design

Hat-trick Design Consultants
for Darwin200

Darwin Poster
Launched in September 2008, Darwin200 is a national programme of events celebrating Charles Darwin's scientific ideas and their impact around his 200th birthday on 12th February 2009. We were asked to design a poster promoting the programme for schools, colleges, universities and partner museums around the country. The iconic image of Darwin was created using his travels, discoveries, theories and observations in one continuous lifeline.

Illustrator
Ken Miki
Creative Directors
Gareth Howat
David Kimpton
Jim Sutherland

Designers
Gareth Howat
Jim Sutherland

Design Group
Hat-trick Design
Consultants

Marketing Manager
Bob Bloomfield
Client
Darwin200

Graphic Design
Abbott Mead Vickers BBDO
for The Economist

Cuckoo Land
Readership of The Economist is a select club. The client wanted to widen that club by telling potential readers that they were more of an Economist reader than they thought. So the perceived negatives of dullness, UK-centricity and only being about economics had to be tackled. We produced this advert as part of a campaign that built on the tonality of the famous red and white campaign but made the ads more accessible, by using illustrations by leading illustrators and copy that extolled the virtues the target market didn't yet realise about 'The Economist'. We also used more personal media than the usual 48-sheets.

Illustrator	**Copywriter**	**Creative Group**	**Advertising Agency**
Paul Davis	Mark Fairbanks	**Heads**	Abbott Mead Vickers
Art Director	**Creative Director**	Paul Cohen	BBDO
Paul Cohen	Paul Brazier	Mark Fairbanks	**Client**
			The Economist

Graphic Design
Jason Ford
for Heart Artists' Agents

2008 Heart Diary Cover
Heart's annual diary showcases their artists' work from the previous year, and is sent out as a gift to the agency's clients. This Gotham-like cityscape created by Jason Ford provides an environment within which signage, street architecture and advertising hoardings were used to typographically reference the seasons. Owing to the Canadian fold, the front and back cover appear in the centre of a wide landscape format.

Illustrator	**Art Directors**	**Designer**	**Client**
Jason Ford	Helen Osborne	Jason Godfrey	Heart Artists' Agents
	Darrel Rees		**Brand**
			Heart Diary

Graphic Design

Disturbance
for I.D. Magazine

I.D. Disturbance Cover
We were asked to shoot a studio portrait to accompany a feature I.D. Magazine was going to run. The article touched on some of the peculiarities and challenges involved in working in a small African city; we thought it would be fun to communicate a little of this in the portrait. Unable to convince any real-life hijackers, monkeys or flying heads to join us for the shoot, we simply turned a corner of the studio into an oversized illustration and posed next to it.

Illustrator
Richard Hart
Art Director
Thomas Porostocky

Photographer
Roger Jardine

Design Agency
Disturbance

Client
I.D. Magazine

Magazine & Newspaper Design

Yulia Brodskaya
for The Guardian

A Thrifty Christmas
Christmas on a budget. A very simple idea executed beautifully by the illustrator.

Illustrator
Yulia Brodskaya

Art Directors
Joanna Cochrane
Richard Turley

Designer
Joanna Cochrane

Client
The Guardian
Brand
G2

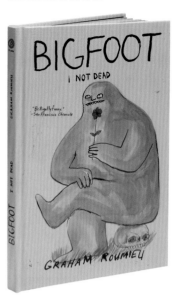

Illustrator
Graham Roumieu

Author
Graham Roumieu

Editor
Emily Haynes

Client
Penguin Group US
Brand
Plume Books

Book Design
Graham Roumieu
for Penguin Group US

Bigfoot: I Not Dead
Bigfoot shares reflections on his life as a shadow-dwelling outcast, a G-list celebrity, and as a truly sensitive soul in conflict with his giant, filthy, primitive killing-machine instincts.

Illustrator
Geoff Grandfield

Art Director
Eleanor Crow

Design Director
Joe Whitlock-Blundell

Client
The Folio Society

Book Design
Geoff Grandfield
for The Folio Society

Touching the Void
Our brief was to make a contemporary set of monochrome illustrations and two-colour cloth jacket design for the factual account of a legendary mountaineering accident.

Design Director
Angus Hyland

Designers
Masumi Briozzo
Kyle Wheeler

Editors
Helen Osborne
Darrel Rees

Design Company
Pentagram Design
Client
Heart

Book Design

Pentagram Design
for Heart

Beat IV – The Rime of the Ancient Mariner
'Beat IV: The Rime of the Ancient Mariner' is an illustrated edition of Samuel Taylor Coleridge's epic poem published by the Heart Agency to showcase their illustrators' work. Pentagram based its design concept around the idea that Heart wanted to produce a contemporary rendition of a classic, creating a design inspired by the graphic language of old books. Heart's edition of Coleridge's supernatural tale spans 82 pages, with each of Heart's 36 illustrators producing a double-page spread to accompany the text. The illustrators were provided with classically inspired page layouts involving empty picture frames to incorporate into their artwork. The dust jacket has the appearance of an old book that has been defaced by Jimmy Turrell, the cover artist.

Illustrator
Julia Ziegler
Art Director
Julia Ziegler
Copywriters
Frank Hose
Henning Müller-
Dannhausen
Oliver Voss

Creative Directors
Holger Jung
Jean-Remy von Matt
Götz Ulmer

Advertising Agency
Jung von Matt
Hamburg

Brand Manager
Meike Runschke

Client
Jung von Matt

Book Design

Jung von Matt Hamburg

Aquarium
The main objective was to change the public opinion about advertisers in general, and in particular about Jung von Matt. The challenge was to create a beautiful book that didn't feel like advertising, but felt authentic and real, although it was produced by advertisers. The book was created partly to satisfy our own dream, and for people interested in advertising, artists and students, who are also curious about or possibly intimidated by Jung von Matt.

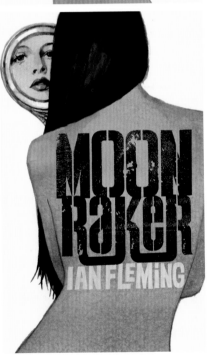

Book Design

Michael Gillette
The Estate of Ian Fleming & Penguin

From Russia with Love / Diamonds Are Forever / Dr. No / Goldfinger / Octopussy and the Living Daylights / Thunderball / Casino Royale / You Only Live Twice / Live and Let Die /Moonraker

Michael Gillette was commissioned to produce a set of covers for a series of James Bond novels published to commemorate the 100th anniversary of Ian Fleming's birth. It was decided that the Bond Girls would be the linking theme. Each cover was assigned a different colour to create a diverse range of moods within the concept. A loose painting technique was employed to enhance the sultry tone of the portraits. Bespoke hand drawn type was designed by the artist and became integral to the image, affording the covers a distinct unity.

Illustrator	Art Director	Creative Director	Clients
Michael Gillette	Jon Gray	John Hamilton	The Estate of Ian Fleming Penguin

430

The jury:
Tony Chambers, Wallpaper* (Jury Foreman)
Dave Bell, KesselsKramer
Simon Morris, Lowe London
Chris Frazer Smith, Wyatt-Clarke & Jones
Dan Tobin Smith, Freelance
Gustavo Sousa, Mother

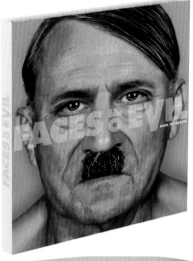

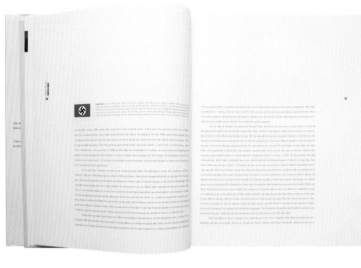

Photographers
Janet Riedel
Hans Weishäupl

Image Manipulator
Hans Weishäupl
Art Director
Hans Weishäupl

Copywriter
Dirk Silz
Typographer
Gunta Lauck

Advertising Agency
Das Comitee
Account Handler
Helen Zeggai

Book Design

Das Comitee

Faces of Evil

This book presents the 13 cruelest dictators of the last century as they have never been seen before: naked, uncensored, close-up and vulnerable. Portraits were created from photographs of over 350 people from the countries that suffered under their dictatorial regimes. Do these composites demonstrate that under the right circumstances, there is, if not a Hitler, a potential accomplice in every one of us? At the very least, they show that cruel men were made of flesh and blood, they are not the abstract monsters we try to disguise them as to distance ourselves. This book challenges us to deal with the human nature of tyrants, and the fact that many helpers hide behind the head of a dictator.

Poster Advertising

Leo Burnett London
for Shelter

Evening
This execution was developed to raise awareness of the housing crisis currently gripping the UK, and explain Shelter's unique positioning as a support to the many thousands of households affected. The fragility of a house of cards is used in this work to explain the complexity of different housing issues. Such are the UK's housing problems that this creative idea can be used to explain the truth about repossessions or temporary and social housing, as well as Shelter's call for the basic human right to have a place to call home.

Photography Blinkk	**Copywriters** Daniel Fisher	**Executive Creative Director** Jonathan Burley	**Account Handler** Gary Simmons
Image Manipulation Saddington Baynes	Peter Gooselin	**Advertising Agency** Leo Burnett London	**Acting Head of Brand & Marketing** Rachel Murphy
Retouching Saddington Baynes	**Typographer** Lance Crozier	**Planner** Gary Simmons	**Client** Shelter
Art Directors Richard Brim	**Print Producer** Simon Keyworth		
Jay Hunt			

Poster Advertising

Abbott Mead Vickers BBDO
for Kids Company

Wrong in the Head
Everyone tells us that the answer to knife crime is to punish the offenders (ASBOs, prison etc.), but this only makes the situation worse: 80 per cent of these kids will re-offend. Kids Company has years of psychological research that proves there is a different solution whereby over 50 per cent will not re-offend. Because we had to change the majority perception, we decided to go straight for the heartland. We placed long copy ads in the Daily Mail, Daily Telegraph and The Times. These featured images that showed the kind of kids responsible for knife violence. However the headlines and copy were designed to show that the viewer's first reaction to the shots was not necessarily the right one.

Photographer Thom Atkinson	**Copywriter** Mark Fairbanks	**Creative Group Heads** Paul Cohen	**Advertising Agency** Abbott Mead Vickers BBDO
Art Director Paul Cohen	**Print Producer** Ed Hoadley	Mark Fairbanks	**Client** Kids Company
Designer Paul Cohen	**Creative Director** Paul Brazier		

433

Photographer	Typographer	Planners	Marketing Manager
Fernando Nalon	José Roberto	Fernanda Barone	João Paulo Lucena
Photography	Bezerra	Valter Bombonato	**Client**
Conteúdo Expresso	**Creative Directors**	Cintia Gonçalves	Pepsi
Getty Images	Dulcídio Caldeira	**Media Planners**	**Brand**
LatinStock	Luiz Sanches	Gisele Carnielli	Gatorade Kids
Art Director	**Executive Creative**	Flávio de Pauw	
Renato Fernandez	**Director**	Maíra Toledo	
Copywriter	Marcello Serpa	**Account Supervisors**	
Gustavo Sarkis	**Advertising Agency**	André Furlanetto	
	AlmapBBDO	Ricardo Taunay	

Poster Advertising

AlmapBBDO
for Pepsi

Soccer / Basketball / Boxer
Gatorade Kids is a campaign where we've re-shot some classic photos in the world of sport, replacing the sacred athletes with children. This shows how a child's dream of becoming a great champion can one day become a reality.

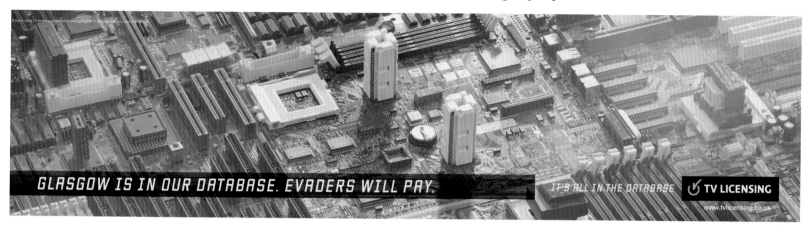

Photographer
Max Oppenheim
Art Director
Mike Bond
Design Director

Neil Craddock
Copywriter
Bern Hunter
Print Producer
Mark Lambourne

Creative Director
Paul Brazier
Advertising Agency
Abbott Mead Vickers
BBDO

**Creative Group
Heads**
Brian Campbell
Phil Martin

Client
TV Licensing

Poster Advertising

Abbott Mead Vickers BBDO
for TV Licensing

Council Flats
The new TV Licensing database contains the address of every home in the UK. To dramatise this we used the visual similarity of a circuit board and a city grid. We manipulated and constructed our own section of circuitry which we lit and shot to imitate a city shot at dawn from the air. If you're in the city, you're in the database.

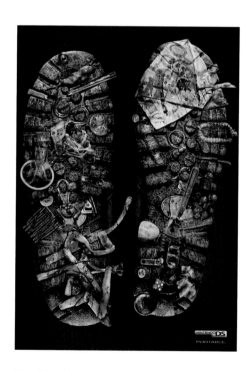

Press Advertising

Leo Burnett Milan
for Nintendo DS

Photographer
Giacomo Biagi
Image Manipulator
Giacomo Biagi
Image Manipulation
Studio Ros

Art Director
Rosemary Collini
Bosso
Copywriter
Paolo Guglielmoni

Creative Directors
Enrico Dorizza
Sergio Rodriguez
Advertising Agency
Leo Burnett Milan

Account Handler
Romeo Repetto
Marketing Manager
Sandro Benedettini
Client
Nintendo DS

Shoes
Nintendo DS is a portable gaming console. Gamers are so into it that they play outdoor with no distraction and no interruption. The print ad shows the soles of a gamer's shoes. The visual exaggerates a real insight: gamers come a long (undistracted and uninterrupted) way while playing.

Photographer
Jonathan de Villiers
Art Directors
Graeme Hall
Noah Regan
Copywriters
Graeme Hall
Noah Regan
Typographer
Pete Mould

Creative Director
Jeremy Craigen
Advertising Agency
DDB London
Project Manager
Caroline Tripp
Planner
Georgina Murray-
Burton

Art Buyer
Sarah Thomson
Account Handlers
Philip Heimann
Briony Small
Marketing Manager
Fran Page
Marketing Director
Julia Bowe

**Advertising &
Promotions Manager**
Shona Campbell
Client
Harvey Nichols

Press Advertising
DDB London
for Harvey Nichols

Bathroom / Café / Fountain

Photographer
Kelvin Murray
Image Manipulator
Clive Biley
Art Directors
Clark Edwards
Nick Pringle
Design Director
Dan Beckett

Designer
Craig Ward
Copywriters
Clark Edwards
Nick Pringle
Typographers
Dan Beckett
Craig Ward

Print Producer
Alan Wood
Creative Director
Ewan Paterson
Advertising Agency
CHI & Partners
Account Handler
Melanie Portelli

Brand Manager
Rosemary Gillespie
Client
Roy Castle Lung
Cancer Foundation

Press Advertising

CHI & Partners
for Roy Castle Lung Cancer Foundation

Sam / Molly / Charlotte
The Roy Castle Lung Cancer Foundation is the only UK charity wholly dedicated to defeating lung cancer. When the government banned smoking in public places, it was crucial that the public didn't assume the problem was solved. In fact, passive smoking in the home became even more relevant; the home was really the only place where people could smoke in a relaxing environment. We wanted to highlight the harm that secondhand smoke in the home does to children. By showing a child in their home surroundings but with the subtle addition of an adult arm smoking, we aimed to intrigue the viewer and communicate the fact that 17,000 children are hospitalised because of secondhand smoke in the UK every year.

437

Photographers	Creative Directors	Art Buyers	Marketing Manager
Paulo Martins	Carlos Furnari	Kristina Florén	Karen Zuccala
Gus Powell	Paulo Martins	Maria Perez	**Brand Manager**
Art Director	Dean Maryon	**Project Manager**	Kieran Riley
Paulo Martins	**Advertising**	Piers Bebbington	**Client**
Designer	**Agencies**	**Account Handlers**	adidas International
Emile Wilmar	180 Amsterdam	Caroline Britt	**Brand**
Copywriter	180/TBWA	Geoff Coyle	adidas
Carlos Furnari	**Production Company**	**Business Affairs**	
Artworker	2D Productions	**Manager**	
Emile Wilmar	**Planning Director**	Kindra Schoemaker	
Print Producers	Andy Edwards		
David Corfield			
Marlon Lee			

Press Advertising

180 Amsterdam & 180/TBWA
for adidas International

Gold is Never a Given – Haile Gebrselassie / Yelena Isinbayeva / Tyson Gay
Gold is never a given. In February 2008, six adidas athletes flew to Beijing – six months before the Olympic Games. Why? Because as gold medal favourites they knew winning is never guaranteed. That's why they were there in sub-zero temperatures training and familiarising themselves with the host city. Adidas and 180 Amsterdam went there to capture this.

Photographers
Mario Daloia
Hugo Treu
Art Directors
Marcus Kawamura
Ary Nogueira
Copywriter
Eduardo Andrietta
Illustrators
Daniel Battaini
Hugo Cafasso
José Cortizo Junior
Ellyson Lifante

Typographer
José Roberto
Bezerra
Creative Directors
Dulcídio Caldeira
Luiz Sanches
**Executive Creative
Director**
Marcello Serpa

Advertising Agency
AlmapBBDO
Media Planners
Laerte Mendonça
Zuleide Rampazzo
Cássio Soares
Account Supervisors
Filipe Bartholomeu
Fernão Cosi
Camila Figueiredo

Marketing Managers
Ricardo Alouche
Ricardo Barion
Ana Maria Oliveira
Client
Volkswagen Trucks

Press Advertising

AlmapBBDO
for Volkswagen Trucks

Volkswagen Customised Trucks – Beer Box / Egg Box / Fruit Box / Milk Box
The aim of this campaign is to remind the audience that Volkswagen trucks are 'the only ones in Brazil tailored for your business'. Throughout the campaign, the main element is packaging designed to look like Volkswagen trucks. Wooden boxes contain large amounts of produce and have paintings on the side; they are transformed into trucks designed specifically to transport delicate products, such as milk, drinks or eggs.

439

Photographer
Guy Farrow
Image Manipulator
Mike Roberts
Art Director
Mike Roberts
Designer
Mike Roberts

Copywriter
Lionel Hatch
Typographer
Mike Roberts
Print Producer
Duarte Goncalves

Creative Directors
Ben Casey
Steve Royle
Design Group
The Chase
Account Handler
Eileen O'Leary

Brand Manager
Steve Mapley
Client
The Manchester and
Cheshire Dogs'
Home

Graphic Design

The Chase
for The Manchester and Cheshire Dogs' Home

Dogs' Home Brochure
The Manchester and Cheshire Dogs' Home required a document that outlined the positive work the organisation had been doing in and around the Manchester and Cheshire community. They had a new initiative that tackled not only the welfare of stray and abandoned dogs but also causes of abandonment, through offering training, education and support, and working with owners to help keep dogs in a loving home. The brochure will also help to encourage people to donate and support the charity.

Photographer
Peter Ginter
Art Directors
Diane Bergmann
Jinhi Kim
Vera Mueller
Kathrin Wetzel
Design Director
Wolf Schneider

Creative Director
Wolf Schneider
Design Group
Scholz & Friends
Identify
Advertising Agency
Scholz & Friends
Agenda

Account Handlers
Jenka Pankau
Bettina Prange
Katharina Söchtig
Constanze Zinner
Marketing Manager
Matthias Nagel
Brand Manager
Thomas Naumann

Client
Bundesministerium
für Bildung
und Forschung
Brand
World Machine

Graphic Design

Scholz & Friends Agenda
for Bundesministerium für Bildung und Forschung

World Machine
What happens when two particles collide? What happened during the Big Bang? What is the origin of mass? Scientists are using the Large Hadron Collider to answer these questions. Mankind's biggest experiment, the World Machine, will take place at CERN, the European Organisation for Nuclear Research in Geneva. The identity of this World Machine involves particles, symbolising the world's largest particle accelerator, a documentary visual language, and surprising marketing approaches such as an exhibition at Bundestag U-Bahn station in Berlin.

Photographers
Corey Arnold
Peter Beste
Immaculada Diaz
Gustav Karlsson
Frost

Nick Haymes
Alex Hoerner
Jouko Lehtola
Mark Likosky
Horacio Salinas
John Short
Ebbe Stub Wittrup

Illustrators
Jared Buckhiester
Jenny Mörtsell
Prop Stylists
Victoria Granof
Chrissie MacDonald

Creative Director
James Casey
Publisher
Swallow
Publications

Magazine & Newspaper Design

Swallow Publications

Swallow Magazine

Swallow Magazine is a hardbound food and travel publication with a unique sideways glance. Taking cues from outside the realms of foodie faddism, it is a magazine for those who like their dinner dirtier and a whole lot more exciting. The inaugural issue digests the Nordic countries, a region often overlooked in terms of gustatory delights. Swallow Magazine is published annually in New York City, and distributed to select locations worldwide.

Photographer
Knut Egil Wang
Art Director
Kjell D Ramsdal

Designer
Kjell D Ramsdal
Copywriter
Hilde Sandvik

Design Group
VJU Brand and
Business Innovation
Brand Manager
Jan Økland

Client
Bryne Stavanger
Offset

Book Design
VJU Brand and Business Innovation
for Bryne Stavanger Offset

Traktorland
There is nothing elegant about tractors. They are bow-legged and loudmouthed, just like in the myth about the farmers of Jaeren, an area along the south west coast of Norway. They are sluggish, hot-tempered and can destroy peoples' sleep. But they are dependable when you need them. This book is an affectionate tribute to the tractor-life of Jaeren. With beautiful and ambient photographs, 'Traktorland' illustrates the central role the tractor has played, and more, still does play, in Jaeren. Who said tractors don't have souls?

Photographer
Christopher Griffith

Design Director
Rebecca O'Donnell

Publisher
Auditorium Editions

Book Design
Auditorium Editions

BLOWN
This is an abstract study of blown out tyres collected from highways across America.

442

The jury:
Nick Bell, Nick Bell Design (Jury Foreman)
Walter Bohatsch, Bohatsch Visual Communication
Sara de Bondt, Sara de Bondt Studio
Guy Featherstone, Wieden + Kennedy London
Julian Melhuish, Saatchi & Saatchi Sydney
Sean Murphy, Value and Service
Scott Williams, A2/SW/HK

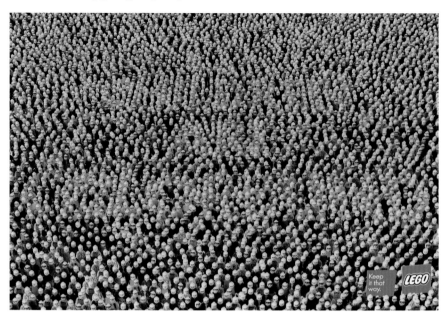

TBWA\Vietnam
for Lego

Colour Blind
Kids don't care about race. All that matters is whether other kids are good playmates or not. Let's keep it that way.

Typographer	**Copywriter**	**Creative Director**	**Account Handler**
Birger Linke	Birger Linke	Birger Linke	Meng Heok Chia
Art Directors	**Photography**	**Advertising Agency**	**Client**
Birger Linke	Teo Studio	TBWA\Vietnam	Lego
Apol Sta Maria			

Wieden + Kennedy London
for Nike

Torres 9
Nike signing Fernando Torres allowed the brand to talk to Liverpool fans. In his first season, Torres proved himself a world-class striker. With 34 goals, he is the first striker since Fowler to score more than 20 in a season, enabling us to celebrate Torres and build Nike's affinity with the fans. Greats like Ian Rush and Robbie Fowler wore the legendary Liverpool number nine shirt. Drawing on this, we elevated Torres' achievement and highlighted Nike's knowledge of the club's history. Each goal scored was unique, so we recreated them with copy, all within nine lines. The home shirt is red. The final line 'and counting' captures Nike and Torres' drive to surpass each achievement, giving hope and moving forward.

Art Director	**Print Producer**	**Advertising Agency**	**Account Handler**
Ben Everitt	Martin Fahey	Wieden + Kennedy	Karelle Dixon
Copywriter	**Creative Directors**	London	**Client**
Darren Wright	Guy Featherstone		Nike
	Stuart Harkness		

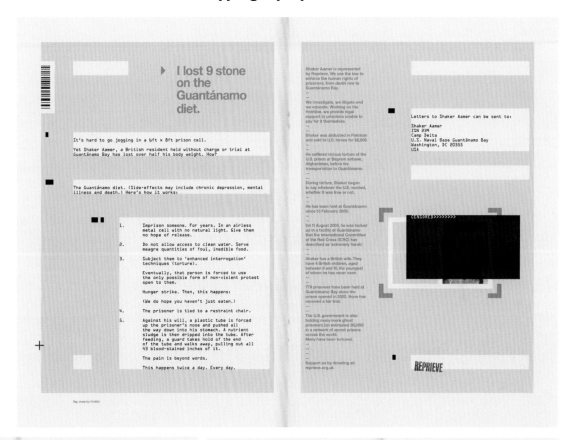

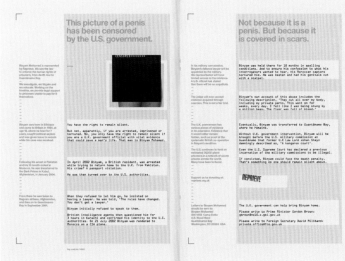

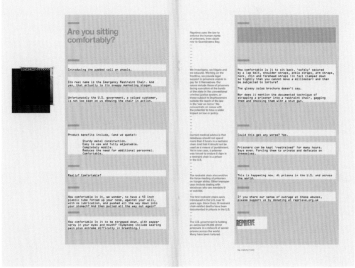

Typographer
Paul Belford
Art Director
Paul Belford

Copywriter
Paul Belford
Advertising Agency
This is Real Art

Account Handler
Kate Nielsen
Client Executive Director
Clare Algar

Client
Reprieve

Press Advertising

This is Real Art
for Reprieve

Diet / Scars / Chair
This is a press advertising campaign for Reprieve, a global legal charity.

Typographer	Copywriters	Creative Director	Account Handler
Karen Jane	Chris Groom	Chris Groom	Elizabeth Kerfoot
Art Directors	Paul Jordon	**Advertising Agency**	**Client**
Chris Groom	Angus Macadam	Wieden + Kennedy	The Guardian
Paul Jordon	**Print Producer**	London	
Angus Macadam	Anna Blom		

Press Advertising

Wieden + Kennedy London
for The Guardian

Basically / Firing Line / Goths
Following a week-long 'How to Write' promotion, The Guardian decided to truncate its 'Guardian Style' journalistic language rule book into a 'Book of the English Language' to give away to readers. Since this was a quirky look inside the process of a great newspaper, filled with its famous wit and irreverence, we decided to pull out real examples from the book. This gave a true flavour of what to expect, and gave us the perfect tone of voice around which to build interesting typographical solutions. Staying true to the brand's white space/colour look and feel, we worked up a series of bold executions, which built up intrigue each day of the week until the book came out on Saturday.

446

Typographer	Designer	Publisher	Brand Manager
Koji Iyama	Yoshiko Akado	Koji Iyama	Hiroshi Suganuma
Art Director	**Photographer**	**Design Group**	**Client**
Koji Iyama	Sachie Abiko	iyamadesign	Guardian Garden

Book Design

iyamadesign
for Guardian Garden

Typescape

This is an experimental book to consider the meaning and shape of the Chinese characters Kanjis. I disjointed Kanjis and extracted the smallest elements, then placed them in a common scene to link them. These continuing scenes with Kanji elements enable you to think about the origins of these characters. Kanji characters are ideograms developed from hieroglyphics; the shapes and combinations of the elements have their own meaning. By placing the elements in a suitable situation, I aimed to visually explain the origin of Kanji.

Typographer	Copywriter	Creative Group	Account Handler
Paul Pateman	Mike Nicholson	**Heads**	James Drummond
Art Director	**Print Producer**	Mike Nicholson	**Client**
Paul Pateman	Linda Carlos	Paul Pateman	Museum of
Designer	**Creative Director**	**Advertising Agency**	Childhood
Paul Pateman	Paul Brazier	Abbott Mead Vickers	
		BBDO	

Graphic Design

Abbott Mead Vickers BBDO
for Museum of Childhood

Memory Back Guarantee

Our brief was to encourage the public to visit the Museum of Childhood. The museum really takes you back to your youth. To dramatise this, we devised this poster as part of an integrated campaign to promote the museum that literally encouraged you to relive your childhood.

Typographers
Geoff Francis
Isaac Nana
Art Director
Chris Bleackley
Designer
Geoff Francis

Writer
John Plimmer
Illustrators
Murray Ball
Geoff Francis
Evan Purdie
Photographer
Steve Boniface

Creative Director
Paul Nagy
**Executive Creative
Director**
Philip Andrew
Advertising Agency
Clemenger BBDO

**Group Account
Director**
Kevin Stroud
Client
New Zealand Post

Graphic Design

Clemenger BBDO
for New Zealand Post

A-Z of New Zealand
In this digital age of emails, text messages, Facebook and Twitter, New Zealand Post asked us to remind people about the joys of sending a real letter with a real stamp. Instead of doing an ad, our idea was to create the A-Z of New Zealand stamps. An issue of 26 stamps is very rare indeed, and this number gave us the scope to add real breadth to our brief summation of great New Zealand people, events and cultural icons. The initial release sold out in less than a week. A subsequent reprint also sold out so quickly that a third reprint is now under way.

The jury:
Adrian Shaughnessy, ShaughnessyWorks (Jury Foreman)
Maf Bishop, Freelance
Jim Davies, totalcontent
Andrew Gorman, Radley Yeldar
Mike Reed, Reed Words
Richard Scholey, Elmwood Design
John Simmons, The Writer

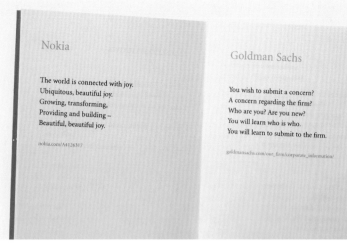

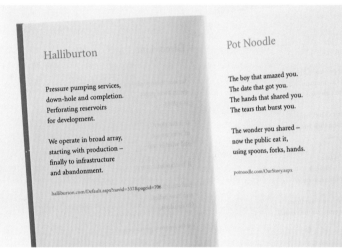

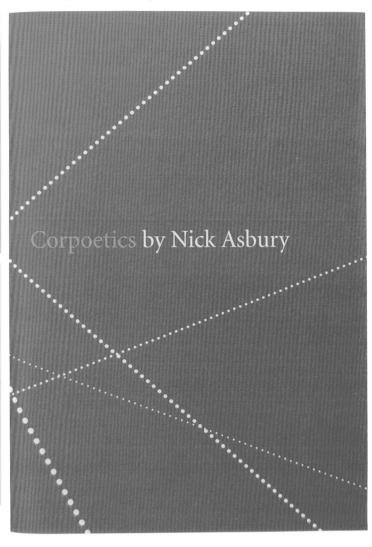

Copywriter	Designer	Design Group	Client
Nick Asbury	Sue Asbury	Asbury & Asbury	Asbury & Asbury

Graphic Design

Asbury & Asbury

Corpoetics
Corpoetics is a collection of found corporate poetry created by rearranging the text from company websites and mission statements. The results range from limericks and haikus to ballads and syllabics, often playfully subverting their source material. Designed to promote the writing side of a new creative partnership, the project demonstrates the ability of the writer to work within the tightest restrictions, unlocking creativity in even the least promising material. Originally sent out as a mailer including a postcard reinterpreting the writer's own homepage, copies were then sold online, with proceeds going to the National Literacy Trust.

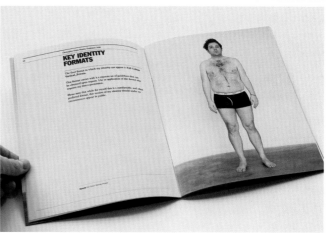

Copywriter
Christopher Doyle
Designer
Christopher Doyle

Photographer
Ian Haigh
Creative Director
Christopher Doyle

Client
You, me & everyone
I know

Brand
Christopher Doyle

Graphic Design

Christopher Doyle

Christopher Doyle Identity Guidelines
Everybody defines themselves differently. My name is Christopher Doyle. I am a designer and a vegetarian. I have engaged with more identities than I can remember, but none more regularly or more intensely than my own. My identity is how I act, look, feel and sound as a person. It has taken 30 years to get to this solution. This is a guide to who I am today, and who I will be in the future. There are things I like about myself and things I hate. Things will happen to my identity that I'm not even aware of yet. I will continue to evolve. Hopefully.

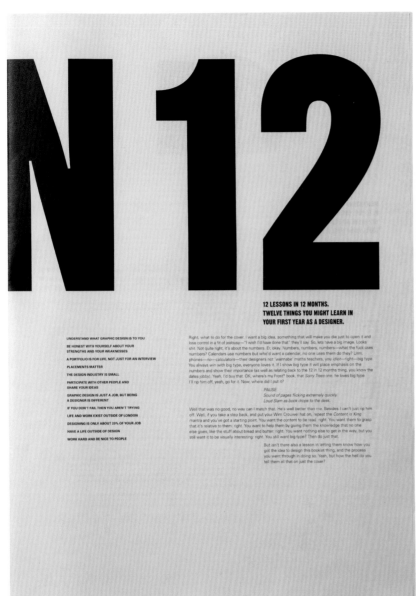

Copywriter
Craig Oldham
Designer
Craig Oldham

Typographer
Craig Oldham

Creative Consultancy
The Chase
Account Handler
Sharron Bardsley

Client
University College
Falmouth

Graphic Design

The Chase
for University College Falmouth

12 in 12
12 in 12 is an accompaniment to a lecture given to University College Falmouth graphic design students. Steering away from the usual 'show and tell' approach, it tells the students what they really want to know about the industry they're entering. Thus, an account of 12 things you might learn in your first year as a designer was given. The 12 lessons are discussed openly to engage the students and create accessibility between them and the subject. With this in mind many mistakes were allowed to remain uncorrected. The booklet was written, by the designer, in a conversational tone (which, you'll find, reads with a Yorkshire accent); it is now free for all graphic design students.

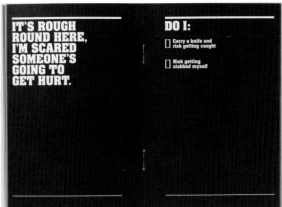

Copywriters
Simon Dean
Paul Hogarth
Jonathan Holt
Art Director
Paul Hogarth

Designer
Anna Nicolo
Junior Designer
Paul Hewett
Typographer
Anna Nicolo

Creative Directors
Paul Hogarth
John Holton
Design Group
Figtree

Account Handler
Scott Chan
Client
Catch 22

Graphic Design

Figtree
for Catch 22

Stuck
For some young people, life can seem like one bad decision after another. Without help these young people can get stuck in their circumstances, making it harder for them to achieve in life. Catch 22 is a charity dedicated to helping these young people out, and 'Stuck' was its first chance to address the world with its new purpose. In this book we put the reader face to face with the issues, presenting them as real catch 22 scenarios with seemingly impossible solutions. After each catch, we show the reader how the charity helps in that instance. The book concludes by revealing the identity of the charity and expressing its beliefs as an organisation.

Copywriters
Keith Cullen
Howard Fletcher

Design Director
Keith Cullen

Creative Director
Andrew Gorman
Design Group
Radley Yeldar

Client
Radley Yeldar

Graphic Design

Radley Yeldar

The Sad Story of the Newsletter
The newsletter as a piece of internal communication is often poorly put together with the wrong sort of content, and fails to communicate. This direct mail piece made that point clearly and simply.

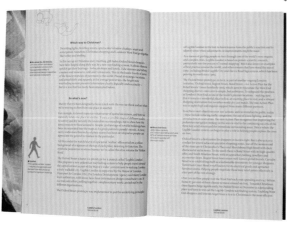

Copywriter	**Editor**	**Design Group**	**Client**
Jim Davies	Kasper de Graaf	Applied Information	Transport for London
Design Director	**Creative Director**	Group	**Brand**
Ben Acornley	Tim Fendley	**Brand Manager**	Legible London
		Jennifer Calvert	

Graphic Design

Applied Information Group
for Transport for London

The Yellow Book

Produced by Applied Information Group and published by Transport for London, 'The Yellow Book' explains the Legible London way-finding prototype installed in the West End in November 2007. 'The Yellow Book' tells the story in plain and compelling language, from the viewpoint of the users for whom the system is designed. The first half is an overview by Jim Davies outlining the background, research and development that culminated in the installation of the prototype. The second half is a visual summation of the theories, concepts and findings behind the system. Documenting and storytelling, in books, movies and exhibitions, form an important part of AIG's project approach, helping inform the design process and gain public support.

454

Graphic Design

300million
for Reed Words

And...
For his self-promotional mailer, freelance copywriter Mike Reed decided to focus on what he'd found to be his biggest bugbear in copywriting: the use of 'and' to begin a sentence. This apparently tiny detail was nevertheless the single most common issue clients raised about his copy. So Mike decided to use his mailer as a sledgehammer to crack this especially tough old chestnut. Marshalling an army of authorities, from Kingsley Amis to H W Fowler, he collected a string of quotations dispelling the myth about 'and'. Then 300million created the nifty mechanism of a booklet that opened and opened and opened. And opened. And opened.

Copywriter	**Designer**	**Typographers**	**Printer**
Mike Reed	Kerry White	Gareth Rutter	Phil LeMonde
Design Director	**Design Group**	Kerry White	**Client**
Matt Baxter	300million		Reed Words

Graphic Design

True North
for Royal Mail

Royal Mail Special Stamps 2008
The Royal Mail yearbook is produced at the end of every year as a celebration of the special stamp issues of the previous 12 months. This edition featured all 14 stamp issues of 2008, together with the stories behind the stamps and their design. As with all Royal Mail stamps, these 14 issues celebrated a diverse range of subjects close to the hearts of many, and as we soon realised, engendering genuine passion in a very special few. So with our theme taken care of, we entitled the book 'Fourteen Passions' and travelled across Britain to meet these fascinating people and allow others to share both their stories and their passion.

Copywriter	**Photographers**	**Creative Director**	**Brand Managers**
Steve Yelland	Stuart Hendry	Ady Bibby	Marcus James
Designers	Ranald Mackechnie	**Design Group**	Dean Price
Sarah Dutton	**Image Manipulation**	True North	**Client**
Kevin Lee	Matt Maurer	**Account Handler**	Royal Mail
Typographer		Tree Wakeling	
Ady Bibby			

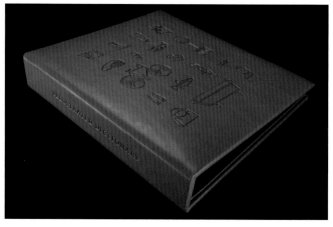

Copywriters
Ruth Gavin
Vivienne Hamilton
Art Direction
GBH

Design Directors
Jason Gregory
Peter Hale
Creative Directors
Mark Bonner
Jason Gregory
Peter Hale

Design Group
GBH
Marketing Manager
Theresa Fatino

Client
SBE Entertainment
Brand
SLS Hotel at Beverly
Hills

Graphic Design

GBH
for SBE Entertainment

Compendium for SLS Hotel at Beverly Hillss
SLS is an international luxury hotel brand that combines elegance and excellence with creativity and a playful wit. As part of a comprehensive identity for their new hotel in Beverly Hills, this compendium marries the gravitas of a functional directory with a mischievous twist – reinventing the idea of a traditional almanac.

Copywriter
Simon Griffin
Art Director
Adam Rix
Design Director
Adam Rix
Designers
Emma Morton
Steve Owen
Ravi Sohanpal

Typographers
Emma Morton
David Palmer
Phil Skegg
Rory Sutherland
Illustrators
Emma Morton
Tim Sinclair
Artwork
Jonathan Robertson

Photographers
Mark Ingram
John Morrison
Tim Sinclair
Jane Stockdale
Luke Watson
Ben Wedderburn
Creative Director
Phil Skegg
Creative Heads
Simon Griffin
Adam Rix

Design Group
LOVE
**Production
Managers**
Jason Munslow
Shelley Wood
Account Handlers
Sarah Benson
Ali Johnson
Client
Silver Cross

Graphic Design

LOVE
for Silver Cross

It's a Boy/It's a Girl
This book was designed and written not only to showcase Silver Cross products, but also to reflect their ethos of 'passionate about parenting' by giving expectant parents a few lighthearted tips and advice.

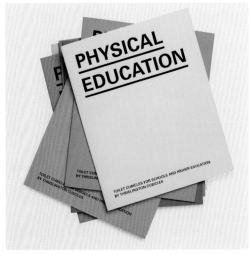

Copywriter	Illustrators	Creative Directors	Advertising Agency
Allan Topol	Andrew Rae	Joe Amaral	TBWA\Toronto
Art Director	Pete Ross	Scott Couture	**Client**
Pete Ross		Allen Oke	Skittles

Graphic Design

TBWA\Toronto
for Skittles

Skittles Brand Experience Now
The Skittles brand kit was sent to agency partners. Since Skittles is a fun and bizarre brand, we felt the brand kit should be too. The kit contained a brand book (with brand guidelines) and a portable cassette recorder with a pre-recorded tape inside. Partners were instructed to listen to the tape after they finished reading the book. The tape was narrated by a character named Reginald. Its contents include a study of the modern teen, a rendition of the Skittles Song (penned by Reginald), and the sound of a rainbow. Hopefully fun was had by all.

Copywriter	Designer	Creative Director	Project Director
Robert Ball	Leon Bahrani	Greg Quinton	Hannah Kirkman
Design Director	**Photographer**	**Design Agency**	**Client**
Robert Ball	Louis Wilson	The Partners	Thrislington Cubicles

Graphic Design

The Partners
for Thrislington Cubicles

Physical Education
The brief was to promote a range of Thrislington toilet cubicles to busy headteachers, who are inundated with marketing material from other manufacturers. You're a headteacher – overworked, overstressed and underpaid. Another direct mail lands on your desk, this one trying to sell you a new toilet cubicle system. Unusually, it makes an effort to understand your workplace, be honest about the problems you face and offer you practical solutions. The writing is humorous, gets to the point and cuts the crap.

The hidden cost of a T-shirt

A 100% cotton T-shirt like this one, needs 200 grammes of cotton.

Cotton grows best on rich, black soil that in its wild state is covered by grassland.

And that grassland is populated with herds of grazing animals: deer, wild horses, antelope, asses, gazelle.

But business is business. And the land is sold to farmers. They move in with noisy, diesel-powered, relentless machines that clear the land.

Square mile after square mile is laid bare and made ready for the plough.

The herds, birds and insects that aren't mowed down are driven from the land.

With no habitat to survive on, within a few fashion seasons, they simply die out.

And end up paying for it with their lives.

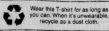 Wear this T-shirt for as long as you can. When it's unwearable, recycle as a dust cloth.

The hidden cost of a T-shirt

This cotton T-shirt has criss-crossed our planet many times to get to you.

First, the raw cotton was shipped from a farming country, to a low-cost manufacturing country. Here it was spun into yarn, and woven into cloth.

Then the finished cloth was loaded onto a ship and transported to an industrial city, in a low-wage, high-skill country.

Here the cloth was cut and sewn into T-shirts. This is one of the batch.

Finally, your T-shirt was packed, and shipped to a port close to you.

Each ship it travelled on left a wake of garbage, oil and exhaust fumes. As the sludge and debris sank in the water, it settled on the plankton, fish and coral, choking them of oxygen and sunlight.

They ended up paying the highest price of all; Their lives.

 Wear this T-shirt for as long as you can. When it's unwearable, recycle as a dust cloth.

The hidden cost of a T-shirt

The fabric of this cotton T-shirt is woven in a mill.

And most mills are located beside rivers.

At the mill, workers treat the fabric with bleaching agents, dyes and chemical softeners. Both these processes need gallons and gallons of water.

Some of the waste water, contaminated with bleach, dyes and chemicals, enters the river.

In the developing world, rivers have plants, and insects, and fish. And crocodiles.

The poisonous chemicals now begin their journey up the food chain.

First the plants and plankton are poisoned.

Then the insects and small fish begin to die.

The bigger fish eat them and die next.

Finally, the crocodiles disappear.

They all pay for our T-shirts with their lives.

This is the real price.

 Wear this T-shirt for as long as you can. When it's unwearable, recycle as a dust cloth.

Copywriter
Neil Johnson
Designer
Joel Chin
Creative Director
Neil Johnson

Advertising Agency
DDB Singapore
Production Manager
Steven Chin

Account Handlers
Rowena
Bhagchandani
Jolene Quek

Marketing Manager
Amy Ho
Client
WWF Singapore
Brand
WWF

Graphic Design

DDB Singapore
for WWF

Deer / Shark / Crocodile
The humble T-shirt that we pay $15 for, and which we casually wear and then discard, actually costs a lot more. The real price is paid for by the wildlife that suffers at every step along the production chain. This fact is heightened by the irony that many fashion brands use animals as their logos. For WWF it has all come together in a series of T-shirt designs that tell the truth simply and eloquently. They are both the medium and the message.

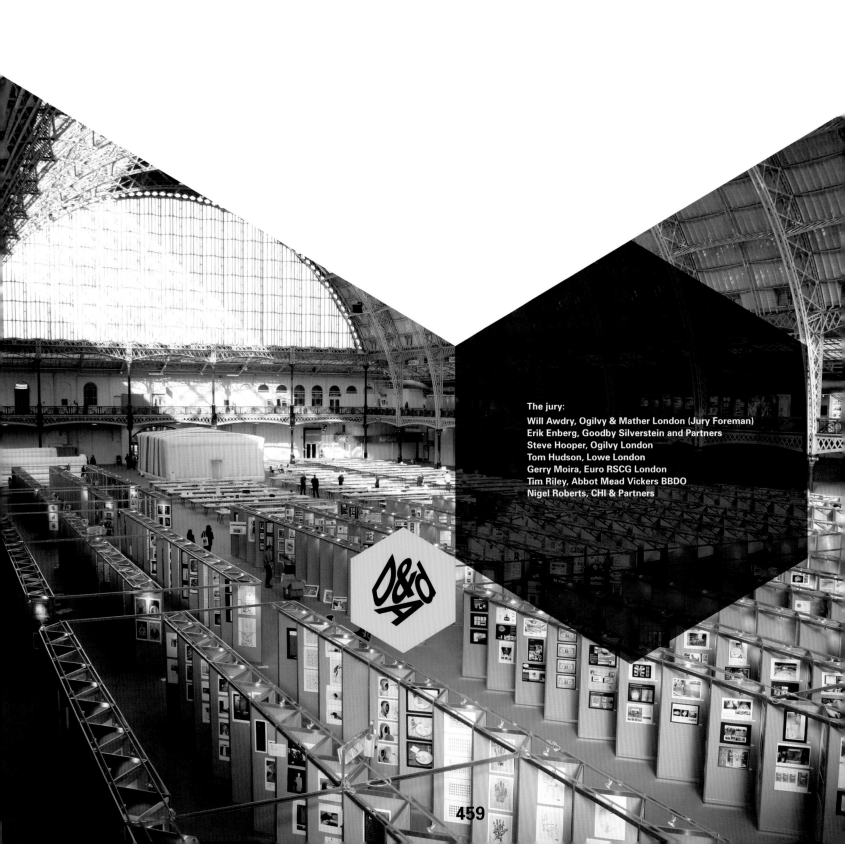

The jury:
Will Awdry, Ogilvy & Mather London (Jury Foreman)
Erik Enberg, Goodby Silverstein and Partners
Steve Hooper, Ogilvy London
Tom Hudson, Lowe London
Gerry Moira, Euro RSCG London
Tim Riley, Abbot Mead Vickers BBDO
Nigel Roberts, CHI & Partners

Snoop Dogg

Rob Lowe

Anjelica Huston

Director	Art Directors	Producer	Lighting
Bryan Buckley	Rob Doubal	Mino Jarjoura	**Cameraperson**
Copywriters	David Kolbusz	**Production Company**	Scott Henrickson
Rob Doubal	Robert Saville	Hungry Man	**Music Composer &**
David Kolbusz	Augusto Sola	**Advertising Agency**	**Arranger**
Robert Saville	Mark Waites	Mother	Ted Chung
Augusto Sola	**Creative Directors**	**Agency Producer**	**Account Handler**
Mark Waites	Stephen Butler	Juliet Pearson	Kerrianne Clem
	Robert Saville	**Editor**	**Client**
	Mark Waites	John Smith	Orange

TV & Cinema Advertising

Mother
for Orange

Snoop Dogg / Rob Lowe / Anjelica Huston
The aim of the 2008 'Goldspot' campaign was to continue the work of Orange in forging a relationship with cinema-goers by reminding them to turn their phones off during the movie. This campaign offered humorous insights into the film-making industry. Furthermore it gave cinema-goers the chance to enjoy the role reversals that meant top Hollywood talent appeared vulnerable as the insensitive and ever corporate Orange film board laid waste to their creative ambitions. The campaign aimed to engage cinema-goers by featuring enticing stars, namely Snoop Dogg, Rob Lowe and Angelica Huston. As the last in the series, it aimed to cap off a six-year campaign that has cemented Orange's relationship with film.

Director Noam Murro	**Associate Creative Director** Nick Spahr	**Advertising Agency** Goodby Silverstein and Partners	**Editor** Avi Oron	**Voice Over Mix** Rohan Young		
Copywriter Mike McKay	**Producer** Jay Veal	**Agency Producer** Tanya LeSieur	**Telecine** Dave Hussey	**Sound Design** Trinitite		
Art Director Nick Spahr	**Senior Executive Producer** Shawn Lacy	**Visual Effects Producer** Nerissa Kavanagh	**Final Mixer** Eben Carr	**Graphics** Superfad		
Creative Director Jamie Barrett	**Production Company** Biscuit Filmworks	**Visual Effects Editor** Bruce Carter	**Director of Photography** Jo Willems	**Client** Comcast		
Group Creative Directors Chris Ford Mike McKay	**On-Line Company** Brickyard VFX	**Visual Effects** Animal Logic Australia	**Sound Designer** Brian Emrich			

TV & Cinema Advertising

Goodby Silverstein and Partners
for Comcast

Rabbit

To make the point that Comcast never stops making the internet faster, 'Rabbit' opens on a rabbit. A rabbit that is then genetically modified and bred with a panther. A rabbit, that once genetically modified and bred with a panther, has turbines attached, is backed by an unusually strong tailwind and placed on ice. Continuing on, the rabbit panther thingy with turbines and tailwind on ice is then shaved with a cold-forged, high-glide surgical-grade razor, and driven by an over-caffeinated fighter pilot with a lead foot. The spot concludes with the whole rabbit panther turbine tailwind hairless razor pilot scenario travelling down a ski jump in Switzerland under better-than-ideal conditions.

Baby Trading

Baby Mobile

Baby Banking

Director	**Art Director**	**Advertising Agency**	**Marketing Manager**
Randy Krallman	Steve Krauss	Grey New York	Nick Utton
Copywriters	**Creative Directors**	**Agency Producers**	**Client**
Ari Halper	Noel Cottrell	Alison Horn	E*Trade
Jimmy Heekin	Tor Myhren	Bennett McCarroll	
Ben Huser			
Randy Krallman			

TV & Cinema Advertising

Grey New York
for E*Trade

Baby Trading / Baby Mobile / Baby Banking
People thought it was tough to trade online. Whatever. If I could do it, they could do it. I kicked it all off on the financial blogs as pukingbaby42, and a week later bum-rushed Super Bowl 42. Yeah, I tossed my stuff in front of the biggest audience ever. At least I wasn't rocking a nipple shield. And who would have guessed I'd blow up that big: Letterman, Leno, Whoopi, Seacrest – big fans. And online, 20 million desktop jockeys saw my busted grill. The dudes at E*Trade's phones blew up: after the Bowl they had their best day ever, best month ever and best year ever. Babies in advertising – we just never get old.

462

Season Opener

All-Star Break

Playoff Time

World Champs

Director Jesse Peretz **Copywriter** Ryan Inda **Art Director** Jay Morrison **Creative Director** Peter McHugh	**Producers** Tracie Norfleet Lynne Pateman **Set Designer** Dan Estabrook **Production Company** RSA Films	**Advertising Agency** Leo Burnett Los Angeles **Agency Producers** Scott Gould Charlie Maas **Editor** Haines Hall	**Lighting Cameraperson** Dariusz Wolski **Worldwide Chief Creative Officer** Mark Tutssel **Marketing Manager** Steven Rosenblum	**Brand Manager** Mary Kubitskey **Client** GMC **Brand** Yukon Denali

TV & Cinema Advertising

Leo Burnett Los Angeles
for GMC

The Players Lot – Season Opener / All-Star Break / Playoff Time / World Champs
A four-episode story of the relationship between an overzealous car park attendant who operates a special 'players' only' lot beneath an NBA basketball stadium, and a star player who drives a GMC Yukon Denali, the car of choice for many professional players. Episode one: Season Opener. The carpark attendant offers encouragement to the player for the upcoming season. Episode two: All-Star Break. The attendant advises the star after his return from the mid-season NBA All-Star game. Episode three: Playoff Time. The attendant counsels the player as he enters the playoffs. Episode four: World Champs. The star exits the stadium after winning the championship, with the attendant encouraging him to do it again next year.

463

Director	Creative Directors	Advertising Agency	Account Handler
Adam Johnson	Enrico Dorizza	Leo Burnett Italy	Gaia Gilardini
Copywriter	Anna Meneguzzo	**Agency Producer**	**Brand Manager**
Anna Meneguzzo	Sergio Rodriguez	Veronica Pasi	Helene Dusseaux
Art Director	**Producer**	**Editor**	**Client**
Milos Obradovic	Ross Saunders	Valeria Baldassarri	Procter & Gamble
	Production Company	**Music Composer**	**Brand**
	Production	George Thorogood	Tampax
	International		

TV & Cinema Advertising

Leo Burnett Italy
for Procter & Gamble

Mother Nature Best Deliveries
In this advert, the naughty side of Mother Nature is captured as she delivers a period to every girl. She sarcastically calls the period her monthly gift. The idea was to make people talk more about periods and have fun with the subject, freeing it from the usual taboo. The spot talks the way people talk, without ad-land speak, conveying that Tampax is in tune with people, and that periods are not a big deal. It was the key to opening up YouTube and Facebook to the brand. The spot has been viewed over 69,000 times on YouTube, and the Facebook page has nearly 16,000 views. The words 'gifted' and 'monthly gift' now have a new definition on urbandictionary.com.

Director
Jim Gilchrist
Copywriter
Sue Higgs
Art Director
Sue Higgs
Creative Director
Alasdair Graham

Producer
Philippa Thomas
Production Company
Thomas Thomas
Films
Advertising Agency
Ogilvy London

Agency Producer
Russell Benson
Editor
Amanda James
**Lighting
Cameraperson**
Robbie Ryan
Account Handler
Matt Pye

Marketing Manager
Jean-Laurent Ingles
Brand Manager
Clare Dolan
Client
Unilever
Brand
Comfort

TV & Cinema Advertising

Ogilvy London
for Unilever

Naturist
This campaign targets the housewife. We wanted to show her how soft Comfort makes your clothes in as entertaining a way as possible. We created a film that really dramatises how good clothes can feel. Clothes don't just feel great, but irresistible. Irresistible enough for even seasoned naturists to abandon a life of nudity and return to the pleasure of wearing skirts, shirts and a 'fawn, lambs wool turtle neck sweater'.

Director
Jim Jenkins
Copywriters
Darren Wright
Matthew Zaifert
Art Director
Rodney White
Creative Directors
David Skinner
Darren Wright

**Chief Creative
Officers**
David Lubars
Bill Bruce
**Executive Creative
Director**
Susan Credle
Production Company
O Positive

Advertising Agency
BBDO New York
Executive Producers
Julie Andariese
Bob Emerson
Editor
Avi Oron
Editing House
Bikini Edit

Music Producer
Melissa Chester
Music House
Big Foote
Account Handler
Gayle Weiss
Client
AT&T

TV & Cinema Advertising

BBDO New York
for AT&T

Scorsese
This advert is the result of a simple idea: instead of moviegoers interrupting movies with phone calls, what if movie people interrupted people's lives with what they do? In this case, Martin Scorsese is directing. How would Martin Scorsese direct a timid suburban mom and her son at bedtime? He'd make it a lot darker, a lot more uncomfortable, and hopefully, for the movie audience, it would be pretty funny.

HOW DO YOU GET INSIDE
First get inside
THE HEAD OF A 16-YEAR OLD
the head of a 16-year old
KNIFE-WIELDING THUG?
bed-wetting boy.

Evil bastard. Thug. Needs locking up. Be honest, when you look at this picture, aren't they the kinds of thoughts running through your head? But it's the thoughts running through his head that we should be more concerned with.

Trying to punish these kids only adds to their resentment and anger. 80% of those given ASBOs, or any other punishment, will go on to re-offend. There's no simple answer. But there is an answer.

Kids Company has known for a long time that the only way to help these kids change is by changing the way we look at them. We have to get to know them. To draw out the past experiences in their lives that have made them the way they are.

And you find the same stories keep coming out. Tales of abuse, drugs, a broken family unit in which these kids never had access to a properly functioning parent. They've suffered appallingly at the hands of family members or their parents' drug dealers and pimps. They've spent all their young lives so afraid they've hardly slept. Even now, they may still wet the bed at the memories of their past traumas. But they survive. Just.

It's this survival mentality they take onto the streets. To them, power and aggression equals safety. So they carry weapons. And a child that struggles to survive for too long can get to a point where they don't care if they live or die. Perversely this makes them very brave and capable of

great harm – if you don't care about your own life how can you care about anyone else's?

So we have to help repair their damaged minds. The only way we can do this is by being the positive role models they never had. We have to spend time with them, love them, make them see that they mean something to someone. Make them cherish life – theirs and everyone else's.

But this takes years of hard effort. Kids Company is working with 12,000 kids. Nationwide there are hundreds of thousands who need proper care. Something drastic has to be done. We have this one chance so let's not waste it. There are a lot of ways you can help. Join us at kidsco.org.uk. Before we can make the public feel safe, we need to make these kids feel safe.

KIDSCOMPANY
supporting vulnerable children

BLAME THE PARENTS?
If only more kids had some.

The problem with kids today? So many of them never get the chance to be kids. No one picked them up when they cried. No one taught them the difference between right and wrong. No one protected them.

Poverty, drug dependency, prostitution and other horrors robbed their parents of the ability to cope. And robbed their kids of the ability to grow up in a 'normal' way. They were savagely beaten by the constant stream of their mothers' 'boyfriends'. They became easy prey for drug dealers and others out on the streets.

So what can they do? They have to protect themselves. They learn that by carrying a knife people will think twice about attacking them. But the day someone does they can't rationalise the situation – no one's ever taught them how. So they lash out in a desperate act of self-preservation. Suddenly they get the reputation of someone who will kill. They get respect. They feel strong. They become increasingly anti-social.

And then a member of the public stands up to them. In their underdeveloped mind it takes them back to that feeling of being weak and afraid when they were shouted at and beaten at home.

The adrenalin kicks in and they lash out. You know the rest.

This isn't to condone violent behaviour. It's just to give you a better insight into the boy holding the blade. Because only by properly understanding them can we help these kids change. The simplistic solutions to street violence you may have read elsewhere don't work. 80% of 'punished' kids re-offend.

But there is another solution that does work. Arrest rates have halved where Kids Company has been involved. 91% of kids have been reintegrated into education or employment.

It's because we've earned their trust. We've become the positive role models they never had. So much so, that 90% of them have chosen to come here themselves or were told to come along by a friend.

By nurturing more and more of these neglected kids we can make huge inroads into teenage street violence. But we can't do it on our own. There are lots of ways you can help and support us. Join us at kidsco.org.uk. If we don't work together now to solve this problem we'll have no one to blame but ourselves.

KIDSCOMPANY
supporting vulnerable children

Copywriter	**Photographer**	**Creative Group**	**Advertising Agency**
Mark Fairbanks	Thom Atkinson	**Heads**	Abbott Mead Vickers
Art Director	**Creative Director**	Paul Cohen	BBDO
Paul Cohen	Paul Brazier	Mark Fairbanks	**Client**
Designer		**Print Producer**	Kids Company
Paul Cohen		Ed Hoadley	

Press Advertising

Abbott Mead Vickers BBDO
for Kids Company

Bed Wetting Boy
Everyone tells us that the answer to knife crime is to punish the offenders (ASBOs, prison etc.), but this only makes the situation worse: 80 per cent of these kids will re-offend. Kids Company has years of psychological research that proves there is a different solution whereby over 50 per cent will not re-offend. Because we had to change the majority perception, we decided to go straight for the heartland. We placed long copy ads in the Daily Mail, Daily Telegraph and The Times. These featured images that showed the kind of kids responsible for knife violence. However the headlines and copy were designed to show that the viewer's first reaction to the shots was not necessarily the right one.

It's one thing to find matches or condoms in your son's pocket.

But what if you find a knife?

If your son's started having sex, or getting up to no good, wouldn't you want to talk to him? It's the same if he's started carrying a knife. There may be safe sex, but there are no safe knives. Maybe he's grown up with violence around him. It's not your fault. But you'd blame yourself if he got in with the wrong crowd. What he needs is to know you're interested. Tell him how upset you'd be if anything happened to him or if he ended up in jail. Get to know his life more, while he still has one. Talk to him calmly. Many other parents are worried too, talk to them. Because finding a knife on your son is far better than finding one in him.

Visit direct.gov.uk/talkaboutknives or call 0845 600 4171 for a leaflet.

Home Office

Copywriter
Mike Boles
Art Director
Jerry Hollens
Photographer
Nick Georghiou

Typographer
Lee Aldridge
Creative Director
Damon Collins
Advertising Agency
RKCR/Y&R

Planner
Megan Thompson
Account Handler
Nick Fokes

Strategic Communications Advisor
Emma Roberts
Client
The Home Office

Press Advertising

RKCR/Y&R
for The Home Office

Condom

Knife crime amongst teenage boys is a big problem in the UK, and is constantly in the headlines. Research revealed that mothers are just about the only people these youths will listen to. This ad was part of a campaign, in women's magazines, that talked directly to mothers. We needed to get under the skin of the problem, and show empathy and understanding without being patronising. Instead, we needed to empower mothers, to persuade them that they be the difference between their son getting involved with a street gang or staying out of trouble. And even the difference between their son being knifed to death or being safe.

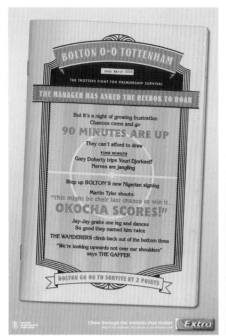

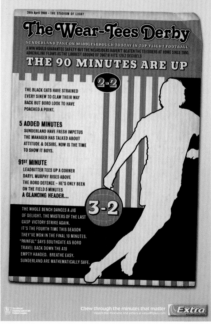

Copywriter	Designers	Creative Group	Advertising Agency
Laurent Simon	Neil Craddock	**Heads**	Abbott Mead Vickers
Art Director	Dingus Hussey	Dave Buchanan	BBDO
Aiden McClure	Aaron Moss	Mike Hannett	**Client**
	Creative Director	**Image Manipulator**	Wrigley's
	Paul Brazier	Mark Deamer	**Brand**
			Extra

Press Advertising

Abbott Mead Vickers BBDO
for Wrigley's

Bolton / Everton / Fulham / Middlesbrough / Newcastle / Sunderland
The brief was to promote Extra's sponsorship of the Premier League to football fans whilst delivering the benefit of tension relief through chewing. We wanted to resonate with genuine football fans so we individually tailored these ads for Bolton Wanderers, Everton, Fulham, Middlesbrough, Newcastle and Sunderland, as these clubs wanted to be involved with the promotion. This allowed us to recount a classic added time moment for each specific club and art direct them in a style sympathetic to their colours and old programmes. The benefit of tension relief through chewing is delivered through encouraging the audience to relive agony of the moment. The ads ran (full page) in the match-day program of the corresponding club.

468

Passengers

① Dead passengers should be conveyed in the boot or 'TRUNK' of the vehicle.

② Hidden passengers MUST be seated directly behind the driver. They should only make themselves known part-way through the journey, in desolate areas of highway.

③ When involving backseat passengers in existential conversation, AVOID driving over bumps in the road. In case of accident, contact Mr W. Wolf.

④ When talking, drivers should ALWAYS keep their eyes on their passenger whilst wildly turning the steering wheel back and forth.

Fig 5.3 Choose fellow travellers with care

Driving abroad

Foreign countries have different rules of the road from us. The following are a small number of examples.

Italy: Cars have the right of way everywhere, including inside houses, churches and sewers.

Australia: All cars must be modified and fitted with fully customised heavily armoured components to comply with all post-apocalyptic wasteland vehicle standards.

UK: Cars invariably have ejector seats, revolving number plates, tracking devices and surface-to-air missiles. Do pay attention to instructions when taking custody of these vehicles.

Fig 7.6 New Zealand: Not all road users are to be trusted

Copywriter
Will Lowe
Art Director
Victor Monclus
Illustrator
Tobatron
Typographer
Pete Mould

Creative Director
Jeremy Craigen
Retoucher
Andy Walsh
Advertising Agency
DDB London
Planner
Damien McKeown

Art Buyer
Daniel Moorey
Project Managers
Craig Neilson
Sophie Simonelli
Account Manager
Jessica Huth
Account Director
Charlie Elliot

Communications Manager
Sal Chapman
Client
Volkswagen
Brand
Independent Film Sponshorship

Press Advertising

DDB London
for Volkswagen

Hollywood Highway Code
To promote Volkswagen's support of independent cinema, we created this booklet, 'The Hollywood Highway Code', a guide to the cinematic rules of the road.

MAKE A GREAT TELEVISION AD AND WIN £20K

INCLUDE	*AVOID*
Doritos	Ambassadors' receptions
	Annoying jingles you can't get out of your head
	Odious condescending one-time hack directors telling us to 'calm down dear'
	Penta-bloody-peptides
	Annoying jingles you can't get out of your head
	Talking about ooh-yeah-food in the yeah-right-there style of ahh, ahh a phone sex worker
	The suggestion that shampooing your hair can somehow induce a multiple knee trembler
	Badly dubbed four-year-old brats gassing themselves on the bog
	Trying to be like well street blood just coz you is advertising to the yoof, innit
	The talky-walky bit that treats you like you have the itsy-bitsy mind of an ickle wickle child
	Caterwauling tone-deaf former bank clerks having a singsong
	Bev and sodding Kev
	Moronic lactose-obsessed muppets skydiving for balls of cheese
	Dried-up 'not fit enough to actually be a model' celebrity beauty editors
	'Ever-so-arty' hippy-dippy soundtracks
	Dancing around like a cat having a fit just because you've consumed a pot of curdled milk
	Lispy company presidents vain enough to think their pigeon English will sway us into buying a two-bit timeshare in some craphole nobody's ever heard of
	Barry Scott
	Annoying jingles you can't get out of your head

FOR MORE INFORMATION VISIT DORITOS.CO.UK

Copywriter
Mike Nicholson
Art Director
Paul Pateman

Creative Director
Paul Brazier
Creative Group Head
Mark Fairbanks

Advertising Agency
Abbott Mead Vickers
BBDO

Client
Pepsico
Brand
Doritos

Press Advertising

Abbott Mead Vickers BBDO
for Pepsico

How to Make a Great TV Ad
The brief was to encourage creatives to enter the 'You Make It We Play It' competition, in which Doritos invited creative talents to create their next TV ad. To be brief, we wrote a brief. Who says planning can't be fun.

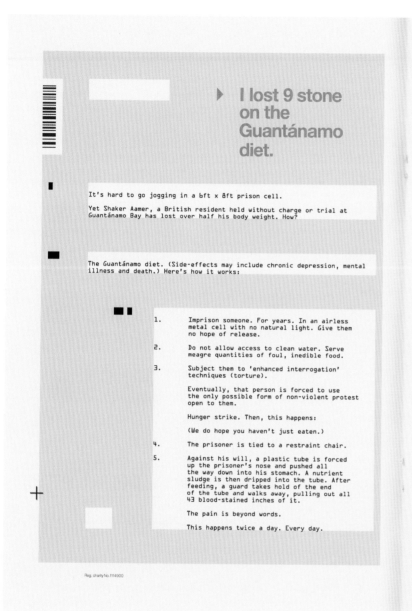

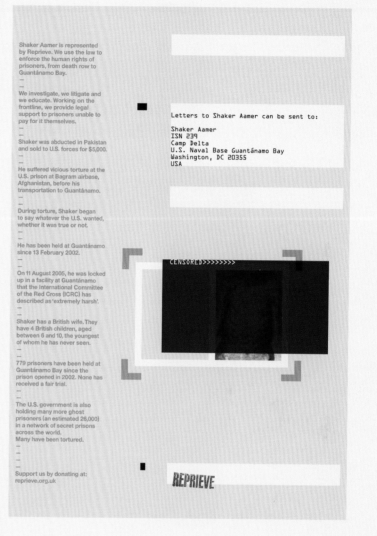

Copywriter
Paul Belford
Art Director
Paul Belford

Typographer
Paul Belford

Account Handler
Kate Nielsen

Advertising Agency
This is Real Art
Client
Reprieve

Press Advertising
This is Real Art
for Reprieve

Diet
This is a piece of press advertising for Reprieve, a global legal charity.

I never took for granted the life the Ahmeds gave me. The day they took me into their London home, I instantly felt warm and safe. My favourite memories were of Saturday afternoons when the women of the family gathered together to gossip and cook. Sonja and I started in the kitchen at the crack of dawn and by mid-morning, the three girls, Farah, Adiva and Nadja would saunter from their bedrooms to join us. Together we would chat about our week's work while preparing an enormous feast for the family. It was as much a day of therapy as it was of productivity, as by late afternoon we were all up to date on each other's business and the house was filled with the mouth-watering aroma of roast lamb, lentil soup and baking aubergines.

On these Saturdays, Omar stayed out of the kitchen. He knew better than to get in the way of women's business. But more importantly, he and Uncle Naveed had business of their own. After breakfast they would head to their rented garage in Greenwich to spend the day working on their cars, but they would always be home for dinner at six o'clock sharp because that was the rule and Omar was nothing if it were not for his rules. Yes indeed, Omar ran a tight ship and whilst he was mostly authoritative and staunch he was complex at the same time.

As a husband, Omar remained distant and aloof, but as a father, I knew he was softer. Underneath that hard exterior there was a man full of compassion and sincerity. It would not be wrong to say that he loved his girls more than life itself and it was no secret he was fiercely protective of them.

As for me, however, I was nothing to Omar. He hardly gave me any attention - rarely a glance, and in fact, not once over all the years even a "hello". But I understood. It was clear we had nothing in common, except of course our place of abode, within which we managed to stay out of each other's way with hardly any effort at all. In fact, our paths never crossed until one day in December, four years ago, which I will never forget.

That Saturday afternoon we were all in the kitchen enjoying its warmth while outside the first sprinklings of snow danced in the air. The girls were bickering over who left the butter to burn and Sonja and I were chopping vegetables for the lamb roast. Suddenly Omar and Uncle Naveed stormed into the kitchen in a rage. They marched straight up to Nadja, the youngest and in my opinion, the prettiest of the girls. Nadja looked up at her father, terrified.

"Nadja!" Omar yelled into her face. "Did you forget the rules? I know what you've been doing." His fist shook just centimetres from his daughter's nose. "The neighbours tell me you have been seeing a boy. Sneaking out in the middle of the night.

You are only sixteen years old, Nadja." Omar lowered his voice. "People have been talking. They think you are a whore." He began to tremble. "Do you know how this makes our family look?"

Omar's face reddened to the shade of a beetroot. He grabbed Nadja's neck and shook her violently sending Sonja into a screaming fit. Omar slapped his wife hard across the face before turning back to Nadja. "You have ruined our family name. What am I going to do?" he screamed.

Suddenly, Omar stopped and closed his eyes, and everybody froze with fear. When he came to, he stared into his daughter's eyes and took in a long deep breath. He turned around and that's when he saw me by the kitchen sink. I was terrified for what was about to happen. Omar made me do something, something I will never forget.

He made me kill Nadja. I cut her throat wide open so the blood poured freely covering the kitchen floor like a red carpet. Omar said it was the price that she had to pay for dishonouring the family name.

I will never forget what I did that day. But what could I have said? What could I have done? I am only a rusty old kitchen knife.

Thousands of honour killings go unreported every year. If you know something please speak out. Because if you don't, who will?

www.stophonourkillings.com

Copywriter	Creative Directors	Account Handler	Client
Susie Chow	Christen Monge	Jessica Davey	Iranian and Kurdish
Art Director	Andrew Reznik	**Marketing Managers**	Women's Rights
Alex Noble	**Advertising Agency**	Diana Nammi	Organisation
Photographer	Ogilvy & Mather	Joanne Payton	**Brand**
Brendan Fitzpatrick	Asia Pacific		International
Typographer			Campaign Against
Alex Noble			Honour Killings

Press Advertising

Ogilvy & Mather Asia Pacific
for Iranian and Kurdish Women's Rights Organisation

Knife
The brief was to raise awareness about so called 'honour killings' that take place all over the world, yet are rarely spoken about. Our solution actually demonstrates this problem, urging people to speak out if they know something or if they can help.

U4

The jury:

Simon Learman, McCann Erickson London (Jury Foreman)
David Angelo, David&Goliath
Sean Atherton, Adelphoi Music
Matt Buels, Hungry Man
Mick Ebeling, The Ebeling Group
Matthew Fone, Eponymous
Doug Foster, Freelance
Guy Manwaring, Sonny London
Mike McGee, Framestore
Hernán Ponce, Ponce Buenos Aires
Jim Radford, MPC
Jonnie Scarlett, The Quarry
Jack Sedgwick, Wave
Kris Wixom, TBWA\Chiat\Day New York

the Coke side of life™

Special Effects
Angus Kneale
Andrew Proctor
Dan Williams
Director
Nicolai Fuglsig
Art Director
Hal Curtis
Copywriter
Sheena Brady

Creative Directors
Sheena Brady
Hal Curtis
Producers
Eric Stern
David Zander
Production Company
MJZ
Advertising Agency
Wieden + Kennedy
Los Angeles

Agency Producer
Matt Hunnicutt
Editor
Russell Icke
Lighting
Cameraperson
Ellen Kuras
Set Designer
Robb Buono
Music Arranger
Robert Miller

Sound Designer
Gus Koven
Account Handler
Ryan Peterson
Client
Coca-Cola

Special Effects

MJZ
for Coca-Cola

It's Mine
Set against the backdrop of the Macy's Thanksgiving Day Parade in New York City, the balloons Underdog and Stewie tussle over a giant Coke balloon, only to have the balloon of Charlie Brown pop up and claim the bottle. This was also selected by the jury in the Direction category.

Director
Antoine Bardou-
Jacquet
Copywriters
Frank Ginger
Sam Heath
Art Directors
Robin Brown
Frank Ginger
Sam Heath

Creative Directors
Tony Davidson
Kim Papworth
Producer
Russell Curtis
**Production
Company**
Partizan
Advertising Agency
Wieden + Kennedy
London

Agency Producer
Rachel Hough
Editor
Bill Smedley
**Lighting
Cameraperson**
Olivier Cariou
**Production
Manager**
Miranda Johnstone

**Production
Assistant**
Laura Jones
Account Handler
Jonathan Tapper
Client
Honda

Production Design

Partizan
for Honda

Problem Playground
The new Honda FCX Clarity is the first zero-emission hydrogen fuel cell car to go into production. In this ad, an army of Honda workers builds a sculpture of Honda's hybrid engine using thousands of Rubik's cubes. The team also complete similarly challenging puzzles, each one representing an engineering problem solved by Honda, such as building energy efficient solar panels. The crowd moves on to build an enormous jigsaw model of the new Honda FCX Clarity, as Garrison Keillor's voice-over explains that when you love finding solutions, every problem becomes a playground. This was also selected in the Editing category.

Director
David Fincher
Copywriter
Jason Bagley
Art Director
Ryan O'Rourke
Creative Directors
Alberto Ponte
Tyler Whisnand
Jeff Williams
Producer
Robin Buxton
Executive Producer
Jeff Baron

Associate Producer
Juliana Montgomery
Production Company
Anonymous Content
Advertising Agency
Wieden + Kennedy
Portland
Agency Producer
Matt Hunnicutt
**Agency Head of
Production**
Ben Grylewicz

Special Effects
Asylum Visual
Effects
Editor
Angus Wall
**Director of
Photography**
Emmanuel Lubezki
Sound Designer
Ren Klyce
Sound Producer
Misa Kageyama
Mixer
Loren Silber

Mix Producer
Jessica Locke
**Visual Effects
Producer**
Mark Kurtz
**Visual Effects
Executive Producer**
Mike Pardee
**Visual Effects
Production
Coordinator**
Emily Hoovler

**Visual Effects
Supervisor**
Sean Faden
**Compositing
Supervisor**
James Allen
Account Handler
Matthew Hernholm
Brand Manager
Mike Crowell
Client
Nike

Direction

Anonymous Content
for Nike

Fate
The life-long journeys of professional American football players LaDainian Tomlinson and Troy Polamalu are chronicled as their destinies collide in a National Football League game. This was also nominated in the Cinematography and Use of Music categories.

Director
Vince Squibb
Copywriter
Dinesh Kapoor
Art Director
Michael Ashley
Creative Director
Axel Chaldecott

Producer
Spencer Dodd
Set Designer
Christopher Oddy
Production Company
Gorgeous Enterprises

Advertising Agencies
JWT London
JWT New York
Agency Producer
Dean Baker
Editor
Paul Watts

Director of Photography
Alwin Kuchler
Client
HSBC

Direction

Gorgeous Enterprises
for HSBC

Lumberjack
HSBC has always sought to celebrate people's differences – from their cultures and customs to individuals' points of view. By now focusing on what people value, HSBC wants to take a closer look at what drives and motivates them in the lives they choose to lead.

Director
Guy Ritchie
Creative Directors
John Boiler
Glenn Cole
Jason Norcross
Bryan Rowles
Producer
Dave Morrison
Line Producer
Aris McGarry

Production Company
Anonymous Content
Advertising Agency
72andSunny
Agency Producers
Sam Baerwald
Angelo Ferrugia
Erika Madison
Special Effects
The Mill

Editor
Robert Duffy
Lighting Cameraperson
David Higgs
Music Composers
Eagles of Death
Metal
Music Arranger
Michiel Groeneveld

Sound Designer
Matt Collinge
Client
Nike
Brand
Nike Football

Direction

Anonymous Content
for Nike

Next Level
The brief was to inspire footballers around the world to become better footballers. Our solution was to show what it takes at the highest level: successes, failures, hard work, knocked-out teeth, all of it. Viewers are directed to nikefootball.com where they can find products and training programmes to help them achieve their goals.

Director
Ringan Ledwidge
Copywriter
Olivier Camensuli
Art Director
Frederic Royer
Creative Director
Olivier Altmann
Producers
Patrick Barbier
Nancy Gabriel

Production Companies
Rattling Stick
Wanda
Advertising Agency
Publicis Conseil
Agency Producers
Muriel Allegrini
Pierre Marcus
Editor
Richard Orrick
Post Production
Antoine Daubert
Jeanne Raibaut

Lighting Cameraperson
Jess Hall
Music Composer
Amelia Warner
Music Arranger
Eric Cervera
Telecine
Mick Vincent
Account Directors
Maylis Pajot
Marie Wallet
Account Executive
Emilie Alalof

Strategic Planning General Manager
Valerie Henaff
Sponsorship & Commercial Communications Manager
Alice Holzman
Advertising Director
Isabelle Quinlan
Brand Director
Nicolas Guiramand
Broadband Communication

Manager
François Baroin
Client
Orange
Brand
La TV d'Orange

Direction

Rattling Stick
for Orange

Rewind City
Orange Rewind City shows us the weepy, parting moment when two young travellers go their separate ways on the streets of a busy Indian town. This execution however sees our young lovers reunited by turning back the course of events. Traffic reverses and pedestrians step backwards until finally our young couple are gobsmacked to find themselves back together again. This was also selected in the Editing category.

a moment of

Schweppervescence

Schweppes

Director of Photography
Greig Fraser
Director
Garth Davis
Copywriter
Jim Ingram
Art Director
Ben Couzens

Creative Director
Ben Coulson
Producer
Karen Sproul
Production Company
Exit Films
Advertising Agency
George Patterson
Y&R Melbourne
Agency Producer
Romanca Jasinski

Editor
Jack Hutchings
Colourist
Edel Rafferty
Senior Flame
Compositor
Richard Lambert
Music Supervisor
Karl Richter
Director's Assistant
Clea Cregan

Marketing Manager
Paul Donaldson
Brand Manager
David Phillips
Client
Cadbury Schweppes
Brand
Schweppes

Cinematography
Exit Films
for Cadbury Schweppes

Burst
This campaign captures and brings to life the feeling of 'Schweppervescence' using super high speed photography of water balloons bursting in slow motion.

Lighting Cameraperson
Alwin Kuchler
Director
Jeff Labbe
Copywriter
Jon Fox
Art Director
Rik Brown
Executive Creative Directors
Nick Gill
John Hegarty

Producer
Ran Holst
Production Company
Sonny London
Advertising Agency
BBH London
Agency Producer
Davud Karbassioun
Editor
Rich Orrick

Music Artists
Isobel Campbell
Mark Lanegan
Sound Designer
Aaron Reynolds
Post Production Company
Absolute
Agency Planning Director
Patricia McDonald

Business Director
Patricia McDonald
Senior Director of Wholesale Strategy
Jennifer Sey
Client
Levi's
Brand
501

Cinematography

Sonny London
for Levi's

Secrets & Lies
Secrets & Lies is one of four films in the Levi's 501 Live Unbuttoned campaign. The campaign celebrates the 501's most distinctive product feature, the button-fly, but makes the act of unbuttoning the symbol of a free, open, uninhibited and unrestrained approach to life. Secrets & Lies dramatises what it means to live life unbuttoned. After meeting on a night out, a young couple reveal they haven't been entirely honest with each other. As they unbutton their 501s the truth is exposed. The more they reveal about themselves, the closer they become.

Editor
Bill Smedley
Director
Steve Hudson
Copywriter
Laurence Quinn
Art Director
Mark Norcutt

Executive Creative Director
Russell Ramsey
Producer
Tim Nunn
Production Company
Hungry Man
Advertising Agency
JWT London

Agency Producer
Lisa Colchester
Lighting
Cameraperson
Ian Murray
Post Production Companies
Framestore
Kpost
Account Handler
Musa Tariq

Press & Campaign Manager
Louisa Mullan
Client
The Foundation for the Study of Infant Deaths

Editing

Hungry Man
for The Foundation for the Study of Infant Deaths

Pain
This commercial shows a succession of women in labour. Through a series of cuts it creates a powerful reminder of the pain endured in childbirth. Towards the end a title fades up to the voice-over saying, 'Nothing is as painful as losing a baby'. You are then directed to the FSID's website for information and donations.

Editor
Bill Smedley
Director
Antoine Bardou-Jacquet
Copywriter
Dave Henderson
Art Director
Richard Denney

Creative Directors
Richard Denney
Dave Henderson
Producer
David Stewart
Production Company
Partizan

Advertising Agency
Saatchi & Saatchi
London
Agency Producer
Rebecca Williams
Lighting Cameraperson
Damien Morisot

Account Handler
Michelle Greenhalgh
Client
Visa Europe
Brand
Visa Debit

Editing

Partizan
for Visa Europe

Running Man
This advert dramatises the role Visa plays in people's lives, taking the hassle out of financial transactions of any value, and making life flow better.

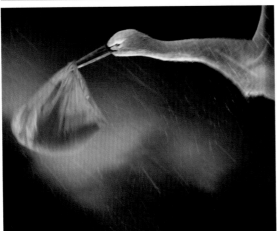

Special Effects
Framestore
Director
Daniel Kleinman
Copywriter
Reuben Hower
Art Director
Gerard Caputo
Creative Director
Eric Silver
Producer
Johnnie Frankel

Production Company
Rattling Stick
Advertising Agency
BBDO New York
Agency Producers
Anthony Curti
Ed Zazzera
Animators
Nicklas Andersson
Michael Mellor
Dale Newton
Visual Effects Producer
Helen Stanley

Visual Effects Supervisor
William Bartlett
Lead Compositor
William Bartlett
Lead Technical Director
David Mellor
Computer Graphics Supervisor
Dan Seddon
Editor
Steve Gandolfi

Music Arranging
Human
Sound Designer
Gus Koven
Sound Engineer
Tom Jucarone
Sound Mixer
Tom Jucarone
Client
Monster.com

Special Effects

Framestore
for Monster.com

Stork
Created by BBDO New York and directed by Daniel Kleinman for Rattling Stick, this spot features an amazing CG stork that is the latest breathtakingly lifelike creature to be hatched by the Framestore commercials 3D team. The spot was supervised by Kleinman's long-time associate at Framestore, William Bartlett, who also led the compositing of the work. The 3D team was headed by Dan Seddon. The biggest single challenge was the feathers, which are always tricky, and never more so than on a stork, whose plumage appears more loosely packed than many other birds', with many of its large feathers individually discernable. Seddon's team developed a new grooming system for the feathers, which gave greater flexibility in changing their size and shape.

Special Effects
Michal Podhradsky
Director
Martin Krejci
Copywriters
Richard Bullock
Samuel Coleman
Dario Nucci
Art Directors
Samuel Coleman
Dario Nucci

Creative Directors
Richard Bullock
Andy Fackrell
Producer
Molly Pope
Production Company
Stink London
Advertising Agencies
180 Amsterdam
180/TBWA

Agency Producers
Cedric Gairard
Cat Reynolds
Animator
Michal Podhradsky
Editor
Filip Malasek
Lighting Cameraperson
Ivan Vit
Director of Photography
Stepan Kucera

Music Composers
Viktor Erkt
Xavier Mosley
Sound Designer
Raja Seghal
Production Designer
Marketa Korinkova
Post Production Company
Glassworks
Post Production Supervision
The Pool

Planner
Alison Stewart
Account Handler
Kyle Marquis
Brand Manager
Nicole Vollebregt
Client
adidas International
Brand
adidas Originals

Special Effects

Stink London
for adidas International

Adi Dassler's Workshop
This is the story of Adi Dassler, the founder of adidas. He handmade his first shoe in 1925. Not many people know this, but adidas is a shortened version of his name. That's why we wanted to make the film to tell the world about the heritage of the adidas brand. The entire film is a 1:3 recreation of Adi Dassler's world. Using stop frame animation, the viewer is taken on a journey through the history of adidas as told by its founder. The set itself took 30 people over one month to build in miniature, and is a masterpiece of craftsmanship.

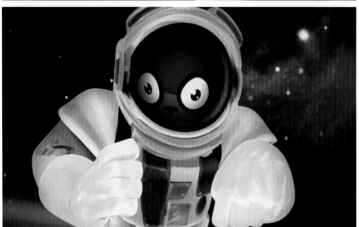

Director	**Creative Director**	**Agency Producers**	**Account Manager**
Yoann Lemoine	Alexandre Hervé	Sophie Mégrous	Thomas Granger
Copywriter	**Production Company**	Florence Potiée	**Brand Manager**
Matthieu Elkaim	Wanda	Sperry	Emmanuelle Guilbart
Art Director	**Advertising Agency**	**Illustrator**	**Client**
Pierrette Diaz	DDB Paris	Pierrette Diaz	Lagardère Active
		Music	**Brand**
		THE	Tiji

Animation

Wanda
for Lagardère Active

The Voyage
Where do balloons go when they fly away? Tiji, the leading French TV channel for children under seven, proposes an explanation as imaginative as children.

Animation Director
Andreas Pohl
Copywriter
Paul von
Muehlendahl
Art Directors
Petra Delitsch
Fedja Kehl
Creative Director
Ralf Heuel

Producers
Steffi Beck
Tobias Ziegler
**Production
Company**
OPTIX Digital
Pictures
Advertising Agency
Grabarz & Partner
Agency Producer
Anne Hoffmann

Sound Designers
Florian
Lakenmacher
Felix Mueller
Maximilian
Olowinsky
Compositing Artists
Daniel Brylka
Marcel Lemme
Lead 3D Artist
Markus Geerts

CGI 3D Artists
Marc Goecke
Michael Gottschalk
Florian Weyh
Music Composers
Supreme Music
Marketing Manager
Christoph Wesche
Client
Bontrust

Animation

OPTIX Digital Pictures
for Bontrust

Money Love
Multiplying money – we have taken this expression rather literally. An almost X-rated animated film shows famous faces from banknotes obviously enjoying the act of multiplication. Everything in the film is made of paper, from the protagonists to the buildings and even the backgrounds. The soundtrack also entirely comprises noises generated with paper. Make your money multiply with us.

Golf. Enjoy the everyday.

Das Auto.

Sound Designer
Paul Hartnoll
Director
Scott Lyon
Copywriters
Graeme Hall
Noah Regan
Art Directors
Graeme Hall
Noah Regan

Creative Director
Jeremy Craigen
Producer
Zeno Campbell-
Salmon
Production Company
Outsider
Advertising Agency
DDB London
Agency Producer
Richard Chambers

Editor
Art Jones
Lighting
Cameraperson
John Matthieson
Music Composer &
Arranger
Paul Hartnoll
Account Handlers
Louise Garnar
Jonathan Hill

Marketing Manager
Rod McLeod
Brand Manager
Morna Steel
Client
Volkswagen
Brand
Golf

Sound Design

Outsider
for Volkswagen

Enjoy the Everyday
Enjoy the Everyday is a visual and lyrical composition depicting the everyday life of one man and his Golf. The advert re-edits a man's experiences in and around the Golf to form a soundtrack. Composed and produced by Paul Hartnoll of Orbital, the track was built from sounds recorded on the shoot. Essentially, the ad shows that the accumulation of all your everyday Golf driving experiences is something very special.

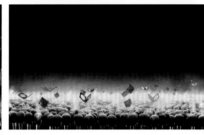

Production Designer
Guillaume Amosse
Director
Johnny Green
Copywriter
Diane Leaver
Art Director
Simon Rice
Creative Director
Paul Brazier

Creative Group Heads
Diane Leaver
Simon Rice
Producer
Fergus Brown
Production Company
Knucklehead

Advertising Agency
Abbott Mead Vickers BBDO
Agency Producer
Yvonne Chalkley
Animator
Drew Lightfoot
Special Effects
Glassworks

Editor
Ted Guard
Music Arrangers
Nick Foster
Peter Raeburn
Sound Designers
Toby Griffin
Owen Griffiths
Client
Royal Mail

Production Design

Knucklehead
for Royal Mail

Grow
To communicate how Royal Mail's business services can help all kinds of organisations expand and grow, we showed various businesses literally growing and flourishing with the use of these services. The commercial is a combination of stop frame animation, live action and CGI. CGI was used in the printing press scene to lay the wrapping paper onto the printing press and to animate the fish. CGI was also used to create the vase sequence: the growing vases are computer generated, as is the vase flower.

Production Designer
Carl Sprague
Director
Neil Gorringe
Art Directors
Patrick Lyndon-Stanford
Alice Tonge
Adam Zoltowski

Creative Director
Neil Gorringe
Advertising Agency
4Creative
Producer
Selena Cunningham

Special Effects
MPC
Editor
James Rosen

Sound Designer
Rich Martin
Client
Channel 4
Brand
Skins

Production Design

4Creative
for Channel 4

Skins, Series 2
While the trailer for the first series of Skins reflects its hedonistic, reckless tone, the aim of this trailer was to echo the more sombre, introspective tone of the second series of Skins, in which the lead character suffers brain damage, a main character dies, and another character is stalked. As the characters were now established, we hinted more at the journey they would be taking. The spot offers clues as to what will happen to each character. The jury has also selected this advert in the Cinematography category.

Production Designer	Creative Directors	Editor	Client
Kate Quinn	Siri Bunford	Adam Rudd	More4
Director	Brett Foraker	**Director of**	**Brand**
Siri Bunford	**Advertising Agency**	**Photography**	Stanley Kubrick
Art Director	4Creative	Alex Barber	Season
Kate Quinn	**Producers**	**Sound Designer**	
	Shananne Lane	Rich Martin	
	Louise Oliver		

Production Design

4Creative
for More4

Stanley Kubrick Season

This spot was designed to promote a season of Stanley Kubrick films and a Channel 4 documentary about Kubrick on More4. It was important to us that the technique of shooting was faithful to Kubrick's – there could be no post production work, special effects or invisible edits. It needed to be shot entirely in camera with a steadicam, a technique Kubrick pioneered in 'The Shining'. Kubrick possessed a fearsome presence on set, and an obsessive-compulsive attention to detail. The objective of the trail was to convey those idiosyncrasies, while at the same time revering his genius.

Director	Creative Directors	Production Company	Editor
Mark Romanek	Alberto Ponte	Anonymous Content	Robert Duffy
Copywriter	Tyler Whisnand	**Advertising Agency**	**Lighting**
Caleb Jensen	Jeff Wiliams	Wieden + Kennedy	**Cameraperson**
Art Director	**Producer**	Portland	Adam Kimmel
Taylor Twist	Erika Madison	**Agency Producer**	**Music Composer**
	Executive Producer	Erika Madison	Andrew Eksne
	Dave Morrison	**Special Effects**	**Client**
	Set Designer	Digital Domain	Nike
	Dominic Watkins		

Direction

Anonymous Content
for Nike

Chalk

Mark Romanek of Anonymous Content directs an inspiring spot featuring Cleveland Cavaliers superstar LeBron James promoting his sixth signature shoe: the Nike Zoom LeBron VI. As the spot opens, the NBA's leading scoring phenomenon, LeBron James, is seen following his pre-game ritual. James approaches his fans with a handful of chalk and launches an explosion of powder into the air. As the flakes settle on the shoes, faces, and applauding hands of the crowd, the spot flashes to a baker, a student, a barber and a street baller performing their personal versions of the lucky ritual.

490

Director
Ringan Ledwidge
Copywriter
Gavin Torrance
Art Director
Danny Hunt
Creative Director
Danny Brooke-Taylor
Producer
Sally Humphries

Production Company
Rattling Stick
Advertising Agency
Miles Calcraft
Briginshaw Duffy
Agency Producer
Lorraine Geoghegan
Editor
Rich Orrick

Lighting Cameraperson
Alwin Kuchler
Music Composers
Ed Hulme
Phil Kay
Music Consultant
Abi Leland
Planner
Andy Nairn

Account Handler
Michael Pring
Marketing Manager
Jon Goldstone
Client
Premier Foods
Brand
Hovis

Direction

Rattling Stick
for Premier Foods

Go on Lad
This is a simple story of a boy running home with a loaf of bread under his arm. The twist is that his journey takes him through all the major events of the last century – from the suffragettes and the First World War to the Blitz and the 1980s Miners' Strike. It's a 122 second epic, covering the 122 years that Hovis has been baking its bread. And the moral of the story? That Hovis is 'As good today as it's always been'. This advert was also selected by the jury in the Cinematography category.

Director
Jim Jenkins
Copywriters
David Skinner
Darren Wright
Matthew Zaifert
Art Director
Rodney White
Creative Directors
David Skinner
Darren Wright

Executive Creative Director
Susan Credle
Chief Creative Officers
David Lubars
Bill Bruce
Production Company
O Positive

Agency
BBDO New York
Executive Producers
Julie Andariese
Bob Emerson
Editor
Avi Oron
Music Producer
Melissa Chester
Editing House
Bikini Edit

Music House
Big Foote
Account Handler
Gayle Weiss
Client
AT&T

Direction

O Positive
for AT&T

Scorsese
This advert is the result of a simple idea: instead of moviegoers interrupting movies with phone calls, what if movie people interrupted people's lives with what they do? In this case, Martin Scorsese is directing. How would Martin Scorsese direct a timid suburban mom and her son at bedtime? He'd make it a lot darker, a lot more uncomfortable, and hopefully, for the movie audience, it would be pretty funny.

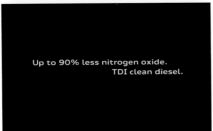

Up to 90% less nitrogen oxide.
TDI clean diesel.

Sound Design

DMDA Method Design Markenfilm Berlin
for Audi

Director	**Producer**	**Animators**	**Music Composers**	**Brand Manager**
Andrew Ruszala	Simona Daniel	Tim Borgmann	MassiveMusic	Michael Finke
Art Directors	**Production**	Chris Keller	Amsterdam	**Client**
Florian Schimmer	**Companies**	**Special Effects**	**Account Handlers**	Audi
Julia Wolk	DMDA Method	Niko Papoutsis	Andrea Bison	**Brand**
Creative Directors	Design	Andrew Ruszala	Niklas Kruchten	Audi TDI Clean
Jens Theil	Markenfilm Berlin	Dirk Urbaniak	**Marketing Manager**	Diesel
Gerrit Zinke	**Advertising Agency**	**Editor**	Lothar Korn	
	kempertrautmann	Hendrik Smith		

Filter
With the innovative TDI clean diesel filter system, Audi is reducing nitrogen oxide emissions by up to 90 per cent. We had 50 seconds to get this rather dry message across in a clear, dramatic way. The advert 'Filter' gives the subject of emissions a whole new look while using a simple analogy to explain the highly complex system behind one of the cleanest diesel cars in the world. This was also selected in the Animation category.

So the RSPCA run programs
that teach kids to respect animals.

37% of violent criminals admit to
being cruel to animals in their childhood.

youneedtherspcaneedsyou.com.au
RSPCA

Sound Design

Nylon Studios
for RSPCA NSW

Sound Designer	**Creative Directors**	**Agency Producers**	**Marketing Manager**
Simon Kane	Laurie Ingram	Jacqui Gillies	Steve Coleman
Sound Design	Andrew Town	Meredyth Judd	**Brand Manager**
Nylon Studios	**Producer**	Kaija Wall	Paige Gibbs
Director	Jane Liscombe	**Editor**	**Client**
Glendyn Ivin	**Production Company**	Jon Holmes	RSPCA NSW
Copywriter	Exit Films	**Lighting**	**Brand**
Laurie Ingram	**Advertising Agency**	**Cameraperson**	RSPCA
Art Director	The Campaign	Adam Arkapaw	
Andrew Town	Palace	**Planner**	
		Dave Hartmann	

Hit
The RSPCA was well respected with a loyal supporter base of animal lovers, however it was struggling to survive due to limited government funding. We needed to appeal to a broader market for support, by showing the RSPCA helps people (not just animals) and the wider community, to prove the charity is relevant and vital to everyone. One RSPCA programme teaches children to have empathy for animals, as kids who are cruel to animals are more likely to commit violent criminal acts, like domestic violence, as adults. To shock and motivate non-animal lovers into action, we developed the idea of a man savagely beating a woman, with her screams replaced by the sounds of an animal being beaten.

Sound Designers
Ashley Bates
Andrew Sherriff
Sound Design
Adelphoi Music
Director
Matthias Zentner
Copywriter
Raymundo Lopez

Creative Directors
Yosu Aranguena
Raymundo Lopez
Producer
David Chipon
Production Company
ACA Films Mexico
City
Advertising Agency
DDB Mexico City

Agency Producers
Elda Bravo
Marcelo Genel
Animators
Dagmar Ammon
Christian Deister
Sylvie Roessler
Christian Stanzel
Martin Tallosy

Special Effects
Abdelkareem
Abonamous
Editor
Jochen Kraus
Music Composer
Andrew Sherriff
Client
Casa Cuervo
Brand
Gran Centenario

Sound Design

Adelphoi Music
for Casa Cuervo

The Calling
This epic 90 second spot, for one of Mexico's premier tequilas, required mind-blowing sound design to complement the spectacular visuals. For the sound designer, the most interesting and challenging part of the work was trying to pitch the sound design elements so that they were in key with the horn note (which runs throughout). The result is a stunning and cohesive mixture of sound and musical elements.

Music Arranger
Jakko
Music Composer
Steve Winwood
Director
Noam Murro
Copywriters
Feargal Ballance
Dylan Harrison
Art Directors
Feargal Ballance
Dylan Harrison

Creative Director
Sam Oliver
Producers
Richard Packer
Shishir Patel
Jay Veal
Production Company
Independent
Advertising Agency
DDB London
Agency Producer
Lucy Westmore

Animator
Dale Newton
Special Effects
Stephane Allender
Computer Graphics Lead
Diarmid Harrison-Murray
Editor
Tim Thornton-Allan
Lighting Cameraperson
Matthew Libitique

Account Handlers
Jonathan Hill
Matt Ross
Marketing Manager
Rod McLeod
Brand Manager
Sarah Luckcraft
Client
Volkswagen
Brand
Volkswagen Polo

Use of Music

DDB London
for Volkswagen

Dog
This is the story of a nervous dog who feels so confident when he rides in the VW Polo that he sings his heart out. It's the feeling you get when you're in the shower – you don't have a care in the world and, regardless of your ability, you can belt out any song that comes to mind. In the case of this nervous dog it's 'I'm a man' by The Spencer Davis Group. This is how it feels to drive around in the safety of the Polo.

493

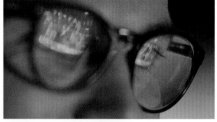

Music Composer
Gustavo Santaolalla
Director
Steve Reeves
Copywriter
Mike Boles
Art Director
Jerry Hollens

Creative Director
Mark Roalfe
Producer
Ella Littlewood
Production Company
Red Bee Media
Advertising Agency
RKCR/Y&R

Music Performers
Kronos Quartet
Sound Designer
Parv Thind
Editor
Scot Crane
Lighting Cameraperson
Alex Melman

Account Handler
Fiona Richards
Marketing Manager
Nicki Sheard
Client
BBC

Use of Music

RKCR/Y&R
for BBC

Places
We all remember where we were when a significant news event happened, and through the decades, the BBC has been the place to go to for important news. Next time a significant event happens, find out with BBC News on your mobile. By using naturalistic filming, we recreated defining news moments. We wanted to make viewers relive the experience, to make the hairs stand up on the back of their necks. This was achieved with the help of the music, a track called 'When our wings are cut, can we still fly?' by Kronos Quartet.

Director of Photography
Alwin Kuchler
Director
Peter Thwaites
Copywriter
Sophie Farquhar

Art Director
Catherine Lennon
Creative Director
Mal Stevenson
Producer
Anna Hashmi

Production Company
Gorgeous Enterprises
Advertising Agency
Irish International BBDO

Editor
Rick Russell
Client
Diageo
Brand
Guinness

Cinematography

Gorgeous Enterprises
for Diageo

Light Show
In the darkness of night, a group of artists converge inside a tower block. Using all the light sources within the building, they create a choreographed light show that from the exterior reveals the image of a surging and settling pint of Guinness within the frame of the building.

Lighting Cameraperson Joost van Gelder	**Creative Director** Paul Brazier	**Advertising Agency** Abbott Mead Vickers BBDO	**Music Composers & Arrangers** Nick Cave
Director Johnny Green	**Creative Group Head** Tim Riley	**Agency Producer** Yvonne Chalkley	Warren Ellist
Copywriter Tim Riley	**Producers** James Bland	**Special Effects** Glassworks	**Sound Designers** Johnnie Burn
Art Director Paul Brazier	Matthew Brown	**Editor** Ted Guard	Aaron Reynolds
	Production Company Knucklehead		**Client** Mercedes

Cinematography

Knucklehead
for Mercedes

Presence
Mercedes-Benz is a well-respected marque. But some people see it as a car for older drivers. The aim was to demonstrate that Mercedes isn't just about luxury, efficiency and comfort. These are dynamic, exciting cars too.

Lighting Cameraperson Crille Forsberg	**Producer** Ran Holst	**Visual Effects Supervisor** Bill McNamara	**Marketing Managers** Ligia Concalves
Director Fredrik Bond	**Production Company** Sonny London	**Music Composer** Steve Sidwell	Ricardo Marques
Copywriter Augusto Sola	**Advertising Agency** Mother London	**Post Production** ABInBev	Adam Oakley
Art Director Gustavo Sousa	**Agency Producer** Richard Firminger	**Producers** Julie Evans	**Client** ABInBev
Creative Directors Robert Saville	**Editor** Rich Orrick	Scott Griffin	**Brand** Stella Artois 4%
Augusto Sola	**Colourist** Jean-Clement Soret	**Planner** Laurence Horner	
Gustavo Sousa			
Mark Waites			

Cinematography

Sonny London
for ABInBev

Triple Filter Fall
The launch of Stella Artois 4% was an opportunity to address some of the negative user imagery surrounding the brand by creating a new definition of the Stella Artois drinker. It was therefore necessary to move away from the classic 'rural village' setting of past Stella campaigns and create a new brand world for this new drinker to occupy. The 60s French Riviera, with its smooth characters and escapades, was chosen as the perfect home for the smoothest four per cent lager. It cleverly retained the brand's association with European film while updating it for a modern audience. The first 60s Riviera spot, 'Triple Filter Fall', marked the start of the campaign.

495

Director of Photography
Daniel Landin
Director
Chris Palmer
Copywriter
Graham Daldry

Art Director
Steve Loftus
Producer
Rupert Smythe
Production Company
Gorgeous Enterprises

Advertising Agency
Specsavers Creative
TV Producer
Sam Lock
Editor
Paul Watts

Client
Specsavers Optical Group
Brand
Specsavers

Cinematography

Gorgeous Enterprises
for Specsavers Optical Group

Collie Wobble
Collie Wobble tells the tale of veteran sheep shearing champion Arthur Arthurson. We see him bringing his sheep from the hills for their spring shearing, just as he has done every year for the last 60 years. This year, however, will be a little less traditional. Arthur accidentally shears his faithful dog, Ben. Should've gone to...

Special Effects
Kirsty Cleminson
Ben Cronin
Simon French
Direction
Dom & Nic
Copywriters
Daniel Fisher
Peter Gosselin

Art Directors
Richard Brim
Jay Hunt
Executive Creative Director
Jonathan Burley
Producer
John Madsen
Production Company
Outsider

Advertising Agency
Leo Burnett London
Agency Producer
Graeme Light
Music Composers
Radiohead
Sound Designer
Ben Leeves

Account Handler
Gary Simmons
Acting Head of Brand & Marketing
Rachel Murphy
Client
Shelter

Special Effects

Outsider
for Shelter

House of Cards
This commercial was developed to raise awareness of the housing crisis currently gripping the UK, and explain Shelter's unique positioning as a support to the many thousands of households affected. The fragility of a house of cards is used in this work to explain the complexity of different housing issues. Such are the UK's housing problems that this creative idea can be used to explain the truth about repossessions or temporary and social housing, as well as Shelter's call for the basic human right to have a place to call home.

Special Effects
Justin Lane
VFX Supervisor
Cedric Nicolas-
Troyan
Lead Flame Artist
Cedric Nicolas-
Troyan
Director
Rupert Sanders

Copywriter
Steve McElligott
Art Director
Jerome Marucci
Creative Director
Eric Silver
Producers
Angela Bowen
Nancy Nina Hwang
Eric Stern

Production Company
MJZ
Advertising Agency
BBDO New York
Agency Producers
Anthony Curti
Ed Zazzera

Animators
Sarah Eim
Chris Staves
Editor
Bill Smedley
Sound Designer
Ren Klyce
Client
Monster.com

Special Effects
MJZ
for Monster.com

Legs
The project combined technical expertise and an eye for well integrated visual effects to create a quirky world with esoteric touches that define the spot. Testing and resolving the design process for the massive legs that dwarf the hero's body was critical, as the character is seen walking towards us, in profile and close up. Cedric Nicolas-Troyan (VFX supervisor and lead Flame artist) and Rupert Sanders tested different approaches and devised a technique using stilts and prosthetics for some scenes, combined with Flame ingenuity to create the look. The cavern sequence required a world representing Earth's centre with a large bicycle rig suspended above it. The actual gyroscopic rig was extended with computer graphics to create the desired epic scale, and put together in Flame for a seamless match.

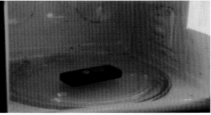

Special Effects
The Mill
Director
David Frankham
Copywriter
Kevin Brady
Art Director
Alex Lea

Executive Creative Director
Ted Royer
Creative Chairman
David Droga
Producer
Jeff Rohrer
Production Company
Smuggler

Advertising Agency
Droga5
Agency Producer
Dana May
Head of Integrated Production
Sally-Ann Dale

Editor
Geoff Hounsell
Sound Designer
Bill Chesley
Client
TracFone
Brand
NET10

Special Effects
The Mill
for TracFone

Microwave
People love to blow things up. A large portion of internet bandwidth is taken up by people who are blowing things up. Our video begins as a typical blow-up-your-cell-phone-in-the-microwave video. But after a few sparks and bubbles, a hideous monster appears out of the cell phone. The true evil lurking in every cell phone has finally been revealed in all its horror. Millions of people watched this public exorcism and were sent to the NET10 website to learn more about the one cell phone company with no bills, no contracts and no evil.

Visual Effects
Animal Logic
Australia
**Visual Effects
Producer**
Nerissa Kavanagh
Visual Effects Editor
Bruce Carter
Director
Noam Murro
Copywriter
Mike McKay
Art Director
Nick Spahr

Creative Director
Jamie Barrett
**Group Creative
Directors**
Chris Ford
Mike McKay
**Associate Creative
Director**
Nick Spahr
Producer
Jay Veal
**Senior Executive
Producer**
Shawn Lacy

Production Company
Biscuit Filmworks
Advertising Agency
Goodby Silverstein
and Partners
Agency Producer
Tanya LeSieur
Editor
Avi Oron
**Director of
Photography**
Jo Willems
Sound Designer
Brian Emrich

Telecine
Dave Hussey
Final Mixer
Eben Carr
Voice Over Mix
Rohan Young
Sound Design
Trinitite
Graphics
Superfad
On-Line Company
Brickyard VFX
Client
Comcast

Special Effects
Animal Logic Australia
for Comcast

Rabbit
To make the point that Comcast never stops making the internet faster, 'Rabbit' opens on a rabbit. A rabbit that is then genetically modified and bred with a panther. A rabbit, that once genetically modified and bred with a panther, has turbines attached, is backed by an unusually strong tailwind and placed on ice. Continuing on, the rabbit panther thingy with turbines and tailwind on ice is then shaved with a cold-forged, high-glide surgical-grade razor, and driven by an over-caffeinated fighter pilot with a lead foot. The spot concludes with the whole rabbit panther turbine tailwind hairless razor pilot scenario travelling down a ski jump in Switzerland under better-than-ideal conditions.

Special Effects
Chris Batten
Lead Flame Operator
Richard DeCarteret
Director
Mitch Stratten

Creative Director
Andy Amadeo
Producer
Sally Newson
Production Company
Hungry Man
Advertising Agency
Grey London

Agency Producer
Rebecca Pople
**Post Production
Company**
The Mill
Editor
Christophe Williams

Telecine
James Bamford
Mick Vincent
Client
Toshiba

Special Effects
The Mill
for Toshiba

Time Sculpture
Using a groundbreaking filming technique, Toshiba's Time Sculpture is the world's first 360 degree, moving image 'bullet time' commercial. The Mill team supervised a shoot that relied on a purpose-built rig supporting 200 Toshiba Gigashot HD camcorders. These were aligned and linked to create a 360 degree inward view of the circular set, allowing for the capture of a series of separate moving images. The images were later brought together to form one seamless action sequence using the highest number of moving image cameras ever in a film sequence, earning the team a Guinness World Record.

Animation

Animatório
for Amnesty International

All Against Each Other
The objective was clear and simple – tell everyone that Amnesty International is an organisation that fights for human rights. Everyone's human rights. Not just a few. Everyone's. It doesn't matter on which side of a fight they are. What really matters is making sure that human rights are respected. We've created an animation where we can see all the battles that have taken place on the planet. Together, the images show in detail every region in the world and its conflicts, present and past.

Animation	**Art Director**	**Executive Producer**	**Agency Producer**
Animatório	Mico Toledo	Alberto Lopes	Christina Almeida
Director	**Creative Director**	**Production**	**Sound Designer**
Mateus de Paula	Chacho Puebla	**Companies**	Paulo Beto
Santos	**Creative Advisor**	Animatório	**Client**
Copywriters	Tura	Lobo	Amnesty
Chacho Puebla	**Producer**	**Advertising Agency**	International
Bruno Ribeiro	Loic Lima Dubois	Leo Burnett Lisbon	

Animation

Wanda
for Nestlé France

KitKat Ultimate Break
KitKat launched its first new recipe in 35 years. Video teasers, a website, games and events were used to gradually build up a story over several months. The idea was to create an interactive link with the consumer, based on the idea of the ultimate break – the most extraordinary break that we can imagine. A website allowed people to share their vision of the ultimate break by uploading videos and story lines. And as part of the campaign, KitKat ran a competition to win a trip into space.

Direction	**Production Company**	**Music Composer**	**Client**
Akama Studio	Wanda	Xavier Berthelot	Nestlé France
Copywriter	**Advertising Agency**	**Account Handler**	**Brand**
Hadi Hassan	JWT Paris	Stéphane Billard	KitKat
Art Director	**Agency Producer**	**Marketing Manager**	
Xavier Beauregard	Elisabeth Boitte	Murielle Koch	
Creative Directors		**Brand Manager**	
Olivier		Frédérique Delahaye	
Courtemanche			
Ghislain de			
Villoutreys			

Animation	**Creative Directors**	**Production Company**	**Music Arrangers**
Shy the Sun	Bob Barrie	DUCK Studios	Elizabeth Myers &
Direction	Stuart D'Rozario	**Advertising Agency**	John Trivers
Shy the Sun	**Producer**	Barrie D'Rozario	**Sound Designer**
Copywriter	Nina Pfeiffer	Murphy	Ken Chastain
Phil Calvit	**Executive Producer**	**Agency Producers**	**Client**
Art Director	Mark Medernach	Jack Steinmann	United Airlines
James Zucco		Holly Stone	

Animation

Shy the Sun
for United Airlines

Sea Orchestra

A United Airlines plane crossing the ocean is serenaded by an orchestra of fantastical animated sea creatures delivering their own version of United's anthem, 'Rhapsody in Blue'. This sea orchestra introduces United's sumptuous new international first and business classes. The animated characters were a combination of hand-drawn textures and computer animation, married together with photographic elements of water, reefs and skies. The quirky score was performed using instruments ranging from tubas and violins to French horns and an Indonesian gamelan.

The jury:

Mauricio Mazzariol, Wieden + Kennedy
   Portland (Jury Foreman)
Mark Ashley-Wilson, Three Drunk Monkeys
Andrew Brown, Swamp
Gemma Butler, Agency Republic
Chris Clarke, LBi
Tom Evans, Mook
Eduardo de Felipe, Pirata
Ricardo Figueira, Isobar Latin America
Jeremy Garner, Weapon7
Rachel Hunt, Hi-ReS!
Kris Kiger, R/GA
Sean Lam, Kinetic Singapore
Jason McCann, TAXI Canada
Ben Mooge, Work Club
Thiago de Moraes, CHI & Partners
Enric Nel-lo, Shackleton
PJ Pereira, Pereira&O'Dell
Blanca Piera, Doubleyou
Edu Pou, Wieden + Kennedy Amsterdam
Alistair Robertson, Abbot Mead Vickers BBDO
Yasuharu Sasaki, Dentsu Tokyo
Duncan Swain, BBC Worldwide
Jakob Swedenborg, Farfar

Creative Directors
Rick Condos
Hunter Hindman
Associate Creative Directors
Hartley Rusen
Marc Sobier
Art Director
Henrik Rosander
Copywriter
Michelle Hirschberg

Creative Co-Ordinator
Karen Land
Chief Digital Officer
Mike Geiger
Advertising Agency
Goodby Silverstein and Partners
Interactive Producer
Maggie O'Brien
Executive Producer
Amanda Cox

Production Company
B-Reel
Communication Strategist
Stephanie Charlebois
Communication Strategy Director
Sidney Bosley
Account Director
Liz Kaiser

Account Manager
Mary Ashley Chenoweth
Assistant Account Manager
Amy Taylor
Brand Strategy Director
Ted Florea
Client
Doritos

Microsites

Goodby Silverstein and Partners
for Doritos

Hotel 626
In honour of Doritos bringing back two intense flavours from the dead, we created an intensely scary website. You're trapped in a haunted hotel and have to complete challenges – like singing a demon baby to sleep – to get out. Hotel 626 uses several groundbreaking techniques to dial up the experience. Your webcam sneaks a picture of you and shows it to you later, inside the lair of a madman. Your one salvation is a phone call on your actual mobile phone with directions on how to get out. To make it scarier, you have to play in the dark: Hotel 626 is only open from 6pm to 6am.

 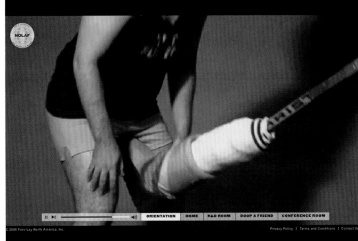

Creative Directors	Dave Cole	Sound Designer	Editors	Production
Jim Paul	**Art Directors**	Jeremiah Moore	Mike Cavanaugh	**Companies**
Peter Rhoads	David Daugherty	**Sound Mixer**	TM Faversham	Element 79
Max Stinson	Mike Lyons	Jeremiah Moore	Caitlin Parker	Mekanism
Interactive Designer	Max Stinson	**Producer**	**Colour Correction**	**Client**
Marcelo Viana	**Copywriters**	Lindsay Fa	SpyPost	Frito-Lay
Interactive Producer	Kevin Mulroy	**Executive Producers**	**Stylist**	**Brand**
Jeremy Leeds	Jim Paul	Velvy Appleton	Chris Aysta	Tostitos
Designers	**Executive Creative**	Jason Harris	**Advertising Agency**	
Emmett Feldman	**Director**	**Director**	Element 79	
Richard Krolewicz	Dennis Ryan	Tommy Means	**Agency Producer**	
Technology	**Interactive Group**	**Director of**	Katie Juras	
Developers	**Creative Director**	**Photography**	**Head of Production**	
Jamal Berkely	Todd Crisman	Andy Lilien	John Noble	

Microsites

Element 79 & Mekanism
for Frito-Lay

NOLAF
This full-screen video site showcases the fictional organisation NOLAF (National Organisation for Legislation Against Fun) and their on-going crusade against all things fun, especially Tostitos. The shorts include Q&A sessions with seven hopeful NOLAF recruits, meetings, and demonstrations that reveal how and why we should fight fun. Mekanism developed the concept, site and content syndication strategy. The Mekanism syndication programme worked well, with over three million views on YouTube alone. Element 79 tapped Mekanism for the NOLAF collaboration.

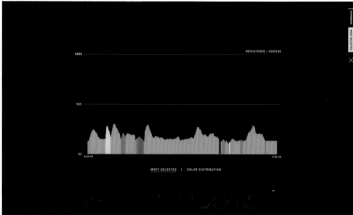

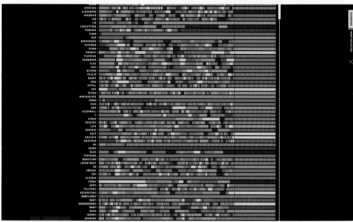

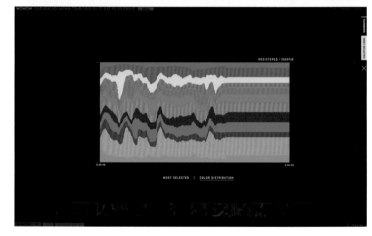

Creative Director	Art Director	Content Strategist	Brand
Kampei Baba	Tomomi Motose	Nobuo Hara	Radiohead Japan
Technical Director	**Digital Agency**	**Client Producer**	Tour
Kampei Baba	Bascule	Yusuke Maeda	
Designer	**Agency Producer**	**Client**	
Tomomi Motose	Masayoshi Boku	WOWOW INC.	

Interface & Navigation

Bascule
for WOWOW INC.

12 Cams, Create Your Rainbow
This is the promotional website for the TV programme 'Radiohead Japan Tour' by the Japanese pay television channel WOWOW INC. We produced publicity for the programme and branding for WOWOW INC. By combining the TV programme and the website we created a way for users to interact extensively with both media. Every user's action is recorded as a piece of a rainbow and accumulates into this bigger rainbow to respond to the message from the artist. At the end, we aimed for the rainbow containing everyone's feelings to become a single piece of art.

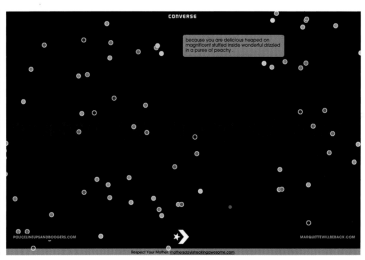

Executive Creative
Director
Mike Byrne
Art Directors
Ross Aboud
Ian Ghent
Advertising Agency
Anomaly

Copywriters
Sean McLaughlin
Beau Unruh
Executive Producer
Andrew Loevenguth
Creative Strategist
Stan Chin

**Communication
Strategist**
Adam Leibsohn
Media Strategist
Chet Gulland
Media Director
Justin Barocas

Account Director
Stanley Lumax
Account Supervisor
Derek Lo
Client
Converse

Websites
Anomaly
for Converse

Domaination
Somewhere out there is a kid that brushes off viral videos and megasites. We had to find him. We had to live in the moment like he does. Believe in taking down the system like he does. And there's no bigger system than Google. So we disrupted Google. We discovered what kids are searching for through meticulous creative research. Using these insights, we invented a new method of purchasing adwords for searches nobody else was buying. For each search we delivered an optimistic message in a tailor-made dot com. We created a network of 100 dot coms, each with wildly creative content that encourages that kid to stick to his convictions.

505

Creative Director	Website Director	Film Directors	Hair & Make-Up
Koichiro Tanaka	Hiroshi Koike	Shizuka Kurokawa	Shinji Konishi
Technical Director	**Website Producer**	Takeshi Nakamura	**Shoot Co-Ordinator**
Qanta Shimizu	Tatsuaki Ashikaga	**Film Production**	Maki Osada
Interactive Designer	**Producers**	**Manager**	**Client Supervisor**
Satoshi Horii	Hiroko Asano	Yuko Ishii	Kentaro Katsube
Designer	Takeshi Fukuda	**Cinematographers**	**Client**
Kohei Kawasaki	**Website Production**	Shigeki Akiyama	UNIQLO
Art Director	**Manager**	Yoshikatsu Yasaki	
Kohei Kawasaki	Izumi Horio	**Stylist**	
Creative Boutique	**Project Manager**	Tetsuro Nagase	
Projector	Yuuri Ogawa		

Websites

Projector
for UNIQLO

UNIQLO Meets Corteo

Cirque du Soleil is a touring circus group that has dazzled over 80 million spectators in 200 cities on five continents. They have come together with uniqlo to collaborate in a new way. Through this joint effort, UNIQLO aims to expand its brand awareness globally. We documented performers, who sported Uniqlo fashion, during training sessions of 'Corteo', Cirque du Soleil's touring production in Miami and Ottawa. These offstage shots lead to a sensational event in Tokyo. UNIQLO, 'Corteo', and invited users were united in a physical and spiritual sense. The campaign culminated in the upload of event shots onto the site, allowing users to share the experience.

Microsites

Colenso BBDO
for New Zealand Book Council

Read a Book at Work

The New Zealand Book Council challenged us to find a fun new way to make books more accessible, and to encourage people to fall in love with reading again. These days, people spend far too much time working in front of their computers and not enough time reading books, so we figured that people would rather read books than do work. We disguised books as everyday office computer documents and released them online. You can now read Oscar Wilde through to DBC Pierre, anywhere, anytime, without anyone ever knowing. Even at work, where your boss and co-workers will be none the wiser. And all these books are housed in our online library, which is designed to look like a Windows desktop.

Creative Directors
Richard Maddocks
Nick Worthington
Interactive Designers
Simon Koay
Phil Newman
Developer
Tim Smith

Designers
Ainsley Waite
Raffaella Wilson
Art Directors
Lisa Fedyszyn
Jonathan McMahon
Copywriters
Lisa Fedyszyn
Jonathan McMahon

Interactive Producer
Hamish Wanhill
Advertising Agency
Colenso BBDO
Agency Producer
Paul Courtney
Account Director
Joanna Wealleans

Group Account Director
Michael Redwood
Client
New Zealand Book Council

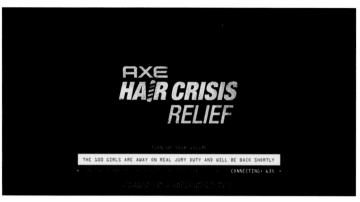

Creative Directors
Calle Sjoenell
Pelle Sjoenell
Art Director
Erik Holmdahl
Copywriter
Beth Ryan

Advertising Agency
BBH New York
Agency Producer
Chad Utsch
Digital Agency Producer
Fabien Pichler

Chief Creative Officer
Kevin Roddy
Production Company
B-Reel
Agency Account Director
Chris Wollen

Client
Unilever
Brand
AXE

Microsites

BBH New York
for Unilever

100 Girls
To launch Axe's range of men's hair products, we had to let guys know how much bad hair hurts their game. So we put 100 girls in a room to judge guys' hair. And waited. When guys uploaded a photo to our site, it was immediately sent live to moderators working in 24/7 shifts, who responded not only to a guy's hair, but to other characteristics like his expression, facial hair and accessories. The guy's photo was then sent back in a personalised, online evaluation from the 100 girls, with a product recommendation to help them get girl approved hair.

Creative Director
Björn Höglund
Technical Director
Per Rundgren
Flash Programmers
Malin Ekman
Erik Sterner

Designer
Anders Johansson
Developer
Stefan Hållen
Art Director
Jonas Hedeback
Copywriter
Anders Gustafsson

Advertising Agency
Daddy
Agency Producers
Oscar Corsvall
Robert Waern
**Production
Company**
Bombay Works

Account Handler
Martin Gustafsson
Brand Manager
Katarina Möller
Client
Heinz

Microsites

Daddy
for Heinz

Talk to the Plant
To prove Heinz's new tagline 'No one grows ketchup like Heinz' and not just say it, we created this interactive ketchup growing experiment. At talktotheplant.com, visitors could talk to a tomato plant in real-time via voice synthesis to find out if it resulted in better growth. Anything told to the plant was broadcast live on the site. A behind-the-scenes blog kept track of technical stuff, problems, the messages and how they affected the plant growth.

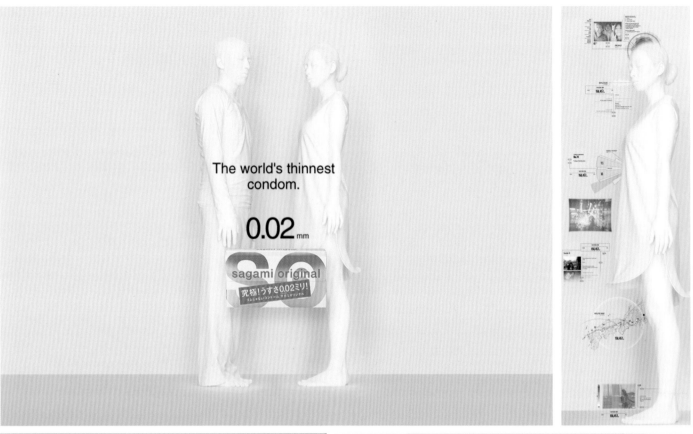

Creative Director Naoki Ito	Kenichi Takahashi **Art Director**	Masanori Mori Seiichi Saito	Rock & Roll Japan **Video Engineers**	Atsuki Yukawa **PR Executive**	

Creative Director
Naoki Ito
Technical Director
Qanta Shimizu
Designers
Atsushi Fujimaki
Saiko Kamikanda
Takeshi Yoshimori
Shigeki Yuriko
Yamane
Flash Programmers
Hiroki Hara
Hiroaki Kitamura
Yukihiro Sasae

Kenichi Takahashi
Art Director
Naoki Ito
Copywriter
Naoki Ito
Sound Designer
Takahisa Mitsumori
System Engineers
Jun Kuriyama
Takuho Yoshizu
Device Producers
Katsuhiko Harada
Hiroyuki Hori
Noriko Matsmoto

Masanori Mori
Seiichi Saito
Photographer
Kenshu Shintsubo
Production Manager
Tetsuji Isayama
Director
Kan Eguchi
Lighting Director
Kimitaka Kajihara
Cameraman
Takahiro Konomi
Advertising Agencies
GT Tokyo

Rock & Roll Japan
Video Engineers
Hiroyuki Watanabe
Eitaro Yamamoto
Music Composer
Ryuichi Sakamoto
Retoucher
Teruyo Murayama
Mixer
Kazune Masutomi
Editor
Keisuke Ohta
Producers
Masaki Endo

Atsuki Yukawa
PR Executive
Koji Torigata
Planners
Masaki Endo
Naoki Ito
Takayuki Rokutan
Qanta Shimizu
Atsuki Yukawa
Client
Sagami Rubber
Industries
Brand
Sagami Original 0.02

Microsites

GT Tokyo & Rock & Roll Japan
for Sagami Rubber Industries

Love Distance
We used a genuine long distance couple for this campaign. They ran a 1,000km marathon, and images of the two were broadcasted live on the internet for a whole month. The couple were allowed to keep in contact only through blog, TV phone and SMS messages. Thus all correspondence between the couple was displayed to the public on the internet. This also provided users with a simulation of a long distance relationship. The men's site and the women's site were created separately; on the day of completion, the two sites come together as one. And that was when the name of the client and the product was revealed.

Copywriters	**Design Director**	**Design Group**	**Director**
Ben Mooge	Tom Hartshorn	Fat-Man Collective	Theo Delaney
Nick Strada	**Art Directors**	**Advertising Agency**	**Marketing Manager**
Nico Tatarowicz	Rodrigo Lebrun	Work Club	Richard Ferguson
Creative Directors	Greg Mitchell	**Agency Producers**	**Client**
Ben Mooge	**Sound Designer**	Frida Detter	Nokia
Andy Sandoz	Anthony Moore	Jo Dillon	**Brand**
			Nokia N-Gage

Writing

Work Club
for Nokia

N-Gage/Fifa 08

Nokia's gaming service N-Gage gave away 120,000 free copies of Fifa 08 for compatible phones. It's a very playable version of Fifa, and perfect for N-Gage users, 20 to 40-year-old men (boys) in quick dead-time situations. Football games are football games: you're happy when you score, swear when you miss, develop ticks and screams, and sometimes don't move for hours at a time. Take this usually private gaming behaviour out of the living room, and combine it with public transport that's suitable for N-Gage, hidden cameras and a gamer stooge. All the films are collected on a CCTV style site.

511

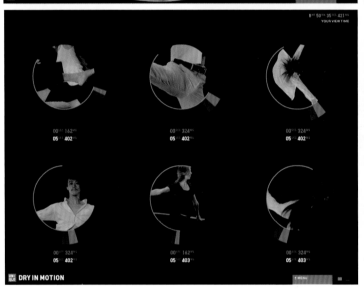

Music Composer	Art Directors	Director of	Project Manager
Steve Reich	Jeong-ho Im	**Photography**	Shinichi Saeki
Creative Director	Koichiro Tanaka	Shoji Uchida	**Client Supervisor**
Koichiro Tanaka	**Creative Boutique**	**Stylist**	Kentaro Katsube
Interactive Designer	Projector	Shinichi Mita	**Client**
Takeshiro Umetsu	**Producer**	**Choreography**	UNIQLO
Designer	Takeshi Fukuda	air:man	
Jeong-ho Im	**Director**	**Hair & Make-Up**	
	Daisuke Shimada	Shinji Konishi	

Sound Design & Use of Music

Projector
for UNIQLO

Dry in Motion
We wanted a fresh way to present Uniqlo's quick-drying clothing line. The site we developed featured human bodies arranged in a circle, moving endlessly and at varying speeds, to the beat of a single drum. The tempo of the drum gradually picks up speed, becoming increasingly vigorous and intense, creating a hypnotic effect. As viewers were drawn further into this pulsating world of energy and dance, they began to gain a physical understanding of UNIQLO's 'Dry' concept. This website was also selected in the Microsites category.

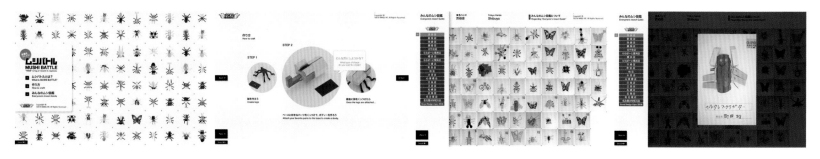

Creative Director
Isamu Nakamura
Executive Creative Director
Masao Miyashita
Designers
Takatoshi Kaneko
Mio Kawashima
Tetsuro Kubota
Keisuke Miyajima
Web Designer
Yuki Sakurai

Art Director
Mikito Nunome
Copywriter
Isamu Nakamura
Web Director
Daisuke Sugita
Web Producers
Takamasa Hirai
Toru Usami
Photographer
Takuya Uroku

Web Photographer
Daisuke Sugita
Web & TV Movie Director
Yoji Akiba
Advertising Agency
McCann Erickson Japan
Graphic Producer
Koichiro Takahashi
TV Producer
Tetsuya Kinouchi

Product Design Company
ZariganiWorks
Account Supervisor
Miho Fukushima
Marketing Manager
Nagumu Terui
Client
Tokyu Hands

McCann Erickson Japan
for Tokyu Hands

Mushi Battle Project
Our aim was to draw more people to Tokyu Hands (a department store which stocks a wide variety of raw materials) during a long holiday weekend when store traffic normally decreases. We created a game called 'Mushi Battle' using the resources available in Tokyu Hands. The motto of Tokyu Hands is to encourage 'handcraft', and collecting insects is a popular hobby for kids in Japan, so we handcrafted mushi (bugs). An official website was launched. During the holiday, more than 3,000 kids and parents visited Tokyu Hands to create their own battling insects, and over 3,000 types of mushi were collected and shown on the mushi encyclopedia on the website.

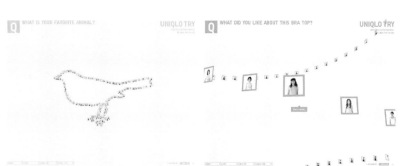

Creative Director
Hiroki Nakamura
Technical Directors
Takeshi Kanamaru
Hiroshi Koike
Interactive Designer
Hiroyuki Misono
Flash Programmer
Hiroyuki Misono

Art Directors
Shin Masuda
Hiroyuki Misono
Yuta Sejima
Sound Design
Cornelius
Digital Agency
Dentsu Tokyo

Agency Producers
Osamu Kimura
Shinsaku Ogawa
Account Handler
Akiko Yamada
Marketing Manager
Shuhei Eguchi

Brand Manager
Kentaro Katsube
Client
UNIQLO
Brand
UNIQLO Bra Top

Dentsu Tokyo
for UNIQLO

UNIQLO Try
This execution is part of a campaign to launch UNIQLO's new product, 'Bra Top', standing for bra and tank top. Women in their 20s to 40s were recruited via mail magazines. Respondents were asked to not only fill out the questionnaire, but also share their own videos. The results are shown online with the respondents' real voices and videos, statistical information and music. With the filtering function, users can select opinions from women who are the closest to them in terms of height, age, size and body type.

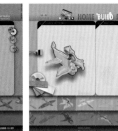

Creative Directors
Lars Eberle
Carsten Schneider
Technical Director
Thomas Meyer
Interactive Designer
Patrick Juchli

Flash Programmers
Max Kugland
Will Kuo
Luis Martinez
Birk Weiberg
Designer
Carsten Schneider

Developer
Oliver List
Sound Designer
Taeji Sawai
Illustrator
Hawken King

Video Animator
Juan Romero
Design Agency
Less Rain
Client
Red Bull

Microsites

Less Rain
for Red Bull

Red Bull Flugtag Flight Lab
Bring on the wood and sheet metal! Break out your saw! Cut the pieces to size, assemble them, paint them and... voila! You've built your own aeroplane. Now it's time to get it off the ground. Will it fly?

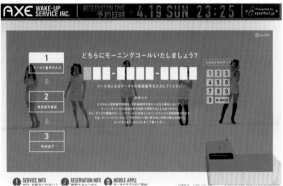

Creative Directors
Masayoshi Boku
Nobuo Hara
Technical Director
Ken-ichiro Tanaka
Programmers
Ikuo Kawai
Tomoko Wada
Designers
Hironobu Ryo
Shoji Takaoka
Yuko Tomioka

Art Director
Megumu Kasuga
Copywriter
Soichiro Yamamoto
Advertising Agency
Bascule
Agency Producer
Ken-ichiro Tanaka
Production Managers
Akira Imafuku
Hirokazu Sawai

Director
Nobuo Hara
Film Production Companies
flapper3
MONSTER ULTRA
Sound Production Company
sin.inc.
Concept Planner
Masayoshi Boku

Concept Planning
BBH Tokyo
Server Side Development
mitsubachiworks
Client
Unilever Japan
Brand
AXE

Microsites

Bascule
for Unilever Japan

AXE Wake-Up Service
Waking up is the tipping point of the day, when guys decide whether to use AXE or not. We wanted to ensure brand experience at that important time, and promote the use of AXE every morning. By making a reservation on the website, the user can get a wake-up call from a charming girl at an appointed time. The system therefore involves the use of a PC and a mobile phone. When making the reservation, the user is made to feel as though he is talking to the girl on a TV-phone. This original brand experience created an online buzz.

Websites

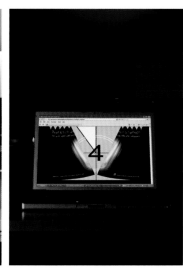

Shalmor Avnon Amichay/Y&R
Interactive Tel Aviv
for Orange

When the Lights Are Off the Site Is On
Orange wanted to promote 'Orange Time', a new online entertainment and movies portal pay service. Our challenge was to prove to surfers that watching a movie on the internet is just as good as watching one at the cinema. Using the insight that when the lights go out in the cinema it's the signal that puts us in the mood, we created a site that opens only if you physically switch off the room lights. When surfers switched off their lights, the site opened up and a trailer of one of the movies offered by the portal was revealed. To see another trailer, users had to switch the lights on and off again.

Creative Directors	**Art Director**	**Account Handlers**	**Client**
Gideon Amichay	Lena Feldman	Amichay Kattan	Orange
Eran Gefen	**Flash Programmer**	Rona Rozental	**Brand**
Interactive Designer	Dimitry Patt	**Marketing Manager**	Orange Time
Dimitry Patt	**Digital Agency**	Iris Ifrach	
Copywriters	Shalmor Avnon	**Brand Manager**	
Roy Cohen	Amichay/Y&R	Tali Cohen	
Rani Sebag	Interactive Tel Aviv		

The Barbarian Group
for Getty Images

Moodstream
Moodstream was built to showcase Getty Images' three main product offerings: still images, footage and music. Getty Images specifically wanted to raise awareness of the latter two, for which it was not as well known. The target audience were creatives involved in rich media communications in a maturing digital landscape. To reach this audience, whose passion and livelihood is creativity on the web, Moodstream was developed as equal parts art piece, usable tool and exploratory toy. The site is a brainstorming tool enabling users to input moods related to a project and see a stream of relevant media to help develop their ideas. It also allowed them to share the work with colleagues and the wider creative community.

In-House Creative	Freya Barea	Miles Hunter	**Digital Agency**
Consultants	Jim Craig	Eric McConnaughay	The Barbarian Group
Rebekah Audic	James Halada	Richard Soar	**Client**
			Getty Images

515

Music Composition	Photographer	Production	Advertising	Client
Dead Mono	Gösta Reiland	**Companies**	**Supervisors**	IKEA
Director	**Advertising Agency**	Chamdin/Stohr	Christine Eliasson	
Amir Chamdin	Forsman &	Kokokaka	Nizze Larsson	
	Bodenfors		Beatrice Siöstrom	

Sound Design & Use of Music

Forsman & Bodenfors
for IKEA

Come in to the Closet. Let's Dance
This is a campaign to promote IKEA's wardrobe solutions. IKEA wanted to display its huge range of styles and all the smart features on the inside. All the movements on the website are controlled by sound and music, so change songs, upload your own music, play on your keyboard or sing into the microphone.

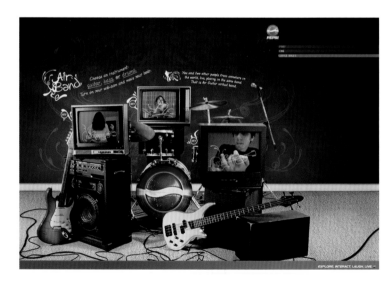

Soundtrack Designer	Executive Creative	Art Directors	Advertising
Marcelo Mandaji	**Director**	Thiago Balzano	**Supervisor**
Soundtrack Design	Marcello Serpa	Guilherme Giacomo	Guillermo Roman
Cromo.sônica	**Programming**	**Copywriter**	**Client**
Creative Director	Sapien	Luciana Haguiara	Pepsi
Sergio Mugnaini		**Advertising Agency**	
		AlmapBBDO	

Sound Design & Use of Music

AlmapBBDO
for Pepsi

Airband
Pepsi needed to offer fun and entertainment to the public. On this microsite, the user can put a virtual band together. He or she will play along with two other people from anywhere in the world. How it works: the user chooses an instrument, then turns on the webcam and plays live, alongside those who are using the tool at that same time. The faster they move, the better the music is.

Websites

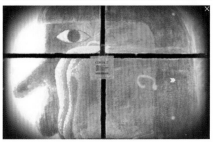 

Animator
Kazuki Nakata
Creative Director
Jumpei Miyao

Flash Programmer
Kazuki Nakata
Designer
Atsushi Hashimoto

Art Director
Atsushi Hashimoto
Design Agency
YAMA

Sound Designer
Shojiro Nakaoka
Client
Coltex

Animation

YAMA
for Coltex

Coltex
This is the corporate site of Coltex, an ad production company in Japan. The site plays out weird, enigmatic animation along with corporate information. The unusual characters appearing on the site include 'the man who's constantly setting up dominoes' and 'the mysterious man who appears in the window'. To maximise the expressive appeal of the site, the animation is made to look as if it were shot in analogue film. Featuring original background music and an imaginative world view, the site is designed to mesmerise our audience.

Animator
Kristofer Strom
Creative Director
Warren Moore
Digital Creative Director
Thiago de Moraes
Interactive Director
Alex Jenkins

Art Directors
Alexei Bertwitz
Rick Standley
Copywriters
Tom Skinner
Angus Wardlaw
Illustrator
Kristofer Strom

Advertising Agency
CHI & Partners
Agency Producers
Sian Parker
Jim Phizacklea
Account Handlers
Simone Dahl
Anna Fettes
Nick Howarth
Camilla Knight

Client
The Carphone
Warehouse
Brand
X Factor Challenge

Animation

CHI & Partners
for The Carphone Warehouse

The X Factor Challenge 2008
We created 'The X Factor Challenge' for the Carphone Warehouse's sponsorship of Europe's biggest singing contest. For the campaign, we asked viewers to sing and draw themselves online for a chance to star on TV during the show's ad breaks. By going online, choosing a song and singing on their mobile or computer, people could draw a character which was then animated to their voice. These animations were judged by the public, and the best, or worst, would make it onto TV each week. The campaign generated over 9,000 performances – judged over 150,000 times – and 30 TV ads.

517

Websites

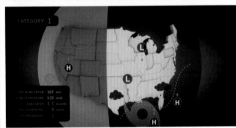

Animators
Andy Kim
Ian Mankowski
Dylan Spears
Glen Suhy
Creative Directors
Christian Haas
Justin Leibow
Rich Silverstein
Paul Stechschulte
Franklin Tipton

Designer
Kevin Lau
Compositor
Claudia Yi Leon
Art Directors
Rudi Anggono
Shane Fleming
Will Johnson
Senior Art Director
Kevin Lau

Copywriters
Larry Corwin
Will Elliot
Sound Designer
Dan Pritikin
Design Group
Superfad
Advertising Agency
Goodby Silverstein
and Partners

Producer
Danielle Hazan
Agency Producer
Rob Sondik
Executive Producers
Kevin Batten
Josh Reynolds
Client
Sprint Nextel
Brand
Sprint

Animation
Goodby Silverstein and Partners
for Sprint Nextel

Sprint Katrina
These spots were created for the Sprint Nextel site. Online campaigns don't fit into the 15/30/60 second time slots, which allows for breathing space in the story telling. We were excited by the opportunity to explore a greater depth of narrative, visual tone, mood and expression. Our challenge was to bring hard-core information graphics about a highly technical service into an entertainment context: to be fun yet tech. We spent a lot of time setting the mood of the spots and finding a personal narrative; one that would walk the line between the serious nature of the topic at hand (the Hurricane Katrina disaster relief) and the humorous mainstream appeal needed to engage.

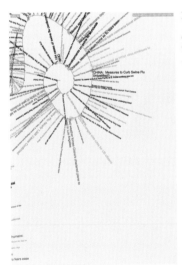
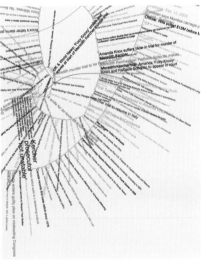
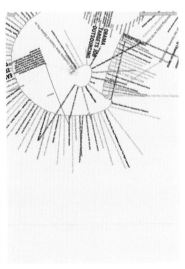

Designer
Brendan Dawes

Programmer
Brendan Dawes

Creative Director
Brendan Dawes

Interface & Navigation
Brendan Dawes

DoodleBuzz
The web is full of top-down scrolling websites that are great for viewing information linearly, but not so good at fun things like chance and exploration. DoodleBuzz was born out of an idea to create a new way of exploring information, allowing for 'quiet chaos' that gives everyone the opportunity to explore unthought-of paths along their news gathering journey. The interface for DoodleBuzz is simply a scribbled line. Draw a straight line. Draw a curved line. Draw a crazy, chaotic, all-over-the-place messed up line. It's up to you how you want to lay out the information. You may start at Iraq but end up finishing on Britney, while taking in the Catholic Church, global warming and 50 Cent.

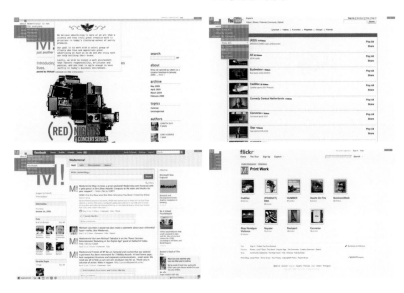

Programmers
Tim Blount
Michael Jordan
Art Director
Tim Blount

Executive Creative Directors
Lance Jensen
Gary Koepke

Advertising Agency
Modernista!
Agency Producer
Paul Lenzi

Account Manager
Eric Freedman
Client
Modernista!

Interface & Navigation
Modernista!

Modernista.com
These days, brands are experiencing less control over how they are defined as power shifts to consumers and community. Additionally, a brand's website is only one of the endless places the brand can exist on the web. Many brands are leveraging the best social networks to build communities. The relaunch of modernista.com addressed these challenges by opening the brand up and allowing people to have a say in defining who Modernista! is. Our website is simple navigation menu lying on top of and highlighting our participation within the living, breathing, and collaborative, social web.

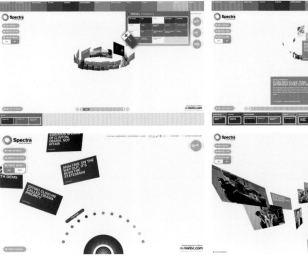
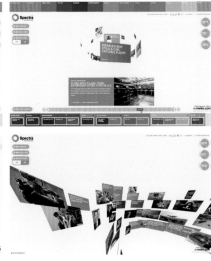

Interactive Designer
Remon Tijssen
Programmer
Marco Christis
Creative Directors
Matt Ferrin
Sam Mazur

Design Director
Remon Tijssen
Art Directors
Matt Ferrin
Sam Mazur
Copywriters
Matt Ferrin
Sam Mazur

Digital Agency
Fluid
Chief Creative Officer
Marty Cooke
Advertising Agency
SS+K

Account Executive
Katie O'Kane
Marketing Manager
Catherine Captain
Client
msnbc.com

Interface & Navigation
SS+K
for msnbc.com

Spectra Visual Newsreader
Typical visitors to msnbc.com don't get a quick fix and leave. They hang around the site and explore its diverse news content. As part of the 'A Fuller Spectrum of News' branding campaign, Spectra Visual Newsreader was created to amplify the msnbc.com experience with colour, customisation and experimental navigation. Site elements include news menu (over 100 channels), autoplay, newscollector, image toggle, orbital settings, word filter, audio sensor and colour sensor. Spectra Visual Newsreader is on spectramsnbc.com. For a fuller spectrum of news, go to ssk.com/spectrum.

519

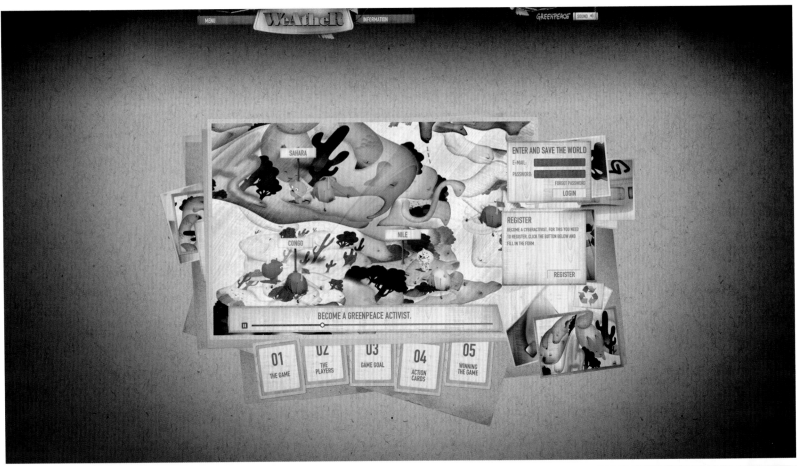

Illustrator	Motion Graphic	Art Directors	User Experience	Marketing Managers
Fabio Cardoso	**Designers**	Fábio Cardoso	**Analysts**	Gladis Éboli
Creative Director	Rafael Araújo	Rafael Kfouri	Dante Calligaris	Joanna Guinle
Sergio Mugnaini	Robson Victor	Caio Sartori	Vinicius Vidal	Clélia Maury
Technical Director	**Game Concept**	Gustavo Sonoda	**Project Managers**	Mariana Schwarz
Fabrizio Barata	**Developers**	**Copywriter**	Vânia São José	Daniela Soares
Flash Interface	Maurício Gibrin	Luciana Haguiara	Juliano Tosetto	**Client**
Developers	Fabiano Onça	**Advertising Agency**	**Account Managers**	Greenpeace
Edgar Akiyama	**3D Artist**	AlmapBBDO	Patricia Gerard	
Flavio Ensiki	Gabba	**Executive Producers**	Muriel Meira	
Developers	**Sound Production**	Eduardo Camargo	Alessandra	
Arhur Lima	Cromo.sônica	Kazi	Sevzatian	
Cauê Passero	**Production Company**	Andre Passamani		
Eduardo Silva	Colméia			

Illustration

AlmapBBDO
for Greenpeace

Weather

Despite being a concern all over the world, global warming is still treated like a distant problem in Brazil, the world's fourth largest emitter of polluting gases. This situation is the result of deforestation, slashing and burning. In order to ensure the government takes the necessary measures, people need to act together. 'Weather' was developed in Brazil to try to attack this problem by mobilising young people – the ones who will suffer the consequences of these climate changes in the future. It is a multiplayer strategy game where players become activists to fight against climate change. This is, of course, a global issue, and Greenpeace 'Weather' has attracted a huge number of players from around the world.

Photographer	Designer	Advertising Agency	Marketing Manager
Nick Turpin	Mark Beacock	Lean Mean Fighting	Blake Harrop
Creative Directors	**Art Directors**	Machine	**Client**
Sam Ball	Sam Ball	**Agency Producer**	Samsung
Dave Bedwood	Mark Beacock	Rachel Bishop	
Technical Director	Dave Bedwood	**Account Handler**	
David Cox	**Copywriters**	Chris Condron	
Flash Programmers	Sam Ball		
David Cox	Dave Bedwood		
James Hay			
Jez Houghton			

Photography

Lean Mean Fighting Machine
for Samsung

The Photographic Adventures of Nick Turpin
Our brief was to launch the 8 megapixel Samsung Pixon Camera phone which is perfect for capturing unexpected moments. A street photographer named Nick Turpin took a photo in his home town of East Dulwich, London, and uploaded it to a website on 22nd October. The public could then click on anything in that photograph. The object with the most clicks then became the subject that Nick had to show in his next photograph. Nick's adventure lasted 28 days with the public sending him across Europe, America and Asia.

521

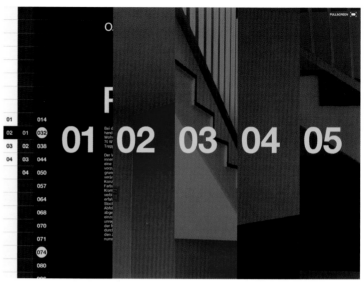

Creative Director
Fred Flade
Interactive Designer
Leigh Hibell

Flash Programmer
Jamie Owen
Programmer
Brandon Paluzzi

Digital Agency
de-construct
Brand Manager
Florian Schmidhuber

Client
O.S.A. Ochs
Schmidhuber
Architects

Graphic Design

de-construct
for O.S.A. Ochs Schmidhuber Architects

www.ochs-schmidhuber.de
This is a website for German architect firm O.S.A. Ochs Schmidhuber Architects. It features
a grid system tightly structuring not only the site as a whole, but all typographic elements in
particular, instilling a definitive sense of order and visual structure. The aim, of course, is to
underline the integrity of the architects' work itself.

The jury:
Dave Bedwood, Lean Mean Fighting Machine (Jury Foreman)
Mark Chalmers, Perfect Fools
Ben Clapp, Elvis Communications
Lars Cortsen, TRIPLE Copenhagen
Dominic Goldman, BBH London
Aaron Griffiths, OgilvyOne Worldwide New York
Naoki Ito, GT Tokyo
Stephen Reed, Beattie McGuinness Bungay
Hugo Rodrigues, Publicis São Paulo
Fernanda Romano, JWT London
James Woods, Grand Union

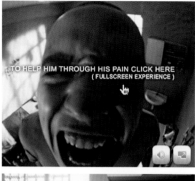

For thousands of
children in the UK
the story will
keep repeating itself,
until someone stops it.

Behind every
troubled youth
is a child
who needs
help.

Creative Directors
Nick Gill
Dominic Goldman
Interactive Designer
Oli Cole
Flash Programming
Stopp
Development
Stopp
Art Director
Dominic Goldman

Copywriters
Nick Allsop
Dominic Goldman
Simon Veksner
Digital Agency
Stopp
Advertising Agency
BBH London
Production Company
Sonny London
Post Production Company
Work

Director
Jeff Labbé
Producer
Nancy Hallam
Editor
Rich Orrick
Sound Designer
Stuart Welch
Agency Producers
Victoria Baldacchino
Ellen Ch'ng

Account Handler
Lucy Kennedy
Marketing Manager
Diana Tickell
Brand Manager
Collette Collins
Client
Barnardo's

Online Advertising

BBH London
for Barnardo's

Break the Cycle
This interactive advert demonstrates the cycle of crime, domestic violence, drugs and despair that many children are caught up in, and invites the consumer to stop the cycle. Being interactive, this ad asks viewers to play the role of Barnardo's and literally intervene to stop the vicious and destructive cycle that thousands of children are trapped in. 'Break the Cycle' was awarded a D&AD Yellow Pencil while the overall campaign was awarded a Nomination.

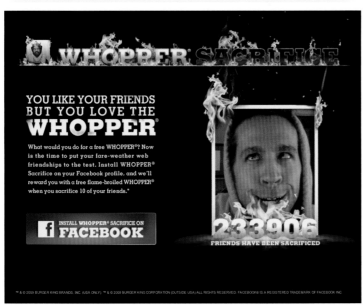

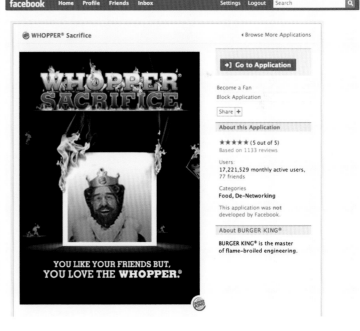

Creative Directors	Interactive Designers	Technical Lead	Director of Integrated Production	Integrated Head of Interactive Production
James Dawson-Hollis	Jordan Clayton-Hall	Oscar Llarena	David Rolfe	Winston Binch
Bill Wright	Nathan Reuss	**Co-Executive Creative Directors**	**Interaction Director**	**Development**
Interactive Design Director	John Whitmore	Andrew Keller	Matt Walsh	Ascent Marketing
Pelun Chen	**Interactive Art Director**	Rob Reilly	**Advertising Agency**	Refresh Partners
Technical Director	Saman Rahmanian	**Interactive Executive Creative Director**	Crispin Porter + Bogusky	**Quality Assurance**
Scott Prindle	**Interactive Copywriter**	Jeff Benjamin	**Integrated Producer**	James Lukensow
Flash Designer	Joel Kaplan	**Associate Creative Directors**	Rob Allen	Stewart Warner
Andrew Kennedy	**Associate Technical Director**	Nuno Ferreira	**Executive Integrated Producer**	**Client**
Programmers	Mat Ranauro	Neil Heymann	Robert Valdes	Burger King
Robert Christ				
Jimmy Pino				

Digital Innovations

Crispin Porter + Bogusky
for Burger King

Whopper Sacrifice
We have too many Facebook friends. Too many childhood buddies, ex-lovers and random co-workers, and we never want to delete any of them. Whopper Sacrifice gave people an excuse to clean up their friend list. All you had to do was answer this question: what do you love more, your friends or the Whopper? And people had no trouble answering it. Only four days after the launch, tens of thousands of people had been sacrificed, and the number was growing quickly. The faster the sacrifice spread, the more it proved that people love their favourite burger, the Whopper, more than their friends.

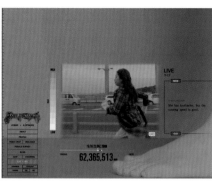
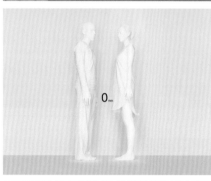

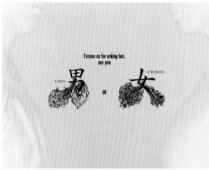

Creative Director Naoki Ito	Kenichi Takahashi **Art Director**	**Music Composer** Ryuichi Sakamoto	**Masanori Mori** Seiichi Saito	**Editor** Keisuke Ohta
Technical Director Qanta Shimizu	Naoki Ito **Copywriter**	**Mixer** Kazune Masutomi	**Producers** Masaki Endo	**Planners** Masaki Endo
Designers Atsushi Fujimaki	Naoki Ito **Sound Designer**	**Advertising Agencies**	Atsuki Yukawa **Production Manager**	Naoki Ito Takayuki Rokutan
Saiko Kamikanda	Takahisa Mitsumori	GT Tokyo	Tetsuji Isayama	**Qanta Shimizu**
Takeshi Yoshimori	**Retoucher**	**Rock & Roll Japan**	**Cameraman**	Atsuki Yukawa
Shigeki Yuriko	Teruyo Murayama	**Photographer**	Takahiro Konomi	**Client**
Yamane	**Director**	Kenshu Shintsubo	**Lighting Director**	Sagami Rubber
Flash Programmers	Kan Eguchi	**Device Producers**	Kimitaka Kajihara	Industries
Hiroki Hara	**System Engineers**	Katsuhiko Harada	**Video Engineers**	**Brand**
Hiroaki Kitamura	Jun Kuriyama	Hiroyuki Hori	Hiroyuki Watanabe	Sagami Original 0.02
Yukihiro Sasae	Takuho Yoshizu	Noriko Matsmoto	Eitaro Yamamoto	

Digital Advertising Campaigns

GT Tokyo
for Sagami Rubber Industries

Love Distance
We used a genuine long distance couple for this campaign. They ran a 1,000km marathon, and images of the two were broadcasted live on the internet for a whole month. The couple were allowed to keep in contact only through blog, TV phone and SMS messages. Thus all correspondence between the couple was displayed to the public on the internet. This also provided users with a simulation of a long distance relationship. The men's site and the women's site were created separately; on the day of completion, the two sites came together as one. And that was when the name of the client and the product were revealed.

Creative Director	Flash Programmer	Art Directors	Agency Producer
Iain Tait	Caroline	Marc Davies	Mike Pearson
Technical Director	Butterworth	Nicky Gibson	**Planner**
Igor Clark	**Designers**	**Copywriter**	Lise Lauritzen
Programmers	Dickon Langdon	David Cadji-Newby	**Client**
Nilesh Ashra	Andrew Zolty	**Digital Agency**	Orange
Mattias Gunneras	**Developer**	POKE	**Brand**
Greg Reed	Derek McKenna		PAYG

Digital Advertising Campaigns

POKE
for Orange

Orange Balloonacy

We knew there were going to be lovely animal-shaped balloons around because they were in the TV ads. We can't see how we could have done anything other than set up a balloon race across the internet. The thing that got us really excited was creating a complex and mutually beneficial relationship between sites, players and Orange, something fun for racers, yet rewarding for site-owners. We built a bespoke 'ad-serving' environment, managing relational data between each individual balloon and the sites. The reward: 40,000 balloons, 3,000 sites and 3.2million free exposures to Orange through the race itself.

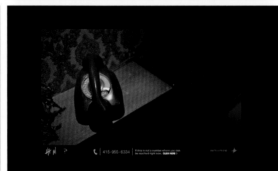

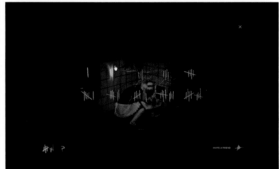

Creative Directors	**Associate Creative Directors**	**Advertising Agency**	**Account Planner**
Rick Condos	Hartley Rusen	Goodby Silverstein and Partners	Ted Florea
Hunter Hindman	Marc Sobier		**Account Director**
Art Director	**Creative Co-Ordinator**	**Agency Producer**	Liz Kaiser
Henrik Rosander		Maggie O'Brien	**Client**
Copywriter	Karen Land	**Executive Producer**	Frito-Lay
Michelle Hirschberg	**Production Company**	Amanda Cox	**Brand**
Chief Digital Officer	B-Reel		Doritos
Mike Geiger			

Digital Advertising Campaigns

Goodby Silverstein and Partners
for Frito-Lay

Hotel 626
In honour of Doritos bringing back two intense flavours from the dead, we created an intensely scary website. You're trapped in a haunted hotel and have to complete challenges – like singing a demon baby to sleep – to get out. Hotel 626 uses several groundbreaking techniques to dial up the experience. Your webcam sneaks a picture of you and shows it to you later, inside the lair of a madman. Your one salvation is a phone call on your actual mobile phone with directions on how to get out. To make it scarier, you have to play in the dark: Hotel 626 is only open from 6pm to 6am.

Creative Director	Copywriter	Advertising Agency	Account Handler
Shankun Sun	Wei Huang	JWT Beijing	Daniel Ingall
Art Director	**Chief Creative Officer**	**Agency Producer**	**Client**
Dechun Qiu	Polly Chu	Lin Ma	Nokia

Digital Advertising Campaigns

JWT Beijing
for Nokia

Bruce Lee Power Campaign
2008 marked the 35th anniversary of Bruce Lee's death. As a tribute to the legend, Nokia launched the Nokia N96 Bruce Lee limited edition. To generate interest, we decided to bring Bruce Lee back to life. We seeded a viral teaser video of never-seen-before footage. Within 24 hours, it had received over 700,000 views and generated huge debate. Two days later, we released the full-length version, then another viral video. The viral videos directed consumers to the campaign microsite nokia-lee.com.cn, which included 3D animation, game and demos of the phone. What started as an exclusively Chinese promotion spread around the globe like wildfire.

529

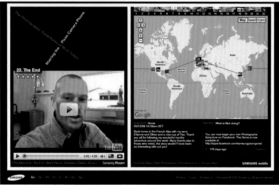

Creative Directors	Flash Programmers	Copywriters	Agency Producer
Sam Ball	David Cox	Sam Ball	Rachel Bishop
Dave Bedwood	James Hay	Dave Bedwood	**Account Handler**
Technical Director	Jez Houghton	**Photographer**	Chris Condron
David Cox	**Art Directors**	Nick Turpin	**Marketing Manager**
Designer	Sam Ball	**Advertising Agency**	Blake Harrop
Mark Beacock	Mark Beacock	Lean Mean Fighting	**Client**
	Dave Bedwood	Machine	Samsung

Digital Advertising Campaigns

Lean Mean Fighting Machine
for Samsung

The Photographic Adventures of Nick Turpin
The brief was to launch the 8MP Samsung Pixon Camera phone which is perfect for capturing unexpected moments. A street photographer named Nick Turpin took a photo in his home town of East Dulwich, London, and uploaded it to a website on 22nd October. The public could then click on anything in that photograph. The object with the most clicks then became the subject that Nick had to get in his next photograph. Nick's adventure lasted 28 days with the public sending him across Europe, America and Asia.

Online Advertising

Creative Director
Koichiro Tanaka
Technical Director
Qanta Shimizu
Interactive Designer
Satoshi Horii
Designer
Kohei Kawasaki
Art Director
Kohei Kawasaki
Website Director
Hiroshi Koike

Website Producer
Tatsuaki Ashikaga
Website Production Manager
Izumi Horio
Creative Boutique
Projector
Producers
Hiroko Asano
Takeshi Fukuda
Photographer
Katsuhide Morimoto

Film Directors
Shizuka Kurokawa
Takeshi Nakamura
Cinematographers
Shigeki Akiyama
Yoshikatsu Yasaki
Stylist
Tetsuro Nagase
Hair & Make-Up
Shinji Konishi
Project Manager
Yuuri Ogawa

Film Production Manager
Yuko Ishii
Shoot Co-Ordinator
Maki Osada
Client Supervisor
Kentaro Katsube
Client
UNIQLO

Digital Advertising Campaigns

Projector
for UNIQLO

UNIQLO Meets Corteo
Cirque du Soleil is a touring circus group that has dazzled over 80 million spectators in 200 cities on five continents. They have come together with UNIQLO to collaborate in a new way. Through this joint effort, UNIQLO aims to expand its brand awareness globally. We documented performers, who sported UNIQLO fashion, during training sessions of 'Corteo', Cirque du Soleil's touring production in Miami and Ottawa. These offstage shots lead to a sensational event in Tokyo. UNIQLO, 'Corteo', and invited users were united in a physical and spiritual sense. The campaign culminated in the upload of event shots onto the site, allowing users to share the experience.

531

Creative Directors	Interactive Art	Interactive Executive	Integrated Producer
James Dawson-Hollis	**Director**	**Creative Director**	Rob Allen
Bill Wright	Saman Rahmanian	Jeff Benjamin	**Senior Integrated**
Flash Programmer	**Interactive**	**Interactive Associate**	**Producer**
Andrew Perry	**Copywriter**	**Creative Director**	Anthony Nelson
Programmer	Joel Kaplan	Nuno Ferreira	**Executive Integrated**
Jim Alexander	**Senior Copywriter**	**Technical Director**	**Producer**
Interaction Designer	Andy Ure	Scott Prindle	Robert Valdes
Jordan Clayton-Hall	**Interaction Director**	**Associate Technical**	**Integrated Head**
Development	Matt Walsh	**Director**	**of Interactive**
Steady	**Co-Executive**	Mat Ranauro	**Production**
WorkPlayWork	**Creative Directors**	**Advertising Agency**	Winston Binch
	Andrew Keller	Crispin Porter +	**Client**
	Rob Reilly	Bogusky	Burger King

Digital Advertising Campaigns

Crispin Porter + Bogusky
for Burger King

Whopper Virgins

Which tastes better, Whopper or Big Mac? To answer the age-old question once and for all, Burger King travelled to some of the remotest parts of the globe to conduct the world's purest taste test. Only people who'd never eaten a burger could give an honest, unbiased opinion based on taste alone. Teaser TV, print and banners directed the curious to WhopperVirgins.com. Visitors saw just how far we were prepared to go to prove the universal appeal of the Whopper. Immediately, the internet and international media were buzzing with the news. After one week and countless blog comments and news stories, the online documentary disclosing the results debuted. New TV, print and banners announced its release.

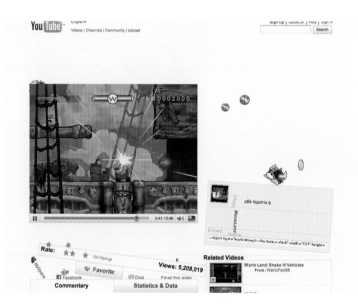

Creative Director	Advertising Agency	Communication	Director
Erik Enberg	Goodby Silverstein	**Strategy Director**	Rebecca Stambanis
Programmer	and Partners	Grace Kao	**Client**
Mike Kellogg	**Agency Producer**	**Account Manager**	Nintendo
Art Director	Jennifer Wilson	Ellen Byron	**Brand**
Bryan Houlette	**Interactive**	**Brand Strategy**	Wii
Copywriter	**Production Director**		
Nat Lawlor	Mike Geiger		
Chief Digital Officer			
Mike Geiger			

Online Advertising

Goodby Silverstein and Partners
for Nintendo

Wario Land Shake It!

The first place kids look to research a new video game is YouTube, which is loaded with hundreds of videos from all kinds of games. In order to make Wario stand out, we created a video that perfectly reflects Wario's love for destroying everything in his path. It starts out like any other game footage montage, but takes an unexpected turn when Wario's smashing begins to affect the entire YouTube page, eventually reducing it to rubble. For YouTube, this was an interactive first which has received over four million views in one month and praise all over the gaming blogs.

Dallas STHLM & Akestam Holst
for Playground Outdoor Equipment Stores

The Playground Barometer
Playground is a specialist retailer of outdoor equipment in Stockholm. This banner advert suggests the best suitable outdoor jacket (from a choice of over 70) based on your local weather forecast.

Creative Director	**Designer**	**Digital Agency**	**Account Handler**
Andreas Ullenius	Yvan Archimbaud	Dallas STHLM	Jerker Winther
Interactive Creative	**Copywriter**	**Advertising Agency**	**Marketing Manager**
Director	Adam Reuterskiold	Akestam Holst	Jonas Gidlund
Paul Collins	**Assistant Art**	**Agency Producer**	**Client**
Interactive Designer	**Director**	Sofia Swedenborg	Playground Outdoor
Ellinor Bjarnolf	Annika Frankel		Equipment Stores

BBH London
for Barnardo's

Education
In this piece of interactive online creative, users take on the Barnardo's perspective as they witness a young boy struggling to read a series of words in the statement 'Many of our projects deal with kids in trouble with education'. As they select words for the boy to read, the user is exposed to the boy's frustration, embarrassment and even anger as he struggles to read. Although basic literacy is something most of us take for granted, the bold statement 'Not every child in the UK will get an A or a B today. Congratulations to the thousands of troubled children who successfully held down full-time education this year', pays tribute to the daily battle faced by many children with learning difficulties, some of whom are helped by Barnardo's.

Creative Directors	**Developer**	**Advertising Agency**	**Account Handler**
Nick Gill	Oli Cole	BBH London	Lucy Kennedy
Dominic Goldman	**Art Director**	**Agency Producers**	**Marketing Manager**
Interactive Designer	Dominic Goldman	Victoria Baldacchino	Diana Tickell
Oli Cole	**Copywriter**	Gudrun Kendall	**Client**
Flash Programmer	Dominic Goldman	Michelle Kendrick	Barnardo's
Oli Cole			

Creative Directors
David Gamble
Simon Labbett
Flash Programmer
Theo Chandon

Art Director
James Manning
Copywriter
Richard Barrett
Director
Colin O'Toole

Digital Agency
Saint
Agency Producers
Caroline Green
Chris Jefford

Account Handler
Katie Zeitlin
Marketing Manager
Laura Trendall
Client
The Home Office

Online Advertising

Saint
for The Home Office

Pick It Up
Our brief from The Home Office was to create awareness around the dangers of carrying a knife. Our solution was simple: make people realise that picking up a knife when you go out is not like picking up a set of keys – it can have dire consequences. As the user engages with the banner a hand appears to pick up the knife. If the user clicks to pick it up, they are instantly thrown into the terrifying reality of a stand off involving that knife. At the end of the video, the following on-screen message appears: 'Pick up a knife, and you're more likely to get stabbed'.

Executive Creative Director
Richard Ting
Associate Creative Director
Andrew Hsu
Executive Technical Director
Nick Coronges
Designers
Juyoung Ryu
Ray Sison

Senior Visual Designer
Chadwick Shao
Senior Interaction Designers
Chris Dugan
Ryan Romero
Presentation Code Developers
Jack Bishop
Lee Walling

Senior Presentation Code Developers
Peter Knif
Sunny Nan
Techonology Team Leader
Thomas Chan
Copy Director
Jason Nichols
Advertising Agency
R/GA

Agency Producers
Amy Chuang
Ghazal Haque
Senior Producers
Kyle Bunch
Marc Maleh
Production Group Director
Jennifer Allen
Production Managing Director
Sean Lyons

Quality Assurance Executive Director
Michael Shagalov
Quality Assurance Associate Engineer
Jane Yang
Client
Nike
Brand
Nike Basketball

Digital Innovations

R/GA
for Nike

Ballers Network
To help players everywhere get into the game, and meet and challenge other players at every skill level, anywhere in the world, Nike partnered with R/GA to create Ballers Network. This application harnesses the social networking power of Facebook to make it easier for players to stay connected to the game, their teammates and the competition, 24/7. Players, coaches and organisers can create leagues, invite teams, set the season schedule, and organise a tournament, revolutionising how the game is played. Ballers Network is the first application for Facebook that connects with mobile phones – because the game doesn't begin and end on the court. Find courts and games any place, send and receive invites any time, or check your profile to see schedules and messages.

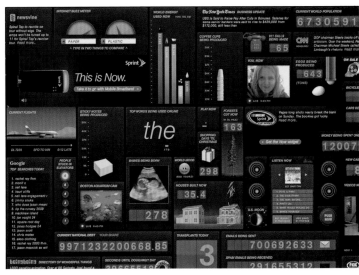

Creative Director
Christian Haas
Flash Programmer
Mike Kellogg
Developer
Mike Kellogg
Art Director
Aaron Dietz

Copywriter
Mandy Dietz
Chief Digital Officer
Mike Geiger
Advertising Agency
Goodby Silverstein
and Partners

Agency Producer
Tena Goy
Senior Producer
Margaret
McLaughlin

Account Handler
Jen Fox
Account Manager
Zoe Kretzschmar
Client
Sprint

Digital Innovations
Goodby Silverstein and Partners
for Sprint

NOW Widget
The internet is right now, whether you can find a way to get on it or not. It's happening as you read this. Sprint's mobile broadband site displays what Now actually looks like. A digital curator of live feeds, cams and streaming data constitutes the world's most elaborate widget. A downloadable version allows people to take the site with them. In the absence of a single dollar spent on media, it was picked up by over 100,000 blogs, with people spending an average of five minutes on it.

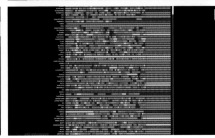

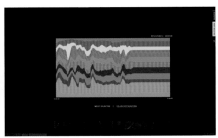

Creative Director
Kampei Baba
Technical Director
Kampei Baba
Designer
Tomomi Motose

Art Director
Tomomi Motose
Producer
Yusuke Maeda
Digital Agency
Bascule

Agency Producer
Masayoshi Boku
Content Strategist
Nobuo Hara

Client
WOWOW INC.
Brand
Radiohead

Digital Innovations
Bascule
for WOWOW INC

12 Cams, Create Your Rainbow
This is the promotional website for the TV programme 'Radiohead Japan Tour' by the Japanese pay television channel WOWOW INC. We produced publicity for the programme and branding for WOWOW INC. By combining the TV programme and the website we created a way for users to interact extensively with both media. Every user's action is recorded as a piece of a rainbow and accumulates into this bigger rainbow to respond to the message from the artist. At the end, we aimed for the rainbow containing everyone's feelings to become a piece of art.

Creative Director	**Art Director**	**Digital Agency**	**Client**
Chacho Puebla	Mico Toledo	Leo Burnett Lisbon	Diageo
Interactive Designer	**Copywriter**	**Agency Producer**	**Brand**
Federico Bosch	Juan Christmann	Antonio Junior	Pampero Rum
Flash Programmer	**Creative Advisor**	**Account Handler**	
Federico Bosch	Tura	Inês Almeida	
Designer	**Illustrator**	**Brand Manager**	
Mico Toledo	Bruna Guerreiro	Ana Teixeira	

Digital Innovations

Leo Burnett Lisbon
for Diageo

World's First Ephemeral Museum
To launch Pampero Rum in Portugal, we focused on a young social tribe consisting of trendsetters. Traditional advertising just doesn't get to this group, but art does. Using Pampero Fundación, a foundation that supports alternative artists, we've created the world's first ephemeral museum. First, the best pieces of street art in the Bairro Alto district were tagged. Then we created a website where you can download an audio guide and a map with the pieces' locations. So you can go out with your mp3 player and walk the museum streets.

Creative Directors	**Art Directors**	**Advertising Agency**	**Brand Manager**
Sam Ball	Miranda Abbs	Lean Mean Fighting	Clare Vaughan-
Dave Bedwood	Zoe Hough	Machine	Davies
Technical Director	**Copywriter**	**Agency Producer**	**Client**
David Cox	Zoe Hough	Rachel Bishop	Emirates
Flash Programmers	**Director**	**Account Handler**	
David Cox	Benton Roman	Amy Hancock	
James Hay	**Producer**		
Designer	Claire Jones		
Mark Beacock			

Digital Innovations

Lean Mean Fighting Machine
for Emirates

The Exposure of Tom King
Emirates launched a route between Dubai and Los Angeles, the home of movies. To celebrate the new route, we shot the short movie 'The Exposure of Tom King' in LA with no people in it whatsoever. People from around the world then auditioned for a role via webcam. Avy Kaufman, Hollywood casting director of 'Brokeback Mountain' and 'The Sixth Sense', selected the cast, who were then composited into the original LA movie. The final movie has a global cast, acting via webcam in the same scenes, who have never met. The movie premiered at 8pm on 7 November in LA and was streamed to www.theexposureoftomking.com

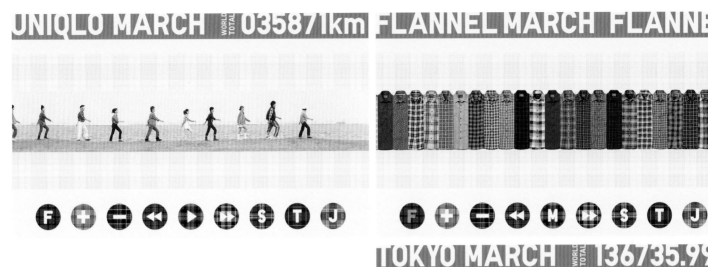

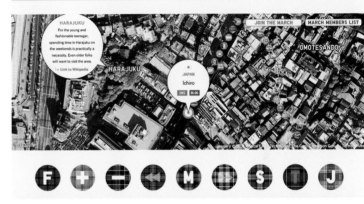

Creative Director	**Art Director**	Yuta Komatsu	**Production**	**Director**	**Digital Innovations**
Naoki Ito	Naoki Ito	Shuta Shimmyo	**Companies**	Kentaro Katsube	
Technical Directors	**Director**	**Video Engineer**	IMG SRC	**Project Co-Ordinator**	# GT Tokyo
Takashi Chiba	Naoki Ito	Tsuyoshi Takahashi	Pictures	Space Hyakka	## for Fast Retailing
Yuma Murakami	**Photographer**	**HTML Writer**	Rock & Roll Japan	**Planners**	
Qanta Shimizu	Kenshu Shintsubo	Taku Ichihara	**Choreographers**	Masaki Endo	
Flash Programmers	**System Engineers**	**Advertising Agency**	Yuriko Imamura	Naoki Ito	
Hidenori Chiba	Koichi Arakawa	GT Tokyo	Yoko Yamanaka	Takayuki Rokutan	
Hiroyuki Hori	Hiroyuki Hanai	**Editor**	**Stylist**	Qanta Shimizu	
Kosuke Sagara	**Music Artist**	Masaki Takehisa	Toshio Takeda	Atsuki Yukawa	
Shin Yamaharu	Cornelius	**Movie Encoder**	**Hair & Make-Up**	**Client**	
Designers	**Production**	Noriko Matsumoto	Mayumi Aota	Fast Retailing	
Saiko Kamikanda	**Managers**	**Production Assistant**	**Creative**	**Brand**	
Takeshi Yoshimori	Naoki Ishikawa	Seitaro Miyachi	**Management**	UNIQLO	

UNIQLO March
With H&M hitting Japan this winter, the project aimed to protect the market position for the number one casual brand, UNIQLO. The shops had to strengthen their connection with the online store as well. The target was all age groups, from kids to elders. This innovative online presentation format is designed to meet the needs of a long-running project. Models of different age groups, sexes and occupations march through the online catalogue, encouraging users to purchase directly online. The project culminates in Tokyo March, where all the online users around the world march virtually in a line on Google Maps.

Creative Director
Nick Turner
Technical Architect
Adam Creeger
Head of Technical Architecture
Neville Kuyt
Creative Developers
James Hay
Tristan Holman
Harald Krefting
Lead Creative Developer
Rick Williams

Creative Development Director
Andy Hood
Art Director
Richard Baxter
Associate Creative Director
Chris Williams
Chief Creative Officer
James Hilton

Senior Software Engineers
Richard Szalay
Kevin Watkins
Digital Agency
AKQA London
Senior Strategists
Paul Bello
Paul O'Neill
User Experience Analyst
Alison Rushworth

Quality Assurance Analysts
Zahid Chohan
Martin Harlow
Head of Quality Assurance
Anthony O'Brien
Technical Delivery Manager
Stuart George
Technical Account Director
Miriam Healy

Account Director
Bonnie Boodram
Group Account Director
Livia Bernardini
Brand Manager
Luis Cilimingras
Client
Fiat

Digital Innovations

AKQA London
for Fiat

eco:Drive

eco:Drive is the very latest in digital integrated technology. It is an easy-to-use computer application that connects your car to your PC. Using cutting-edge analytical software, eco:Drive dissects and evaluates your driving style and shows you ways to cut down on fuel consumption, reducing your CO_2 emissions and saving you money. The eco:Drive application analyses your acceleration, deceleration, gear changes and speed. It then awards you a mark out of 100, according to how efficiently you have driven. Step-by-step tutorials then help you improve your score, giving you practical advice on how to perfect your driving style, using information from your own journeys.

Creative Director
Sergio Mugnaini
Technical Director
Fabrizio Barata
Programmer
Yves Apsy

Art Directors
Fabio Cardoso
Diego Cardoso de Oliveira
Copywriter
Juliana Borges

3D Producer
Geninho
Advertising Agency
AlmapBBDO

Client
Pepsi
Brand
Gatorade

Animation

AlmapBBDO
for Pepsi

Waggle Boy
The goal was to create a campaign with an interactive element to support the Gatorade brand. The idea of the piece is to show very clearly how Gatorade helps to restore your energy.

The jury:
Dan Rosen, AKQA (Jury Foreman)
Tim Ash, Nokia UK
Cheryl Calverley, Unilever Foods UK
Derek Handley, The Hyperfactory
James Hilton, Inside Mobile
Masaru Kitakaze, Hakuhodo
Dominick O'Brien, glue London

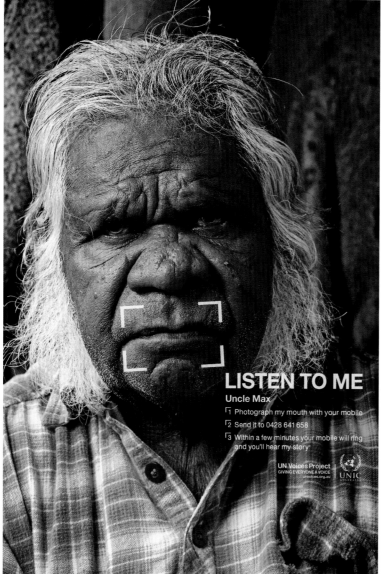

LISTEN TO ME

Uncle Max

1 Photograph my mouth with your mobile

2 Send it to 0428 641 658

3 Within a few minutes your mobile will ring and you'll hear my story

UN Voices Project
GIVING EVERYONE A VOICE
unvoices.org.au

UNIC
AUSTRALIA

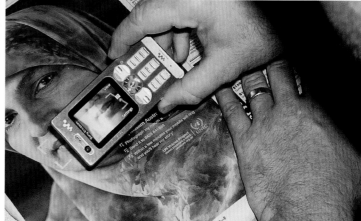

Mobile Marketing

Saatchi & Saatchi Australia
for United Nations

UN Voices Project

The UN Voices project was created to give everyone a voice. Really give them a voice. By using revolutionary mobile technology, we made posters and press ads talk for the very first time. How it works: After taking a mobile phone photo of the featured person's mouth, you send it to the number shown as a text message. Almost instantly your mobile will ring and you'll hear their story in a brief pre-recorded message. You are then directed to unvoices.org.au where you can hear other stories or add your own.

Creative Directors	**Director**	**Producer**	**Agency Producer**
Dave Bowman	Ralph van Dijk	Tom Eslinger	Kate Whitfield
David Nobay	**Photographers**	**Sound Engineering**	James Tracy Inglis
Digital Creative	Tim Gibbs	Sandcastle Studios	**Brand Manager**
Director	Petrina Hicks	**Executive Creative**	Julia Dean
Brian Merrifield	Sean Izzard	**Director**	**Marketing Manager**
Technical Direction	David Knight	Steve Back	Abdullah Mbamba
Dialect	Scott Newett	**Advertising Agency**	**Client**
Hyperfactory	Daniel Smith	Saatchi & Saatchi	United Nations
Mobot	**Copywriter**	Australia	
Mobile Developer	Steve Jackson	**Project Manager**	
Shaun O'Connor	**Mobile Designer**	Paul Worboys	
Art Director	Christina Lock		
Vince Lagana			

540

Creative Directors	Mobile Copywriters	Advertising Agency	Producers
Yasuharu Sasaki	Hiroshi Koike	Dentsu Tokyo	Morihiro Harano
Hirozumi Takakusaki	Yasuharu Sasaki	**Production**	Toshifumi Oiso
Mobile Developers	**Mobile Designer**	**Companies**	Takashi Omori
Minoru Araki	Rie Fujinaka	Engine Plus	**Brand Manager**
Shozo Okada	**Game Designer**	Hi-Posi	Chie Muranaka
Art Director	Keiichi Tozaki	Memokami	**Client**
Yusuke Kitani			Honda

Mobile Marketing

Dentsu Tokyo
for Honda

Ke-tai Traveler K-TRA

In Japan, young people stopped buying cars. They now spend their money on mobile phones to communicate with friends. To foster brand loyalty to Honda, and to remind young people of the joy of mobility, we launched a new mobile community application K-TRA (Ke-tai Traveller). K-TRA changed mobile phones into vehicles. Players have their own 'movatar' (mobile avatar), and it hitchhikes on the mobile phones of other people. The movatars travel around Japan riding someone's mobile phone, collecting souvenirs and talking with other players. Sometimes movatars send emails to the owners about their activities. Using K-TRA, people experienced the joy of mobility and wanted to 'move' more to lift movatars.

Creative Director	Art Director	Animation Company	Brand Manager
Gavin McLeod	Hannes Ciatti	Sixty40	Debbie Mills
Technical Director	**Mobile Copywriter**	**Project Manager**	**Client**
Aaron Wallis	Genevieve Hoey	Megan Wooding	Sydney Dogs
Mobile Developer	**Mobile Designer**	**Account Handler**	& Cats Home
Hannes Ciatti	Genevieve Hoey	Kirsty Smith	**Brand**
Web Developers	**Head of Copy**	**Digital Account**	Animal Rescue
Gilmore Davidson	Hamish Stewart	**Director**	Shelter
Rebecca Roach	**Advertising Agency**	Lee Bachar-Alder	
Flash Developer	M&C Saatchi/Mark		
Peter Vink			

Mobile Marketing

M&C Saatchi/Mark
for Sydney Dogs & Cats Home

Throw Us a Bone
In Australia, 'throw us a bone' means 'please help us'. We created our own entertaining content, Frankie the wonder dog, then pioneered a convergent technology platform that enabled people to interact in real-time with him. People 'threw' Frankie a bone via SMS and received an instant dog trick in return. Every bone thrown was a $5 donation. We achieved great results in just three days: 1327 bones were thrown, 17.4 per cent of people threw twice or more, 25 per cent of dogs needing homes were adopted. We witnessed a 600 per cent increase in new volunteers and over $150,000 worth of free media was generated from Optus, Inspire, Fairfax, News Limited and JCDecaux.

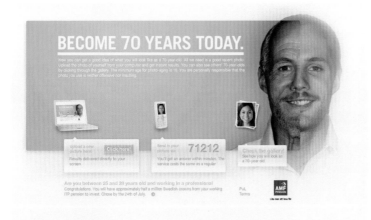

Mobile Development	Retouching	Technical Supplier	Client
Unwire	C2	Crossmedia Avenue	AMF
Photographer	**Advertising Agency**	**Advertising**	**Brand**
Erik Undéhn	Forsman & Bodenfors	**Supervisors**	AMF Pension
Production Company	**Media Agency**	Åsa Ambuhm	
Perfect Fools	Mindshare	Maria Jonsson	
		Maria Molnar	

Forsman & Bodenfors
for AMF

MMS

All advertising from AMF Pension focuses on the idea that the future is bright and there are reasons to look forward to it. We wanted to make the idea of a pension important for younger people by getting them to think about the future. This campaign employed phone messaging and a web-based service where visitors could have their photos aged, so that they looked 70 years old. The campaign included film spots (with Peter Siepen and Charlotte Perelli), outdoor boards, internet banners and a website. During October only, 322,946 photos were submitted by visitors that wanted to see how they might look as 70-year-old retirees. The initial target was 50,000 visitors.

543

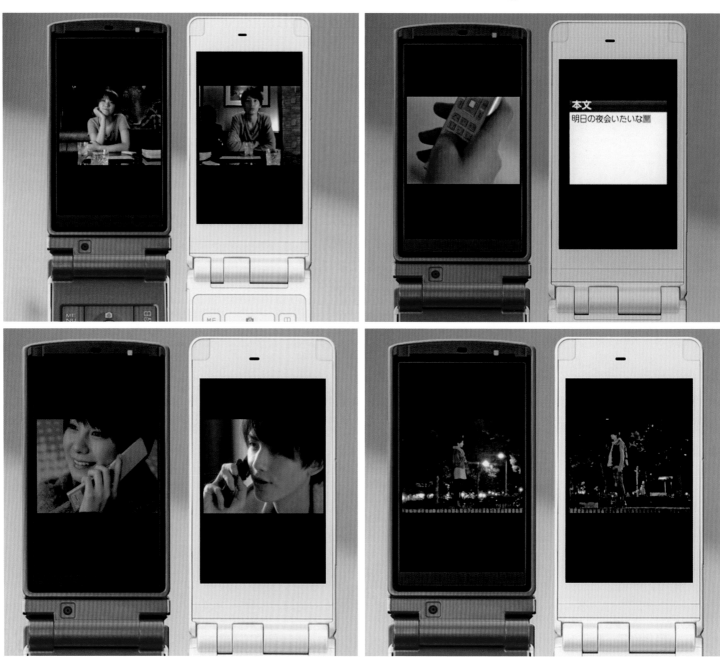

Creative Director
Yuki Kishi
Technical Director
Tomoko Tanaka
Mobile Copywriter
Yosuke Murai
Film Director
Takahiro Miki

Cinematographer
Hiroyuki Hourin
Advertising Agency
Dentsu Tokyo
Project Manager
Shinya Kishiro

Account Handler
Kei Terasaki
Brand Manager
Takeshi Kimura

Client
SONY Music
Associated Records
Brand
JUJU feat.
Spontania

Mobile Marketing

Dentsu Tokyo
for SONY Music Associated Records

Pair Movie 'Sunao ni Naretara' (Wish I Could be True to Myself)
The purpose of this campaign was to advertise the Japanese singer-songwriter Juju's new song, 'Sunao ni Naretara' (Wish I could be true to myself). We were challenged by the client to develop an innovative mobile campaign that no one had ever tried before. We developed a brand new type of mobile movie called 'Pair Movie'. We leveraged this technique for the song promotion, and have produced the original movie in five episodes. It was streamed for free on the campaign site from 1 December 2008 to 14 February 2009.

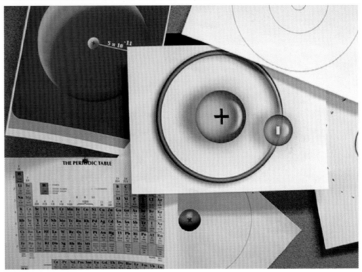

Digital Creative Director	Copywriters	Advertising Agency	Engagement
Tim Cheng	Rowan Dean	Euro RSCG	Strategy Planner
Direct Creative	Jamal Hamidi	Australia	Eric Phu
Director	**Head of Design**	**Executive Producer**	**Group Account**
Peter Maniaty	Darren Cole	Skye Lanser	**Director**
Art Directors	**Executive Creative**	**Senior User**	Tim Boys
Janine Poon	**Director**	**Experience**	**Client**
Heather Stewart	Rowan Dean	**Manager**	SONY
		Robert Muller	

Euro RSCG Australia
for SONY

Quantum Code

Using QR technology for the first time in Australia, Sony created a mobile promotion that recruited tech-savvy 'spies' for a thrilling real-world treasure hunt and adventure leading to a promotional tie-in with the James Bond movie Quantum of Solace. A series of complex cryptic clues unlocked a safe containing $15,000. Activated via mobiles, the search for clues revolved around a cast of villains and a beautiful spy, Constance Newlove. To complete their tasks, recruits competed using social networking platforms such as blogs, forums and Facebook. With over 8,000 dedicated players and thousands of comments posted on forums and blogs, Constance Newlove's YouTube and Facebook channel gained tens of thousands of fans.

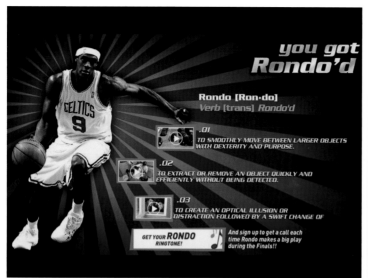

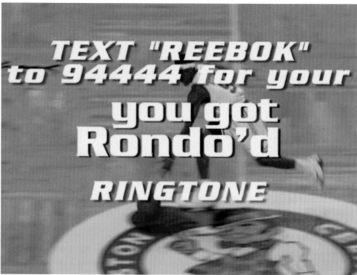

Creative Directors	Art Director	Mobile Marketing	Marketing Manager
Dusan Hamlin	Chris Cannacott	Agency	Catherine Thomason
James Hilton	Mobile Copywriter	Inside Mobile	Client
Technical Director	Chris Steedman	Account Handler	Reebok International
Eric Mugnier	Mobile Designer	Matthew Wilkinson	Brand
Mobile Developer	Jenny Kimmerich	Brand Managers	Reebok
Jon Kwan	Project Manager	Richard Prenderville	
	Ryan Lafleur	Marcus Spurrell	

Mobile Marketing

Inside Mobile
for Reebok International

You Got Rondo'd!
In 2008, the Boston Celtics reached the NBA finals. Reebok had just eight days to create an engaging campaign, targeting Celtics and basketball fans around the world. The 'You Got Rondo'd' concept was based around key player Rajon Rondo. Basketball fans were encouraged to adopt the 'You Got Rondo'd' slogan and share it via their mobiles. Every time Rondo made a great game play, opted-in fans would hear the custom ring tone and on answering the call, receive unique motivational messages from celebrity basketball players. The viral mechanic behind the ringtone and call back service ensured global success for the campaign. The term 'You Got Rondo'd' became a popular catchphrase for basketball fans.

Creative Director
Jon Carney
Mobile Developers
Savvas
Constantinides
Terence Mbano

Technical Director
Alex Matthews
Art Director
Chris Mount

**Mobile Marketing
Agency**
Marvellous
Account Handler
Nick Fisher

Brand Manager
Barry Moore
Client
adidas

Mobile Marketing

Marvellous
for adidas

adidas Marathon Run Tracker
Nobody runs a marathon on their own – runners depend on the support of friends and family to reach their ambition. So adidas launched their marathon service that brought together RFID chips in runners' shoes, with timings at every 5km on the course, within an adidas run tracker application, where supporters could enter a runner number to get the latest information on that competitor's progress. This included a mapped location, average speed and estimated finish time, allowing friends and family to be in the right place at the right time. Supporters could also send personalised messages of encouragement to large digital displays around the course; the messages came up as runners approached, helping them reach their 'impossible is nothing'.

Creative Director	Motion Graphics	Advertising Agency	Senior Account
Duan Evans	**Producer**	AKQA London	**Director**
Mobile Technical	Jim Birchenough	**Mobile Strategy**	Geoff Northcott
Producer	**Associate Creative**	**Director**	**Client**
Andrew Burgess	**Director**	Jonathan Hum	Nike
Art Director	Nick Bailey	**Senior Project**	**Brand**
Davor Krvavac	**Chief Creative**	**Manager**	NIKEiD
Motion Graphics	**Officer**	Joel Godfrey	
Director	Daniel Bonner		
Greg Mullen			

Mobile Marketing

AKQA London
for Nike

Nike PHOTOiD

Nike briefed AKQA London to connect young, style-conscious consumers with the brand's online shoe customisation service via their mobiles. We created Nike PHOTOiD: a world-first application of colour recognition technology that turns mobile photos into customised Nike Dunks within seconds. Whenever, wherever inspiration strikes, simply shoot your picture, send it via MMS and receive your shoe design featuring the main colours in your photo – with a unique code to go online and buy. Nike PHOTOiD – 'Shoot Your Colours' launched in nine territories, propelling Nike into an exciting new space, helping creative youth connect with NIKEiD in an innovative way and setting a new standard for mobile marketing.

Clemenger BBDO
for New Zealand Transport Agency

Distracted Driverss
Driver distraction is a growing problem in New Zealand. Each year a staggering number of serious crashes are caused by drivers using their mobile phones behind the wheel. A recent study reported that two thirds of young people admitted to taking their eyes off the road to read and send text messages while driving. Our challenge was to inform people of the dangers, but our idea went one step further, and created a way to let them actually experience how something as simple as texting while driving can have fatal consequences.

Creative Director
Paul Nagy
Art Directors
Sarah Jackson
Lisa Scott
Copywriters
Tammy Keegan
Paul Nagy
Editor
Jason Martin

Programmer
Marc Broad
Executive Creative Director
Philip Andrew
Head of Digital
Scott Sinclair
Advertising Agency
Clemenger BBDO

Mobile Technology
Run the Red
Agency Producers
Martin Gray
Lisa Scott
Production Manager
Martin Gray
Account Manager
Linda Reuvecamp

Group Account Director
Sean Keaney
Business Director
Annabelle Wilkinson
Client
New Zealand
Transport Agency

Hakuhodo
for SONY Computer Entertainment

Siren New Translation
The latest series of 'Siren', a legendary horror game, was released. Our aim was to make the release campaign feel very real, so we created content with the assumption that Hanyuda Village, where the game is set, actually exists. A 'webisode' site was developed, showing TV crews sneaking into the village. Another 24-hour live camera site showed images from the cameras that the TV crews set up. The two sites had 3,770,000 accesses over 50 days. We produced mobile content too: when fans phoned a deadly number, they were connected to Hanyuda Village via TV phone. There were 57,000 connected calls in 50 days.

Creative Director
Yutaka Hayashi
Technical Director
Takuji Ujiie
Flash Developer
Keitarou Takahashi
Art Director
Yuni Yoshida
Copywiters
Yutaka Hayashi
Akira Kojima
Designer
Jyun Ino

Producer
Takanori Hayashi
Photographer
Kenichi Negishi
Director
Kenji Murakami
Executive Creative Director
Masaru Kitakaze
Advertising Agency
Hakuhodo
Sound Designer
Hajime Ehara

Stylist
Minori Niizaki
Hair & Make-Up
Nishimura Eizou
Akiko Kawano
Project Managers
Haruko Kato
Hiroaki Mizutani
Kazuki Shiraki
Planners
Akira Kojima
Osamu Ooshima

Account Executives
Satoe Izu
Kaoru Kato
Brand Manager
Hiroyoshi Beppu
Client
SONY Computer
Entertainment

Creative Director	**Mobile Copywriter**	**Advertising Agency**	**Brand Manager**
Masaru Kitakaze	Yutaka Hayashi	Hakuhodo	Noriko Shibayama
Technical Director	**Mobile Designer**	**Project Manager**	**Client**
Kyohei Tsuji	Ryo Miyawaki	Yoshiki Miura	Tohato
Art Director	**Illustrator**	**Account Handler**	**Brand**
Ryo Miyawaki	Bunpei Yorifuji	Yoshiki Miura	Chibi-Poli

Mobile Marketing

Hakuhodo
for Tohato

Chibi-Poli Mobile Hunting!
We named the product Chibi-Poli because in Japanese 'chibi' means 'small' and 'poli' is an onomatopoeia for a light, crisp texture. Since 'poli' also means 'cops', we developed cop and robber characters with a well-known illustrator. We then carried out an electronic cops and robbers game using mobile phones, entitled 'Chibi-Poli Mobile Hunting', in Shibuya, one of Tokyo's largest entertainment centres for young people. The simple game design, which allowed participants to find the robbers (QR codes) hiding in the streets of Shibuya and win a digital prize, proved extremely successful.

Creative Director	**Mobile Copywriter**	**Account Handler**	**Client**
Alasdair Graham	Jon Morgan	Tom Shattock	Coca-Cola
Technical Director	**Advertising Agency**	**Brand Manager**	**Brand**
Scott Seaborn	Ogilvy London	Prinz Mathew	Fanta
Art Director		Pinakatt	
Mike Watson			

Mobile Marketing

Ogilvy London
for Coca-Cola

Stealth Sound System
Fanta believes teens should have the right to play. The brief was to produce a mobile phone application that teens can play without their fun being spoilt by adults. This idea was inspired by the controversial ultra-sonic alarms used to disperse teenage groups, which play high-pitch sounds that only young people can hear. When you get older, you can't hear these sounds any more as your hearing naturally deteriorates. We turned the technology on its head. The mobile application we invented, the Fanta Stealth Sound System, enables those same teenagers to communicate between themselves using frequencies that adults can't hear.

Viral

The jury:

Michael Lebowitz, Big Spaceship (Jury Foreman)
Oli Christie, Inbox Digital
Paul Clements, TBWA\DENMARK
Piero Frescobaldi, Unit9
Christian Haas, Goodby Silverstein and Partners
Chris Hassell, Ralph
Chuck McBride, Cutwater
Philippe Meunier, Sid Lee
Matthew Smith, The Viral Factory
Zeke Tastas, Naked Sweden
Ben Wheatley, Mr and Mrs Wheatley Ltd

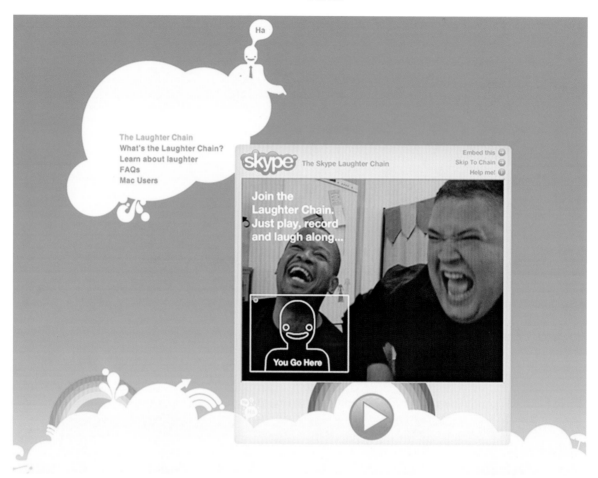

Creative Direction	Advertising Agency	Programming	Head of Experience
The Viral Factory	The Viral Factory	Franki & Jonny	**Design**
Production Company	**Design Group**	**Marketing Manager**	Henrique Penha
The Viral Factory	Franki & Jonny	Nick Wright	**Client**
			Skype

Interactive Virals

The Viral Factory
for Skype

Skype Laughter Chain
The main film shows how hysterical laughter is contagious. It aims to demonstrate that talking over video provides a richer communication experience. The film was supported by an interactive element that let people simultaneously watch and record their reactions, which they could then add to the chain. The player and interactive experience could be embedded into anyone's blog, social network profile page or website. Viewed over nine million times, with an extraordinary rate of viewer engagement, the chain is approximately one hour and 45 minutes long now, with over 8,000 submissions. The campaign generated overwhelming positivity; in some cases it was actually considered inspirational.

Creative Directors
Phil Clandillon
Steve Milbourne

Creative Agency
Sony Music
Creative

Developer
Svetozar Batoev
Marketing Manager
Matt Reynolds

Client
Columbia Records
Brand
AC/DC

Viral Films

Sony Music Creative
for Columbia Records

AC/DC Rocks the Office

Our brief was to reach 30 to 40-year-old men with 'a genuine blow-out moment in these serious times'. We decided to offer them a moment of rock 'n' roll escapism at work. Most office workers are subject to a restrictive internet policy which essentially stops them from having fun. We decided to raise two fingers to the IT department by including AC/DC's music in an Excel spreadsheet, a file type allowed through every corporate firewall. Now we just had to make the spreadsheet compelling enough for people to pass it on. To achieve this, we created the world's first music video in Excel with the video playing back real time, frame by frame in ASCII.

Director
Keith Schofield
Creative Direction
The Viral Factory
Producer
Jon Stopp

Post Production
Producer
Tracey Khan
Production Company
The Viral Factory
Advertising Agency
The Viral Factory

Animators
Dom Del Torto
Neil McFarland
Editor
Rob Hill
Senior Dubbing
Mixer
Kim Storey

Music Composer
Dominic Nunns
Marketing Managers
Miguel Ares
Richard Holley
Client
Diesel

Viral Films

The Viral Factory
for Diesel

SFW XXX

We often protest that not all great virals are about sex, but sometimes a brief comes along that just begs for it. SFW XXX was created to celebrate Diesel's 30th birthday and promote that the brand was throwing parties around the world. Our viral is a direct tribute to the internet meme 'SFW' (safe-for-work) from somethingawful.com, where people paint over rude photos with animation. Our film features clips of 80s porn films, however the naughty bits are covered with animation showing non-sexual activity, such as eating corncobs or playing pinball. In the first week the film was viewed over four million times and has since generated widespread international press coverage.

554

諾基亞N96李小龍限定版勁爆登場

Nokia N96 Bruce Lee Limited Edition

Director
Jinjing Zhu
Copywriter
Wei Huang
Art Director
Dechun Qiu

Creative Director
Shankun Sun
Chief Creative Officer
Polly Chu

Producer
Jade Tang
Advertising Agency
JWT Beijing
Agency Producer
Lin Ma

Account Handler
Daniel Ingall
Client
Nokia

Viral Films

JWT Beijing
for Nokia

Bruce Lee Ping Pong
2008 marked the 35th anniversary of Bruce Lee's death. As a tribute to the legend, Nokia launched the Nokia N96 Bruce Lee limited edition. To boost sales, we decided to bring Bruce Lee back to life. We seeded a viral teaser video of never-seen-before footage. Within 24 hours, it had received over 700,000 views and generated huge debate. Two days later, we released the full-length version then another viral video. The campaign captured attention around the world, creating a Bruce Lee wildfire on the net. At the same time, it drove consumers from the web to Nokia stores to experience the phone for real.

Director	**Producer**	**Lighting**	**Head of Group**	Viral Films
Chris Palmer	Rupert Smythe	**Cameraperson**	**Marketing**	
Copywriters	**Production Company**	Ben Seresin	**Communications**	# WCRS
Simon Aldridge	Gorgeous	**Sound Designer**	Chris MacLeod	## for Transport for London
Tom Spicer	Enterprises	Pav	**Group Account**	
Art Directors	**Advertising Agency**	**Account Director**	**Director**	**Awareness Test**
Vince Chasteauneuf	WCRS	Jenny Bust	Fergus Adam	To cut down on cycling fatalities, this ad allowed both drivers and cyclists to experience
Kit Dayaram	**Agency Producer**	**Group Marketing**	**Client**	first hand how seemingly obvious things can become totally invisible to the human eye.
Creative Directors	James Lethem	**Manager**	Transport for London	One of the few virals that lived up to the name, it was viewed by over ten million people
Yan Elliott	**Editor**	Nigel Hanlon		online in its first year.
Luke Williamson	Paul Watts			

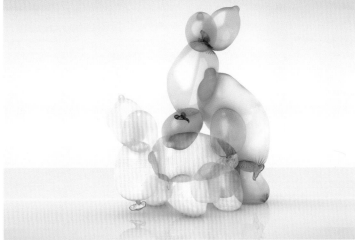

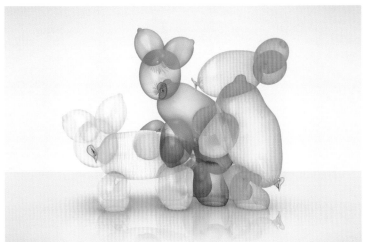

Have fun. Be Safe. Wear a condom.

Animator
Dave Thomlison
Director of
Animation
Mike Wharton
Direction
Superfad
Art Director
Andrew Stubbs
Johnston
Creative Director
Rob Rugan

Group Creative
Director
Fernando Lecca
Associate Creative
Director
Jerry Williams
Chief Creative
Officer
Eddie Synder
Producer
Mike Tockman

Executive Producer
Geraint Owen
Production
Company
Superfad
Advertising Agency
Fitzgerald &
Company
Modelling
Domel Libid
Sound Designer
Joel Raabe

Senior Sound
Designer
Joe Mendelson
Compositor
Adrian Winter
Chief Broadcast
Officer
Christine Sigety
Client
Durex

Animation

Fitzgerald & Company
for Durex

Get It On!

The Superfad creative team employed much close scrutiny of inflated rubbers, and careful study of animals 'at it', during extremely thorough pre-production. We quickly figured out that timing was everything. Giving each little joke time to breathe (and squeak) was essential to the humour. We played with this early on with a rough 2D animatic. From there the 3D department, compositor and sound designers took the production quality to a whole new level, adding little jokes along the way. Originally commissioned for the US market, the campaign quickly went global, earning the Durex brand and its safe sex message over three million hits within two weeks of its release.

Director	Creative Directors	Special Effects	Editor	Marketing Manager
Guy Ritchie	John Boiler	Chris Badger	Robert Duffy	Adam Collins
Copywriter	Glenn Cole	Giles Cheetham	**Sound Designer**	**Senior Advertising**
Jason Norcross	Jason Norcross	**Production Company**	Matt Collinge	**Manager**
Art Director	Bryan Rowles	Anonymous Content	**Music Composers**	Colin Leary
Bryan Rowles	**Producers**	**Advertising Agency**	Eagles of Death	**Client**
	Aris McGeary	72andSunny	Metal	Nike
	Dave Morrison	**Agency Producers**	**Account Handlers**	**Brand**
		Sam Baerwald	Alex Schneider	Nike Football
		Angelo Ferrugia	Evin Shutt	

Viral Films

72andSunny
for Nike Football

Next Level
Our brief was to inspire footballers around the world to become better footballers. The film shows what it takes at the highest level: successes, failures, hard work, knocked-out teeth, all of it. Viewers are directed to nikefootball.com where they can find products and training programmes to help them achieve their goals.

Director	Production Company	Special Effects	Group Account
Joseph Kosinski	Anonymous Content	Vernon Wilbert	**Director**
Copywriter	**Advertising Agency**	**Editor**	Peter Goldstein
Mat Bunnell	T.A.G.	Russ Glasgow	**Group Account**
Art Director	**Agency Producer**	**Sound Design**	**Supervisor**
Ben Wolan	Vince Genovese	Lime	Lyndsey Corona
Creative Directors	**Executive Producer**	**Previsualisation**	**Client**
Scott Duchon	Jeff Baron	**Artist**	XBOX
Geoff Edwards	**Animators**	David Rosenbaum	**Brand**
John Patroulis	Jack Kasprzak	**Computer Graphics**	Gears of War
Producer	Marc Perrera	**Supervisor**	
Melanie la Rue	Roy Sato	Peter Plevritis	
	Andrew Tamandl		

Viral Films

T.A.G.
for XBOX

Rendezvous / Last Day
This viral piece combines 'Rendezvous' and 'Last Day', two promos developed for 'Gears of War 2' from XBOX. 'Rendezvous' and 'Last Day' were created entirely in the Gears of War 2 game engine to deliver the realism, detail, texture and physics of the actual game; all animation was done in-engine to enhance the role-playing experience. It was first storyboarded and previsualised; motion capture was done to detail the characters' movements. Designed for a wider audience, it is contemplative and set to a haunting ballad, to give gamers a new piece of content to share for greater exposure.

Creative Directors	Assistant Producer	Advertising Agency	Account Handler
Jim Elliott	Christine Oh	Goodby, Silverstein	Leslie Barrett
Margaret Johnson	**Executive Producer**	and Partners	**Account Manager**
Executive Creative	James Horner	**Editing**	Erin Fromherz
Director	**Production Company**	Barbary Post	**Client**
Jeff Goodby	Bob Industries		Häagen-Dazs

Viral Films

Goodby Silverstein and Partners
for Häagen-Dazs

Krumpin'

As Colony Collapse Disorder threatened the US bee population, agency planners recognised that 40 per cent of the natural flavours used in Häagen-Dazs ice cream could disappear – and with it, one third of all the natural products we eat. This viral film was one aspect of an integrated campaign created to help bring the honey bee back. The film was awarded the coveted FWA favourite viral video of 2008. The campaign resulted in one of the fastest moving media and PR stories of 2008, real contributions to bee research, renewed revenue growth and, ultimately, testimony before Congress to save the honey bee.

Director	Production Company	Director of	Brand Manager
Benjamin Wolfl	Markenfilm	**Photography**	Anne-Catherine
Copywriters	**Advertising Agency**	Lutz Hattenhauer	Paulisch
Edgar Lindscheid	Scholz & Friends	**Account Handlers**	**Client**
Fabio Straccia	**Agency Producers**	Anna Kubitza	Amnesty
Art Director	Nina Heyn	Penelope	International
Sara Vieira	Nele Juergens	Winterhager	
Creative Directors	Daniel Klessig	**Marketing Manager**	
Oliver Handlos		Markus N Beeko	
Martin Pross			
Wolf Schneider			
Matthias Spaetgens			

Viral Films

Schloz & Friends
for Amnesty International

Crazy-Leader-Commercial

We released a viral film with documentary scenes of George W Bush, Vladimir Putin and Mahmoud Ahmadinejad. What at first looks like all those typical politician speeches soon becomes an absurd rivalry of doing handicrafts. Putin is carefully folding a poodle out of a red balloon, Bush replies with a nice piece of origami, and finally Ahmadinejad gives his personal best with two lovely potholders. All this ends with an on-screen message telling us, 'We can change what they do. Amnesty International'. By clicking on the final screen, users are forwarded to the donation page of Amnesty International's website.

Director	Creative Director	Producer	Account Handler
Jinjing Zhu	Shankun Sun	Jade Tang	Daniel Ingall
Copywriter	**Chief Creative**	**Advertising Agency**	**Client**
Wei Huang	**Officer**	JWT Beijing	Nokia
Art Director	Polly Chu	**Agency Producer**	
Dechun Qiu		Lin Ma	

Viral Films

JWT Beijing
for Nokia

Bruce Lee Match

2008 marked the 35th anniversary of Bruce Lee's death. As a tribute to the legend, Nokia launched the Nokia N96 Bruce Lee limited edition. To boost sales, we decided to bring Bruce Lee back to life. We seeded a viral teaser video of never-seen-before footage. Within 24 hours, it had received over 700,000 views and generated huge debate. Two days later, we released the full-length version then another viral video. The campaign captured attention around the world, creating a Bruce Lee wildfire on the net. At the same time, it drove consumers from the web to Nokia stores to experience the phone for real.

Director	Producer	Agency Producer	Head of Integrated
Jaron Albertin	Stephanie Scire	Dana May	**Production**
Copywriter	**Special Effects**	**Editor**	Sally-Ann Dale
Isaac Silverglate	Method New York	Dustin Stevens	**Client**
Art Director	Riot Los Angeles	**Sound Designers**	Activision
Jeff Anderson	**Production Company**	Marshall Grupp	**Brand**
Executive Creative	Smuggler	Phan Visutyothapibal	Guitar Hero World
Director	**Advertising Agency**	**Director of Digital**	Tour
Ted Royer	Droga5	**Services**	
Creative Chairman		Craig Batzofin	
David Droga			

Viral Films

Droga5
for Activision

Bike Hero

Guitar Hero is a social videogame that is played and beloved by millions of people around the world. So we produced a video in which it appears that a Guitar Hero fan has made his own homage to the game, by playing it on a bike. We made this video for hardcore fans to enjoy and discuss, and perhaps even inspire them to pay their own creative homage to Guitar Hero.

Pony   Clown   Lollipop

Copywriter	Creative Directors	Advertising Agency	Music Composer
Michael Dawson	Richard Maddocks	Clemenger BBDO	Dee Taylor
Art Director	Guy Rooke	**Agency Producer**	**Client**
Chris Berents	**Producer**	Denise McKeon	SEGA Australia
Designers	Harley Tesoriero	**Editor**	**Brand**
Brett Bimson	**Production Company**	Joe Morris	SEGA
Kevin Phillips	Yukfoo Animation	**Sound Designer**	
		Andrew Stevenson	

Viral Films

Clemenger BBDO
for SEGA Australia

Pony / Clown / Lollipop
New games and content were created to help gamers recover from the mental trauma of playing the twisted and horrifying 'Condemned 2' game from SEGA.

Viral Films

Wieden + Kennedy Portland
for Electronic Arts

Walk on Water

There's a large crop of YouTube videos showing amusing glitches in EA Sports' Tiger Woods PGA Tour video game; bizarre stances, putts that spin endlessly around the lip of the cup and players that bend impossibly in half. Rather than trying to ignore the fact that even the best games have a few hiccups, we decided to embrace one of the funnier glitch videos. YouTube user Levinator25 posted an in-game clip of the Tiger Woods character hitting a shot while standing on the surface of a pond. We attached a video response to his post to demonstrate that, when it comes to Tiger, EA Sports had actually gotten this feature right. It's no glitch.

Director	Creative Directors	Advertising Agency	Sound Designer
Matthew Cullen	**Jed Alger**	Wieden + Kennedy	Charlie Keating
Copywriter	Aaron Allen	Portland	**Account Handler**
Eric Samsel	**Producer**	**Agency Producers**	Andrew Schafer
Art Director	Stanny Park	Ben Grylewicz	**Client**
Rob Kendall	**Special Effects**	Jeff Selis	Electronic Arts
Interactive Designer	Bryan Godwin	**Editor**	**Brand**
Marcelino Alvarez	**Production Company**	Colin Woods	Tiger Woods PGA
	Motion Theory		Tour

Sound Design & Use of Music

Grey London
for Toshiba

Timesculpture

Timesculpture was created to promote Toshiba's upscaling technology which converts images on ordinary televisions to HD quality. To represent this step-change, we took 200 ordinary Toshiba camcorders and recorded an evolution of the 'bullet time' technique. Rather than showing a 3D rotation of a still moment, Timesculpture manipulated moving snapshots of time. The soundtrack was a remix of 'Air War' by Crystal Castles, known for their technology inspired sound. The film was watched more than 250,000 times in its first five days on YouTube, and was the number three entertainment clip during its first month. It was recently awarded a Guinness World Record for the most cameras ever used in a composite film sequence.

Sound Designer	Creative Director	Advertising Agency	Account Handler
Owen Griffiths	Andy Amadeo	Grey London	Hugo Feiler
Director	**Chief Creative**	**Agency Producer**	**Marketing Managers**
Mitch Stratten	**Officer**	Rebecca Pople	Matt McDowell
Art Director	Jon Williams	**Editor**	Rupert Standley
Andy Amadeo	**Production Company**	Christophe Williams	**Client**
Copywriter	Hungry Man	**Music Composer**	Toshiba
Andy Amadeo	**Post Production**	Crystal Castles	
	Company		
	The Mill		

The jury:

Matt Clark, United Visual Artists (Jury Foreman)
Joshua Davis, Joshua Davis Studio
Daniel Hirschmann, Jason Bruges Studio
Andreas Müller, Nanika
Chris O'Shea, Freelance
Eva Rucki, Troika
Joachim Sauter, ART+COM

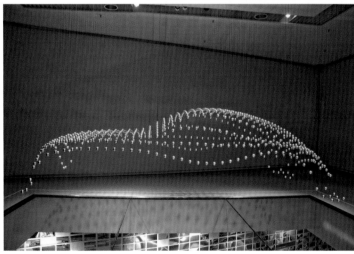

Creative Director	Designer	Design Agency	Client
Joachim Sauter	Susanne Traeger	ART+COM	BMW Group
Technical Designers	**Art Directors**	**Museum Director**	**Brand**
Simon Schießl	Patrick Kochlik	Dr Ralf Rodepeter	BMW
David Siegel	Petra Trefzger		

Digital Installations

ART+COM
for BMW Group

Kinetic Sculpture for the BMW Museum
The Kinetic Sculpture is a metaphorical translation of the process of form-finding in design. Covering an area of six square metres, it comprises 714 metal spheres, hanging from thin steel wires attached to individually controlled stepper motors to animate a seven-minute long mechatronic narrative. Moving chaotically at first, the sculpture evolves through several competing forms and eventually resolves into a final shape whose profile hints at one of many well-known, historic and current, BMW cars. Shortly after the opening of the BMW Museum, the Kinetic Sculpture became the most watched video worldwide in the automotive category on YouTube for a week.

564

Design Studio	Curating Practice	Client
Troika	Artwise Curators	British Airways

Digital Installations

Troika
for British Airways

Cloud

Troika was commissioned by Artwise Curators to create a signature piece for the entrance of the new British Airways luxury lounges in Heathrow Terminal 5. In response, we created 'Cloud', a five metre long digital sculpture whose surface is covered with 4,638 flip-dots that can be individually addressed by a computer to animate its entire skin. Flip-dots were conventionally used in the 70s and 80s to create signs in train stations and airports. By audibly flipping between black and silver, the flip-dots create mesmerising waves as they chase across the surface of 'Cloud'.

565

Creative Director
Joachim Sauter
Associate Creative Director
Uwe R Brückner
Designers
Christine Paech

Jens-Ove Panknin
Susanne Traeger
Art Director
Dennis Paul
Architect
Eberhard Schlag

Design Agency
ART+COM
Architecture Agency
Atelier Brückner
Museum Director
Dr Ralf Rodepeter

Client
BMW Group
Brand
BMW

Digital Installations

ART+COM
for BMW Group

Mediatecture for the BMW Museum
The objective was to create a dynamic environment for a museum of mobility. The mediatecture, a symbiosis of media and architecture, enlarges the space by extending it virtually through three-dimensional moving images. It also sets the exhibited 'parked' cars in motion relative to the animated walls. In the switched reactive mode, the pattern of illumination changes according to the mere presence of visitors, actively involving them in the scenario.

Creative Director
Benjamin Tomlinson
Designers
Amanda Gaskin
Alex James
Interactive Designer
Immo Blaese
Art Director
Steve Lloyd

Copywriter
Gerard Ivall
Developer
David Ashman
Software Developer
Chris O'shea
Electronics
Benjamin Tomlinson

Creative Agency
ico Design
Project Manager
Sandra Dartnell
Chief Flapper
Steve Lloyd

Assistant Flappers
Viv Bhatia
Gerard Ivall
Client
Victoria & Albert
Museum

Digital Installations

ico Design
for Victoria & Albert Museum

Flap to Freedom
The Victoria & Albert Museum village fête is a contemporary take on the traditional English fête, providing an extraordinary array of creative, fun, engaging and imaginative events and games, by leading as well as up-and-coming designers. Ico Design devised an interactive game based around the idea of racing battery hens to freedom. Through the clever use of hidden technology, our custom-built robotic chickens were controlled by the frenzied movement of flapping participants. No one worked out how it was done but everyone had fun trying to be the fastest flapper.

Creative Directors
Catherine Botibol
Mo Saha
Technical Director
Paul Tully
Designer
Gareth Paul Jones
Architectural Designers
Jason Bruges
Gabby Shawcross

Interaction Designers
Jason Bruges
Gabby Shawcross
Industrial Designer
Tom Sloane
Installation Art
Jason Bruges Studio

Art Director
Gareth Paul Jones
Writer
Peter Kirby
Production Manager
Amanda Barnes
Digital Agency
Less Rain
Brand Experience Manager
Mark Schulz

Brand Experience
pd3
Head of Brand
Shadi Halliwell
Head of Campaigns
Richard Murfitt
Head of Advertising
Katrina Ward-Smith
Client
O2

Digital Installations

Jason Bruges Studio & pd3
for O2

The Memory Project
Over time, we have kept our personal memories safe in diaries, photo albums and shoeboxes. We are now increasingly relying on hard drives, servers, websites and mobile phones to capture and store our digital memories. O2 Bluebook offers O2 customers online storage of texts, numbers and photos, ensuring nothing is lost. Devised to create awareness and spur engagement, the Memory Project was an immersive offline and online digital experience. The installation, a 10ft tall interactive structure, housed 11 cameras recording a digital panorama of its location every minute. These captured digital memories were stored on built-in hard drives. Visitors could explore them on screens inside the installation, or at home on the website. The Memory Project toured to London, Edinburgh and Liverpool.

Start Creative
for adidas

adidas miCoach Core Skills

Adidas miCoach Core Skills is a totally new retail experience that invites visitors to adidas sport performance stores to test their core athletic skills using a range of exciting, interactive tools. The aim was to create an engaging brand experience that would reinforce the adidas brand promise of 'enabling a better you'. Core Skills turns high-end sports technology into an accessible, fun on-brand experience, in an innovative way. Latest touch-screen technology, an intriguing environmental design and a media-rich website are combined to help customers understand sport and improve fitness. Core Skills is now being rolled out internationally, following its successful launches in Berlin and Paris in 2008.

Creative Director David Judge	**Interactive Designers** Paul Kyndt	**Interactive Programming**	**Brand Manager** Lisann Costello
Technical Directors Steve Blyth	Dan Potter **Copywriter**	**Agency** Engage Production	**Client** adidas
Stuart Ledden	Dan Radley	**Retail Experience**	**Brand** adidas miCoach
Designer Ben Barton	**Digital Agency** Start Creative	**Agency** Judge Gill	Core Skills
Art Director Matt Wheatcroft		**Marketing Manager** Chris Aubrey	

Universal Everything
for Victoria & Albert Museum

Forever

The Victoria & Albert Museum commissioned Matt Pyke to create the second winter installation in the John Madejski Garden at the museum. 'Forever' was a large moving image wall installation of endless animations responding to an ever-changing soundtrack. The bespoke generative design system at the heart of 'Forever' did, and still could, spawn different audiovisual films every day, forever. A live online installation, generating an endless series of downloadable video podcasts, coincided with the display, which opened on 21 November 2008. This project was supported by Creativesheffield and Apple.

Creative Directors Matt Pyke	**Design Group** Universal Everything	**Project Managers** Guillaume Olive	**Client** Victoria & Albert
Simon Pyke		Philip Ward	Museum
Karsten Schmidt			

Index

Advertising Agencies
(180/TBWA) 132, 438, 485
180 Amsterdam 438, 485
4Creative 115, 172, 174, 176
72andSunny 164, 478
Abbott Mead Vickers BBDO 46, 252, 277, 395, 426, 433, 435, 447, 466, 468, 470, 489, 495
AIM Proximity 101
Akestam Holst 533
AKQA London 548
Albion 372
AlmapBBDO 70, 71, 74, 91, 151, 248, 416, 417, 434, 439, 516, 520, 538
Anomaly 505
Arc Worldwide Thailand 403
Arnold 66, 162
Barrie D'Rozario Murphy 500
Bascule 504, 514, 535
Bates Taiwan 41
BBDO Bangkok 53
BBDO New York 120, 338, 465, 484, 491, 497
BBDO/Proximity Malaysia 30, 31, 47, 93, 388
BBH Asia Pacific 49, 98, 99
BBH China 413
BBH London 28, 29, 41, 54, 83, 117, 395, 415, 481, 524, 533
BBH New York 126, 127, 143, 412, 508
Big Ant International 23, 134,
BJL Manchester 56, 117
BMF 111, 324
Callegari Berville Grey 47
CHI & Partners 397, 414, 437, 518
Clemenger BBDO Melbourne 112, 156, 163
Clemenger BBDO Sydney 561
Clemenger BBDO Wellington 62, 106, 448, 549,
CLM BBDO 78, 79, 389, 410
Coleman Rasic Carrasco 194
Colenso BBDO 108, 109, 161, 507
Creativeland Asia 123, 259, 260
Crispin Porter + Bogusky 145, 146, 154, 155, 162, 525, 532
Daddy 509
Das Comitee 432
David&Goliath 50, 258
DDB Berlin 88
DDB Chicago 202, 203
DDB London 24, 25, 38, 76, 77, 80, 81, 84, 157, 169, 436, 469, 488, 493
DDB Mexico City 493
DDB Paris 55, 486
DDB Singapore 458
DDB Vancouver 158
Del Campo Nazca Saatchi & Saatchi 61
Dentsu Kansai 218, 267, 369
Dentsu Tokyo 345, 360, 513, 541, 546
Draftfcb Johannesburg 42, 205
Droga5 19, 22, 139, 497, 560
Dye Holloway Murray 216, 390, 391, 402, 406
Element 79 503
Euro RSCG Duesseldorf 236
Fallon London 163, 164
Family Business 374
Fitzgerald & Company 557
Forsman & Bodenfors 516, 543
George Patterson Y&R 165, 480
good design company 223, 276
Goodby Silverstein and Partners 119, 150, 336, 461, 498, 502, 518, 528, 532, 535, 559
Grabarz & Partner 487
Grey Beijing 396, 400, 422
Grey Istanbul 209
Grey London 185, 405, 498, 562
Grey Melbourne 52
Grey New York 462
GT Tokyo 510, 526, 537
gürtlerbachmann Werbung 235, 320
Hakuhodo 550
Hakuhodo Kettle 96
Happy 374
HEIMAT, Berlin 140
Inside Mobile 546

Irish International BBDO 494
Jung von Matt Hamburg 131, 429
Jung von Matt Stuttgart 226, 420
JWT Beijing 529, 555, 560
JWT Cape Town 114
JWT Chile 48
JWT India 398
JWT London 94, 477, 482
JWT New York 85, 128, 164, 477
JWT Paris 499
JWT San Juan 119
JWT Shanghai 40, 411
JWT Singapore 51, 72
JWT Sydney 68
kempertrautmann 492
Kinetic Singapore 269, 283, 319, 421
Kolle Rebbe/KOREFE 373, 421
Lean Mean Fighting Machine 521, 530, 536
Leo Burnett Argentina 136
Leo Burnett Brazil 404
Leo Burnett Brussels 209
Leo Burnett India 375
Leo Burnett Italy 468
Leo Burnett Lisbon 499, 536
Leo Burnett London 43, 65, 433, 435, 496
Leo Burnett Los Angeles 463
Leo Burnett Manila 39, 118
Leo Burnett Milan 435
Leo Burnett Mumbai 367
Leo Burnett Sydney 39
Leo Burnett Thailand 403
Leo Burnett Toronto 69, 87
Leo Lin Design 266
Lowe & Partners Malaysia 284
Lowe Bangkok 104
Lowe Bull Gauteng 138
Lowe New York 221
Lowe/Draftfcb Amsterdam 116
M&C Saatchi/Mark 119, 542
Marcel Paris 90
McCann Erickson Japan 513
McCann Erickson London 338, 409
McCann Worldgroup Hong Kong 34, 35, 224, 225
McCann Worldgroup India 124
Media Consulta TV & Filmproduktion 121
Miles Calcraft Briginshaw Duffy 167, 168, 491
Modernista! 519
Mortierbrigade 117
Mother London 167, 168, 460, 495
Net#work BBDO Cape Town 210, 285
Ogilvy & Mather Asia Pacific 472
Ogilvy & Mather Hong Kong 282
Ogilvy & Mather Mumbai 418
Ogilvy & Mather Thailand 55
Ogilvy Amsterdam 116
Ogilvy Cape Town 67, 423
Ogilvy Frankfurt 39, 105, 115, 118, 133, 213, 271, 366, 401
Ogilvy London 465, 550
Ogilvy New Zealand 129
Ogilvy Shanghai 394
Ogilvy Singapore 50, 92
Ogilvy Stockholm 36, 37, 102, 103
Ogilvy Toronto 131
ponce buenos aires 161
Projector 506
Publicis Ambience 117
Publicis Conseil 479
Publicis London 42
Publicis Mojo 130, 141
RAPP London 209
R/GA London 336
R/GA New York 534
Red Bee Media 173, 175
Rediffusion Y&R 114
RKCR/Y&R 56, 57, 94, 170, 176, 177, 178, 467, 494
Saatchi & Saatchi Australia 113, 229, 540
Saatchi & Saatchi Frankfurt 118
Saatchi & Saatchi London 135, 216, 483
Saatchi & Saatchi Los Angeles 59, 144, 415

Saatchi & Saatchi Malaysia 54, 58, 63, 86, 268
Saatchi & Saatchi New York 44, 45, 89, 152, 153, 204, 206
Saatchi & Saatchi X 122
Santo Buenos Aires 165
Scholz & Friends 559
Scholz & Friends Agenda 440
Scholz & Friends Berlin 228, 325
Serviceplan 119, 245, 375
Shalmor Avnon Amichay/Y&R
Interactive Tel Aviv 515
Specsavers Creative 496
SS+K 519
Syrup Stockholm 100
T.A.G 558
TBWA\Berlin 132, 266
TBWA\Chiat\Day New York 148, 158
TBWA\ESPAÑA 85
TBWA\NEBOKO 160
TBWA\Tequila Singapore 64, 87, 392, 393
TBWA\Toronto 457
TBWA\Vietnam 444
TBWA\WHYBIN\TEQUILA 116
The Brand Agency 207
The Campaign Palace 109, 160, 492
The Chase 452
The Classic Partnership Advertising Dubai 258
The Furnace 73
The Jupiter Drawing Room Johannesburg 121
The Viral Factory 552, 554
This is Real Art 445, 469
Three Drunk Monkeys 120
VCCP London 142, 159
Vitruvio Leo Burnett 115
WCRS 162, 556
Wieden + Kennedy Culver City 490
Wieden + Kennedy London 60, 82, 399, 444, 446, 475
Wieden + Kennedy Los Angeles 149, 474
Wieden + Kennedy Portland 157, 215, 476
Work Club 511
Young & Rubicam France 26, 27, 419

Animation
A Large Evil Corporation 216
Animatório 499
Curious Pictures 162
Frater 195
Passion Pictures 176, 177
Shy the Sun 500
Sixty40 542
Why Not Associates 175

Architectural Firms
Atelier Brückner 566
Design Research Lab 343
Dewhurst MacFarlane and Partners 352
dRMM 347
Foster+Partners 351
Jump Studios 357
LOT-EK 350
Nex Architecture 343
Perkins Eastman 352
PKSB Architects 352
Rieder 343

Audio Companies
POP 154, 155
Sound Lounge 158
Wave Productions 158

Brands
13th Street 226
501 481
8 Magazine 298
A diamond is forever 128
Absolut Vodka 374

Index

AC/DC 553
Acme Climate Action 316
adidas 438
adidas miCoach Core Skills 567
adidas Originals 232, 485
Air Action Vigorsol 117
Airtel Mobile Phone Data Backup 114
Alka-Seltzer 78, 79, 389, 410
AMF Pension 543
Anchor Butter 397
Animal Rescue Shelter 542
Antalis 244
Anthony's Honeytube 373
Anthony's Oil Change 373
Architectural Association School 343
Arnet 165
Au 345
Audi TDI Clean Diesel 492
AUDITORIUM Editions 442
AXE 98, 99, 161, 514
Banged Up 405
BBC iPlayer 176
BBC Sport 177
Beijing Capital International Airport 351
BMW 21, 564, 566
Bonanza Coffee Heroes 284
Breeze Excel 104
Brownfield Catering 354
Bud Light 202, 203
Canelé 51
Capitu 174
Cardinal Café 340
Carlton MID 156, 163
Cavalleria Rusticana & Pagliacci 415
Cheerios 45, 89
Chibi-Poli 550
Cia. de Bolso 70
CITC 239
Coca-Cola 149, 212
Comfort 465
Crest 152, 153
Cycle Safety 556
Dairy Milk 163
Defender 94
Designing Naturally 249
DIE ZEIT 298
Distracted Driver Safety 549
Doktor Möller's Quince Brandy 375
Doritos 470, 528
Dove Pro-Age 131
Earth Garbage Bag 264
Earth Hour 39
Extra 468
Fanta 550
Fedrigoni 124
FHM 92
Film 4 174
Filtainer: Clean Water for All 385
Flannel Shirts 537
Flash 344
Flora 138
Four'N Twenty Meat Pies 112
Fudkor Lemon Flavoured Tea 375
Gallery 447
Gatorade 538
Gatorade Kids 74, 434
Gaymers Original 406
Gears of War 558
Glenfiddich 341, 357
Gnarls Barkley 191
Golf 488
Goo Home 96
Google 209
Gran Centenario 493
Guardian Newspapers 427
Guided Visits 61
Guinness 54, 396, 422, 494
Guitar Hero World Tour 560
Handycam Alpha 164
Harvey Nichols 24, 25, 76, 77
Havaianas 248, 416, 417
Head & Shoulders 204
Heart Diary 426
HeartWorks 384

Heinz Ketchup 509
Herbal Essences 115
Honda Environment 82, 399, 475
Hornbach 140
Hot Chip 262
Hovis 167, 168, 491
Howard Smith Paper Graphic Design
    and Print Awards 265
HSArchitecture 268
Huggies 85
Humanglobaler Zufall 301
Hungerproject 219
IFAW UK 108
IKEA 39, 115, 213, 286
Independent Film Sponshorship 469
Indiana Motors Auto Repair 260
International Campaign Against
    Honour Killings 472
International Premium Travel
    Experience 500
Jake & Dinos Chapman 315
James Boag's Draught 130, 141
James Ready 69
Jealous Lovers 129
Jeep 30, 31, 93, 388
Jme 371
John West 52
Johnnie Walker 87
JUJU feat. Spontania 546
Kandinsky 330
KFC 395
KitKat 499
Know Your Limits 142, 159
La TV d'Orange 479
LAUS 2009 272
Le Grand Mix 26, 27
Leave Nothing 476
Lee 374
Legible London 454
Letter Writing Campaign 268
Levi Strauss 28, 29, 49, 83,
Lily's Kitchen 372
Logan 363
Lokart Paint Thinner 367
M&M's 64, 392, 393
Made by Bob 370
Magnatec 423
MAMEW 223
Marie Claire 285
Marie Curie Actions 121
Mark Six 282
Marmite Snacks 84
Marunouchi Cafe 218, 267
Matrix 144
McDonald's 24-Hour Delivery 118
Million 22
NBA 119
NET10 497
New Street Square 331
Nike 224, 225
Nike Athlete Message 444
Nike Basketball 534
Nike Football 164
NIKEiD 548
No Frizz 378
Nokia N-Gage 511
Not For Commercial Use 235
NV10 208
nycgo.com 412
O&M 377
Oasis Dig Out Your Soul 126, 127, 143
Office Games 272, 327
Old Spice 157
Orange Goldspots 460
Orange Time 515
Oxfam 57
Pampero Rum 536
Panadol 91, 400
Passat 169
Passport 205
PAYG 527
Peace Campaign 32, 33
Pedderzine Power 229
Peezy 385
Penguin Books 58, 86, 240, 321

Penguin Classics 312, 313
Piccadilly Lights 358
Piece Together for Peace Project 266
Play-Doh 283
Plume Books 428
Ply 345
Polo 157
Polytrade Paper 244
Portable 435
Powerfuel 421
PSP 85
Public Service 40
PUMA 350
Quantum 381
QUIT 109, 160
Radiohead 504, 535
Reaffirmation & Renewal Campaign
    280
Recipease 329
Reebok 546
Rellana Hair 366
RNS 510 Navigation System 88
Rolling Stone Magazine 398
Routan 145
RSPCA 492
Safeguard Antibacterial Soap 63
Sagami Original 0.02 510, 526
Schweppes 480
SCRABBLE 48
SEGA 561
Skins 176, 489
Skittles 148
SLS Hotel at Beverly Hills 456
SOLERNO 376
SONY Cyber-shot 164
Soso 362
Specsavers 496
Spiritualized 263
Sprint 518
Stanley Kubrick Season 172, 490
Stella Artois 4% 495
Stilo 404
Stuffit Deluxe 206
Supporting Vulnerable Children
    433, 466
Swanswell 334
Tampax 464
tesapack® ultra strong 420
Tesco Lotus 53
The 11th International Architecture
    Biennale Venice 340
The Deptford Project 253, 355
The Great Schlep 19, 139
The Gruen Transfer 120
THINK! 65, 162
Tide 44
Tiji 486
TKTS 352
Tooheys Extra Dry 696ml 324
Tostitos 503
Touareg 67
Touching the Void 428
Trafic 276
Transport for London 162
Travel Oregon 215
truth 162
UK Definitive Circulating Coinage 20
Ultra Zoom SP-570 68
Unilever 508
UNIQLO Bra Top 513
United Nations 36, 37, 102, 103
Upload Cinema 116
Upscaling 562
Urban Play 227
USPA 377
Visa Debit 483
Volkswagen 493
Vorwerk Vacuum Cleaners 105
WERK Magazine 214, 408
White Road 342
White Season 177
Wii 532
wine 255
WMF 405
Wonder Performance 111

571

Index

World Machine 440
Wptt Contraceptive 361
WWF 55, 418, 458
X Factor 518
Yearpack 285
Yukon Denali 463

Clients
.jp 223
123fleurs.com 47
3.14 CREATIVE 273
60|40 279
ABC 119, 120
ABInBev 495
ABSA Capital 121
Action World Solidarity 271, 401
Activision 560
ADCN (Art Directors Club Nederland) 317
ADG-FAD 272
adidas 132, 547, 567
adidas International 438, 485
adidas Originals China 232
Alexander McQueen 248
All Japan Federation Printing Industry Associations 310
Alzheimer's New Zealand 109, 161
American Legacy Foundation 162
AMF 541
Amnesty International 107, 167, 228, 268, 325, 499, 559
Anheuser-Busch 202, 203
Aniboom 200
Antalis Hong Kong 244
Arla Foods 397
Arnet Broadband 165
Artisan Cellars 349
Asbury & Asbury 452
Associated Magazines 285
AT&T 465, 491
Atlantic Records 191
Audi 492
AXE Hair Crisis Relief 508
Axel Springer Verlag 302
Barnardo's 54, 524, 533
Bayer 78, 79, 389, 410,
BBC 177, 178, 494
BBC MC&A Future Media and Technology 176
BBC News 175
BBC Two 173
Beijing Capital International Airport Company 351
Bharti Airtel 114
Bistrotheque 344
Bloomberg 357
BMW Group 21, 564, 566
BOCCI 382
Bontrust 487
British Airways 565
British Army 42
British Heart Foundation 185
British Library 56
Bryne Stavanger Offset 442
Bundesministerium für Bildung und Forschung 440
Burger King 146, 154, 155, 525, 532,
Cadbury Schweppes 163, 480
Calgary Society for Persons with Disabilites 242
Cancer Patients Aid Association 117
Canelé Chocolate Pâtisserie 51
Car Mall Used Cars 259
Casa África 313
Casa Cuervo 493
Casa do Zezinho 151
Castrol 423
Catch 22 453
Centennial PR 118
Centre de Fotografia Documental de Barcelona 276
Century Fiesta Costume Shop 47
CEPF 40, 411
Channel 4 174, 489

Channel 5 Broadcasting 405
China Environment Protection Fund 40, 411
Chocolate Research Facility 350
Christopher Griffith Studio 442
Chrysler Korea 30, 31, 93 388
Church of St Peter & St Paul 319
Cia. das Letras 70
City Council of Ljubljana, Slovenia 355
City of New York 352
Coalition for Father Duffy 352
Coco de Mer 258
COI 42
Coltex 517
Columbia Records 553
Comcast 150 461, 498
Conect (Specialised Council of Pay TV Thematic Channels) 110
Converse 505
Crimestoppers 94
Cycle Safety 162
Danish Crafts 231
Darwin200 273, 425
Das Comittee 432
Das Hunger Projekt 219
De Uitkijk 116
DeBeers 128
Design Research Lab 343
Deutsche Stiftung Denkmalschutz (German Foundation for Monument Protection) 118, 133
DHL 116
Diageo 87, 494, 536
Diesel 90, 554
Dom and Helena 220
Doritos 502
Drive Alive 42
Droog Design 227
Durex 555
Durty Nellies Irish Pub Beijing 396, 422
E.ON Energi, Munich 330
E4 176
Ekchai Distribution Systems 53
EMI Records 262
Emirates 536
Enablis 241
English National Opera 415
Environment & Public Health Organization, Nepal 385
Ermida Nossa Senhora da Conceição 222
ESPN 119
Etrade 462
Eurocamp 56
European Commission DG Research 121
Eye Bank Association, Kerala 123
FAST RETAILING 537
FHM Singapore 92
Fiat 404, 538
Fiell Publishing 281
Financial Times 38
Fondazione La Biennale di Venezia 353
Foster's Group 156, 163
Fria Tidningen Newspaper 100
Friedrich Wilhelm und Karin Reller OHG 366
Frito-Lay 503, 528
Frontiers Magazine 270
Fudkor India 375
FUEL Publishing 305
Funnelly Enough 385
G2 427
Garmin 394
Gavin Martin Associates 246
Gaymer Cider Company 406
General Mills 45, 89
Generalitat de Catalunya 234
Generation Press 235
Genfiddich Single Malt 339, 357
Getty Images 515
Global Coalition for Peace 32, 33, 134
Globo 174
GMC 463

Good Worldwide 296
Goodman Fielder Baking 111
Google Turkey 209
Graflex Directions 266
Greenpeace 444, 520
GSK 50, 400
Guardian Garden 318, 447
Guardian News & Media 286, 446
Guinness Anchor Berhad 54
Häagen-Dazs 559
Hanqingtang Design 233
Happy Forsman & Bodenfors 264
Harvest 238
Harvey Nichols 24, 25, 76, 77, 80, 81, 348, 436
Hasbro Singapore 283
Heart 429
Heart Artists' Agents 426
Heineken 160
Heinz 509
Henry Iddon Photography 257
Honda 82, 115, 399, 475, 541
Hornbach Home Improvement Superstores 140
Hotels.com 158
Howard Smith Paper Group 265
howies 402
HSBC 477
HuaSen Architecture 268
I.D. Magazine 427
Ichida Garden 360
IDEE 218, 267
IKEA Germany 39, 115, 213, 284, 516
Indiana Motors 260
International Fund for Animal Welfare 108
Inventive Medical 384
Iranian and Kurdish Women's Rights Organisation 472
Italasia Thailand 403
ITV 41
Jack Daniel's 66
James Ready Beer 69
Jamie Oliver Enterprises 329, 371
JAQK Cellars 365
Jealous Lovers Productions 129
Jewish Council of Education & Research 19, 139
johnson banks 252
Kaleidoskop Theatre 275
KDDI CORPORATION 345
Kids Company 433, 466
Kiduk Reus & Yumi Choi GbR 284
Kimberly-Clark 85
Kouzu Embroidery 369
Laforet 276
Lagardère Active 486
Land Rover 94, 170
Land Securities 331, 340, 358
Levi Strauss 28, 29, 41, 83, 481
Lion Nathan 130, 141, 324
Live Poker 55
Living Proof™ 378
Lo Recordings 260
Logan Wines 363
Lokart 367
London School of Economics, The Urban Age Project 307
London Vision Clinic 335
Lurpak 60
Lv Shanchuan 316
Manchester City Football Club 239
Mars 64, 148, 392, 393
Mattel Chile 48
McCann Erickson London 338, 409
McDonald's 118
Mediterranean Sculptors' Symposium 342
Mencap 281
Mercedes 495
Metallica 262, 364, 376
Midas 158
Mimi Hajime Ueoka 254
minä perphonen 239
Ministry of Economy, Trade and Industry 310

Index

Mitsubishi Estate 218, 267
Modernista! 519
Monster.com 484, 497
More4 172, 490
Morton & Peplow 278
msnbc.com 519
MTV 166
MTV Exit Asia 194
Museum of Childhood 46, 252, 277, 395, 447
Museum of Sex 221
MW.com India 398
Mytton Williams 245
National Basketball Association 119
National Portrait Gallery 230
NB: Studio 251, 424
NBC Universal Global Networks 226
NESTLÉ France 499
New York City Department of Education 22
New York Magazine 290
New Zealand Book Council 108, 507
New Zealand Post 448
New Zealand Transport Agency 62, 106, 549
Nike 34, 35, 164, 224, 225, 444, 476, 478, 490, 534, 548
Nintendo 435, 532
Nokia 336, 511, 529, 555, 560
Not For Tourists 318
Nova Radio 26, 27, 419
NTNU 266
NTT Resonant 96
NYC & Company 126, 127, 143, 412
NYTDC 273
O2 567
Ochs Schmidhuber Architects 522
Olympus 68
Orange 97, 168, 460, 479, 515, 527
Oregon 215
Original & Mineral 377
Oxfam 57
Oxford Oratory 280
Patties 112
PAVe 269
Pedder Group Hong Kong 229
Penguin Group 240, 304, 312, 313, 321, 430
Penguin Group US 428
Pepsico 74, 434, 470, 516, 538
Perfetti van Melle 117
Perth Zoo 207
Philharmonic Orchestra of Hamburg 131
Photolibrary 87
Playground Outdoor Equipment Stores 533
Polytrade Paper Corporation 244
Premier Foods 167, 168, 491
Preventing Violence, New Zealand 116
Prism Papyrus 124
Procter & Gamble 44, 63, 115, 152, 153, 157, 204, 464
Provokateur 316
Publishing & Design Group 299
PUMA International 339, 350
Quad 230
Quantum Saddle Company 381
Quirin Bank 236
QUIT 122, 135
Quzhou Seezo Trading 361
Radford Wallis 247
Radley Yeldar 457
Red Bull 514
Red Cross Argentina 136
Reebok International 546
Reed Words 455
Reprieve 217, 445, 471
Richard House Children's Hospice 272, 327
Roca 358
Röhsska Museum 233, 278
Roland Berger Strategy Consultants 235, 320
Roman Catholic Diocese of Oakland 356

Roy Castle Lung Foundation 437
Royal Opera House 106
RSPCA NSW 492
Sagami Rubber Industries 510, 526
Samsung 521, 530
Samsung Ortmans 208
São Paulo Alpargatas 248, 416, 417
SBE Entertainment 326, 456
Schnapsbrennerei Doktor Thorsten Möller 375
School of Visual Arts 240, 322
Schott Solar 118
Schweppes 165
Scottish Opera 280
SEGA Australia 561
Sense International 424
SGW 384
Shelter 43, 433, 496
Silver Cross 236, 368, 456
Silverfish Books 58, 86
Simplot Australia 52
Skins™ 73
Skittles 457
Skype 552
Smith Micro Software 206
SONY 164, 545
SONY Computer Entertainment 85, 549
SONY Music Associated Records 546
SosoFactory 362
Sour Sally 421
Spaceman Recordings 263
Specsavers Optical Group 496
SpringerWienNewYork 319
Sprint 336, 535
Sprint Nextel 518
St Mary's Church 279
Städtische Galerie im Lenbachhaus 330
Steelcase 383
Studio Brussel 117
Suntory Museum, Osaka 320
Surfrider Foundation 59
Swallow Magazine 441
Swanswell Trust 334
Sydney Dogs & Cats Home 119, 542
Sydney Writers' Festival 2008 229
Taiwan Smoker's Helpline 41
Tátil Design 249
TDC, Taipei 266, 420
The Absolut Company 374
The Cancer Council Victoria 109, 160
The Carphone Warehouse 518
The Caseroom Press 321
The Cathedral Group 253, 355
The Coca-Cola Company 149, 212, 348, 474
The Comedy Store 274, 328
The Creative Circle 216, 308
The Deli Garage 373, 421
The Economist 120, 338, 426
The Estate of Ian Fleming 430
The Folio Society 428
The Foundation for the Study of Infant Death 482
The History of Advertising Trust 390, 391
The Home Office 142, 159, 467, 534
The Hong Kong Jockey Club 282
The International Architecture Biennale Venice 340
The Manchester and Cheshire Dogs' Home 238, 440
The Royal Mail 285, 455, 489
The Royal Mint 20
The Star Inn 317
The Swedish Museum of Architecture 241, 263, 366
The Warehouse Limited 101
Theatre Development Fund 352
Thrislington Cubicles 246, 457
Tiger Beer 414
Time Magazine 299
Times Square Alliance 352
TNT 119, 254

Tohato 550
Tokyu Hands 513
Toshiba 498, 562
Toyota 144, 415
TracFone 497
Transport for London 162, 454, 556
Treader 261
TV Licensing 435
U Corporation 377
UK Government – Department for Transport 65
Unilever 84, 99, 104, 131, 138, 161, 465, 514
UNIQLO 506, 512, 513, 531
Unit F büro für mode 298
United Airlines 500
United Nations 36, 37, 102, 103, 113, 540
Universal Studios Hollywood 50
University College Falmouth 452
Utrecht 306
Velocity Films 114
Verlagsgruppe Lübbe 119
Versus Cancer 117
VF Arvind Brands 374
Victoria & Albert Museum 567, 568
Virgin Atlantic 210
Virgin Galactic 332
Visa Europe 483
Vodacom 205
Vodafone 333
Volkswagen 67, 71, 88, 91, 145, 157, 169, 439, 469, 488, 493
Vorwerk Germany 105
Warner Brothers 126, 127, 143, White Cube 315
Wigan Little Theatre 237, 337
William Grant & Sons 376
WORK 214, 408
WOWOW INC. 504, 535
Wrigley's 468
Wuesthof 245
WWF 39, 55, 72, 413, 418, 458
XBOX 558
Xero 364
Yorkshire Sculpture Park 237
Yum! Restaurants International 395
Zapruder's Other Films 120
ZEITmagazin 298
Zoo de Buenos Aires 61

Colour Correction
SpyPost 503

Curating Practice
Artwise Curators 565

Design Groups
300million 455
702 Design Works 273
A2/SW/HK 230, 231
ALT Design 413
Alt Group 364
Apple Industrial Design Team 380, 386
Applied Information Group 454
ART+COM 564, 566
Asbury & Asbury 450
Asylum Creative 349, 354
Atelier Works 307
Browns 265
Build 235
Cartlidge Levene 286
ChauhanStudio. 384
Codesign 244
Container 377
Coy! Communications 216
David Pearson Design 304
De Designpolitie 254
Design Center 355
DFraile 362
Disturbance 427
Eric Chan Design 244
e-Types 275

Index

Euro RSCG New York 299
Face 317
Farrow 263, 281
Fat-Man Collective 511
Figtree 453
Franki & Jonny 552
Fraser Muggeridge Studio 242
GBH 326, 332, 339, 350, 456
Glassworks 384
Grafica 276
Graflex Directions 266
Gucci Group 248
HanTang Communications Group 361
Happy Forsman & Bodenfors 233, 241,
   263, 278, 366
Harvey Nichols Display Production
   Team 348
Hatch Design 365
Hat-trick Design Consultants 273, 280,
   309, 331, 335, 340, 358, 425
Héctor Serrano Studio 358
ico Design 567
Identica 241
iriver 386
iyamadesign 318, 447
johnson banks 252, 334, 339, 357
Jones|Kroloff 353
Judge Gill 567
Ken-Tsai Lee Design Studio 238
Kinetic Singapore 319
Less Rain 512
LOVE 236, 368, 456
Maddison Product Design 385
Magpie Studio 246, 278
MARK 237, 257, 274, 328, 337
Marksmith 256
MASAMI DESIGN 310
Mash 220
Mister Walker 234
MIT (KAF) Project Team 385
moodley brand identity 298
MR_DESIGN 264
Murray & Sorrell FUEL 305, 315
Music 250, 259
Mytton Williams 245
NB: Studio 230, 251, 424
Open 296
Pearlfisher 371
PearsonLloyd 383
Penguin Group UK 314
Pentagram Design 429
Provokateur 316
Purpose 279
R2 design 222
Radford Wallis 247, 424
Radley Yeldar 240, 321, 453
Rockwell Group 353
Rose 279
Scholz & Friends Identify 228, 325, 440
SenseTeam 268
Seymourpowell 381
Skidmore, Owings & Merrill LLP 356
Steelcase Design Studio 383
Stranger & Stranger 376
Studio8 Design 299
Studio Astrid Stavro 234
Studio mk27 346, 356
Studio Myerscough 253
Studio Rasic 342
Superfad 518, 557
Tátil Design 249
The Brand Union 333
The Chase 238, 285, 440
The Hong Kong Polytechnic
   University School of Design 385
The Partners 272, 327, 457
The Stone Twins 317
This is Real Art 217, 308
Thomas Mayfried Visual
   Communication 330
Thonik 227, 340
Troika 565
True North 256, 455
Turner Duckworth: London and San
   Francisco 212, 262, 364, 376

Universal Everything 568
Visual Arts Press 240, 322
VJU Brand and Business
   Innovation 442
Wallzo 262
War Design Studios 363
WAX 242
Wieden +Kennedy Studio 215
Williams Murray Hamm 329
Wolff Olins 228, 325, 378
WORK 408
ZariganiWorks 513
ZERO PER ZERO 243

Development
Ascent Marketing 525
mitsubachiworks 514
Refresh Partners 525
Steady 532
WorkPlayWork 532

Digital Agencies
AKQA 538
Bascule 504, 514, 535
Dallas STHLM 533
de-construct 522
Dentsu Tokyo 513
Fluid 519
Leo Burnett Lisbon 536
Less Rain 567
Liberty Concepts 19, 139
Liquorice 138
POKE London 97, 527
POKE New York 22
Saint 534
Shalmor Avnon Amichay/Y&R
   Interactive Tel Aviv 515
Start Creative 567
Stopp 524
The Barbarian Group 515
VCCP Digital London 142

Editing Houses
Barbary Post 559
Bikini Edit 465, 491
MacKenzie Cutler 148, 158
Prime Focus 200

Fabrication
Enclos Corp 356
Mare Island Woodworks 356
Pohl 356
Thomas Swan Sign Company 356

Finishing
RIOT 154, 155

Illustration
6B Studio 70
A Large Evil Corporation 216
Am I Collective 26, 27, 419, 423
Corbis 70
Kinetic Singapore 283
Magic Cube 92
Production Plein Soleil 26, 27, 419

Image Manipulation
Magic Group 317
Saddington Baynes 43, 433
Studio Ros 435

Letterpress
Yee Haw Industries 67

Livery Application
Start Design 332

Media Agencies
BBC Media Planning 176
Carat Hamburg 132
Mindshare 543

Mobile Marketing Agencies
Inside Mobile 546
Marvellous 547

Music
Amber Music 146
Baker/Smith/Butler 163
Beacon Street Studios 157
Big Foote 465, 491
Dead Mono 516
Human 484
Junkie JXL 164
MassiveMusic Amsterdam 490
Scandal 202, 203
Supercharango 165
Supreme Music 487
THE 486

On-Line Company
Brickyard VFX 150, 461, 498

Photography
Attic Fire Photography 52
Conteúdo Expresso 74, 434
Corbis 47, 70
Flickr 228, 325
Fotolia 246
Getty Images 74, 94, 434
LatinStock 74
Layoutsatz 2000 245
Magnum Photos 228, 325
Missouri State Highway Patrol 262, 364
Photolibrary 87

Post Production Companies
Absolute 481
Barnsley 142, 159
Company 3LA 161
Final Cut 161
Finish 173
Framestore 482
Glassworks 485
Kpost 482
Molinare 110
MPC 142
Saatchi Design 229
School 158
The Mill 176, 498, 562
Work 524

Pre-Press
Cromotex 314
Straight Premedia 317

Printing Companies
alsoDominie 214, 229, 408
Spinhex & Industrie 317
Tf Artes Gráficas 313

Index

Production Companies
2D PRODUCTIONS 438
4Creative 174
Aardman Animations 24, 25, 76, 77, 117
ACA Films, Mexico City 493
Academy Films 167, 170, 190, 196
Animatório 499
Anonymous Content 164, 476, 478
APG Highlight 256
Avex Hawaii 98, 99
Because Music 196
Bendercine 165
Biscuit Filmworks 150, 461, 498
Black Gold Films 19, 139
Bob Industries 119, 559
Bombay Works 509
B-Reel 502, 508, 528
Chamdin/Stohr 516
Cinema Centro 151
Colméia 520
Colonel Blimp 192
Condor 114
CZAR 160
DMDA Method Design 492
Draw Pictures 198
DUCK Studios 500
Eardrum 207
Element 79 503
Engine Plus 541
Exit Films 480, 492
Ferocious Films 106
First Left 210
flapper3 514
Flying Fish 111
Ghost Robot 189
Gorgeous Enterprises 142, 159, 162, 176, 477, 494, 496, 556
Great Guns 175
Hi-Posi 541
HLA 164
Hocus Pocus 118
HSI 126, 127, 143
Hungry Man 166, 168, 460, 482, 498, 562
Independent 142, 157, 493
Joyrider 198
Jungleboys 120
Knucklehead 489, 495
Kokokaka 516
Limes Vertriebsgesellschaft 132
Lobo 174
Markenfilm 492, 559
Mekanism 144, 503
Memokami 541
Mirinda Films 110
MJZ 148, 161, 162, 163, 474, 497
MONSTER ULTRA.INC. 514
Mortierbrigade 117
NonFiction 146, 154, 155
O Positive 158, 465, 491
OPTIX Digital Pictures 487
Outsider 488, 496
Partizan 197, 199, 200, 475, 483
Partizan Lab 195
Perfect Fools 543
Pictures 537
Pinsker Druck und Medien 247
Plaza Films 109, 161
Poolworldwide 197
Prodigy 156, 163
Production International 464
Radical Media 191
Rattling Stick 167, 168, 479, 484, 491
Red Bee Media 173, 175, 176, 177 178, 494
Red Lion 200
Renegade 112
Revolver 194
Rock & Roll Japan 537
RSA Films 463
Saatchi Design 229
Smith & Jones Films 157
Smuggler 145, 497, 560
Soma Films 109, 160
Sonicville 208
Sonny London 481, 495, 524
Sonovision & Noiseroom 205

Station Films 152, 153
Stink London 169, 485
Superfad 557
The Feds Digital 112
The Garden TV 160
The Viral Factory 552, 554
Thomas Thomas Films 465
Tobias Stretch Films 200
Trigger Happy Productions 140
Up The Resolution 193
Urban Brew 138
Velocity Films 114
vertical vision & Co.KG 132
Wanda 479, 486, 499
Yukfoo Animation 561
Zombie Flesh Eaters 177
Zoo Film Productions 188

Programming
Sapien 516
Franki & Jonny 552

Project Management
Conversion Management Associates 356

Publishers
ADCN 317
Church of St Peter & St Paul 321
Face 317
Generation Yacht 235
Not For Tourists 318
Phaidon Press 307
Scribner 311
Swallow Magazine 293
Unit F büro für mode 298

Record Companies
Atlantic Records 196, 200
Deaf Dumb & Blind 198
Ed Banger 196
EMI 199
Modular Records 195
Mute Records 192
Ninja Tune 193
One Little Indian Records 189
SONY 190
Sub Pop Records 197
TBD Records 188, 200
Universal Island 195
Waxploitation 191

Retouching
24+7 132
C2 543
Electric Art 52, 73
Rocket 59
S05 85
Saddington Baynes 43, 433

Sound Design
Adelphoi Music 493
Audioclip 110
Audioforce 140
Beacon Street Studios 157
Cornelius 513
Cromo.sônica 516, 520
First Left 210
Lime 558
Nylon Studios 492
sin.inc. 514
Sonzeira 151
Sound Reservoir 109, 161
Trinitite 150, 461, 498
Wave 142, 159

Special Effects
Abdelkareem Abonamous 493
Asylum Visual Effects 476
Brickyard VFX 162
Digital Domain 490
Framestore 167, 484
Glassworks 169, 489, 495
Machine Molle 196
Method New York 560
MPC 170, 176, 192, 489
PPL 200
Riot Los Angeles 560
Rushes 167
Smoke & Mirrors 167
The Mill 161, 478, 497
Technical Direction
Dialect 113, 540
Hyperfactory 113, 540
Mobot 113, 540

Visual Effects
Animal Logic Australia 150, 461, 498
Brickyard VFX 119
The Mill New York 148

Acknowledgements

© 2010 D&AD
9 Graphite Square, Vauxhall Walk
London SE11 5EE
www.dandad.org

D&AD is a registered Charity
(Charity No. 3050992) and a
Company limited by Guarantee
registered in England and Wales
(registered number 883234)
with its registered office at 9
Graphite Square, Vauxhall Walk,
London, SE11 5EE, UK.
Phone: +44 (20) 7840-1111.

The D&AD logo and the
pencil are the registered
trademarks of D&AD.

© 2010 TASCHEN GmbH
Hohenzollernring 53
D-50672 Köln
www.taschen.com

To stay informed about
upcoming TASCHEN titles,
please request our magazine
at www.taschen.com/magazine
or write to TASCHEN,
Hohenzollernring 53,
D-50672 Cologne, Germany,
contact@taschen.com,
Fax: +49-221-254919.

We will be happy to send you
a free copy of our magazine
which is filled with information
about all of our books.

Design
Jeremy Leslie
Photography
Christine Donnier-Valentin
Noel da Costa

Awards Director
Holly Hall
**Editorial & Production
Coordination**
Jana Labaki
Editorial Content
Holly Hall
Maeve O'Sullivan
Victoria Perrot
Artwork
Kim Browne
David Pollack
Josephine Spencer
Senior Editorial Assistant
James Wormald
Editorial Assistance
Marta Bacardit
Pablo Brandao
Kim Harrison
Will Marsden
Lewis Proudfoot
Tomoko Suzuki
Sanne Winderickx
Image Production
Gemma Martí O'Toole

Editor in Charge
Julius Wiedemann
Editorial & Production
Coordination
Daniel Siciliano Bretas
Jutta Hendricks

Production
Thomas Grell
Stefan Klatte

German Translation
Jürgen Dubau
French Translation
Aurélie Daniel
for Equipo de Edición

Printed in China

ISBN: 978-3-8365-2083-6